THE REAL LIFE OF LAURENCE OLIVIER

Why, even I myself, I often think, know
little or nothing of my real life. Only
a few hints — a few diffused faint
clues and indirections...

—*Ellen Terry*

To H.B.

who met a fool in the forest

THE REAL LIFE OF
LAURENCE OLIVIER

Roger Lewis

APPLAUSE
THEATRE & CINEMA BOOKS

The Real Life of Laurence Olivier by Roger Lewis

ISBN 978-1-4930-8685-6

Library of Congress Cataloging-in-Publication Data

Lewis, Roger
The real life of Laurence Olivier / Roger Lewis
p. cm.
Includes index.
ISBN 978-1-4930-8685-6
1. Olivier, Laurence, 1907- . 2. Actors--Great Britain--Biography. I. Title.
PN2598.O55L48 1997
792'.028'092
[B]--DC21 97-31702
CIP

APPLAUSE
THEATRE & CINEMA BOOKS

An imprint of Globe Pequot, the trade division of
the Rowman & Littlefield Publishing Group, Inc.
ApplauseBooks.com

Distributed by NATIONAL BOOK NETWORK

Contents

Preface

To criticise is to appreciate, to appropriate, to take intellectual possession.

Henry James

There are two ways of making an attempt on Laurence Olivier's life. The first, and most obvious, is the multi-volume biography, with his long and wonderful career meticulously mapped out – a chronological plod inspissated by quotations from contemporary reviews (e.g. 'The Sir Toby seemed to be a cousin not of Falstaff but of Bardolph, and was played very much in the vein of one of Sir Cedric Hardwicke's tooth-sucking yokels' *Jack O' London's Weekly*, 5 March 1937); the reminiscences of colleagues (e.g. 'In addition to his initial genius for acting, his imagination and meticulous concentration with which he approaches every part he plays, he has always had and still has the physical attributes of a romantic star,' intoned Noël Coward to a reporter – when the tape recorder was turned off, Coward would be more apt to ask his interviewer if he 'took it up the arse' or whether he knew it for a fact that one could become excited sexually by sitting naked in a cake); a rounding up of diaries, letters, memorabilia (e.g. 'Darling, don't forget the potted plant and the summer pudding in the larder,' jotted Vivien Leigh); and all of this garlanded with the obligatory Angus McBean photographs, stills from the BBC Hulton Picture Library, a snapshot or two of the young Larry larking about. Exemplars of this apparently objective style: Holroyd on Shaw; further back in time, Gibbon on the fall of Rome.*

But biography, the science of who we are, of what we ought to be, needn't come across as gossip or monumental alabaster; and the traditional cradle-to-the-grave approach can be paradoxically patternless and antiseptic, like the reconstruction of the plot of a play that has not survived. For where are the epiphanies? The digressions and curlicues?

* 'Another damned thick, square book! Always scribble, scribble! Eh! Mr Gibbon?' (The Duke of Gloucester, to Edward Gibbon, upon accepting the second volume of *A History of the Decline and Fall of the Roman Empire*.)

The vivid signs and smells and tints that we cherish about a man? In real life, the intensity of recall is not sequential, and yet the long scholarly biography, with its Newtonian laws of action and reaction, beginning with genealogy and concluding with cuttings from the obituaries, diligently charts careers, as if for a newsreel, and quite misses colour and tone. (*Where* was Olivier in Cottrell's book? Or Holden's? Or Spoto's?) There is no suspense, going year by year from obscurity and childhood – that 'forgotten boredom' in Larkin's phrase – to early success, to fame, to illness and death. That is not an interesting narrative; it is a death sentence, and we know the verdict all along. ('Early on Tuesday, 11 July 1989, a priest was called. During the prayers, Olivier's respiration became more laboured, but he was beyond pain' – Spoto.)

Why, I might look at themes and cross-currents and make my arrangement of scenes backward-reaching! To understand Olivier, his controlling principles and his sensibility, better, we could go towards his roots, his origins, not leave them behind in the opening chapters. We'd start with what we all know he was and see the inevitability and force of destiny; we'd see the evolution of genius, its stem and leaf and flower. It would be an exciting way of watching him change, and given that the duty of an author is not simply to review or explain art, but, through a passionate description of performances, to rival it, occasionally to surpass it; given that the duty of the critic is to be an artist, turning emotion into thought, then my task with Olivier is not to tell his story but, as if using cinematic cuts and fades, to evoke it.

The Real Life of Laurence Olivier – and his life has been in his art – is a personal essay dashed down as it were in pink chalks on sheets of foolscap. Here are my opinions and impressions, an expression of my feelings, formed after having read the dozens of memoirs and volumes devoted to him – the pharaoh's tomb was first looted by Felix Barker in 1953 ('As I write news comes that sudden illness has prevented [Vivien Leigh] from completing this film [*Elephant Walk*: she was replaced by Elizabeth Taylor], and the play which the Oliviers were planning for the Coronation [Rattigan's *The Sleeping Prince*] will have to be postponed'); and after having made my own archival delvings across the world. This book is my meditation on Olivier's roles, and how they related to his psychological and emotional needs. I have got to know him – and the truth of him – through his body of work. Why do we attend to him? Why can't people be indifferent to him? Though in his voice there was the clamour of a forge, Olivier wasn't larger than life, but he did enlarge life, its sadness and its valour. And though Salvador Dali claimed to have encountered a fellow schizophrenic, Olivier was rather more than two-faced; he was many-sided.

His intricacies, his shape: here is my subject. In writing about Olivier I will be writing a provocative history of the performing arts in this century, for if his origins were in the mossy, mildewed Victorian theatre – the world of Beerbohm Trees, assorted Terrys, and strands of dust like Harcourt Williams and Cedric Hardwicke – he ended up in Derek Jarman's unorthodox *War Requiem*, playing an old soldier. (He was *always* an old soldier – he would have been declamatory, but for the rage, the lashing out, which was part of his nature.) Between came his youthful success as a matinée idol, alongside Noël Coward in the first production of *Private Lives** – which led to Hollywood ('He has no chance – he tries

* Not only will this be the first book on Olivier *not* to tell the 'You great clob' anecdote, about corpsing during the run of *Private Lives*, I also manage not to tell the 'This is the end – you're all finished! It's all over!' story (when Olivier heard that war had been declared). Olivier in the Garrick Club pretending to be an Italian ('I am Papa Zoffany') is also given a miss. This alone will make me the more merchandisable, and yet perhaps you should know that I had an altercation with the publishers over these omissions. 'You write as if the reader has read at least one of the conventional biographies, which may not be the case,' was the criticism I received from a hop-o'-my-thumb at Random House when the manuscript was delivered.

To whom was this remark the most discourteous? The reader – assumed to be an ignoramus? To me – because it implied people wouldn't want to take the trouble to tackle the formal density of my prose? (*n.b.* writers are pathetically easily affronted – far more vain, mad, drunk, etc., than actors.) Well, as it is my belief that because you are holding this book in your hands you'll know the salient facts, and that you are unlikely to be asking 'Laurence Olivier? The actor?', I have told my editors that they can tickle my tits until Friday and I'll still not insert a 'potted history' of my subject 'at the beginning', for the benefit of slow-coaches unaware that after an illustrious career on stage and screen Olivier was recognized as the greatest performer ever ('The greatest Macbeth – since Macbeth'); that he was knighted in 1947; that at the age of fifty-five he became Director of the National Theatre; that after a divorce from Jill Esmond he married Vivien Leigh; that he then went on to marry Joan Plowright; and that he's not to be confused with T. E. Lawrence, D. H. Lawrence, or Vic Oliver, the comic pianist.

Though I may fail to be as gripping as Sheridan Morley or Alexander Walker, I have spent many years developing a baroque and multi-layered manner that is characteristic – my texts full of trapdoors through which the reader falls to find surprising things; a tone that in equilibrium keeps the giddy line midway (Browning) – and if you enter into the spirit of my quest all shall be revealed about the highs and lows of Olivier's life; whether or not he was a star at drama school; his first big break; attitudes towards money; rising through the ranks; recognition as a great actor; and so on. (If you still want to know what this book is 'about' I can but quote Graham Greene: 'Save your obviously valuable time and read only the epigraph' – Ellen Terry, as quoted by Virginia Woolf, misremembering Walt Whitman: Christ, what a pile-up!) Anyway, in my own fashion, I omit nothing.

to look like Ronald Colman,' said a report on his screen-test), where he was *the* Heathcliff in Wyler's *Wuthering Heights* ('The Mark of Hell was in his Eyes' ran the posters), *the* moody and taciturn Hitchcock hero in *Rebecca;* he played Shakespearian heroes at the Old Vic with Ralph Richardson; he alternated Mercutio and Romeo with John Gielgud – Edith Evans was the Nurse, Peggy Ashcroft was Juliet. He was *the*

There have been Olivier biographies galore (amounting, I estimate, to *c.* five thousand pages) – after Felix Barker, came Virginia Fairweather (1969), John Cottrell (1975) Margaret Morley (1977), Robert L. Daniels (1980), Thomas Kiernan (1981), Melvyn Bragg (1984), Felix Barker again (1984), Foster Hirsch (1984), Garry O'Connor (1984), Robert Tanitch (1985), Anthony Holden (1988), Lynn Haill (1989) and Donald Spoto (1991); and Olivier himself was aware that he'd become more mined than the Rhondda Valley. When Jill Esmond, his first wife, complained about the reduplication of what she deemed inaccuracies, he assured her that 'Mr Kiernan's book may be the eleventh or twelfth – I cannot be sure – and I have never read one of them . . . I would not believe a word I read about myself, ever!'

In place of reading, Olivier took to writing – *Confessions of an Actor* (in which 'he tells you everything and reveals absolutely nothing,' according to his son, Tarquin) was published in 1982; *On Acting*, reminiscences about his favourite roles, appeared four years later. Yet despite this welter, which encompasses gossip and conjecture (e.g. Spoto's unsubstantiated theory that Olivier was a committed homosexual – as if that had anything to do with the price of tea) and semi-scholarly graft (e.g. O'Connor's step-by-step account of an Australian tour – *Darlings of the Gods*, which was made into a mini-series starring Anthony Higgins), it paradoxically remains the case that until this moment Olivier's story has not been durably told. (O'Connor gave up before he began: 'There exists no outstanding and complete biography of Olivier for the simple reason that the total of the man, his life and his work, is still too great to be embraced by any one individual,' he sighed.)

Books on Olivier are full of awe – the prevailing tone is of glory, amazement, worship – but each is irresponsive; none of them dare to be inspired. Preoccupied with record-keeping, there has been absolutely no attempt at interpretation. Yet it is my belief that facts do not speak for themselves – and that what we want is not more incident or detail (and certainly not a re-traversing of the same ground) – and so my book will, instead, concentrate upon the 'evaluation of relationships, the comprehension of motives, the depiction of persons' (to quote from the creed of Richard Ellmann, formulated when he was fatigued by *another* biography of Hemingway to review for the *New York Times.*)

Having finished writing this book two months before adding this footnote, however, I think I can now say I don't really *believe* in conventional subservient biography. I never did – my Sellers opus was an attempt to blow apart the genre. I feel more strongly than ever that Olivier was analagous to Guy Davenport's description of Picasso: 'Picasso's biography is the simple fact that he has painted since age twelve. In between pictures there were poets, wives, visits to the bullring, the movies. It is obvious that Picasso's *life* is there on the canvasses; all else is lunch (there is photographic evidence that he eats), looking over the newspaper, and endorsing cheques.' (*Hudson Review*, Volume XXIII, 1970.)

Hamlet, *the* Henry V, *the* Richard III, *the* Othello (each put on celluloid). He made a film with Marilyn Monroe, *The Prince and the Showgirl* (Olivier and Monroe: 'the most exciting combination since black and white'); and he surprised everybody, directly after the war by wanting to play Archie Rice, the clapped-out music hall comic in *The Entertainer.* So I will see his limitations; I will decide what his success consisted of; I will ask how he saw himself. (In *Confessions of an Actor,* what did he remember or refuse to confide?)

His ancestors were churchmen and schoolmasters, and his father, Gerard Kerr Olivier, experimented with both avocations. His mother, Agnes Louise Crookenden, a headmaster's daughter, died of cancer in 1920, when Olivier was twelve, and his solitariness – his sense that something essential was missing in his life – stemmed from that moment. 'I've been looking for her ever since,' he said of his absent parent. 'Perhaps with Joanie [Plowright] I've found her again.'

It wasn't a mother he wanted – so much as a Holy Mother. Before going to St Edward's, in Oxford, Olivier had been for at least four years a choirboy at All Saints, in Margaret Street, London. What with those high Anglo-Catholic services and his father's regular sermons and professional admonitions about sin and evil, it is little wonder that there was a deep religious sense in his work. Beyond the Englishness, the heroism, the bravura acting; beyond the changes in his appearance – noses/wigs/walks: the playacting aspects of acting – what mattered was *inside*: the sensibility, the spirit. His autobiography had a quasi-religious aura; his final roles, in *Brideshead Revisited, A Voyage Round My Father,* and *King Lear,* were priestly and other-worldly. So what was the nature and extent of his guilt? Why do I feel that he believed he had not lived his life as he ought to have done so?

The answer involves Vivien Leigh. The human tragedy of their relationship is at the centre of Olivier's life (and mystery); theirs was a supreme mutually destructive twentieth-century love affair. They were at their happiest before their marriage (in August 1940); and once a couple they were already divided. Prior to the wedding, their erotic adventures had been surreptitious and fun; once conjoined, however, they began to bicker. Vivien lost the role of Cathy in *Wuthering Heights* (to Merle Oberon); but when she won the role of – and screen immortality as – Scarlett O'Hara in *Gone With the Wind,* Olivier was jealous. He subsequently failed to encourage David O. Selznick to have her cast as the second Mrs de Winter in *Rebecca*; nor was she his Elizabeth in *Pride and Prejudice,* when he was (wonderful as) the arrogant Darcy.

They did appear as Romeo and Juliet on Broadway, but it was a catastrophe. Her voice was inaudible in the huge American theatre (though there was no misunderstanding her words when she jostled through crowds of autograph-hunters at the stage door: 'Fuck off – now fuck off!'); and the roles Olivier did choose for her, Shaw and Shakespeare's Cleopatra, for instance, were beyond her range. Her triumph (and disaster) was as Blanche, the flighty, ageing beauty in Olivier's London production (and subsequently Elia Kazan's film adaptation) of *A Streetcar Named Desire* – a role which 'tipped her over into madness'. She endured electro-convulsive shock therapy, and was also diagnosed as suffering from tuberculosis.

Her illnesses filled Olivier with resentment – and guilt. The more he tried to retreat from her (into his work and affairs with Dorothy Tutin and Sarah Miles), the more devoted and/or outrageous she became. She had extravagant habits and the castle she furnished for their married life, Notley Abbey, in Buckinghamshire, took much of Olivier's money. (Medical costs and Jill Esmond's alimony took care of the rest.) Notley, indeed, like Hearst's San Simeon, was filled with famous guests week after week. The Oliviers played the role of adoring couple in public and dreaded being left alone together – privacy unleashed their savagery (as guests at Notley and fellow actors at Stratford-upon-Avon testify).

His last battles, however, were not, after all, marital; they combined fights against his own illnesses and the shipwreck of age with political and bureaucratic – and Oedipal – problems at the National Theatre: 'Many of us felt both enormous sentiments of love, of longing to be approved by him,' said Jonathan Miller, one of his associates, 'and patricidal feelings at the same time.' The history of the running of the Old Vic and the National seems to me like the Wars of the Roses, with Tynan, Miller and Michael Blakemore as boisterous barons; Peter Hall as a beady-eyed would-be usurper; Olivier as a Lear or Pericles, resenting being made to relinquish his power.

After he'd done so, it still wasn't the end. Olivier made *Sleuth* (with Michael Caine) and his many lucrative Hollywood cameos; he directed and starred in television plays, and in the Mortimer (*A Voyage Round My Father*) and Evelyn Waugh (*Brideshead Revisited*) outings, he had definitive death-bed scenes. Like Ralph Richardson and John Gielgud, his last things are amongst his best. Yet, where Richardson turned acting into daydreaming, and where Gielgud has used the cinema to portray an ironic patrician scorn, Olivier maintained – and refined – his gusto and ferocity. Some performances, owing to illness, never actually flamed into being (Nathan Detroit in *Guys and Dolls*; Don Vito Corleone, no less, in *The Godfather*); but there were enough appearances as princes, generals, dukes and scheming lawyers to prove that he was, ultimately, acting's Picasso. Prodigal, randy, assured, his was a presence few can expect to rival, let alone over-reach. This book concludes with a look at his legacy, at his taste. What effects has he had? What was his influence? He held dominion over the performing arts – but what else?

Our imaginations, for one thing.

Chapter One
Either/Or

Olivier had invited him to play King Lear at Chichester (though as a mother-fixated malcontent, 'fat and scant of breath', he'd have been an eye-opening Hamlet, far better than the other comedian, Peter O'Toole, whom he did direct in the part); they both leased apartments in Roebuck House, Stag Place, Victoria (the fixtures and fittings failed to impress Ingmar Bergman, who noted Lord Olivier's un-Scandinavian shabby-genteel housekeeping: 'the expensive sofas grubby, the wall-paper torn . . . Everything was dusty or stained. The breakfast cups were not properly washed up, the glasses had lip marks on them, the wall-to-wall carpets were worn out, the picture windows streaky');* and on 8 September 1980, Olivier was early to arrive at his memorial service at St Martin-in-the-Fields, Trafalgar Square – where, thirteen years previously, there had been a service of thanksgiving for Vivien Leigh. Olivier was ushered along a pew to sit next to Bernard Cribbins.†

Quite how often they otherwise criss-crossed, I've no idea; but here's a thought. Olivier said that Archie Rice was inspired by the artistes he recalled from his Birmingham Rep days, in the twenties. So what if a Ray Bros revue had been in town or passing through? Peg and Bill and, backstage in a Moses basket, their squalling infant? A switched body! Divided twins! Had Olivier, when in Birmingham, run away to join a music hall company, he'd have grown up to be Peter Sellers; for, turn Olivier and Sellers round and they were reverse sides of each other; and I don't mean that where Sellers recoiled from the colour purple (the

* The hard-to-please Swede's problems began at Heathrow: 'When I arrived in England there was no one to meet me! I am Ingmar Bergman. If I had invited Laurence Olivier to Sweden, not only would I have been at the airport to meet him but my entire company also.'

† Sellers' co-star in *Wrong Arm of the Law* and *Two-Way Stretch*, and Olivier's from *Homage to T. S. Eliot*, recorded at the Globe Theatre on 13 June 1965. Groucho Marx also appeared. Cribbins performed a John Dankworth arrangement of *Sweeney Agonistes*; Olivier read 'Little Gidding'.

shade of death), Olivier adored it (he owned a purple taxi); or that where Sellers' mother was clinging and omnipresent (kept to hand by spiritualists once she'd dropped off the twig), Olivier's was absent, dying when he was a child. It is more that they were both saturated in their work, wholly absorbed in their roles, and it's their imaginative force which envelops us. They were conscious of their separateness – set apart from the rest of us by the scale of their talent, if nothing else* – and excelled at playing solitaries. Sellers' characters are defiant dreamers: Clouseau, the mournful detective; Mr Martin, the Scottish accountant; Fred Kite, the embattled shop-steward; Robert Danvers, in his deserted bachelor pad; or Chance the gardener, puttering off across the surface of a misty lake. Olivier's creations, less impassive and more intent, are isolated by their rank (his many kings and generals or Monroe's consort in *The Prince and the Showgirl*), by their responsibilities (Nelson, in *That Hamilton Woman*, for instance), or by their guilt and intense emotions (Heathcliff, in *Wuthering Heights*, and James Tyrone, in *Long Day's Journey into Night*, would serve as examples). Despite the sense we get that these men are on their own, however, the actors are able to suggest an intimacy, a collusiveness. We are inside Kite's mind with him when he is successively humiliated; Hamlet and Richard III turn and talk to us, include us. We share Clifford Mortimer's anger at being blind, in *A Voyage Round My Father*. When Othello comes on, toying with a long-stemmed red rose, we feel a distinct ripple of pleasure, of sexuality.

Gielgud's heroes used to be sniffily above-it-all, pictures of lamentation, and Chaplin's tumbles seemed to take place behind glass, but Olivier and Sellers' characters have fertile minds and are therefore never boxed in, except perhaps by circumstance, the chance and accident of other people. James Tyrone caterwauls in his damp clapboard house, Captain Edgar dances himself to death on his fogbound island, but like Hamlet prowling the haunted ramparts and staircases of Elsinore, in the nutshell of their heads they can account themselves kings of infinite space – like Evelyn Tremble, in *Casino Royale*, wish-fulfillingly making himself James Bond, or Old Sam, in *The Optimists of Nine Elms*, a decrepit street busker who is also, somehow, grand and impressive. This is because Olivier and Sellers invest their creations with weird inner freedoms, of which the acting gives signals and hints. For the paradox of these two players is that, even when Olivier is gesticulative or Sellers caricatured,

* 'Once you get to the top, the load of staying there is almost superhuman,' claimed Olivier. Sellers, likewise, found success – the burden of public expectation; the need not to let yourself down – quite intolerable. Peter Hall has said that had Sellers possessed the talent to handle his talent, 'he'd be an Olivier'.

they are neither artificial nor fanciful – rather, they disfigure or distort, tilt or splinter reality and raise nature to its height. (In contrast to Ralph Richardson, say, who was not natural but supernatural.) We believe in them – despite acting being make-believe.

That might be the first comparison to strike us, the sheer love of wigs, false noses, outlandish clothes, false teeth (Olivier bequeathed his Shylock snappers to Dustin Hoffman); the excitement of costume and theatrical impedimenta. Sellers and Olivier were always disguising themselves, powdering their faces green or learning new walks, a long brisk stride for Clouseau, a panther's slow, graceful jounce for Othello. This is acting's deep appeal, to be able to alter oneself, and 'I found it the biggest fun,' Olivier said, 'the idea of pretending to be somebody else, of making an audience believe that I was somebody else.'

With Olivier this is an earnest of his versatility – one week Hotspur, next week Justice Shallow; Oedipus before the interval, Mr Puff when you returned to your seat. The showing off is delightful and direct. It is as if, through his successive selves, he represented, or made us attentive to and aware of – with delicacy and accuracy – our own discontinuities, or inconsistency; of how we can be one person, and then we are another. And there is something of the nature of life here, of what's quick and vital. Olivier doesn't seem to be hiding within his myriad manifestations; nor did he dart between roles searching for an identity – as Sellers did. Sellers, infinitely flexible, like moving water, never settled on what he wanted to be. Music hall goon? Ealing or Boulting Bros character actor? Hip and groovy Hollywood star in the Age of Aquarius? Family man, lord of the manor at Chipperfield, or womanizing divorcee inhabiting a succession of penthouse suites? He didn't have his own voice, only a babble of funny accents and impersonations, a polyphony. He was the master mimic, afraid of the vacancy of his core; a hollow man.

There was an element of the great impersonator about Olivier, too; though far from being like the sea ('I am the sea!' wails Titus Andronicus), he was a marble triton amongst the foam, having as his fixed point English history and his place within it, as heir to Kean, Garrick and Irving ('I based my Richard III voice on imitations I'd heard people do of Irving'). He was always pleased with his technical perfection and that the critics had praised the East Side New York accent he learned from Clare Eames for Elmer Rice's *The Adding Machine*, in 1928 ('I made a very careful study of it . . . and Clare very carefully taught me the accent, absolutely precisely, every word of it'). To prepare for *Carrie*, two decades later, he spent time with Spencer Tracy, acquiring an imperturbability for Hurstwood, a toughness, that makes the adulterous flight with Jennifer Jones the more tragic: this is no pleasure trip, undermined with flashes of guilt – Olivier embodies integrity, getting into his voice, for all the outward calm, the man's quiver of panic as he morally lapses. For *Semi-Detached*, at the Saville Theatre, in 1962, he listened to tapes of Nottingham shopkeepers, devoting (recalls John Osborne) 'tremendous care, literal-minded care, on perfecting the accent' – to no avail. 'What part of America are you from, sir?' he was asked innocently, when he tried to blend in in the Midlands. For *Inchon*, an epic about the Korean War, he retreated to Franco Zeffirelli's villa at Positano and endlessly replayed a recording of General Douglas MacArthur making a speech. 'He went at it over and over again. Unfortunately for the rest of us, they weren't awfully interesting speeches and by the end of the hundredth repetition I thought I and my other guests would go mad,' sighed his exasperated host.

Olivier described the accent in the Elmer Rice play as being 'incidentally . . . like no other in the world', and in his late films – *The Jazz Singer, Dracula* or *The Betsy*, amongst many others – he comes out with Germanic/Jewish/Dutch noises that, similarly, are like no others in the world. He became vocally cartoonish – quite rivalling Joan Plowright's Yugoslav squawk in *I Love You to Death*. 'Oh, to have been a fly on the wall when these two meatballs were in the shower at home practicing their bad accents together,' remarked Joe Queenan in his essay 'If You Can't Say Something Nice, Say It In Broken English'.

But Olivier was always mocked for his experiments and inventions (French-Canadian in *49th Parallel*; Russian in *Moscow Nights, The Demi-Paradise*, and *The Shoes of the Fisherman*), perhaps because his impersonations, like Meryl Streep's of Danish, Australian or English accents, are slightly off, over-precise, like elocution lessons. They are put on over the top of their normal tones and rhythms. Ululating in *The Jazz Singer* ('I hef no son') or growling in *Cat on a Hot Tin Roof*, Cantor Rabinovitch and Big Daddy are still Olivier; just as, though he developed what he described as 'the violet velvet that I felt was necessary in the timbre of the voice' in Othello – for which he was much lampooned ('What he gives us is a Notting Hill Gate Negro,' said Jonathan Miller) – he is still Olivier. He was always different – and the same. He could toy with caricature – and not only with how he sounded; look at the length of Richard III's nose or Henry V's haircut; he could literally make a spectacle of himself – yet there's no escaping his grandeur, his refinement. It's the quality Zeffirelli wanted him to bring to the small role of Nicodemus, in *Jesus of Nazareth*, who speaks the prophecy of Isaiah – that Jesus is the true Messiah, who'll take upon himself all the sins of the world. 'The words of the prophet issued from [Olivier's] lips in a whisper. They were not recited, but seemed, rather, born in him,' recalls the director. 'There is that capacity in Olivier to suffuse himself with light. He . . . convinces us of the reality of the human drama that he is going through as a Jew of the ancient faith.' And in an even briefer role, Dr Spaander, who pleads with SS General Ludwig for a temporary truce to remove Allied wounded, in *A Bridge Too Far*, there's that unique quality again. Olivier, and only Olivier, as the director Richard Attenborough knew, could convey by his countenance alone the sorrow and pity of war – which is as well, because his Dutch accent, in his scenes with Liv Ullmann, where we contend with her Swedish one, is out of *The Muppet Show*.

We overlook Olivier's funny voices because his performances, attentive, active and penetrating, are creative rather than imitative. That his intonations are askew is not the issue, as it is when Sellers devised an atrocious French accent for Clouseau. When he was offered the role of the Mahdi, the Sudanese zealot who has General 'Chinese' Gordon killed, in *Khartoum*, Olivier wrote to Michael Relph, the associate of Basil Dearden, the director, asking 'if they were able to be obtained, please send me the tapes of the Mahdi made by any Peter Sellers types from the Sudanese Legation . . .' It is amusing that Olivier went to such trouble, working at the part five weeks before shooting began, hoping to be anthropologically exact in a Hollywood blockbuster which starred Charlton Heston ('THEY SAY THE NILE STILL RUNS RED FROM THE BATTLE FOR KHARTOUM! The City that became a Torch – the Torch that Fired the World!'); and it is interesting that he specifically connects exotic accents with Sellers; but his scenes in the film, though flirting with absurdity – Olivier is wrapped in tribal togs and has ferocious eyebrows – carry weight, authority. 'I shall take Khartoum in blood, and the streets will run in blood, and the Nile will taste of blood for one hundred miles, and every Egyptian will die; every child, woman, man, Sudanese too, who opposes the will of my Lord Mohammad will die . . .' he says – and you believe him.

Khartoum was made in between performances of *Othello* at the Queen's Theatre (where the National Theatre Company was giving a ten-week season), and shortly after the stage production of *Othello* had been filmed for posterity at Shepperton. So no doubt the Mahdi benefits from Shakespearian effects; he is brother to the noble Moor, the one who stayed behind in Africa and got to know the Egyptian who'd given their mother that handkerchief which had magic in the web of it, the worms being hallowed that did breed the silk. But there's more to it than this;

more to the Mahdi than his investiture with Olivier's concurrent Othello – which might be considered a fortuitous accident. What's at issue is that time and again his performances have an air of ridicule – which he checks, or subverts, with his inherent energy. Michael Ingolby, in *Fire Over England*, is impetuous and piratical, until called to the colours by his Queen, Elizabeth I; Heathcliff, the spurned stable lad, moping on the moors, returns as a glowering, taciturn landowner, subjecting his former tormentors, the Lintons, to unspecified violence – perhaps he no more than glares at them, as Richard III glares at Buckingham ('I am not in the giving vein'); or as Ezra Lieberman, the frail Nazi hunter in *The Boys from Brazil*, glares at Dr Josef Mengele's ex-nurse, Frieda Maloney, played by Uta Hagen. These men dare you to laugh at them. Their voice has the colour of stone.

There is a rage about Olivier, which makes him very focused, and the reason why he'd play Romeo as Mercutio, or Hamlet as Hotspur (or Archie Rice as Coriolanus, James Tyrone as Prospero and Clifford Mortimer as Lear); his acting, in effect, would rewrite roles, so that doubters or dawdlers become shrewd and purposeful. He was illusionless, where the significance of Sellers' characters is that they are fantasists. Sellers' characters imagine themselves to be other than they are; Olivier's know in their minds that they are superior and such knowledge gives them a cold strength, so that when he plays evil men, Richard, or the dentist in *Marathon Man*, there is no instability; they are not mad, like Sellers and his creations. There is no – this is what's most alarming – irresponsibility. Indeed, it's Olivier's concentration which draws us to him; he's the principal cause of energy in any scene. This rage? This concentration? It has to do with his joy at being alive and his anger at the facts of death, age, waning powers. Sellers feared death, too, of course, after his heart attacks; and he had a passion for ghosts, spirit mediums and communicating with the dead. But he didn't stand for life *against* death, as Olivier did. (Olivier's death scenes were frequently lively and prolonged.) Sellers could only look back. He was afflicted with nostalgia, for his childhood, when he was grown-up; for *The Goon Show*, when he was a film star; for his first wife, when he'd exhausted three subsequent spouses. He'd revisit houses where he'd once lived, reminisce with old air-force colleagues. Only in his yesterdays was he certain that his troubles were far away; yesterday was his land of lost content – where the impetus with Olivier was to reject the past, to move on. 'If I've finished with something I can't bear to go back,' he said in 1976. 'Take Chichester . . . I can't bear to go back. And at the National Theatre I feel like a ghost. On the opening night I felt like a ghost . . . I don't want to go back. I feel awkward. It feels like harking back.' The past was important only as a measure of how far he'd fled from it, as an index of his ambition. 'I will show them, I will show them, I will show them,' he said of his family when still in his teens. In the fifties he rejected the rustling-chocolate-papers plays of Christopher Fry (*Venus Observed*) and Terence Rattigan (*The Sleeping Prince*) for John Osborne and the Royal Court; selecting a team for the National, he rejected the actors who'd been with him when he managed the St James Theatre, or who had been in the original Old Vic Company, or who were in his Shakespeare films. As Esmond Knight* recalls, to approach Olivier for work was to elicit a firm refusal. 'It was so hurtful, like the King in *Henry V*, casting aside all his old chums, Falstaff and company.'

Instead, founding and running the Chichester Festival and forming the troupe which eventually went up to London, to the Old Vic until the new premises were ready on the South Bank, which they weren't until 1976, he recruited new talent (Jacobi, Hopkins, Stephens, Maggie Smith) and quite deliberately got rid of his former colleagues. His marriage to Joan Plowright, who played his daughter in *The Entertainer*, suggested he was literally espousing a younger generation. Plowright, twenty-two years his junior, 'was part of an entirely new world he wanted to move into,' claimed Tony Richardson. It's like Picasso, a new woman for a new phase in his work – a highly conscious interpenetration of art and life.

Twenty-odd years back again, in the thirties, it was Vivien Leigh who'd represented a new world he'd wanted to possess, and the tragic estrangement was from Jill Esmond, whom he married because he wondered what love felt like, and about whom he later said, 'Poor old Jill, she didn't deserve much, but she deserved better than me.' Vivien transformed him – or at least redefined him – and brought out his bashful streak and flirtatiousness. During the making of *Fire Over England*, in 1936, he was smitten by her prettiness, her will and her frailty. Spoilt, barmy and pampered, Vivien aroused him; in her turn, she was always afraid that she would lose him, and she was always vexed by him. As a woman simultaneously profound, or anyway dreamily remote, and shallow, she was the only person in Olivier's life who was too much for him, and he quickly began to resent her proximity and the ways she had of

* Esmond Knight (1906–87) was Fluellen in *Henry V*, Bernardo in *Hamlet*, Ratcliffe in *Richard III* and Colonel Hoffman in *The Prince and the Showgirl*; he's also a judge in *A Voyage Round My Father*.

tempting him to abandon control. (She went mad for love, as did Lynne Frederick, Sellers' widow.)

But at least she supported his intense belief in himself, and Olivier was conscious of his distinction, and this could make him inadvertently funny.* Notorious for his rigid routine of physical training (Sellers, incidentally, never attempted exercise), he once took a fall on the Brighton sea front. Nobody came to his assistance or recognized him in his tracksuit, and so finally he had to shout, 'I am Sir Laurence Olivier! I need help!' It was as if he was always playing two parts simultaneously, Olivier-the-legend, and then the actual role. There is a sinister painting which captures this, Salvador Dali's dual portrait of Olivier and Olivier-as-Richard-III, commissioned by Alexander Korda in 1955. 'Sir Laurence is two-faced, I see a split personality,' said the artist, who has the actor's head nightmarishly floating and superimposing itself upon the King's face. But what's startling isn't Olivier's resemblance to Richard's sharp, cruel features; it's that what we are looking at is the process of soul-shifting, of a congruence that is to do with cold-bloodedness and calculation.

Another example of Olivier's curious distance from a role, and yet his simultaneous overlap with it, is the famous first rehearsal for *Othello*, where he was bespectacled and in his street clothes, yet the voice was in character. It was 'a shattering experience', remembered Kenneth Tynan. 'Normally on these occasions the actors do not exert themselves . . . [Olivier] delivered the works . . . He fell on the text like a tiger.' He was both the actor *and* the Moor. And because of this discrepancy – the way he doesn't vanish into a role, but gives a commentary on it, which conveys Olivier's presence, his essence – because of this divergence, he is a comic actor. Or more precisely, an ironic one. Though he advised Michael Gambon to 'go for the laughs' when tackling a tragic part, I don't mean comic in the sense of hilarity, and in any case 'clowns have always made me want to cry', he claimed. Nor, particularly, that Olivier

* And an easy target for satirists. Here is his entry in Henry Root's *World of Knowledge* (London, 1982):

> OLIVIER, Lord (b.1906 [*sic*]): Our first player. Burgundy to Gielgud's claret, he gives every word of a part the rasp of danger. Too good an actor to play real people, his Othello had more essential *négritude* than ever Paul Robeson's did . . . Can anyone who saw his Oedipus at the New Theatre . . . forget his terrible cry of anguish . . . ? It was based, I remember reading, on the mating cry of the North American bull moose. Ever a perfectionist, Olivier spent nine months practising it in a forest thirty miles from Quebec. With such success, in fact, that he got shot four times.

absorbed acting tricks from comedians, such as George Robey,* whose 'diction was superb', or Chaplin, who 'talked very pretentiously in his half-American, half-Cockney accent . . . I remember him saying "Hamlet was a young man who was subject to all youth's *stimuli* . . ." Well, years later I used the same rather pompous inflection on the word *anthropophagi* in Othello's speech to the Senators, so Charlie Chaplin got me a nice laugh.'

What I'm getting at is that Olivier's humour is in his understandings, in the way he can inhabit the minds of villains or heroes, and be Macbeth and Macheath; or, in *Becket*, where he could play, with ease and conviction, either the Archbishop or the King; or, in *Romeo and Juliet*, where in 1935 he could share the roles of Romeo and Mercutio with John Gielgud. This dexterity is devilish. He didn't possess (Sybil Thorndike's phrase) 'that tortured egocentricity', that claustrophobia, or tightening in the chest feeling, you need for tragedy. His mind is quicksilvery, inspired, a little absurd. He sees the high comedy of it all. Olivier almost mocks the acting process at times, with his sing-song delivery and scene-stealing (pretending to swat flies or wasps in Shallow's orchard or Clifford Mortimer's garden, to take attention off Ralph Richardson and Alan Bates respectively). His work had a near-facetious aspect. He didn't dissolve away, like Sellers, who'd go around believing he was a Welsh librarian or an Indian doctor. Acting wasn't a mental condition; it curiously remained as acting, as a craft. It was not for him, as it was for the schizoid Sellers, a state of delusion and dissolution; it was, instead, a process of, or it involved, dissimulation, to which he could bring, like a conjuror, his swiftness and certainty.

Where Sellers – a melancholic constrained to wear the cap and bells – was an inchoate mass defined by the roles he played, a nothing who became something when given the framework of a script, Olivier, by contrast, imposed his will and impudence not only on the parts he chose – so that (for example) Archie Rice ceased being an end-of-the-pier flop and wasn't quite such a brittle shell. He was a deposed king. (Interestingly, *The Entertainer* has not succeeded with any actor since.) And Hamlet, too, back in 1937,† was augmented. 'He believed he had a great deal of Hamlet-like anguish and spiritual paralysis to bring to

* Sir George Robey was cast as Falstaff in a flashback scene Olivier interpolated into *Henry V*.

† Michael Redgrave was Laertes and Alec Guinness was both Osric and Olivier's understudy: 'I . . . was outraged at the gymnastic leaps and falls required by his example.' Other stars who understudied Olivier include Albert Finney (*Coriolanus*), Anthony Hopkins (*The Dance of Death*) and Robert Stephens (*The Entertainer*).

the part,' claimed Tyrone Guthrie. But Olivier also imposed his will and impudence on us, the audience. The audience was the enemy, to attack, to subdue. He told John Mills that he made his first entrance thinking, 'You are about to see the greatest fucking performance of your entire life, and I will be giving it – you lucky people.'

Arrogant, yes, and yet we are compelled to accept this; it's inarguable. 'There's always got to be something,' said Richard Burton admiringly, of the rhetoric, sword play, acrobatic leaps and tumbles, 'that pulls a gasp from the audience and turns them into a thunderstruck mob. He loves power over them.' Olivier likened himself to a hypnotist. 'All my life I have known I could stand on a stage and command an audience,' he boasted to Robert Stephens; and when fully confident he could, in fact, pare away attention-grabbing excesses. At the second performance of *Richard III*, at the New Theatre in 1944, 'I felt . . . this complete confidence . . . I felt a little power of hypnotism . . . I felt that I had them, to such an extent that I didn't even bother to put on the limp. I thought, I've got them anyway. I needn't bother with all this characterisation any more.'

If he went in for elaborate make-up early on – 'You hear Macbeth's first line, then Larry's make-up comes on, then Banquo comes on, then Larry comes on,' commented Vivien Leigh waggishly of a 1937 production, for which Olivier devised an ornate ringleted lion mask – the nose putty and greasepaint ('The smell of a stick of greasepaint, No. 5, No. 9, lake, $7^1/_2$, still makes my scalp tingle') diminished with the years, as was the case with Sellers, who as Chance, the Mr Nobody in *Being There*, or as Nayland Smith, the doleful sleuth in *The Fiendish Plot of Dr Fu Manchu*, appeared as himself, white-haired and translucent. It is as if the actors spiritualized themselves, Sellers' swan-song actually being the god-like gnomic Fu, chasing Helen Mirren, Olivier's being white-haired and translucent divinities like Zeus, in *Clash of the Titans*, chasing Maggie Smith, or the Augustus John figure in *The Ebony Tower*, who again has women in the background, and who informs his young rivals, 'You can't have any art without danger.'

The danger is not necessarily physical, though when he catalogued his injuries for William Hobbs' manual, *Techniques of the Stage Fight*, Olivier seemed as calamitous as Clouseau: broken ankle, from jumping over a balcony as Bothwell in *Queen of Scots*, in 1934, followed by torn cartilages, ripped calf muscles, impalements, a broken foot, an arrow in the shinbone, electrocution, and a 'landing from a considerable height, scrotum first, upon acrobat's knee'. Acting, for Olivier, meant action; but the way he completely wins our confidence – the same as Sellers – is by keeping still and alert and letting the other fellows get hectic and flustered. Harry Secombe and Spike Milligan were manic in *The Goon Show*, and Herbert Lom blinks and wheezes throughout the Pink Panther series, and Sellers pockets the scenes by timing his reactions, affecting to be aghast or helpful, taking in the world's perplexity with reproachful, sad eyes. Thus, Astrov, gazing at Michael Redgrave's Vanya cracking up, or Clifford Mortimer, enthroned in his deckchair, monitoring the seasons, or Air Chief Marshal Sir Hugh Dowding, listening to the bombs fall upon London like unrelenting flints, in *Battle of Britain*. Thus, too, Nelson, in *That Hamilton Woman*, enduring the chatter of Vivien Leigh, or Wellington, in *Lady Caroline Lamb*, no doubt finding Sarah Miles more clamorous than a parrot against rain.

Eyes narrowed, nostrils scenting the air for danger: you'll find both Othello and Clouseau doing that; and I can imagine Sellers and Olivier working together, perhaps as Olivier and Danny Kaye worked together, in beautiful routines. (He told Paul Rudd on the set of *The Betsy* that 'I think the most enjoyable night for me as a performer was *The Night of a Hundred Stars*,* when Vivien and Danny Kaye and I got into little schoolgirls' clothes and sang "Triplets"' – a song about precocious siblings.) Indeed, perhaps they did have a spectral association? They both admired the ethereal and melodious Robert Donat. Donat was Gielgud's original choice for the Romeo/Mercutio apportionment; he was Olivier's own original choice for the Chorus in *Henry V* (a duty Donat wanted to discharge 'if it is humanly possible': it wasn't†); and Olivier was Alexander Korda's original choice for the commissar who is actually a British spy in *Knight Without Armour*; but it was Donat, despite chronic asthma attacks, who got to watch Marlene Dietrich strip off her furs – much to the delight of the pubertal Sellers, *Knight Without Armour* being one of his first favourite films. Donat appears in the Notley visitors' book, he was offered the role of the Duke in Olivier's New York production of *Venus Observed* in 1951 and 'turned it down flat', and Olivier read the lesson at his funeral in 1958.

Donat and Olivier did manage to collaborate successfully at least once, in *The Magic Box*, directed by Sellers' mentor, John Boulting,‡ as the film industry's contribution to the Festival of Britain, in 1951.

* At the London Palladium in 1951. It's rather horrible and survives on DRG Records, Archive Series DARC-2-1104, as *Command Performance*.

† Leslie Banks took the role. He appeared with Olivier in *Fire Over England*, as the Earl of Leicester, and as Olivier's elder brother, Keith Durrant, in *Twenty-One Days*.

‡ Boulting, with his twin brother Roy, directed Sellers in, amongst others, *I'm All Right, Jack*, *Heavens Above* and *There's a Girl in My Soup*.

Actually, it isn't a film; it's an hallucination: a Victorian England, of bright-blue skies and snow-white lace antimacassars, canary-yellow corn-fields and jet-black steam trains, populated by its character actors – Joyce Grenfell, Stanley Holloway, Miles Malleson, Bernard Miles, Cecil Parker, Dennis Price, Margaret Rutherford, Thora Hird . . . All it lacks is Sellers, though he is *there*, in Donat's shuffling, pathos-ridden William Friese-Greene, the pioneer of moving pictures. Olivier shares Friese-Greene's big moment, when the scientist puts his projector together – the magic box itself, expensively constructed from sliding mahogany panels, brass screws and hand-ground lenses – and his invention, for which he has undergone penury and imprisonment for debt, works. It works! In his excitement he reels into the street, there to find Olivier as Second Holborn Policeman. The ensuing scene is pantomime. Donat's tears and agitation bring out Olivier's sceptical kindness – he can't be sure these are tears of joy, and the subdued comedy is that the bobby is half expecting a body, or evidence of a misdeed, up in the attic laboratory. All Friese-Greene wants, in fact, is a witness – someone besides himself to testify that pictures can move. And the scene is indeed moving. Olivier goes from bewilderment and caution to professional courtesy and wonder ('You must be a very proud man, Mr Friese-Greene'); Donat glows with pride – his faith has paid off. He's rapt, and rapturous, hardly noticing the copper's departure as he stares ahead at the figures dancing on the sheet. This is the blissful self-absorption of Chance looking at his television screens, and ignoring Shirley Maclaine; of Dr Pratt, in *The Wrong Box*, absent-mindedly using a kitten to blot his ink, and oblivious to Peter Cook.

The scene was adapted for the *South Bank Show* documentary series on Olivier, broadcast in 1982. Instead of Friese-Greene's flickering footage of holiday-makers on the promenade, the Second Holborn Policeman now beheld clips of Olivier's actual movies, overlaid with specially composed patriotic music – a parody, I felt, of Walton's pomp-and-circumstance scores for the Shakespeare films. But if this was a joke – Olivier the great actor mesmerized by the evidence of his own career – it didn't quite come off. Because Olivier wasn't looking at Olivier; just as, in the untampered-with original scene in *The Magic Box*, Olivier wasn't simply goggling at a nutty professor's scratchy strip of celluloid. What registers in the constable's face isn't only an appreciation of what he's seeing; it's an understanding of the effort, the faith, the enduring creative impulse that lies behind, or beyond, what he's seeing. It's the aura he brought to *Jesus of Nazareth* again, or what Sybil Thorndike meant when she said, 'Larry . . . doesn't always know what he can achieve, because that's bigger than himself. He's bigger than he knows.'

She was thinking of his Oedipus ('something in himself made it larger . . . his performance took on higher qualities') and of the Captain in Strindberg's *The Dance of Death* ('grim humour, defiant humour; he understands that'), and she suggests a mystical dimension, or divine afflatus, which Donat himself perceived when he wrote to congratulate Olivier on his Second Holfborn Policeman performance. 'I don't think I told you how much I adored your make-up. [Olivier was adorned with a steel-grey wispy moustache, the tips waxed, and trimmed mutton-chop whiskers, such as he did sprout and sport in real life throughout the seventies.] You looked like a sort of celestial Tiger Tim. The kind of Tiger Tim you might find in the desert instead of the sphinx.'

Which is by way of saying that there is something of the real Olivier – and Sellers – in their brooding silences. Indeed, Olivier is at his worst when impetuous, jumpy, gabbling. As Logan, the barrister who falls for Merle Oberon in *The Divorce of Lady X*, he's too fizzed-up; in *Moscow Nights*, as Captain Ignatoff, there's a good deal of bleating and flippancy, which is unappealing. Olivier is not Olivier if he is unable to contain himself, and this is not exclusively an affliction of the early films and plays, i.e. before Vivien smoothed out his awkwardness. The sneering, snorting, derisive Andrew Wyke, in *Sleuth*, pacing the floors of his mock-Tudor mansion, setting traps and playing games, is not a pleasurable performance. There is nothing to the man. Olivier can do little but bluster. He is a cipher in a thrillerish farce, and is demeaned into concocting a character out of mannerisms, finally relying on quotations from his own repertoire: Wyke puts on a periwig and pretends to throw a fistful of snuff into the air, like Captain Brazen in *The Recruiting Officer* or Tattle in *Love for Love*. Those sneers and derisive snorts derive from *Moscow Nights*.

When not speaking, when not overburdened with disguises, when this actor is responding to a life beneath the text, to the life between the lines, it is then, I think, devoid of gimmickry, stripped of protective camouflage, that we come to realize that his work is a personal record, the theatre and cinema allowing him to demonstrate his state of mind; the theatre and cinema showing his struggle to express some inner force. Hence, his acting is autobiographical. I don't mean that each role paralleled his life, but that acting was an exaggeration, or commentary, or renegotiation of his own experience, its passion and circumstances. Acting was a testament to his rapid imagination, which was relentless. Look how hard he worked! Thousands of roles, hundreds of plays, dozens of films; scores of recordings, voice-overs, narrations. He managed theatres, led companies, toured the world. He was a human industry.

With Sellers, who also in his time played countless parts, industriousness was more evidence of his madness. Hysterical, egotistical, clinically depressed, his ever-shifting forms were an attempt to flee from himself, never to repeat himself. He was haphazard, improvisatory, unable to retake a scene in a film studio, let alone possessing the discipline for theatre. Irresponsibility is never a criticism you'd level at Olivier, who could be painfully professional. Harry Andrews remembers him producing real tears for an emotional scene in *Nicholas and Alexandra*, but the actor refused to accept the praises of cast and crew. 'No, I was too weepy. A bit too weepy. I'd better have another take.' Sellers never developed a capacity to be self-critical. He was too vain for judgement. If he muffed his lines or bungled a gag, he'd sack co-stars, fire directors, stage tantrums and create chaos. He was completely deranged by the end.

In that their life becomes their work – Sellers' a diary of a madman; Olivier's a story of shunning happiness, as if he felt he didn't deserve it – it is necessary to rewrite Eliot. It is my belief that the more perfect the artist, the more completely interconnected – not separate – in him will be the man who suffers and the mind which creates. Sellers and Olivier played the roles they did because of the people they were. Quilty, broad and massy, in *Lolita*, is Sellers himself, supple and evasive; Clouseau is loneliness played for laughs; the characters in *Hoffman* and *There's a Girl in My Soup* demonstrate Sellers' difficulties with girls, whom he treated as adornments or mechanical objects like his cameras or cars – literally, as models.

What happens with Olivier is that somewhere inside his stage people and film performances there'll always be the person, dark and ferocious, coping with the rapture and pain love has caused him. The marriage to Vivien, its break-up and long-drawn-out consequences, is the source of Edgar's life in *The Dance of Death*, of Tyrone's in *Long Day's Journey into Night*; and he himself described *Macbeth*, in which he appeared with Vivien at Stratford,* as 'a domestic tragedy . . . It's the passage of two people, one going up and one going down.' Role after role is a meditation on romantic love, or the responsibilities of paternal love, or the loss of

* Gielgud reckoned Vivien's Lady Macbeth the best he ever saw. '[It] showed an astonishing vocal power and poignancy of feeling.' He was less happy about the idea of her Juliet. When she put forward the suggestion that she might include the potion scene from *Romeo and Juliet* in the wartime revue *Spring Party*, Gielgud said, 'Oh no, Vivien! Only a great actress can do that sort of thing.'

maternal love. Seldom, in Olivier's work, does love bring joy. Perhaps it does at the end of *Love Among the Ruins,* when Sir Arthur Granville-Jones, KC, wins the affections of Katharine Hepburn's Jessica Medlicott, after defending her in a breach of promise suit, but George Cukor's television film is turn-of-the-century whimsy. More usually there's no solace. Can we believe that Darcy and Elizabeth Bennet will be happy for long? Not with Olivier being that saturnine.

From the adulterous shenanigans of *No Funny Business,* in the thirties, to Mr Halpern and Mr Johnson discovering that the woman they lived with and loved all their lives remained a stranger (in Alvin Rakoff's two-hander in 1983); from his Chekhov productions, with their thwarted emotions, to *Henry V,* where the King's courtship of Princess Katherine is warfare – i.e. the laying of a siege – by other means; with *Wuthering Heights, Carrie, The Prince and the Showgirl,* not to mention *Hamlet* and *Othello*: Olivier's work is an exploration of love's destructiveness and the true subject of Olivier's portrayals is Olivier, his fears and fantasies and fulfilments. And we, as the audience, yield to his hunger, to a star's vulgar need for the public's love. With Olivier, or Sellers, acting is much more than a nice night's entertainment; much more than competence. There is mystery to them; we never reach the end of them. Acting brightened them. It was where they could stand, unfold, and be themselves.

Chapter Two
Jupiter

On 7 July 1932, a Western Union telegram from Frank Joyce, his agent in Hollywood, was delivered to Olivier at his flat in Roland Gardens, SW7:

> IMPORTANT YOU CABLE US AT ONCE YOUR MEASUREMENTS AS MGM MUST PREPARE YOUR WARDROBE STOP ALSO LET YOUR MOUSTACHE GROW IN CASE THEY DESIRE TO USE IT REGARDS.

Which was promptly answered:

> MEASUREMENTS FOR COSTUME HEIGHT FIVE FOOT TEN STOP NAPE TO WAIST SEVENTEEN AND A HALF STOP FULL LENGTH JACKET TWENTY EIGHT AND A HALF STOP WIDTH BACK EIGHT AND HALF STOP ELBOW TWENTY TWO STOP FULL SLEEVE THIRTY TWO AND HALF STOP CHEST THIRTY EIGHT STOP WAIST THIRTY STOP HIPS THIRTY EIGHT STOP MOUSTACHE BEING WORKED ON REGARDS.

Joyce, however, pressed for more feet and inches:

> MGM ADVISES MEASUREMENTS NOT SUFFICIENT REQUEST YOU CABLE DETAILED TAILORING MEASUREMENTS URGENT REGARDS.

By 11 July, and yet more enquiries, Olivier was beginning to bridle:

> REFER TO PESTERRE BEVERLY HILLS OR RKO WARDROBE FOR FULL MEASUREMENTS STOP ENGLISH TAILORS DO NOT TAKE MORE THAN I CABLED REGARDS.

We have most of his measurements, therefore (*aet.* twenty-five), but not his measure. For Olivier's was a life that doesn't fit facts. There is about him a feeling of vastness, of strangeness. He was a force of nature: '... this whirlwind. He is an extraordinary whirlwind ... with these eyes and suddenly this genius and fire ... He goes ... up in the stratosphere,' testified Michael Caine, his glasses still steamed up years after making *Sleuth*. 'It was like being on stage with a Force Ten gale,' recalled Billie Whitelaw, one of his Desdemonas. To be in the spotlight with Olivier was to feel a frozen wind, like the lashing hail that whitens green plains as it passes. His King Lear didn't challenge the storm; he'd seized its being and he *was* the storm – the eye of the hurricane; and in *Cat on a Hot Tin Roof* he became thunder and lightning – as Big Daddy describes it himself, 'all my life I've been like a closed-up fist, pounding, smashing'.*

When rehearsing the scene where Maggie tells Big Daddy that she is carrying Brick's baby, 'he just looked at me. And looked and looked,' said Natalie Wood. 'It went on so long I began to feel faint.' As Maureen Stapleton remarked, hearing this story, 'One thing honey, when you've been looked at by Olivier, you know you've been looked at.' Whether his glance is the devil's glint of Richard III, forcing Buckingham to his knees in homage, or Nicodemus, in *Jesus of Nazareth*, witnessing Christ's agony on the cross, and watching the body being taken down in the rain, Olivier's comprehensive penetration is right down into the soul. It's the depth at which the Almighty is meant to peer, or the gaze of the vampire, which can cross oceans of time to find you (as the bogey-man Archie Rice threatens: 'let me know where you're working tomorrow night – and I'll come and see you'). Vivien responded to it, when she was impelled to see him as the flamboyant Tony Cavendish in a play about the Barrymore family, *Theatre Royal*, at the Lyric in 1934. He was like somebody she'd made up inside her head. She promptly announced to her companion, 'That's the man I'm going to marry.' When it was explained to her that she was married already, as indeed was Olivier, she retorted, 'It doesn't matter. I will still marry him one day. You'll see.'

Olivier's intensities – which are erotic – seem to be like the workings of fate, or destiny. Hilde makes answer to them in *The Master Builder* – Ibsen's play, in which Olivier appeared at the National in 1964, being almost embarrassing with its metaphors of thrusting, climbing and scaling sexual heights; its spires, steeples, literal and symbolic erections. 'She trembles and quivers if I even come near her!' says Solness, of the ebullient child-woman who turns up in his house unannounced, claiming she knows him from her dreams; and she herself tries to put the orgasmic shiver into words: 'It sounded like harps in the air . . . And I heard harps in the air . . .' The maidens of Meryton village and Netherfield Hall are

* Despite the suggestiveness of cosmic violence, Olivier remained in perfect control. He was never to my knowledge *overtaken*, as Welles was, when, playing Othello under Olivier's management at the St James's Theatre in 1951, he knocked Gudrun Ure unconscious and, flinging coins at Maxine Audley, lacerated her face.

invigorated by this strange music, too, in *Pride and Prejudice*. 'My goodness, he does have an air about him,' murmurs Greer Garson, as Olivier's Darcy prowls the ballroom, toying with his monocle, frowning. Soldiers from the visiting regiment whoop and carouse, chatting up the girls, flattering them, but Olivier keeps quite out of the party spirit, and appears cross when dancers jostle him, laugh and tread away. Garson's Elizabeth Bennet calls him arrogant, detestable, etc., but there's irony, interest, in her criticisms. He's similar to how he appears in *Rebecca*, when, through scorn and put-downs, Max shows his affection for the second Mrs de Winter, who is gauche, knows she's laughed at; the very opposite of the domineering, pleasure-seeking Rebecca, which is why Olivier's character takes refuge in her.

In *Pride and Prejudice*, Elizabeth apprehends a man who knows his own value – as she does hers – and who, far from being snobbish and supercilious, can tell (as can she) that it's the villagers and the local gentry, with their hats and gowns, and their neurotic need to be taken for people of fashion, who are the ones suffering from pomposity and condescension. Though Darcy (like Max, or Heathcliff) is withdrawn, like the sun, or the bird in the forest, he could only be himself – and Olivier always had a strong sense of himself. Olivier's Darcy has a calm, and graciousness, but for all the civility, what counts with him, as with *Rebecca* and *Wuthering Heights*, is the suggestion of sudden fires. Within him, under the outward respectability and impeccable manners, lurk fantastic agonies and ecstasies, which fought on. In Maxim de Winter we have a portrayal of a man who thinks he may have murdered his first wife. Beneath the romantic drama Olivier plays out a moral allegory, suggesting to us the character's guilt and torment. The flames licking Manderley are hell-fires – and flames of lust. For with his silver hair, Olivier is a devil in disguise. Rebecca was appalling, a scarlet woman who deserved to die, but Max's hatred is so intense, Olivier shows that he loved her; he was her match, like king and queen of the underworld. (What else is Manderley, a moonlit wilderness, tropically overgrown, but the domain of a Dracula?)

A similar destructive passion courses through *Wuthering Heights*. With Olivier, Heathcliff is not an ignorant and rude lout; he's a gypsy baron – indeterminable, and with night hanging in his eyes. David Niven, and the rest of them, don't so much register disbelief at the scale of Heathcliff's emotions, they realize they can't match them, so call him devilish or pagan – they mean perverse. He won't allow Cathy to die. He condemns her to be a ghost, to wait for him, and the film is framed with his communings with her spirit in the snows and heather.

Cathy is impulsive, heedless; Heathcliff is deliberative and apparently harsh. They are the complementary parts of a single, ideal personality, one and equal. 'I am Heathcliff,' Cathy tells Ellen, but with Merle Oberon being coy and shrill, I rather doubt this. Instead of embodying Brontë's romantic absolutes, she is petulant, precise. (She should be flirting at the Meryton Ball.) She is not the Cathy whom Olivier evokes (she's still the fluffy Leslie Steele from *The Divorce of Lady X*); the Cathy who inspires him to understand the order of nature – of mortality – of oblivion. But, paradoxically, Olivier's isolation is Heathcliff's isolation. Who can forget the scene outside the window of Thrushcross Grange, when he's looking at the revellers, at a world that's out of reach, that he cannot live in – not even when he's back and wealthy, and he's still deprived of Cathy, and takes Isabella in revenge? (She's a vampire's willing victim.)

Olivier's power, a freezing stream or motion in the air, is that of an enchanter, from whom nobody can take flight. He makes you defenceless – charming and disarming. We can see him in operation at the garden party, in *Pride and Prejudice,* when Darcy instructs Elizabeth on how to use a bow and arrow – it's like Henry V giving her a private archery lesson, or an encounter between Apollo and Diana the huntress in classical mythology, because she hits the target smack in the bull, and there's by now a rapport between the characters that's strongly sexual. Darcy and Elizabeth delight in each other's skill, as I can imagine the actors admiring each other, for it may be noted here that Olivier and Garson had worked together five years previously, in *Golden Arrow,* at the Whitehall Theatre in 1935, and they had conducted an off-stage affair. Garson's mixture of impudence and confidence, and her wide spontaneous smile, is immensely appealing. You can quite see why she's Mr Bennet's favourite daughter (Edmund Gwenn – Santa Claus himself); why Darcy admits he's 'not ashamed of having loved her'.

But why, then, in *On Acting,* does Olivier disparage the performance? 'Darling Greer seemed all wrong as Elizabeth . . . She was most affected and silly,' he states. Perhaps it still rankled that he'd failed to persuade MGM to cast Vivien in the role – though if it's affectation and silliness you want, Viv's the girl. It is almost as if, by 1986, when *On Acting* was published, Olivier, old and confused, had oddly misremembered who *did* play Elizabeth Bennet, and had substituted Vivien Leigh's style for Garson's. Vivien had also wanted to play Joan Fontaine's part in *Rebecca,* but that was opposed by Selznick, the producer, who wanted an actress with an unformed personality – someone whom Olivier could convincingly order around.* (And with Olivier, women *want* to be subservient to his desires.)

William Wyler had actually offered Vivien Isabella Linton in *Wuthering Heights*, but she'd wanted to be Cathy or nothing. We must be grateful to Geraldine Fitzgerald for stepping in – she's beautiful, bruised, anxious, and she could have announced, 'I am Heathcliff' with the conviction Merle Oberon lacks. Fitzgerald, indeed, is one of the few actresses to stand her ground with Olivier, to accept his challenges. (She goes unmentioned in his memoirs.) I'm thinking of that scene where she implores Heathcliff to look into her eyes and see the depth of her love, and she has a washed-out, shagged-to-death look that is warm and honest, and full of a despairing longing for peace.

What we are registering in Olivier in these Hollywood movies of his first maturity† is a union of the human – the actual – the sensual – and the divine – the spiritual – the ideal. There is nothing ethereal about his divinity. Heathcliff, the changeling, is attentive to the physical, to particularities: look at the way he pats the dogs, or saddles the horses, or frowns into the sunshine when he's lying in the heather, or the way he stands before the fireplace, staring into the coals, or at how he puts down a pewter mug in front of Hindley. Or, in *Rebecca*, the way Olivier scoops up a blob of spilled marmalade (repeating the action identically in take after take, according to Joan Fontaine). You believe in what you are seeing. Indeed, the realism was too much for Sam Goldwyn, who inspected the set and snarled at Heathcliff in the stable-boy sequences and exclaimed to Wyler: 'If this actor continues to look dirty like that, I'm going to close the picture.'

It wasn't the mud or the make-up – what Olivier called 'the paint [which] they just daubed on my face here and there' – that irked the producer. It was the way, in spite of his bashfulness, that the actor gave off power; his emotional charge and essential concentration. Olivier is precise, complete. His paradox – his uniqueness – is that for all his

* Here is David O. Selznick's actual memorandum, dated 18 August 1939: 'I am convinced that we would be better off making this picture with a girl who had no personality whatever and who was a bad actress but was right in type than we would be to cast it with Vivien.' Perhaps she'd fancied her chances at being Rebecca in *Rebecca* – the witch who of course doesn't appear? In fact, her screen test survives and was shown at an Olivier retrospective at the Plitt Century Plaza, Hollywood, on 30 March 1979. Her problem was that she'd failed to throw off Scarlett O'Hara; she was too frantic for a role that requires passivity.

† Precise opening dates: *Wuthering Heights*, 13 April 1939, at the Rivoli Theatre, New York; *Rebecca*, 28 March 1940, at the Radio City Music Hall, New York; *Pride and Prejudice*, 8 August 1940, same address.

disguises and externals, the conscious dignity and pathos, what comes across – and perhaps he scarcely knew what he was doing – is a feeling that his characters are made over and are resolving into the primal elements: snow in *Wuthering Heights*, fire in *Rebecca*, storms and bloody battles for his many heroic roles, dust and shadow and flood. As a force of nature, or as Robert Donat's sphinx, with his sneer of cold command, he makes his entrances in flashes of lightning and golden skies. See how he materializes as Othello, toying with the rose, Blake's rose. Look how he comes out of Elsinore's sepia mists as Hamlet; or how he steps out of the moony blues and faint greens of the flags and livery as Henry V – how, indeed, his voice is intrinsic to the hoof-prints and gallops of Agincourt. In *Richard III*, the King is a creature of thorns and hectic reds; in *The Entertainer*, Archie Rice's music-hall songs are like black-magic dirges – they echo from the house of the dead:

> Why should I care
> Why should I let it touch me,
> Why shouldn't I sit down and cry
> To let it pass over me?

Archie's anthem might be about the shifty abnegation of responsibility – he's dissociating himself from a community he feels is rejecting him, which he'd love to leave. When Olivier sings it, however, there's a power rising through him, and it's a song about defiance. And this happens with Olivier. Such are his relations to the world, you feel the world will always yield. Ghosts come when summoned; kingdoms are handed over and battles won against the odds; the eternity of toil and decay is called into question – and with Richard squirming amongst the dogs of war, Nelson patrolling the *Victory* in full regalia, his Shakespearian duels, and Lord Marchmain or Clifford Mortimer lying in state, the moment of death is always a triumphant moment, because Olivier's death scenes are an expression of life. Solness climbs into the sky and disappears, Hamlet is carried ceremoniously to Elsinore's topmost battlement (a strange destination for a corpse, but the idea of an allegorical ascension is meant), and Olivier returns fallen angels – or demons – to their places in the firmament. In our imaginations, his characters are not dead; there's always more to know about them. Tynan has recorded how, when rehearsing Captain Brazen, in *The Recruiting Officer*, Olivier improvised lines and bits of business, consistent with the character but unmentioned by Farquhar – his illimitable consciousness out-ran the dramatist. And that is how he went on, as a creator, as an actor, evolving from one existence to the next (Malvolio, Macbeth, and Titus Andronicus, say, in

1955), making adjustments, and then escaping from his own performances, gliding off like a phantom.

Worlds exist because of Olivier. I know that the fundamental allure of theatre is its theatricality – Hamlet's blond rinse and pearl-handled dagger; Lord Horatio Nelson and the Prince Regent of Carpathia's decorations and medals. I know that one of the joys of the performing arts is seeing through its contrivances – the toy boats and model London in *Henry V*; a parched Spain standing for Bosworth in *Richard III*; the steam trains racing through the Balkans, and it's the Severn Valley Railway, in *The Seven Per Cent Solution*. But, though quite aware that it is a sham, quite conscious of its deceptions, we allow Olivier to transfigure the contrivances. We don't do this for Ralph Richardson, who was like Merlin passing through, amused by the conventions of stage and screen; we don't do this for Gielgud, warned off by the notes of patrician disdain, or Guinness, who is either a refugee from German expressionist comedy (*Olivier Twist, The Ladykillers*) or on the verge of disappearing (as George Smiley).

The other great actors of Olivier's generation don't *want* us to suspend disbelief. With Olivier, and his blend of solemnity and high spirits, and given that distinct fire he gets to run over people – from Michael Caine to Maureen Stapleton, from Cathy Earnshaw to Hilde Wangel – it is as if he had no choice, obliterating disbelief, and you know something memorable is sure to happen. With a wild beating of wings, his characters embody the struggles – the complexity and callousness – that being alive incurs. Where other actors nurse a character's seven deadly sins or disabling weaknesses, Olivier takes on his roles not for their psychic wounds or besetting flaws, but he plays men for their potential greatness. 'They are part of me and I of them,' he has said of 'my Shakespearian roles', and it's Olivier's own incandescence that's released. He expresses not the loss or absence of hope, but affirmation, aspiration. He managed this even in – or perhaps especially in – *Oedipus Rex*, at the New Theatre, in 1945. When Oedipus blinded himself it was not to wallow in unworthiness; it was almost as if he wanted to know what terrible suffering is like. Other actors may have interpreted Sophocles' tragedy as being about the impossibility of innocence (killing your father; marrying your mother); Olivier made it a play about determination and courage – a man's insistence on knowing the truth, and facing up to the worst.*

* Freud's disciple, Ernest Jones, notoriously wrote that Hamlet had an Oedipus complex; Olivier gave Oedipus Edgar's philosophic insight from *King Lear*, when he, as Mad Tom, meets his blinded father and realises there's always somebody worse off than yourself: 'O gods! Who isn't can say, "I am at the worst"?' (IV, i)

The actor told John Mortimer that he based Oedipus' off-stage howl, as he plucks out his eyes, on what hunters do to animals. 'You know what I had to do to make that pain sound real? . . . I thought of foxes screaming. With their paws caught in the teeth of a trap.' He also recalled the procedures of ermine catching. 'In the Arctic they put down salt and the ermine comes to lick it and his tongue freezes to the ice. I thought about that when I screamed as Oedipus.' Telling these tales, the actor became the animals he had attended to, his wrists stiff and helpless, as the fox; as the ermine, 'he became a small, thirsty animal'. Max Adrian also witnessed the transformation, when Olivier was recounting a Kiplingesque story about a snake and a chicken, and the chicken pecks the snake, which is so surprised it drops dead of shock. 'Not the greatest story perhaps, but as he told it Larry became the chicken and the snake, and he was so convincing that at the end, when he was playing the snake, you thought he was going to have a heart attack himself and pass out on the spot.'

Olivier goes beyond mimicry or anthropomorphism, i.e. Beatrix Potter or Walt Disney's ascription of human personalities to bunnies and mice. And though Tynan said that 'One thinks of Olivier in terms of other species, of panthers and lions' – a conceit belaboured in that critic's essays on the subject, where Olivier is 'a fighting bull' with 'a tender-tigerish smile' and all too often 'the lion's paw may lash out' (*A View of the English Stage* is a jungle book) – what counts is Olivier's alertness to the surge of life, the flame of life, and he can locate this in flowers and leaves (Astrov's maps of the Russian forests; Lord Marchmain's recollection of the Brideshead estates; the inflexion he gives to Clifford Mortimer's line 'the jays have eaten all the peas') just as much as in animals and men.

Olivier's sense of wonder, his acknowledgement, or celebration, of the divine element within men and beasts, which enables his heroes to have their temptations, and to be self-conscious, and yet they'll still seek better things and want to overcome disorder, or at least to swerve away from it, because they are imbued with Olivier's own exhilaration and persistence – all this fortitude would seem not only old-fashioned, but positively archaic. Quite so. The temper of the nineteenth century, the mental atmosphere, say, of Tennyson's *Ulysses* – 'To strive, to seek, to find, and not to yield' – was Olivier's inheritance. He had an Edwardian upper-middle-class core, with the concomitant proprieties and discriminations. He sent his eldest son to Eton, Christ Church and into the Coldstream Guards. His lineage is packed with rectors, rural deans, colonels and politicians. Yet his perspectives are longer than that. Genealogical sources are as maybe; and the precise people to whom Olivier owed his existence I'll discuss in the next chapter. But what about Olivier's origins in fantasy and legend?

It's not so much that, through the connections of kin – e.g. the Revd. Jourdain Olivier, who was chaplain to William of Orange – he had a sense of pomp and circumstance, the power and the glory; it's more that Olivier's elation and energy put me in mind of Ernest Thesiger* in *The Bride of Frankenstein*, drinking a toast to 'a new world of gods and monsters'. Olivier was not, I think, altogether of this world. He was Jupiter, Zeus, King of the Gods, King of Kings, 'dispenser of good and evil in the destinies of men', according to *The Oxford Companion to Classical Literature*. 'He is the giver of the laws that rule the course of events, and he knows the future, and sometimes reveals it by portents and oracles . . . He is the defender of the house, of the hearth, of the rights of hospitality, and of liberty . . . He is supreme among the gods.' He was also a sly old randy-boots and pursued women by changing his shape and form – most famously into that of a swan, to commit intimacy with Leda.

Tameless and swift, physically resplendent, Olivier was clearly there to be identified as a demi-god in his early films, going from role to role, forming and transforming. In Hollywood, in 1940, he even had an Old English Sheepdog named Jupiter, which came with the house on Cedarwood Drive; and Michael Redgrave has noted Olivier's fondness for large premises – Valhalla, or Mount Olympus. Tarquin's christening, for example, in 1936, took place in 'an enormous studio in Chelsea with enormous windows, and enormous fireplaces – a setting that would have dwarfed lesser men; but he was very much in his element'. Thus, Olivier's presence, his scale – all five foot ten of him, waist thirty, moustache being worked on.

The Chelsea pad, once Whistler's workrooms, was succeeded by Notley Abbey, near Thame, Buckinghamshire, and had been preceded, at one time, by a childhood of draughty vicarages. Perhaps because the sky and the breeze is in his acting, Olivier requires room – requires a stage. The very platforms he supervised and designed, Chichester or the National, are tall and wide, panoptic; and his films are light and airy – Elsinore's denuded ramparts, endless corridors and stairways, filled with little but wisps of mist, and the paneless windows opening on to a grey and empty sea; or the English court, in *Richard III*, a series of interconnect-

* Thesiger (1879–1961) played the Duke of Berri in *Henry V.* He also appeared with Olivier in the scene from *The Pickwick Papers* in the command performance *Here's to Our Enterprise*, at the Lyceum in 1938.

ing pale-blue chapels and throne rooms; or *Henry V*, with its rolling green swards and cloudscapes; or the vast pink and purple Carpathian Embassy in *The Prince and the Showgirl*.

You'll not find Olivier allowing himself to be upstaged by scenery. His production of *Uncle Vanya* at Chichester, in 1962, required little save a wall of plain rough timber slats – he took huge pains, apparently, to find exactly the right shade of pale varnish, to signify a Russia that's high and cold; and his version of *Three Sisters*, at the National in 1970, with its skeleton trees and chilly, silent chambers, is another place of frost and a white sun. This is because the heat, the colour, the clutter of character and the bustle of mind – the activity – is what Olivier himself, in person, is there to provide. He fills the stage. It's his nature to be sublime ('so distinguished by elevation or size or nobility or grandeur or other impressive quality as to inspire awe or wonder . . .' *OED*). This is how he is suited to the epic proportions of Netherfield Hall, Wuthering Heights, Manderley, or the Roman villas in *Spartacus* – actually filmed at Hearst's San Simeon, a.k.a. Kane's Xanadu. Even in his later films, he's demonstrating not frailty, diminishment, but gusto; and, whether pottering in his apple orchard (*A Voyage Round My Father*), residing in a Venetian palazzo with his mistress (*Brideshead Revisited*) or luxuriating in rural France with a pair of nymphets (*The Ebony Tower*), Olivier is always playfully retrieving a spirit from the Ancients – he's always Jupiter, figuratively on his marble throne, his glance widened to cover the whole earth seen from space.

And not only figuratively. In *Clash of the Titans*, made in 1981, we have almost a parody – and yet also a direct representation – of Olivier's Olympian, Zeus-like sensibility. As the screenplay for what Robert Stephens, Maggie Smith's first husband, called 'that terrible film' was written by the urbane Beverley Cross, Maggie Smith's second husband, this cannot be a coincidence? The guying of his augustness is its pull – for here Olivier is, up in heaven, an azure vault with cool porticos and fine muslin curtains, dressed in a white negligée and a golden laurel wreath, the most proud and authoritative Jupiter you ever saw. 'Oh! Mighty Zeus!' they call him, 'Great Jupiter', and Olivier is reunited with Dame Maggie, his Desdemona, his Hilde Wangel, as Thetis, and with Claire Bloom, his Lady Anne and Lady Marchmain, as Hera. Also about the place is Flora Robson, from *Fire Over England* and *Wuthering Heights*.

Because the Mount Olympus scenes set off such semi-intentional comic reverberations – heaven is populated by the National Theatre crowd, and the gods bicker and have jealous rivalries, like actors –

Olivier, typically atypical, is grave and commanding. There's none of the high tenor campery of his other old codger roles. His voice has the Othello register, aptly, as much of his dialogue is with his former Desdemona; and in his disputes with the disapproving and narrow Hera, his official wife, we hark back to Richard III, running rings around his future queen ('I'll have her, but I will not keep her long'), and to the chatelaine of Brideshead, suffering and praying non-stop for the soul of her estranged and adulterous husband. You could almost say, this is a send-up of Olivier's famous encounters with women, his marriages prolonged. Had Vivien been alive, she'd be there, perhaps instead of Siân Phillips, dressed in Balmain's latest silk scanties.

The women chuckle about Zeus' disguises and seductions – how he goes around reshaped as a cuttlefish or as a shower of rain, the better to infiltrate female defences. (Thetis countered him by changing herself into a shark.) But there is little of the trickster in Olivier's performance; the prankster doesn't seem much present in the white-bearded and stately old man whose face shines out of Perseus' magic shield, giving advice. Olivier seems to have grasped that if *Clash of the Titans* has any value; if there is anything to salvage from Ray Harryhausen's notoriously tacky special effects (the stop-motion plastic lizards and rubber dinosaurs – actually the charm is in their shoddiness); if there is anything to be made from this assignment without yielding to the camp, then it is to give a strength and integrity to Zeus' understanding of paternal love. Perseus is his son (Thetis being the mother), and the father has to watch the boy learn to be a hero, undergoing trials, facing horrors. The father knows of these dangers, but cannot intervene – he can only do so much to force a destiny. Paternal love, and the knowledge that you must let go, and leave people to their own free will: even Zeus, as played by Olivier, has to agonize about his powerlessness in this department.

Olivier works against the grain of poor material, putting things there that weren't there, never ceasing to be inventive and cramming his characters with nuance. Another father–son bond is *The Jazz Singer*, of 1980; yet another, though a more fulfilling script, Mortimer's *A Voyage Round My Father*. Everybody bar Olivier would leave these cantankerous old despots as they are, and allow us to laugh at, or shrink from, their eccentric ways. Cross, bossy, selfish Clifford Mortimer is yet aware of his effects. Olivier, the actor, plays him *as* an actor, with a fondness for expensive suits, ties, silk handkerchiefs, canes, cologne and panama hats – a fop. In court, as the divorce lawyer, he gives performances. He ought to be horrible, tyrannical (Rex Harrison, who wanted the role, would have been a splendid shit), but Olivier is sympathetic – we sympathize with (a) his rage and frustrations at being blind; (b) his pride, in not wanting blindness to curb his life; (c) his hatred of ever being thought disabled. He rages (literally) at the dying of the light;* and he is vulnerable, too, with his child's fear of losing face. Clifford Mortimer is Olivier's Oedipus, not at Colonus, but growing old in a summery England on the edge of the Chilterns.

These father figures, however, avoid sensuality – they are *beyond* sensuality, as is Ezra Lieberman, in *The Boys from Brazil*, Julius Edmond Santorin, in *A Little Romance*, and Abraham Van Helsing, in *Dracula*. Olivier is a weightless god, fallen to earth to right wrongs; he's divine intervention itself, routing the vampire, hunting Hitler's clones, assisting a pair of young lovers. These are dancing, capering performances, full of flutterings and shrugs and shrinkings and graceful hand gestures. Yet, though performances of twirls, don't mistake them – all this deftness could easily lend itself to swordplay, and the characters still benefit from Olivier's strong, masculine music. Ezra Lieberman, for example, lets out a bray of contempt, when he's sickened by the presence of the evil Nazi nurse. With his rage and loathing, he suddenly has a chilling force – and this aggression, lying in wait beneath his cultivated manner and poses, is linked to Olivier's rigour and appetites, to his rapacity. Hence to the concupiscence of Zeus alluded and attested to by Maggie Smith and Ursula Andress (Aphrodite) in *Clash of the Titans*, and which is exercised fully elsewhere.

Critics are meant to disparage *The Betsy* – 'What makes this movie especially painful is that it exposes this brilliant actor at his very worst in a performance totally out of control' (*New York Daily News*, 10 February 1978); 'It is abysmally depressing to see Laurence Olivier hobbling through this jetsam chuckling and croaking . . .' (*New York Tribune*, same date) – but, like those summary, violent, experimental canvases Picasso knocked out during his last years, full of minotaurs and fauns and a frightening sexuality, which showed how alive and ebullient antiquity was to him – canvases only now being revalued – so, too, I think, *The Betsy* needs assessment, for in it the erotic charge felt in his other performances comes to the surface and gets its softish-core expression.

The settings are those laughably large Rhode Island châteaux built by Vanderbilts, Carnegies, Whitneys, Rockefellers; and Olivier's Loren Hardeman Snr, po-facedly called 'Number One', is a plutocrat of that

* Olivier gives a fiery rendition of Dylan Thomas' poem 'Do not go gentle into that good night' in Patrick Garland's *What Will Survive of Us is Love*, broadcast on television on 6 July 1987 to celebrate Olivier's eightieth birthday. He begins the reading quite ancient and senile. By the end he is robust – the relish he gives the word *rage* rejuvenates him.

kidney – as founder of the giant conglomerate Bethlehem Motor Corporation, I suppose he's inspired by the industrialist and squillionaire Henry Ford, who in 1903 organized a company at Detroit to produce cheap cars. When we meet Olivier, he is a snow-haired nonagenarian, still holding on to his power, and concerned to invent and develop a cheap, eco-friendly car for our century's end. But who cares about the plot, or the cars? Or even the power struggles between junior members of the dynasty, Loren Hardeman Jr (Paul Rudd) and Loren Hardeman III (Robert Duvall), whom logic demands we call Number Two and Number Three? What matters is Olivier's grandiose and monumental characterization, which was meant to be comically and defiantly overblown. 'You can say what you like about that film,' he stated, 'but it was very enjoyable to do. It was a filthily vulgar part, the most awful character I've ever played in my life, and I enjoyed it highly.'

The relish comes out in the accent. Olivier has decided that Hardeman is a first-generation immigrant, so a Highland burr comes and goes with the American yawps and twangs. There's a growling crofter inside the tycoon. It's a trick he devised for *Long Day's Journey into Night*, where James Tyrone reverts to being Irish during emotional outbursts. Only Olivier could get away with this, or would have thought of it, filling his speeches with ancestral voices. It's like Dvořák's New World Symphony, the percussive Manhattan noises interwoven with nostalgic remembrances of Bohemian village square-dance numbers, with their rapid beat. It makes his characters have tumultuous interiors; delve deep enough in their subconscious, and you'll come across all manner of sticks and bones from their past, from their forebears' past. It's vocal archaeology. Archie Rice, you'll recall, given the news that his son has been killed in Suez, leans against the proscenium arch and sings the blues. Osborne's script informs us that this is because he's regurgitating a jazz singer he'd once heard and was impressed by. But Olivier *becomes* 'that old black whore singing her heart out to the whole world'; he *becomes* somebody who 'can stand up and make a pure . . . natural noise' which implies 'there's nothing wrong with them, only with everybody else'.

And, suggesting history, and hearing, in American jazz, the lamentations of the slaves, Olivier embodies pre-history – right back to Jupiter, the paterfamilias, first glimpsed in *The Betsy* frolicking with the French maid, Roxanne. As Olivier's buttocks, in tasteful long-shot, heave in a gathering momentum, attesting to the vinegar strokes – i.e. that approaching crisis during coitus when the face takes on a rictus of concentration, comparable to sucking on something acidic – we have leisure to reflect on how unnecessary it has been, over the decades of

Olivier's career, for us to see him at it to know that he can do it. Indeed, it's an ill omen to catch a glimpse. Horses neigh and ghosts shriek and fierce fiery warriors fight upon the clouds. In *The Seven Per Cent Solution*, Sherlock Holmes finds Moriarty (Olivier – as creepy as hell) in bed with his mother, a trauma that is later linked to his cocaine addiction, perhaps, though I'm surmising, even to his violin playing. In *The Betsy*, whoever it is peeping round the door when Olivier is having it off shortly shoot themselves. It's too private; it's sacrilege.

Richard III's misshapen shadow follows Lady Anne into her bedchamber – that's pornographically suggestive enough. Heathcliff and Cathy have obviously copulated out on the moors. We don't need to see them asprawl, aslant, in the heather, to know this has taken place. That's why Cathy can be dismissive and cruel to him later, when she dolls up to receive Edgar (Niven, agreeably chumpish: without his moustache he's like Stan Laurel). Cathy puts on a frock and puts on airs. She's stirred and embarrassed by Heathcliff's proximity, by the momentousness of having just lost her virginity to him. He's awkward, wanting to be attentive but not daring to overstep the mark in front of the others. It's all there in Olivier's face – a man realizing the world has altered forever. (With Isabella, years later, seduction holds no thrill. He suggests a fast gallop, and he's wearied by his own prowess.)

His Romeo must have shared these virile qualities. Indeed, back in 1935 he was censured for them. He was deemed too 'resonant' for 'Shakespeare's tenderest verse' (*Evening Star*); 'He is a ranting, writhing Romeo' (*The Times*); 'He has not the lyrical quality either of voice or manner' (*Manchester Post*). The critics preferred Gielgud's melodiousness. Olivier, we might say, was too much for his audiences. But surely was he not *life*, was he not the *thing*? He could justify his approach, as he justified *The Betsy*. 'I believe that my attitude, passion, poetic-realism and Italianate silhouette were all aimed in the right direction . . . I was trying to sell realism in Shakespeare – I believed in it with my whole soul.'

Olivier's realism is a kind of surrealism, a heightening, a sharpening, a clarity that comes in dreams. His realism is the mud and dirt that offended Sam Goldwyn; the way he's bewilderingly spiritual and carnal – a blend, incidentally, he adduced in Peggy Ashcroft, his Juliet. She came to see *The Dance of Death*, in 1966, and visited Olivier in his dressing room afterwards. They embraced, exchanged compliments, and she'd barely gone out and shut the door behind her when Olivier turned to Robert Stephens and said, 'She's had more cock than you've had hot dinners.'

You only have to compare Olivier with Gielgud, who is as soft as roses, to appreciate Olivier's vivid moodiness, to understand the sense of tension the latter brings to a role. Gielgud, as Olivier himself commented, is a cerebral actor ('all beauty, all abstract things'), but he meant an emasculated actor: 'I've always felt that John missed the lower half [of the body] . . . I believed that Johnny [as Romeo] was paying attention – to the exclusion of the earthiness – to all music, all lyricism, and I was for the other side of the coin . . .'

This is amusingly on view in *Richard III*. Clarence is in the tower, warbling away about his nightmares, and Olivier – the director as well as the star – simply leaves the camera in a single position and lets Gielgud get on with treating the speech as an aria, his arms operatically waving to signify distress. It is a recital, temperamentally frigid. (You know how sardonically Richard will view it.) Which is how, as Gielgud aged, he came to play civil servants, Whitehall mandarins, diplomats, courtiers, characters who are never unseemly. And why Olivier, having had Clarence unceremoniously dunked in the butt of Malmsey wine, goatishly ended up, in *The Betsy*, rogering Roxanne.

Gielgud is exalted, pale, infertile; Olivier is roguish, a princely eagle – and both of them, it must be said, are self-aware enough to parody their own styles effortlessly (e.g. Gielgud as the butler in *Arthur* or as the poetaster in *No Man's Land*). Tupping the maid, and promising to set her up as a haberdasher, Olivier is the philandering Jupiter who'll make dreams come true. We don't hear of Roxanne again, alas. (She has the twittering accent of a French maid in a bad comedy film.) Unless it's she who runs the boutique the fixtures and fittings of the film come from, the flower baskets, the frilly frocks, the gentlemen's double-breasted concoctions. Though seventy when the movie was made, Olivier has to pretend to be ninety (his eyelashes are bleached white) and, in flashbacks, forty, or even younger. But throughout he wears expensive turn-of-the-century suits, teamed with the maple and satinwood interiors, the upholstery and fine marquetry of his surroundings – his Elysium. Roxanne, like Norman Hartnell, sticks with her classic lines.

Pulp fiction has a habit of constructing itself around myths and fables – of alluding to art under its artlessness, and *The Betsy* contains a version of *Hamlet*. Olivier hops into bed with his son's wife, Sally Hardeman (Katharine Ross) and they loll under the fur rugs as Claudius and Gertrude. (When he reaches out his arm towards a photo in a silver frame, his palm is outspread, like his Othello.) The Paul Rudd character is a studious and impractical weakling, a homosexual prince who kills himself, watched by a boy who grows up to be Robert Duvall. And is the girl, Betsy, with dark curly hair and baby teeth, the Ophelia? Except she doesn't go mad – though I don't know, she has sex with the frog-faced Tommy Lee Jones, and he calls her a 'child' when they are making the beast with two backs.

Olivier's way with women is protective, patriarchal. Roxanne gets her shop; Sally is serviced; Betsy receives his shares in the business. His way with the men is to get them to resemble him. Duvall, who likes to play aggressive squash, and Rudd, his fey father, have deep-set eyes, hollowed sockets, and this is like a cartoon variation, a genetic aberration, of Olivier's own eyeballs, which in *The Betsy* roll and swivel in mock dismay or anger – when he looks glum, it's funny. He's a told-off little boy.

The adorable naughty infant, the grave tycoon in his prime, the dignified baron, older than the century: Olivier is ageless, materializing in different scenes differently proportioned. This isn't versatility – it's regeneration. The explicit rejuvenating randiness of *The Betsy* is explained, perhaps, by *The Ebony Tower*, in which Olivier's Henry Breasley, his last full-length role, shows the actor's affinities with Augustus John and Picasso, i.e. with heterosexual geniuses, who drew their inspiration from the manipulation of women. Olivier's muse, his Dorelia, his Dora Maar or Françoise Gilot, was of course Vivien Leigh, whose mischievousness – and mystery – made every man in the world swagger. Her blandishments, her shining eyes, her voice which held a laugh . . . Yet it was to Olivier whom she offered herself as a standing sacrifice, Scarlett to his Rhett, and everything that had made up his life rushed towards the alliance; everything afterwards rolled away from it, and was an attempt to recover from it.

Love's resentments and destructiveness are the subject of Breasley's art, though Roger Rees' priggish young critic, David Williams, refuses to see any connection between the painter, his day-to-day existence, and the work he accomplishes, the exhibitions he manages by some miracle to mount; between the private truth and the public artifice. Williams turns up at the villa, situated in bright-green idyllic countryside near Limoges,* hoping to secure an interview with his hero – and what does

* The self-same location, in the Haute-Vienne, 250 miles SSW of Paris, was used for Alain Resnais' film *Providence* (1977), in which Gielgud, nearly ten years prior to Olivier, played a boozy and incontinent artist – a novelist, this time. 'You won't get me, you fucking bastards!' he rails, at the shades of death. But where Olivier is an artist full of possibility and danger, Gielgud can only try and pretend to have solidity, boldness. Indeed, in this film, the bits about sexual instincts and artistic expression turn out to be dream or nightmare sequences! The real Gielgud sweet-naturedly comes on at the end to bless his family. 'Just leave. Neither kiss nor touch . . .' Gielgud is the faint Prospero, a role he's played many times, but which Olivier wouldn't countenance, complaining the speeches are 'awfully sonorous stuff and terribly humourless. No laughs in Prospero. Not a fucking smile there.'

he find? Not a magus, not a polymath, but what he takes to be a foul-mouthed old reprobate; and Williams is such a prim, humourless academic, so incapable of veering from the path of high seriousness, he can't see that Breasley is having fun with him. Nor can he see that Breasley's enjoyment of parties and picnics and watching brown-limbed beauties sunbathe nude and splash in the lakes is the source of his art, not a detraction from it.

Olivier is at his most classical, his most Zeus-like, wandering the arbours, feasting off fresh fish and peaches, dashing down the Puligny-Montrachet, and talking of the sexual nature of painting, of creativity. It's the nearest he came, perhaps, to explaining his own theory of art – that you must remain under the influence of passion all your life; that you must be impatient with too much order and security. Hence, his own abandonment of Jill Esmond, who was tender and affectionate, but with whom there was something – turmoil? – lacking. The high-strung Rees' supercilious critic is appalled by the egotism, dismissing it as drunken maundering. He can't understand how the dedicated artist can captivate people and bind them to him, but still need to keep himself free, solitary. He just thinks Breasley lacks refinement. Yet it is the critic who has a want of feeling, who is intolerant and disdainful.

To impersonate Breasley, Olivier was taken to meet John Piper.* Piper, I think, would serve to symbolize in his own work the divisions between the two characters in *The Ebony Tower* – his pictures being, on the face of it, topographical studies of churches, stately homes, castles, often commissioned by their well-off owners, and then – the true subject – the buildings are placed under tempestuous, violent skies. (When Piper unveiled his portrait of Windsor, King George VI said he was 'frightfully sorry about the weather'.) There's always a livid storm brewing. Rees, we might say, is in favour of the austere architectural exactitude; Olivier is the lightning and hail, the black night and shooting stars. There's always something in him that's terrifying, and which has elements of sexual attraction. He always gave the impression of great strength. Acting, with its wonderful freedom, with its appeal to a man who did not wish to be fixed in his form, was his medium – like paint or prose – through which his mind worked.

* Or so says John Mortimer, who appears to believe he made the introduction. In fact, Olivier would have known Piper for forty years – he designed the scenery for the Old Vic *Oedipus*, and he'd been commissioned to do a painting of Notley.

Chapter Three
The Guilty Vicarage

It was a family much given to nicknames and diminutives. His father was Farve; his stepmother, Isobel Buchanan Ronaldson, was Ibo, Ronnie, Izzie, and then again, Monna; Sybille (b. 26 July 1901), his sister, was Baba; Gerard Dacres (b. 5 September 1904), his brother, was Dickie, or Bobo; and when Laurence was little they called their rare and sensitive animal Kim. Of course they did. Kipling's classic was first published in 1901, six years before Olivier's birth. The adventures of Kimball O'Hara (a relative of Scarlett's?), a bazaar-boy in Lahore, whose talent for disguise – 'Remember, I can change quickly' – draws him into a society of spies and secret agents, is a parable of a prototypical actor. At one level, *Kim* is a children's book. Kim is Peter Pan, the rooftops and India's vast countryside, a Never Never Land. On another, it is a spiritual quest – Kim, like Barrie's flying boy, is searching for his identity: 'I am Kim. This is the great world, and I am only Kim. Who is Kim?'

Such existential problems wouldn't have beset the infant Olivier – they'd come later. 'I don't know who I am,' he lamented to his son, Richard, towards the end of his days. 'I've played two hundred characters in my life and I know them all better than I know myself.' But he'd have known, too, that those two hundred characters were facets of himself, fragments of himself, his life's work being a stealthy prowl through the dark gullies and lanes of his personality. He projected his temperament into his roles; and his roles interpret his life, crammed, as it was, with resilience, intractability and a sense of doom.

The point about Kim is that, though a child, he possesses a wisdom beyond his years. He has a child's gaiety, a man's heroism, and a guru's disconcerting clairvoyance – he's superior, and rather sunk in himself. 'I consider in my own mind whether thou art a spirit . . . or an evil imp,' the Tibetan lama says. Elsewhere he is described as 'thoughtful, wise, and courteous; but something of a small imp'. Though the military orphanage at Sanawar can account for his education ('Ye'd be brought up to the Church of England') and his parents – still people who encounter Kim are apprehensive, uneasy. 'It's O'Hara's boy, sure enough. O'Hara's boy leagued with all the Powers of Darkness.' Kim goes along with his alleged supernatural origins (as does Hotspur, in *Henry IV Part One*): 'upon the hour that I cried first fell the great earthquake,' he tells enthralled listeners.

He was a 'young tiger' – and this was Olivier, also. His schoolfellows, at All Saints, Margaret Street, near Oxford Circus, found him one moment a show-off, the next, despondent, melancholy. 'He kept us all off balance in our attitude toward him,' recalled Laurence Johnson, who grew up to become the actor Laurence Naismith – Matt of the Mint in *The Beggar's Opera* and Stanley, the Earl of Derby, in *Richard III*. 'One got the feeling that Larry was on stage all the time . . . testing out roles. It was impossible to tell the real Larry Olivier from some character he was temporarily playing.'

Again, this mutability is Kim's, for whom 'change of scene, service, and surroundings were the breath of his little nostrils'. Kim learns to be lithe and inconspicuous – and self-sufficient – because he is a foundling, or a changeling. He's the artful dodger, scavenging and living off his wits, and he's demeaned, we'd all agree, when captured by well-intentioned adults, who pack him off to school, where he learns how to fold his clothes and set out his boots. Kim's a bright spark we don't want quenched; he'd be a noble savage, like Mowgli, except he didn't even benefit from the example of being raised by wolves. He has a wildness – which is not to say he's delinquent. Far from it. Kipling is at pains to show that a character like Kim's, though tortuous and indirect, is innately good, innately civilized. (He doesn't need a talking panther or bear to inspire him.)* This is why the lama teams up with him, enlisting his aid on the pilgrimage to reach the Sacred River – created when the Buddha drew a bow and the arrow passed out of sight, and where it touched the earth, there broke out a stream . . . And this is why Colonel Creighton can call him 'a man after his own heart'. Edgar Rice Burroughs needed Tarzan to be a genuine blue-blood – the Earl of Greystoke – in order to justify his gumption and kingship amongst the apes. Kim is nature's own aristocrat. Duke's son – cook's son – son of a hundred kings: Kim can keep his head when all about him are losing theirs; he can talk with crowds and keep his virtue; and no doubt he could meet with Triumph and Disaster, and treat those two imposters just the same.

---

* Harold Adrian Russell Philby, known as Kim because he, too, was an infant dissembler, is, however, an example of these talents going to the bad.

What he won't do is belong to anyone. His skills are survival skills – and he's reached a point, with his chameleonic proficiency, where he loves 'the game for its own sake'; he is always 'playing a hidden game', embodying different emotions, keeping himself free and inaccessible. Thus, too, Olivier: 'He was a complete clown,' remembered Sybille. 'He'd have the whole lunch table shaking with laughter, but he had his sombre side too. He would sit for a long time not saying anything at all. You always felt as though Larry worked everything out in his mind before he spoke.'

Deliberative, precise, in charge of himself, Olivier – like Kim – seems to have treated childhood as a time to be got through as quickly as possible; he was curiously detached from what developmental psychologists call its 'booming, buzzing confusion'. Mature when he was young – he was Uncle Vanya at nineteen, King Lear at thirty-nine ('old dodderer parts are easier, somehow, with more recognizable eccentricities to play on') – the defining characteristic of his actual ancients is their youthfulness. In *The Boys from Brazil*, he rolls on the carpet fighting with Gregory Peck; in *A Little Romance*, he enters a bicycle race; in the 1983 television production of *King Lear*, he traps and skins a rabbit. As discussed in the previous chapter, in *The Betsy* and *The Ebony Tower* he gets to glue himself on to lean meat like Katharine Ross, Toyah Wilcox and Greta Scacchi and drain the strength out of them. 'To myself, inside,' he claimed, 'I am seventeen with red lips,' i.e. Orlando, luminous and erotic, whom he played in 1936 (when actually aged twenty-nine) as the Forest of Arden's Robin Hood. (*As You Like It* was adapted by J. M. Barrie, David Lean was the editor, William Walton wrote the music,* and Ninette de Valois was the choreographer.) But it's not that he has a young man's energy and enthusiasm that's at issue; it's that, full of dignity and asperity, he has a lyrical, ageless spirit. Kim, as it were, survives as Puck of Pook's Hill.

Young or elderly at will, little or big, white or (as Othello) black ('the whole thing is tremendously highly sexual because it's a black man'), Olivier is demonstrably Kim, who as a low-caste white could also pass himself off as an authentic native, 'burned black', familiar with the vernacular, eating with the holy men from the same dish. But Olivier wasn't an orphan. He wasn't abandoned in the jungle, like Mowgli, or a castaway, like Greystoke. His mother wasn't a nursemaid who died of

---

* Reviewed in *World Film News* (October 1936) by Benjamin Britten, who said, 'A large orchestra in which strings are very prominent has been used, and in the accompanying pastoral music one is conscious of the energetic ranks of the London Philharmonic sweating away behind the three-ply trees.'

cholera or his father a feckless colour-sergeant who held a post on the Sind, Punjab and Delhi Railway, took to opium and 'died as poor whites do in India'. So why did he feel the need to act – to develop Kim's survival tactics – to turn his life into a non-stop performance? As a child, people said of him, 'Larry Olivier? Oh yes, he was a natural actor all right . . . He was not altogether a nice boy . . . and I have found him much the same in later years . . . He's always been rather a frightening man.' It's the virtuosity, his ability as it were to lift off from the earth, rise above circumstance, that made him seem both angel and demon, companionable or suddenly brusque and private. ('If he was sulking, heaven help all!' said Sybille.) And he himself, in *Confessions of an Actor*, cheerfully informs us that 'people often ask my wife Joan "How do you know when Larry is acting and when he's not?" and my wife will always reply "Larry? Oh, he's acting all the time."'

The reason Olivier is a super-charged Kim, acting all the time and playing the game for its own sake, rushing and lunging, and sociable and solitary, is that, though not an orphan technically, he made himself one emotionally. A certain sort of artist always does. He feels himself to be deliciously apart. He has to make himself anew. Nobody is going to be allowed to hold themselves responsible for him in any way. Because they risk his individuality, he does his best not to be absorbed into that unignorable body of people, his immediate family. They are a background you don't request. Hence, for example, Welles, Burgess, Capote, each a one-off species; each unwilling to be governed by what had gone before; each preferring his origins to seem shrouded in the mysterious – and each, inexorably, inescapably, trapped by fate. (Welles, the child prodigy, remained too clever by half, dropping projects when they bored him, like a spoilt brat discarding toys; Burgess, his name changed from Wilson, traipsed the world, learned many languages, and never shook off his Manchester upbringing; Capote, the gilded butterfly, the wit and sophisticate, never climbed clear of a decadent and sinister Deep South.)

Olivier, with his preternatural awareness of the gap between Olivier and everything that was not Olivier, looked back at his youth and childhood and saw somebody else. 'I was absolutely brainless' (at home and school); 'ingenuous and stupid as I was' (at the Central School of Speech Training and Dramatic Art); 'I was pretty damn stupid' (at the Birmingham Repertory Theatre); 'stupid little idiot that I was' (in his first West End runs, particularly *Private Lives*); 'One thought of oneself, idiotically skinny as I was, as a sort of Tarzan' (in connection with his athleticism in *Queen of Scots* or *Theatre Royal*, in 1934); 'my idiotic, childish reasoning' . . . etc. etc. Perhaps he's trying to convey his innocence, his bashful ignorance? He was somebody newly hatched, a little bird just out of the egg? We can see such a scallywag in the early scenes of *Wuthering Heights*. The child Heathcliff, played by Rex Downing, could be the child Olivier, absorbing and remembering, and growing dark. He's the little changeling boy brought back to the farm by Mr Earnshaw, and in time, and after a fast fade and a lap dissolve, he reverses his fortunes, going from being a stable lad to a frock-coated, white-cravated master. We don't know his origins; nor do we know where he goes off to or quite how he makes his money. As the posters told us that 'THE MARK OF HELL IS IN HIS EYES', and as Olivier, dangling the hurricane lamp at Cathy, announced, 'What do they know of Heaven or Hell, they who know nothing of life,' I think we are to assume he dashes back and forth to the Underworld. He's the self-made orphan incarnate.

The primeval fantasy orphan – who of course *isn't* an orphan – is Oedipus.* The legend, decoded, means that, in revolting against the father, striking him dead, the son, once the authority figure is out of the way, discovers a basis for self-expression, or so he hopes.† He can make a fresh start. Olivier, as an actor, could make fresh starts by assuming new characters. 'There are times when to be James Tyrone in *Long Day's Journey into Night* is heaven compared to being me,' he told *Life* magazine, in August 1972. 'It's a great relief to be in somebody else's shoes – dirtier though they may be and uncomfortable though they may be.' Except, as Joan Plowright divulged, Tyrone's scuffed brogues were Olivier's and Olivier's alone. 'There was a time when they took *Long Day's Journey* out of the repertory for some reason. Larry was relieved that he didn't have to play himself for a while.' Is it such a hidden secret to reveal? That Olivier is continuously present in his characters? And that his life was a continuous sequence of masquerades?

* Welles is Tiresias in a tedious film made in a ruined amphitheatre, in 1967; Burgess' heroes are hobbled by clinging stepmothers, and he adapted *Oedipus the King* for the Guthrie Theatre, in Minnesota. His Oedipus novel is *M.F.*, which stands for 'motherfucker'. Capote's *In Cold Blood*, about the slaughter of a respectable Kansas farming family by a pair of drifters, has a classical inevitability. Olivier's *Oedipus Rex*, in a double bill with Sheridan's *The Critic*, opened in London on 18 October 1945 and played for seventy-six performances, before transferring to the Century Theatre, New York, the following May, as part of the Old Vic Company tour. Ralph Richardson was Tiresias, Sybil Thorndike was Jocasta and Harry Andrews was Creon.

† Both Olivier's sons, Tarquin and Richard, have written books about the weight *they* felt, being the progeny of a demanding and famous parent who, though absent much of the time, because work came first, dominated their existence. (Olivier's children are Hamlets figuring out the Ghost.)

Oedipus Rex is (a) a detective story about a man's discovery of who he is; (b) a family drama about rejection and ill-fated home-coming; and (c) an allegory of the wrongs you do to parents and to the gods. Olivier, with his trapped-ermine scream, which some say reverberates still amongst the rafters of the New Theatre, embodied a hero who faced up to his destiny and, blinding himself, cutting himself off from people, endorsed his damnation. That clear yell (' "Oh, Oh" is given in most editions. After going through all the vowel sounds, I hit upon "Er".' Thanks) was the soul's acceptance of guilt. It terrified the critics. 'A man seeing the horrors of infinity in a trance might make such a sound,' said Tynan. 'One of those performances in which blood and electricity are somehow mixed. It pulls down lightning from the sky. It is as awesome, dwarfing and appalling as one of nature's angriest displays,' wrote John Mason Brown, in the *Saturday Review of Literature.*

Everything to do with Olivier is funnelled into the cry – it's a vortex. His determination, his courage, and chiefly his feelings of guilt, which I'll define as the burden of one's moral shortcomings. Acting, the very thing he was good at, occasioned guilt. As a child, or extra-terrestrial, at 26 Wathen Road, Dorking, or 22 Lupus Street, Pimlico, he said he lied. Well, it's more fun to lie. That's theatre. 'For what is acting but lying, and what is good acting but convincing lying?' he asked boldly, rhetorically. 'The whole theatre is a bloody lie from beginning to end,' he told a shocked press conference, at the Plâce des Arts, Montreal, on 17 October 1967, when the National was in Canada for the Expo 67's World Festival of Entertainment.* I'm sure he'd agree that though acting may not be the real world, neither is it a traduction of it, or a mockery of it. His 'one inveterate and seemingly irresistible sin, that of lying' could be transfigured into imaginative sympathy – as he said in 1964, 'I think almost everybody would find Greek tragedy . . . the furthest removed from natural feeling. I remember, before I played Oedipus I had a talk with Sir Maurice Bowra† . . . He said there's only one thing to do in *Oedipus Rex*. You cannot feel real. The only approach is to feel fated. You have to enter a kind of vacuum, if you're playing parts such as Oedipus. You have to be in a world all your own, of your own imagining, that has its own style of stance, that by its absolute authenticity of purpose looks real, that by an attitude toward the dialogue sounds real.'

---

* With *The Dance of Death*, *A Flea in Her Ear* and *Love for Love*.

† Sir Cecil Maurice Bowra, CH, Kt., FBA, 1898–1971. Warden of Wadham and a classical scholar, author of *Ancient Greek Literature* (1933), *Sophoclean Tragedy* (1944), etc. Surprising his friends by courting an ugly woman, he opined, 'Buggers can't be choosers.'

Art may be a secondary world, or an alternative to the world, but Olivier could enter through its gates, and put his 'early wicked tendencies' to use. Indeed, they'd always come in handy. Orphans, foundlings, changelings, call them what you like – these artists who believe themselves self-created might grow up rejecting others, recoiling from intimacy – loneliness being something to cherish – but, paradoxically, and on their own terms, they need audiences to want them, to take to them. Oedipus is conscious of the presence of the Chorus, 'men before whom he must keep up appearances,' said Yeats, like a king before his court – or an actor before the sharp spectators. Olivier's amateur theatricals, as a child, were directed at his mother: 'I played shamelessly to my mother. She would mouth the words with me, and whenever I stumbled she would urge me on, applauding deliriously when I got it right and suffocating me with hugs at the end.' And this reassurance – from plays and audiences – has to be repeated endlessly.

Olivier's mother, Agnes Louise Crookenden, was born in Kidbrooke, Kent, on 1 December 1871. What is more interesting is her death, forty-nine years later, on 27 March 1920, when her youngest child was coming up for thirteen. She'd suffered from glioblastoma, a malignant central nervous system tumour, that even today leaves a life expectancy for people over forty of only a few months. Its rapid enlargement destroys normal brain cells, with a progressive loss of function, and raises the intracranial pressure, causing headache, vomiting, and drowsiness.* Her last words to her son – the scene sounds as staged as Cathy's deathbed in *Wuthering Heights*, or Lord Marchmain's in *Brideshead Revisited* – were, 'Darling Larry, no matter what your father says, be an actor. Be a great actor. For me.'

Sybil Thorndike – who became his mother-surrogate – remembered Agnes Olivier as being dark and gypsy-ish, competent and vivacious – and Olivier's women were to be cat-ladies in this genre: Vivien, Dorothy Tutin, Sarah Miles, Joan Plowright. 'Mummy was just everything,' said Sybille. 'She was the most enchanting person. Hair so long she could sit on it. She absolutely made our childhood. Always saw the funny side of everything. She adored Larry. He was hers. He always amused her very much.' She was an angel in the house – the kind of woman that men wish women to be, pure, tender, hushed. Olivier's memories of 'my heaven, my hope, my entire world, my own worshipped Mummy', 'my wonderful Mums', 'our beloved but greatly over-stressed Mummy', have the quality of a faded photograph. There she is, arranging flowers,

* *Oxford Concise Medical Dictionary*, 3rd ed., 1990.

running the household, checking the crockery for dust, playing the piano, paying the butcher's bills, writing letters. The kind of woman to be found 'spelling out fairy tales by the nursery fire', as Virginia Woolf would say. Less of a real woman than an ideal of womanhood, she was the perfect Edwardian hostess, flattering, teasing, titillating, drawing people out – and to her, by ministering to their sorrows. (This was Vivien at Notley: the manners, the control, and then the private chaos going on inside.)

Olivier had a strange way of remembering this apparition speak: 'How I wish you wouldn't persist in making this hateful business necessary. I do detest it so.' The hateful business is a spanking. Olivier has to be flagellated for his fibbing. But the line he gives his mother, or decides to recall across a distance of sixty-odd years, is out of Restoration comedy, or a bodice-ripper. It is mildly titillatory. From the beginnings, therefore, sin and guilt – the secret pleasures of naughtiness – are connected with sex. When the prefects beat him at school, 'I suffered pain such as I had not known possible.' His crime: to have spurned homosexual advances ('I was a flirt'). When he starts his affair with Vivien, 'I began to feel sorry for Jill, indeed to feel pain for her and, of course, guilt.' When Vivien began to cuckold him on the Australian tour, again guilt and physical pain are combined – his bad leg is like a psychic wound: 'Pain . . . pain. It was the pain of blood in full flood trying to get out of my knee and through the plaster.' He accepts it as his due.

Guilt, he says, 'was a dark fiend', which especially pursued him when he was first encoiled with Vivien. 'Two years of furtive life, lying life. Sneaky.' He calls himself a 'worm-like adulterer'. Why is this self-abasement off-putting? Because it is merely apparent. He called his autobiography *Confessions of an Actor*, but he only appears to be confiding. His prose, flowery, turgid, righteous, prone to an adjectival clog (divine, sweet, enchanting); the curlicues, the fuss: his book is a version of the kind of performance he was giving at that point in his career, in the seventies and eighties, when he's to be found twirling his moustache, coming out with curious accents, and flourishing his cane in the air. Ornate, verbose – Olivier doesn't fall asleep, for him 'the god Morpheus had applied his gentle pressure to my dormic nerve'; he doesn't go for a quick shag, Olivier has 'tender venturings into the blessed unction of sex'. It's a masquerade. Olivier is dramatizing his life, hiding his life behind (or within) campy mock-feminine mannerisms. We must imagine him talking, acting it out.

Lord Jim, in *A Portrait of the Artist as a Young Man* (1904), was evidently not the only author to get language to mimic the successive stages in the growth and development of a boy's mind. Baby's prattle for the early years, a Stalky and Co. apple-pippin slang for the schooldays chapters, a self-conscious cleverness for the undergraduate era; you get the idea. Language becomes sophisticated as Stephen Dedalus does. Olivier re-invents the technique. The 'baby Bees-bees' for childhood; 'It's no use you sitting there, looking like dried *baddocks*' for schooldays; and Mr Pooter at the Mansion House Ball for dinner with Winston Churchill: 'Excuse me, Sir, but have you ever tried plain water with it? I believe it to be the soda that crawls up the back of our necks the next morning.'

Olivier, reminiscing about his childhood, doesn't refer to Joyce, but he does consciously invoke Joyce's extravagant and fantastic antecedent, Dickens, whom the precentor at All Saints, Father Geoffrey Heald, held to be a treasure house of characterizations. So, early on in *Confessions of an Actor*, he deliberately mimics *David Copperfield*, relishing the genteel poverty of his upbringing, caricaturing the blows and destitution, sketching himself as gangling, threadbare, hirsute, with buck teeth, i.e. he's a Cruickshank engraving. Olivier even quotes the famous opening sentence – 'Whether I shall turn out to be the hero of my own life, or whether that station will be held by anybody else, these pages must show . . .' – and adds, 'I could use the same description with regard to my own birth.' Which is nonsense. Nobody was likely to usurp Olivier. Perhaps he was wondering whether he'd turn out to be the *villain* of his own life, because in the *Life* magazine interview he claimed, 'I'm constantly amazing myself – and not with admiration, either. I do have a self-detestation . . . If [James Tyrone] hated himself the way I hate myself – then at least we have a partnership.'

Tyrone, of course, is an actor, his overweening personality crammed with wiles, stratagems, dissimulation. He's laughably insincere, trying to smile and wince his way through the day, coping with a morphine-addicted wife, a son who's terminally tubercular, and another son, who plays the piano in a knocking shop, who is in the grip of the grog. He has caused their problems, too, by failing to pay for adequate medical treatment, by depriving them of self-confidence – by being, not just the big despotic father, but by being actorishly aware that he's playing this role. He hates his family for the responsibilities they impose upon him, for the money they need and attempt to extract from him. He hates his family for boxing him in – for depriving him of freedom – and most of all, and no other actor, and no other man, only Olivier could bring this out, he hates his family for making him love them so much.

'It's what I call one of my autobiographical jobs,' said Olivier. 'People say, "How did you find that character?" That chap wasn't a stranger to me at all. I didn't have to invent for his eccentricities. I knew them all.' That Olivier could identify with a guilt-ridden baffled old thesp, seeing out his crabby retirement on the fog-bound edge of a river (the Tyrones' cabin is as isolated and oppressive as Vanya's villa), is a clue to what he felt about his own past. For Olivier, in interviews and memoirs, like Tyrone, enthroned on his veranda, affects to find himself intolerable. Reverting to the nursery spankings, Olivier goes into detail about the number of thwacks he used to get; he tells us proudly that he learned to stifle his yelps; and he wonders, if this task was so distasteful to 'my Mummy', why then wasn't it his father – otherwise depicted as Mr Murdstone – who got to be the one to make chase with a slipper or maybe a driving iron, leaving Agnes out of it? Being smacked was the one – the sole – intimate moment between mother and son he decided to record. That she was reticent about the disciplinary action implies she half condoned his crimes; that she nevertheless overcame these scruples and didn't spare the rod – why, 'How much the nobler . . . my mother's voluntary self-punishment.' Beating him, she's hurting herself.

What an odd jumble of emotions. He remembers the pain and the humiliation ('I noticed . . . while I was removing the necessary garments that she was in a state of high distress'); and maternal love and filial devotion is expressed through 'the monotonous exchange of sin and punishment'. He's not really contrite ('my habit of lying ceased . . . for a while, anyway'); her heart isn't in the violence, but none the less she goes through with it. This is theatre. Olivier and his mother are involved in a complex play of feeling, like Hamlet and Gertrude.

Eileen Herlie, the Scottish actress who was the Queen of Denmark in his film, was twenty-seven when she was cast; Olivier, the Prince, was forty. He dyed his hair platinum blond to seem younger, but there is no disguising his furrowed middle-aged brow. (He looks like a forty-year-old Olivier with dyed hair reciting from *Hamlet*.) What was he up to, insisting on a Gertrude thirteen years junior to her own son? It's because Olivier was wish-fulfillingly bringing his mother back. Herlie has long dark tresses, voluptuous, flouncy white nightgowns. She's an Edwardian mother getting ready for bed, surrounded by her combs and hairbrushes, her hand mirror and her bottles of scent. Though she and Hamlet kiss on the lips and fondle, in scenes with many meaningful cuts to the marriage couch – 'a couch for luxury and damned incest' – the mood between them is exasperated, irritable. There's an edginess, a tension, not explained away by the stabbing of Polonius, by Elsinore's political intrigue. They understand each other all too well, and can do little but exchange fleeting expressions of helpless love.

This is more urgent, more felt, than the sentimentality of *Confessions of an Actor*, where Olivier is incumbent to keep up appearances. What his actual mother was like may be further deduced from another Shakespearian character, Kate in *The Taming of the Shrew*. In this play, the disguises-within-disguises are complex by anybody's standards. Hortensio, Lucentio and Tranio swap clothes and dress up as private tutors, or as each other, or as other people again, the better to woo Bianca and Katharina. In the sixteenth century, identity was confused further by boys playing the girls' roles – in the sixteenth century and at All Saints choir school in the twenties. In 1919, Olivier was Maria in an end-of-term extract from the kitchen scene in *Twelfth Night*. One of the cast being suddenly indisposed, Father McGlinchy's daughter, Ethel, who taught the choristers how to dance for a fancy-dress ball, was drafted in to play Sir Toby Belch. She grew up to be the actress Fabia Drake.* They did the bit where Sir Toby, Sir Andrew and Maria, the housekeeper, carouse into the small hours and get told off by Malvolio. Maria ('a beagle, true bred') sides with the gentry against the uppity steward, and she's the one who perfects the plan for revenge ('Sport royal, I warrant you'). She's mischievous – spiteful. Hence, a year later, Olivier could develop his character further as Katharina, the shrew.

Laurence Naismith says there was nothing effeminate about Olivier in drag. He was wholly absorbed in the part and 'The moment he put on those dresses his image and bearing changed completely. He really became a young girl.' Sybil Thorndike, who witnessed these early appearances because her father, Canon Arthur John Webster Thorndike, the vicar of St James the Less in Westminster, was a friend and neighbour of the Olivier family, agrees that 'he could play the girls beautifully . . . He was a wonderful Katharina . . . He was marvellous in women's parts, though he himself is the least effeminate of men. You couldn't have a man less effeminate off-stage. Yet I've seldom seen a better Katharina than the one he did at school.'

The transsexual facility lingered. Dame Sybil appeared with him and Monroe in *The Prince and the Showgirl*, shot at Pinewood in 1956. He was demonstrating how he wanted the Queen Dowager and Elsie Marina to

* Olivier contributed a foreword to her autobiography, *Blind Fortune* (London, 1978). He recalled both the dancing lessons ('I felt a certain elated emotion as she took my hands') and the *Twelfth Night* excerpt: 'Our first and only appearance on any stage together throughout our lives was in a performance for which the casting must forever be regarded as the most unique in all theatre history.'

move, to gesture, and he told his cast, 'You won't be able to do it as well as I could' – and Dame Sybil concedes 'it was true'. Like Shakespeare who, as Keats said, could transform himself into Iago and Imogen, so could Olivier disappear into their different worlds. He had a capacity that felt all things; and as Katharina, aggressive, scornful, high-spirited, and yet with an air of distress and disappointment, Olivier imagined himself, intensely and comprehensively, to be his mother.

Dame Sybil noticed this at once. 'He looked just like his mother in the part.' So did Sybille his sister. 'He modelled his character on Mother, and it was this that enabled him to come across so well as a woman. Father was at one performance . . . and he had to get up and leave, so shaken was he to see Larry recreating Mother down to the last detail. Father, of course, misunderstood. He castigated Larry for his sacrilege in bringing Mother back to life, so to speak.'

Acting is an affair of ghosts, and Agnes' spirit was mingling with Olivier's own. (That the baby Vivien Leigh miscarried in August 1956 was to have been baptised Katherine is somewhat fateful.) His Katharina, despite her temper, secretly enjoyed the game of being tamed by Petruchio. Her sexual curiosity was awakened – as Olivier's had been by his mother, who was to remain a touchstone in this field. Overexcited to be in New York on his first visit with Jill, for example, and hoping for rumpy-pumpy at the Algonquin, he'd chide himself for 'indulging in such idiotic fantasies; my mother should really be around with slipper or hairbrush'. These, we could conceive, would be Katharina's weapons. 'The Shrew was boldly and vigorously played, with dark, flashing eyes and a spiteful voice' (*Birmingham Post*); 'an excellent study of scowling bad temper' (*Birmingham Mail*); 'The boy who took the part of Kate made a fine, bold, black-eyed hussy, badly in need of taming . . .' (*Daily Telegraph*).

If Olivier's family and friends recognized all that as a portrait drawn from life – technically from death – and if Olivier's father ran howling from the theatre (*The Taming of the Shrew* was first performed at All Saints School in 1920 and the production was revived on 28 April 1922, when Geoffrey Heald was invited by the governors of the Shakespeare Memorial Theatre, Stratford-upon-Avon, to stage it as part of the Bard's Birthday Week Festival), then Agnes Crookenden was not the melting paragon of legend. She must have been savage and intransigent. Olivier told Tynan that 'I absolutely worshipped and adored my mother who died when I was thirteen years old, and I often think, and say, that perhaps I've never got over it.' But if he'd not got over it, he was at least conscious enough of the trauma to discuss it openly, which makes me mistrust its later impact and wonder whether it was a misery that must go on forever. He seems so collected about it – there's no seam of vulnerability or helplessness; no appeal. You'd never think Olivier defenceless, and if he was once or for a long time discomposed and aggrieved, the force of all those years, of feeling hopelessly alone, armed him, and lurked in his characters' dark rhythms and impressiveness.

Olivier's mother, one way and another, gave him a layer of hardness. Yet it was his father, Gerard Kerr Olivier, born in Wiltshire on 30 April 1869, whom he called 'a man of ice', 'a sententious old misery who played for effect . . . as if religion were a lie that Farve enjoyed shaming others into believing' – that is to say, a hypocrite (or an actor) – whom he believed was brutal and blighted his existence. Indeed: 'I have always thought that the initial trouble between me and my father was that he couldn't see the slightest purpose in my existence.' Yet since when was it necessary for parents to regard children as being utilities, as having a use, for good or ill? Worth is not a quality parents quantify. 'Everything about me irritated him,' Olivier claimed, though the boot may well be on the other foot. If Olivier resembled and was coddled by his mother, it must have been no joke for Gerard having two termagants in the rectory; and in any event, Agnes fell mortally ill, which didn't exactly engender much heart's ease. Olivier also bemoaned his father's parsimony. Bathwater (hot and cold) was rationed; drink was issued in thimble measures; and meat was carved wafer-thin. When Olivier left home for the Central School, the parting advice he received was, 'You can either walk everywhere and save bus fares, or bus everywhere and save shoe leather; you'll have to try it and see which is cheapest.'

Olivier doesn't see that this remark may have been meant ironically – the penurious parson sending himself up. The son also fails to see the potential for satire when, after the marriage to Jill, they go to stay with Farve, and Farve still offers Kim the top off his boiled egg. Affronted, they take the old fellow to a restaurant. He orders oysters, smoked salmon, lobster, fine wines. 'Well,' he announces cheerfully, 'if I get outside that I won't be doing badly.' His advice on the menstrual cycle is similarly mock-guileless bordering on malice: ' . . . the good Lord has given to mankind a safe period, so that nature can be truly gratified without yielding up the blessed fruit of conception – and this special time, the middle of the month.'

Gerard gave himself theatrical airs, which made his presence ambiguous, unsettling. Olivier was encouraged to denigrate him by Jill's family, who found him stuffy, chilled to the marrow, too fond of laying down the law – he was the kind of man, Olivier was led to believe, who'd forgotten 'all about the days of [his] youth, when [his] blood was warm, and the sunshine was singing in his heart.' It is more likely that this parody of a frosty geezer, emotionally and no doubt actually constipated, was his reaction to, and defence against, the Esmonds, who were rather a high-spirited lot. Jill's father, H. V. Esmond, was a playwright and actor-manager; her mother, Eva Moore,* was a famous West End actress. They had a country house near Marlow, and the Esmond entourage included Noël Coward, Ivor Novello and Gerald du Maurier. A country parson mingling with such names is bound to feel himself ponderous and uninteresting, and would come across as withdrawn and disdainful. Gerard Kerr Olivier, a man concerned with how he seemed to other people, got in first with a caricature of wearisomeness – and Olivier himself made use of this in *Henry IV Part Two*, at the New Theatre in 1945.

Olivier took the small role of Justice Shallow, Falstaff's wizened friend in the Gloucestershire orchard. Shallow, Shakespeare's 'lecherous . . . monkey', was depicted as an old-maidish fuss-budget, prating about 'Clement's-inn, where I think they will talk of mad Shallow yet . . . Jesu, Jesu, the mad days that I have spent!' He's looking back at his boisterous college days, but now it's more likely to be the chimes of midnight that they have heard pealing ('That we have, that we have, that we have') and many of their old acquaintances, Double, Francis Pickbone, and Will Squele, a Cotswold man, are dead. When he scurries off to organize dinner, Falstaff remarks, 'Lord, Lord, how subject we old men are to this vice of lying' – Shallow's recollections are fictions, aggrandisements; he's in his anecdotage, chattering through his lean chops and entwining his bony fingers in greasy wisps of hair. This time, Ibo, Olivier's stepmother, was the one to run weeping from the stalls, taking refuge red-eyed backstage. It had been Gerard she'd seen incarnated up there, beady, cagey, muttering about fatstock prices and the sexual conquest of Jane Nightwork, alongside Ralph Richardson's melancholy Knight and Miles Malleson's Silence – Gerard, who'd died of a stroke at Addington, Buckinghamshire, on 30 March 1939.

Olivier was in Indianapolis, on tour with Katharine Cornell in *No Time for Comedy*, and did not return for the funeral. Though he never said so explicitly, he was always guilty about this. (In his memoirs he is at pains to explain how far off America was from England in those

* She has a crammed two-page four-column entry in *Who's Who in the Theatre* (eleventh ed., 1951). She played characters with names like Felicia Umfraville, Violet Melrose, Ellice Ford, or Wilhelmina Marr, in plays with titles like *Our Boys, Pilkerton's Peerage, Marriages in Mayfair*, etc. She was admired by Queen Mary.

days; he'd have had to go by train to New York, across the ocean by ship; transatlantic flights didn't come in until Churchill had a brainwave; and anyway, Ibo was a great coper . . .) His mixed feelings about his absence indicate his private war, his grudges, his perplexities about his father, the only man on whom he presumed to pass moral judgement.

For the man he didn't want to resemble, he resembled. James Tyrone's past-it suits, frayed watch strap, and mildewed elegance; his bitterness and panic of self-loathing; his meanness, closeness: these are aspects he attributed to his father, and yet when he was in the play he claimed them to be his own. 'On the first night . . . I had a message from my darling, lovely elder daughter. She said, "Darling Daddy, now we know why you have been so strict about turning lights off at home. It is because you were practising for your play." It's just that I hate waste; petty economy, not sensible economy, is my sin. There are some things that, like James Tyrone, you never get over. When I first went on the stage professionally at seventeen, I lacked for food. I was hungry and out of work and terrified. My father was a parson – or a priest as he liked to call himself. We were very, very poor . . .' Cue the shared bath water story; the minuscule slices of chicken story. (In *Long Day's Journey into Night*, Tyrone marks the level on the whiskey bottle and unscrews superfluous low-wattage bulbs from the electrolier.)*

Another thing Olivier would do – turn down the thermostat on the swimming pool. 'I have a switch in my bedroom that turns on a blower in the pool room, and by the time I arrive, it's amply warm,' he said in 1982. 'I like the water to be seventy-seven or seventy-eight degrees, but my wife won't go in at such a low temperature. So I set the thermostat at eighty and tell her it's eighty-two.' Eighty, ninety, what's the odds? It's his cheese-paring precision which is significant. For his father, 'saving was a craving. This is no idle jingle but the plainest statement of fact.' Olivier, too, was afraid of being thought profligate – and there is a connection to be made between the carefulness, the watchfulness, over money and his greed for fame – 'Thank God for the movies . . . I get

* Olivier made niggardliness virtuosic – to be grouped with his death-defying stunts and tumbles. As Ronald Pickup recalls: 'I remember when we were doing *Long Day's Journey into Night* there was a piece of business which involved a very dangerous teeter on the edge of a table, in order to unscrew an overhead lightbulb so as to save electricity. Now this was a man who was no longer young, sharing with the audience the knowledge that he was in a position of danger. But it was also dead right for the character's obsessive, manic miserliness – he was *going* to turn off that light bulb, however dangerous it was. And he would teeter on the edge of the table, turn it off, then step back in a wonderful piece of daring: "Told you so. I could do it!"'

a fortune for doing [them], which is absolutely what I'm after' – and his vigilance as an actor. Edward Petherbridge, who understudied Frank Finlay's Iago, noticed how Olivier could conserve, mete out, calculate exactly how much energy to expend. 'Watching rehearsals . . . I would think he was giving everything. Then there was a run-through, and I realized, no, he hadn't been giving everything . . .' There was always some capital to be kept in reserve for, as he would put it, the fight, the run on his exchequer. Discussing the great Shakespearian roles he said, 'You give them all you've got and the author says to you: "You've given it all you've got? Good. Now, more. Good. Now more. More, damn you. More, more, MORE! MORE!" Until your heart and guts and brain are pulp and the part feeds on you, eating you. Acting great parts devours you. It's a dangerous game.'

It was as if he was having to survive in the wild, and he couldn't afford to be negligent. How he differs from Welles, say, who was bounteous, extravagant, avid in different ways. Olivier could not have made *Citizen Kane* or put Falstaff at the centre of Shakespeare's Histories; Welles wouldn't have been interested in *Henry V*, unless he could have debunked the heroism. Olivier did want Welles to be his Buckingham in the film of *Richard III*: what a duel (of attitude, acting styles, myths; Englishness vs. America; classical-romantic vs. the gothic-baroque) that would have been: 'May it please you to resolve me in my suit?' 'I am not in the giving vein today' – and thwack! down comes the sceptre on the edge of the throne.

There is a deep psychological meaning to Olivier's canny husbandry. Hoarding his resources, mental and physical, he'd not like to give much of himself away, either. Though he surrounded himself with people, in theatres and film studios, in committee rooms and at Notley or his houses in Sussex, he didn't need others to be near. He says he suffered from premature ejaculation – it's the same principle at work: get it over quickly. He didn't like to connect. He was sociable, and he could suggest an aura of intimacy ('Lord Olivier becomes a bit boring you know. Call me Larry'); indeed, though he made himself a social animal, creating and leading companies, needing an organization, within which he'd distribute and withhold rewards, and know everybody's names, like a hostess – nevertheless he was private, reticent, independent. When you watch his early films, especially forgotten photoplays such as *Potiphar's Wife*, *Q Planes*, *Moscow Nights* or *Twenty-One Days*, you realize there are large parts of Olivier he means to keep to himself. That's very enticing, of course, and would evolve into an erotic allure, in *Wuthering Heights* or *The Beggar's Opera*, where he plays Macheath as a good-humoured wolf with glancing, darting eyes. There's a strength in there. Beautiful and inaccessible, he keeps – or gains – control of himself. Yet he's remote.

His acting is expressive of loneliness. Heathcliff, candlelit behind the rain-lashed window panes, would become Shylock, a frock-coated Rothschild, daring you to spurn him, in a cramped and greenish Rialto, illuminated by black lamps. *The Merchant of Venice,* a National Theatre production taped for television in 1973, gets to be about a man who doesn't want you close. Olivier is a distinguished Jewish financier, not the usual hook-nosed Fagin or slavering son of the desert. He has a self-protective mock-flirtatiousness, a curdled kind of charm, which doesn't mean to succeed in winning you over. His fastidiousness, clothes, bearing; the dignity and the cover – the social niceties: he anticipates your prejudices, goes on about being a Jew (he slightly camps up his Jewishness), so as to pre-empt your wanting to notice or remark about such things. He is ingratiating – but this is all diversionary. He is elsewhere, emotionally shut off. And so was Olivier. He had a family, to whom he could be simultaneously devoted and distant. ('He once hoisted me on his shoulders, on a beach – but I only know that because I have seen the photograph,' said his son Richard recently.) And such was Vivien's desire for possession, it was inevitable that he should leave her.

Shylock is a widower. Olivier allowed a stream of secret feeling to flow into his lines when he reminisced about Leah. This is the loss which bruised him, left him vulnerable. Jessica's departure brings back his sorrow in full flood. He's newly bereaved. Gabbling about the ducats she's made off with, he hides his guilt behind, or within, the pretence of worrying about money. Olivier's Shylock is extraordinary: he's not interested in the lucre – indeed, he grimaces at the absurd conscious send-up of himself as a man only worried about money – and what he's remembering isn't the jewel, which Jessica has squandered, but the person to whom he gave that jewel, who was more precious than the jewel ('I would not have parted with it . . .' he entreats). He's remembering when he was younger and happier; before things happened to close him off from people and turn him into a snowfield.

When his mother died Olivier felt she'd abandoned him. His proud spirit underwent a sense of wrong. Lost in an arctic sea, 'I was a sailing ship adrift, lying dead in the water, masts buckled and sails in tatters, at the mercy of the ocean's currents.' Perhaps it really was the case that Olivier spent the rest of his life never knowing quite what his feelings were, this man who was yet precise and exact? He did not know what he thought. His father, similarly, was emotionally paralysed by his wife's death – and where Olivier decided to delight in his struggles, his despair filling him with exhilaration (like Richard III he'd become one to originate and control), Gerard Kerr Olivier – according to his son – was simply a lifelong horror. 'A very frightening father-figure, a Victorian father-figure . . . I was terrified of him.' Sybille backs this up: 'And talk about a temper – a storming, raging tornado which he'd turn on Larry in a way he never did on our brother Dick and me. Father didn't like Larry, and Larry was terrified of him.'

Thus, the inspiration for that sceptre-as-offensive-weapon; or the invective in *Sleuth*, where his voice, all charm to start with, rises and takes on a snarl and snap. It's more than a parade-ground rebuke – there's real violence and contempt in Olivier's tones. The fake joviality and flirtatiousness are not intended to conceal the pressure building up in him – and, if this was Andrew Wyke, it was Olivier too: 'You could be very familiar with Larry, tremendously so,' says Michael Caine, 'but only to a certain extent. He has a quality – I used to think, "He doesn't like me today" . . . On the days he didn't like me, he would call me "baby". Then when he was in trouble, it was Michael – "Michael, can we go through the lines?" When he's not quite sure of something he'll go terribly feminine – and you won't attack him because he's being all nice and soft. But once he got the lines down, he'd say, "Right, baby, let's go on the set, shall we?"'

The cunning child is there, manipulating its parents – a trick which worked with Agnes (she colluded with it), and which manifestly did not with Gerard, who didn't want his young son to keep reminding him of his dead wife – though Olivier comically alleges that his ire went right back to the cradle: 'My father never recovered from the slight disgust that he felt at his first viewing of me.' Nor did Olivier recover from the disgust he felt about his father, whom he turned from a person into a predicament, and who was impersonated, as late as 1976, as a cruel caricature in *The Seven Per Cent Solution*. Professor Moriarty is a cameo – 'vital to me, these cameos, *spiritually* and *financially*. I've always managed to give them all the animation they need' (italics added) – and the joke is meant to be that the criminal mastermind who torments Holmes is, in reality, a feeble old mathematics tutor, a shabby, genteel schoolmaster. But with Olivier handling the reins the chills never stop rippling down your spine. For all the apparent servility and fearfulness and mock-deference, this Moriarty is terrifying. His queasy spirit belongs with Richard III and Dr Szell, in *Marathon Man*, in the gallery of grotesques.

He has only a few short scenes, which took two days to shoot, and for which he received seventy-five thousand dollars. He bustles up to

Watson (Robert Duvall with a preposterous accent),* proffers a sheaf of telegrams, and complains about Holmes' unrelenting obsession with him. He is exasperated and amazed and faintly threatening – he is defensive and has a weird restlessness. He's all long, bony fingers, elbows, thin legs – an insect or bird of ill omen – and Ken Adam, the art director, constructed a tenebrous hidey-hole for this cormorant. Moriarty is to be glimpsed in the cloudy mirror of his musty room, with its low, damp ceiling, its piles of yellowing newspapers; and there's a dark-yellow haze to the walls, a yellowish-brown fug coming from the hissing gas jets, which the Napoleon of crime adjusts and turns down frugally. (The room has jaundice.) This is the beggarly atmosphere of Olivier's childhood vicarages, where 'We were what was called "gentry", though we lived in a slum in Dorking . . . My father had china, masses of it, sitting out all over the house – tablefuls of silver lying out on shelves – none of it properly cleaned and dusted.'

In Holmes' delirium, Moriarty becomes a serpent – the speckled band? – and there's a close-up of a hooded cobra intercut with Olivier's looming, menacing face. His eyes rimmed with red, his lips thin and red, his gums straight, his face, against the black backcloth, vampirishly blanched; with his strands of grey hair overcombed and oiled flat, Olivier is indeed the evil Moriarty, a sadistic pedant torturing his pupils with trigonometry. But Holmes' dementia suggests more than bad cess with differential calculus. Watson, a medical man and no fool (facts we are apt to forget), decides to transport the Baker Street wiz to Vienna, to see what Freud can unravel about the case. Moriarty reappears in hypnotic trances and during a cocaine-induced fit, and Holmes wasn't exaggerating his fears. This black, black Moriarty is a very serpent in the Garden of Eden – the fornicator, in a flashback sequence, who is seen jerking under the eiderdown with Sherlock's mother. Sherlock's father bursts in and fires a gun, and we see Moriarty scuttling away, startled by the light, trying to hide his identity behind the blood-splattered bedsheet – it clings to him like a lace shroud.

He has a look of sheer amazement, a version of which is on his face when he's telling Watson about the persecution and the telegrams; he's affronted, his eyes staring without blinking whilst his brain assesses the extent of any danger. He is defiant, covert; he has an irrepressible rage. What began as a prissy, petty pedagogue becomes – Olivier? Olivier's

* Nicol Williamson, Alan Arkin, Robert Duvall: they *all* have preposterous voices and accents. (Williamson's Holmes goes from falsetto to basso-profundo and back in the space of a word.) Did the ghost of Peter Sellers creep into the sound booth and re-dub the movie?

father? The latter was a bit eccentric, not much of a provider, and he had a restlessness, suggested by his leaving schoolmastering for the church and then shifting from parish to parish, but Olivier always associated him with damnation, rather than salvation; with vengeance and anguish and shame, rather than tenderness; with cruelty and suffering and neglect, rather than love. 'I had the feeling that my father was silently ruing the day I was born, so disgusted did I imagine him to be with me . . . I felt terribly guilty . . .'

Guilty that he'd been born? Guilty that he was not worthy of signs of love? Guilty because he was defiant? Sybille is the expert witness here: 'He tended always to be quiet and withdrawn when Father was in the house, and then burst out into his other much more ebullient self when he was gone, by way of compensation . . . Despite his attachment to Mother, he was in awe of Father. He wanted so for Father to like him.' The complexity of the love/hate relationship was to give depth and dimension to his performances – full, as they are, with his rage and sorrow. An actor may live a pretend life – fantasy, illusion, make-believe – but Olivier's creations were aroused by what he'd observed and felt. His acting was an expression of his intense emotions, and he and his father could never meet. They had confrontations instead.

His amazing senses transfigured *The Jazz Singer*, in which he played 'God forgive me . . . Al Jolson's Jewish father.' Neil Diamond's, actually, though Olivier was contemptuous of the entire exercise, especially when Sidney J. Furie, the director, was replaced by Richard Fleischer, and the film had to be reshot. 'It was damned embarrassing enough to do once. But then they . . . asked me to go through the whole silly thing again. That made it doubly embarrasing. It's trash.' Trash with its own integrity, however. I quite enjoy it. It's terrible – and it's wonderful. In the former category, we have Neil's first wife (Catlin Adams), the childhood sweetheart, who can't face the gregarious show-biz people in the dressing room, so she scurries off down the corridor and we never hear of her again; or the second wife (Lucie Arnaz) welcoming Neil back after he's walked out on her and the baby – he's spent a year thumbing lifts and growing a beard, and a reunion is staged on the beach in merciful dumbshow and longshot.

The cause for wonder is Olivier's Cantor Rabinovitch, the cross and demanding paterfamilias, devoted to the synagogue and its rituals – to tradition. The film is an old-fashioned battle between the generations – a voyage round a father. Neil's Yussel Rabinovitch wants to run away from the chanting and solemnity of the church choir and, as Jess Robin, delight the populace with his pop songs, 'You Baby', 'America', and

'Hello Again', amongst several dozen other ditties. Olivier's character is dead against this, and casts his son into outer darkness. He's a Jewish Lear, betrayed, he believes, by his thankless loved one. His voice shoots up a few octaves, and stays there. His face is shrunk, pinched, grave; he wears huge glasses which miniaturize and yet also enlarge – it's a swimmy effect – his eyes. (I'm reminded of Hardy's phrase: 'the weakening eye of day'.) Olivier is worried, aquiver, alert – a thousand variations on flickers of anguish. He's simultaneously mild and powerful, qualities to the fore in the big reconciliation scene, a scene that outstrips the mad King's reconciliation with Cordelia for spiritual uplift or schmaltz.

The cantor, wrapped in his ritual vestments, totters into the vestry, cold-shouldering his errant son. Yussel/Jess can get no acknowledgement from the old man – Olivier radiates pride, rage, solitude and vulnerability. You know he loves the boy really. Neil insists that his father looks at a photograph of the grandchild he's never seen. 'Look, Pop, look. He has Ma's [as it might be] nose.' Pause. Olivier continues to look stern, and he then says, in a whisper, 'And-he-has-your-eyes.' It makes me weep every time! Olivier is not Jewish like his Shylock; he's a rococo version of Jewish. A Jewish critic in New York said Olivier is so astonishingly Jewish, his performance is 'an act of unintentional yet nonetheless unforgivable anti-Semitism' – but I personally don't find him forced or over-the-top. I see only restraint, which is what makes for the beauty; the touch is so sure.

Olivier shows that love involves embarrassment. Hence it's an awkwardness people try and skirt around or conceal. Which was the case with his father. What to others might have seemed Gerard's reticence, or reserve, Olivier coded as coldness, or indifference. He assumed there'd be a battle, trying to get away and be an actor; he'd thought to follow his brother Richard to India, and plant tea; or join the mercantile marine. 'When we had seen [Richard] off on his boat at Tilbury and got back home to Letchworth where my father was rector, I said, "Well, when can I follow Dickie out to India, Father . . . I don't want to go to the university." And my father said, "You're talking nonsense, Kim, you're going to be an actor." I was amazed that he'd thought things out for me at all and that he'd thought things out that far. I secretly knew he was right, that I ought to be an actor, and I was very surprised that he had the perspicacity, and the observation of my character, to know that finally I was going to be that . . .'

For all that he says against his father, Olivier was aligned with him – over (as we'll see in the next chapter) religion and the classics; his nineteenth-century style of acting. Olivier didn't destroy the past – he perpetuated it. He became himself not by rejecting his father, but by becoming patriarchal, at the National, or Chichester, or by being the figurehead of his profession. On the day he died Judi Dench said, 'Well, he and Dame Edith, Dame Peg, Sir John and Sir Ralph are certainly my generation's heroes and when they start to go . . . it's like when you lose your parents.'

Chapter Four
The Time of the Angels

Ellen Terry said, 'You cannot act without a feeling for religion,' and in his foreword to Fabia Drake's *Blind Fortune*, Olivier claimed, 'I am aware of much religious feeling, but no certain belief.' He did indeed possess what was essentially a religious mind, which revolved around the concepts of sin, confession, punishment, deliverance, and grace. Macbeth, Richard III, Titus Andronicus, Astrov (*Uncle Vanya*), Edgar (*The Dance of Death*), James Tyrone (*Long Day's Journey into Night*): Olivier knew that each of his characters had a soul to save or lose.

He didn't overdo this. Richard's prayers on the night before Bosworth – 'There is no creature loves me;/And if I die no soul shall pity me' – were deleted from the film. I think he found direct appeals for sympathy off-putting, unmannerly – unmanly, even. His method is more backward-curving: you feel for his Macbeth, for instance, owing to the remorse he shows to Macduff ('But get thee back; my soul is too much charged/ With blood of thine already'). His technique was observed by John Mortimer. 'What an impossible character your father must have been,' Olivier told him, munching cake shortly after shooting Clifford's death-bed scene in *A Voyage Round My Father*. 'Of course, it's absolutely vital not to try and play him for sympathy.' Mortimer says he was confident then that, if Olivier was avoiding sympathy, audiences would compensate – they would 'sympathise immediately with the central character, just as he made the audience adore Richard III'. Avoiding self-pity, Olivier has a fearlessness, a certainty – approaching almost impudence – in his relationship to his art. His element of confidence – of simplicity, of austerity – is that of a preacher mounting a pulpit and claiming to be heard. He is a priest of the imagination. 'The theatre is his form of church,' said Joan Plowright, 'a temple to man's knowledge of man, a place where people gather together and somebody talks to them and they are moved.'

The importance of the liturgy and Anglican pieties; psalms and hymns and a sermon's cadence: it was all in his blood. Crockford's *Clerical*

Directory is clogged with Oliviers. The Revd. Dacres Olivier (1831–1919), prebendary of Salisbury, honorary chaplain to the Earl of Pembroke, who married the daughter of the Rt. Revd. Robert Eden, primus of the Scottish Episcopal Church, for example; or the Revd. Henry Eden Olivier (1866–1936), vicar of Epping, rural dean of Chigwell, who married the daughter of the Revd. Cape, rector of St George's, Hanover Square, author of *What Happened at the Reformation*, and whose recreation was listed as motoring.

The family originated in Gascony, near Pau, in the Basses-Pyrénées – and note how it's Laurence, not Lawrence, Sybille, not Sybil; there was an Uncle Arnould, rather than Arnold. 'French spelling for all our names *please*,' Olivier squeals in his memoirs. In 1721, Jerome Olivier turns up in London as minister of the French Chapel of the Savoy; his son married the daughter of Jean Baptiste Massé, Louis XV's court painter, and out of that match came Daniel Stephen Olivier, the rector of Clifton in Bedfordshire. His grandson, the Revd Henry Olivier, the rector of Poulshot in Wiltshire, inherited the Manor House, Potterne, from his parents, Colonel Henry Stephen Olivier and Mary, the daughter of Admiral Sir Richard Dacres. His youngest son was Gerard Kerr, *our* Olivier's father.

Gerard went to Winchester. He was taken on the Grand Tour of France and Italy, where his father assumed the Church of England incumbency in Alassio during the summer. He was interested in the theatre and opera – though any ambitions here were not encouraged – and he went to Merton College, Oxford, claiming that he was sent down for riding a coach and four along the High. I thought this apocrypha worth verifying, and after an afternoon in the archives, examining the Minute Book of the Warden and Tutors' Committee, the admissions register signed by the students, and the Warden Bowman's personal notebooks, I discovered that G. K. Olivier matriculated as an undergraduate in October 1888 and remained until Michaelmas Term 1890, leaving without completing a degree.

On 19 March 1889, Mr Jefferson, Mr Bucknall, Mr Wyld and Mr Olivier were warned 'that the college expects them not to be noisy and disorderly in their rooms and in the quadrangles . . . Mr Wyld [was] directed not to bring his horn into college in future. Mr Olivier was also warned that his work has been unsatisfactory.' Eventually he was rusticated because 'owing to missing a train, [he] remained away for a night'; he was admonished 'being one chapel short, and warned he will be expected to keep one extra next term'. By 7 October 1889 he'd grown impatient with the rules and regulations and requested that he 'be allowed to remain out of residence till October 1890' – which was granted, so long as he returned to sit his Collections at the end of Lent. On 22 March 1890, 'Mr Olivier's Collections were reported to be on the whole satisfactory,' but he never did return to Oxford in the autumn.*

Collections, i.e. college, as opposed to university, tests, were stringent. Gerard was made to sit papers in Latin prose composition; unseen passages for translation from Greek and Latin; Greek and Latin grammar; passages from Euripides' *Hecuba and Alcestis*; Virgil, Aeneid, I–V; arithmetic; Euclid, Books I, II; and algebra. Victorian England not only educated its gentlemen in the ways of the ancient world; the nineteenth century was meant to be a matching high point of civilization. The broken columns and triumphal arches of Athens and Rome were duplicated in railway stations, museums, mansions and municipal buildings. Novels became enormous; paintings were of epic scenes (e.g. Herbert Arnould Olivier's *Juno's Heartless Fowls*, or *The Supreme War Council, Versailles*, which was presented to the nation); there were wars, against the Sikhs, Afghans, Zulus and Boers, that should have been described by Pliny or Plutarch. The tumult of life; life's terrifying grandeur: this is what the Victorians represented, and the classical virtues told them how to behave, no man succeeding better than Gerard's (and Herbert Arnould's) elder brother, Sydney Haldane Olivier, who entered the Colonial Office, having come top in the open competition in 1882, and became a PC, KCMG, CB, LL D, and a baron in 1924. (He's the first Lord Olivier, and was governor of Jamaica and Secretary for India.)†

---

* He went, instead, to complete his education at the University of Durham. Information recorded in the Hatfield College Archives and the Durham University Library confirms that: 'Gerard Kerr Olivier was a member of Hatfield College and registered as an undergraduate student from October 1890 until mid-summer 1895. He was reading Classics and General Literature and obtained a Bachelor of Arts (Class III) degree in June 1895. The regulations at that time did not require him to keep terms continuously and so it cannot be said he was resident in Durham all that time – indeed, it is unlikely that he was as he cannot be found in such Bursar's records that we have for that period. His degree was conferred upon him in person on June 25th 1895. He followed up his studies (probably externally) and was awarded an MA degree (in person) on June 21st 1898. The only other record of him in the College Archives is his address in 1927, which was: Addington Rectory, Winslow, Buckinghamshire.

'Until his death in 1939 he was registered in the University Calendar as a Member of Convocation and as a voter for the University Representative in Parliament.'

† Shaw called him 'handsome and strongly sexed, looking like a Spanish grandee in any sort of clothes, however unconventional . . . I believe he could have carried a cottage piano upstairs; but it would have cracked in his grip.' The *DNB* entry on Sydney Olivier quotes this (though omits the 'strongly sexed' bit), and adds: 'He was a man of

Knights in armour, jousts, chivalry, personal bravery and physical strength, practical wisdom and measure – these are the classical ideals, encroached upon by envy, avarice, lust. This archaic/modern by-play carries on in religion. The point about the Judaeo-Christian church is that the old-style pagan gods are still remembered. Jove, or Jupiter, and his stage thunder is Jehovah; Venus Aphrodite embodies the creed of love; Ruth standing amongst the alien corn is Persephone. Olivier, who as we have seen was good at playing gods, played ordinary men as demi-gods: Archie Rice, the tenacious deposed king of a crumbling empire (literally and figuratively: his music hall is called The Empire); Graham Weir, the schoolmaster in *Term of Trial*, who makes impassioned pleas for truth and innocence (he's Socrates); Inspector Newhouse, in *Bunny Lake is Missing*, God's cerebral policeman, who says 'I'm not questioning you – I'm trying to know you better.' And anyway, what are the gods? What is religion? Human emotions discriminated, particularized, segmented, made flexible. Love, death, wisdom, jealousy, aggression styled as Venus, Pluto, Minerva, Juno, Mars; or as the Holy Trinity: Father, from whom; Son, to whom; and Spirit, through whom are all things.

One of the qualities that makes Olivier unique is that he is curiously old-fashioned. There is a lack of cynicism, irony, indirectness in his work. At one extreme we have the element of juvenile hero-worship in his portrayal of Henry V, which Ralph Richardson described as 'the exaltation of all scout-masters. He's the cold bath kind, and you have to glory in it.' And at the other, there's Olivier's robustness, his rectitudes, as exemplified by his ability to see into the heart of and play with complete conviction both Becket ('If I do not defend my priests, who will?') and Henry II, screaming in anguish, in Jean Anouilh's drama, at the Hudson Theater, New York, in 1961. Simply by an abrupt bending or tilting of the neck, Olivier can register the ideal of duty and/or the problems of pride.

Olivier's manners, and their limitations; his formality and forbearance; his courtliness – which, somehow, can contain his maverick behaviour; his control and technique: all this derives from his nineteenth-century tastes, from his sense of being part of a continuous tradition. 'Burbage, Garrick, Kean and Irving. Great volcanoes as far as I'm concerned . . . Lead me by the nose, Richard, David, Edmund, Henry; lead me by the nose and then release me. Let me make the judges think I am the best bull in the

commanding intellect, and he could, and did, labour terribly, exacting a high standard of performance from himself and those who worked with him.' His field was racial colour problems, and he rejected 'the short-sighted theory that the dividing habits of race are permanently stronger than the unifying power of humanity.'

ring.'* He consciously put himself in their company, as part of the apostolic succession, and he gathered in the heirlooms. At Notley (and later Royal Crescent, Brighton), he had a private museum of old play texts, costumes, props, and model stage-sets; he had a collection of signet rings worn by famous actors (including David Garrick's, inscribed for Irving 'in recognition of the gratification derived from his Shakespearian representations'); he displayed what he believed was 'the earliest known theatre wig – the one Garrick wore as Abel Drugger'; in a glass case reposed the dagger Irving used as Othello; and he owned and used – 'the sense of the past!' – the make-up kit once belonging to William Charles Macready. He collected Edmund Kean memorabilia (including his lace collar and undergarments), and his prize exhibit was the sword flourished by Kean as Richard III – which had been passed to Sir Henry Irving – thence to the Terry family, and from Kate Terry to her grandson, John Gielgud, who presented it to Olivier.†

Richard, his youngest son, says that Henry Irving was 'Larry's hero', and this would seem no more than appropriate, as Irving and Olivier, as men of distinction, with obligations and responsibilities, determined to continue working despite illness, were reincarnations of each other. 'He died two years before I was born,' said Olivier, when opening the gardens near Irving's statue, in July 1951, 'and yet I am as conscious of him as if I had served as a member of his company.' (They are now buried together in Poets' Corner.) Irving's management of the Lyceum, at which he acted and produced, and was sole master, prefigured – though without state subsidy – Olivier's National Theatre; and Olivier *did* appear there, on 23 May 1938, in the 'Henry Irving Centenary Matinee', *Here's to Our Enterprise*, performed in the presence of Queen Mary. Olivier played Jingle in a sketch from *The Pickwick Papers* (also in the scene: Edmund Gwenn, Esmé Percy, and Ernest Thesiger); Vivien

* On 31 May 1987, with the Alzheimer's well advanced, he must have believed their ghosts were actually coming back to get him. The National Theatre put on a ghoulish show called *Happy Birthday, Sir Larry!*. The idea was that his place in the theatrical firmament would be expounded by Burbage (played by Alec McCowen), Garrick (Edward Petherbridge), Kean (Ben Kingsley) and Irving (Antony Sher). Peggy Ashcroft wafted in as Lilian Baylis. Peter Hall played Shakespeare. I'm sure it was an evening well worth missing.

† 'He consciously picked up the threads – almost self-consciously. For example, he has a little private museum with Kean's sword and other pieces. That's typical Larry,' says William Gaskill. Olivier bequeathed his Garrick memorabilia to the Garrick Club, and directed in his will that the following persons could each select an object from the *musée*: John Gielgud, John Mills, Rachel Kempson, Peter Hiley, Laurier Lister, Pieter Rogers, Laurence Harbottle, and Lady (Ralph) Richardson.

Leigh was in a playlet called *The Lyons Mail.* The silk-bound souvenir programme replicated the pages of Irving's Lyceum productions of the 1870s.

Irving was a man of dignity and industry, grandeur and loneliness, who struggled in provincial rep, who struggled with poverty, to become pre-eminent. He was impressed by the Comédie-Française, with its gestures, movement and articulations handed on from Molière, which suggested to him that acting could be one of the fine arts; and his resolution was to bring a grace and finish to the English stage's blundering and bluster – its bewhiskered amateurishness. He had – like Olivier – reserves of power; a romantic way of trembling and advancing – as Edward Gordon Craig said: 'His hovering affectionate care for every line uttered, every move made . . . by jingo! When he did love a piece it began to glow. Oh, not alone his own role – that of course – but everyone's role – and every scene – every bit of scenery and every light.'

He was good at affecting insanity, which won him ovations in mid-scene, and in *The Bells,* buckling his shoes, sitting back in his chair and looking astounded, or in *Macbeth,* muffling his head in his mantle and collapsing beside the throne, he devised a famous dumb-show to signify attacks of conscience and guilt. Hamlet, Shylock, Othello, Coriolanus, Romeo, Lear, Malvolio, Richard III, Macbeth: these were in Olivier's repertory (they both played Shylock as a Rothschild banker), and Irving's lavish production of *Romeo and Juliet,* with Ellen Terry, failed much as Olivier's did, in 1940, because the actor/producer tried to recreate the whole of Italy on stage and the scene changes went on past midnight. A market-place in Verona with real donkeys crossing a bridge; banquet scenes, with pages and serving wenches; dance interludes; real running water, and trees, and lilies; a monastery with dozens of chanting monks. This is theatre as pageantry – as historical spectacle – and it has a connection with Olivier's desire for verisimilitude in *Henry V,* with correct heraldic devices for the English noblemen, accurately researched armorial bearings, weaponry, battle plans, tracery on the tombs. Peter Ustinov remembers that when making *Spartacus,* Olivier insisted on not using a saddle, because this would have been anachronistic. He instead perched precariously on his white horse, which was authentically fitted with a gold bridle, but it was no good – he kept slipping. The scene was completed with Olivier astride a step-ladder.

Irving and Olivier have origins in Victorian painting – William Powell Frith's bustling *Derby Day,* for example, or Sir Lawrence Alma-Tadema's highly finished treatments of classical subjects (he designed the sets for

Irving's *Coriolanus* in 1901), or George Frederick Watt's allegories, such as *Caractacus led in Triumph through the streets of Rome*, or Sir Edward Burne-Jones' sweet choirs of angels. Attention to detail – each flower, each leaf, each fold in the fabric – is one thing, but the pursuit of historical accuracy can create museum exhibits, rather than moving dramas. Olivier's *Romeo and Juliet* was 'pedantically staged', according to the reviewers; 'everything is solid; the doors close with a proper bang; the hardware makes a proper rattle . . . Bells ring off stage. The orchestra is busy all evening . . . An enormous amount of labour has gone into this production [and it is] swallowed up in heavy scenery . . .' The 1948 film of *Hamlet* is prone to this ponderousness. Ladies and gentlemen of the court sweep in and out, carrying fire brands or wine goblets, but they don't *do* anything – they are obviously extras. No activity or business; this is a film set – or a canvas of Herbert Arnould Olivier's – not a household. The costumes – billowing white shirts and tights – are Victorian (they could be out of the Lyceum's wicker hamper); and the death of Ophelia is a staging of the Millais painting. The girl whizzes downstream doing the backstroke in strands of weed.

Olivier's Shakespeare films are like Victorian ballets. (Elsinore has little in the way of furnishings: a spare, empty space, it is a dance floor waiting, in vain, to be filled with leaps and mazurkas.) His acting, like dance, is over-expressive: his moony, moody Hamlet is choreographed to strut the deserted ramparts reading a book. Robert Helpmann had created a one-act *Hamlet* for the Royal Ballet in 1942, and that's Olivier here. Richard III is an evil magician or black swan by Diaghilev or Nijinsky, and his death is a scene from a ballet at the Russian court, as he twists his sword hilt to make the sign of the cross. It is designed to please the eye; and does it offer more than meets the eye? Olivier brings to acting the eroticism of dance. His Romeo (with first Peggy Ashcroft and then Vivien Leigh as Juliet) was about an awareness of the body: moist mouth, hair falling in front of the eyes; the glow and innocence of musculature and physique. Othello, like the Mahdi in *Khartoum*, legs apart, arm pointing at the ground, is a colossus – an emblem of brute beauty.

Olivier's strength and appeal is his nineteenth-century air – his robustness, even his silliness. His ornate prose style, for example, chimes with Irving's, who said things like 'Sir, when I play Charles Surface, I dine off the liver wing of a chicken, moistened by a bumper of sparkling burgundy.' Those who say that his acting seemed greater than it was, who resent him, who complain that he was too technical – a machine manufacturing caricatures and distortions* miss the point that, by being thought through, the joy of his performances is our knowledge that he is in total command. Over-insistence may involve an alienation with other players (who come across as laborious and illusory), but not with Olivier. His fascination is the way he copes with, surmounts, doubt, lack of confidence, insignificance, the lack of pattern or direction – all those anxieties which modern art glories in. Which is not to say that what he did didn't surprise him ('When I played *Antony and Cleopatra* I had a very rare experience at one matinée, and I wrote it down in my diary: "enjoyed the performance this afternoon"'); and it's his joy in acting that is infectious. 'My life's ambition,' he claimed, 'has been to lead the public toward an appreciation of acting, so that they will come not only to see the play but to watch acting for acting's sake.' How like Irving he sounds – who said – who *pontificated*: 'Life, with all its pains and sorrows, is a beautiful and precious gift; and the Actor's art is to reproduce this beautiful thing, giving due emphasis to those royal virtues and those stormy passions which sway the destinies of men.'

I can never quite think of Olivier as a modern man. (He was the last Victorian.) Modern clothes sit on him ridiculously, like costumes. He's best in a robe of rich purple or a golden wreath – a Roman toga, or Hamlet's Danish regalia ('On the day that my Knighthood was announced, I stalked about Denham Studio, got up in Hamlet's glad

---

* I particularly have in mind Russell Davies' pasquinade, *J'Accuse*, broadcast on Channel Four, in which Olivier's old confrères were rounded up to denounce him as a clockmaker or fraud. The *Othello* production is accused of racism and ludicrousness, and a smirking sixth form is made to watch the video and see it as an example of 'how to read a text with maximum insensitivity'.

Attacks on Olivier as a caricaturist and fake – a Great Impersonator (like Sellers) – were particularly prevalent after the publication of *Confessions of an Actor* (1982) and *On Acting* (1986). John Carey said that Olivier had 'a fondness for deeply thought platitudes which come thudding out like stuffed bison.' But he'd always had enemies. Not everybody was enamoured of his style. Here's a letter sent to him at the Palace Theatre, postmarked 15 September 1957, which I unearthed during my research – the interesting fact is that Olivier had bothered to preserve it:

Savoy Hotel
Midnight, Friday

Sir:
I'm just back from enduring your horrible 'Entertainment' [sic]. You cannot give me back my wasted evening but you can give me back my money.
I demand you return it to me at 239 rue St Honore, Paris. I mean what I say.
John Pelzel

Pinned to this: two £1 stalls tickets, Palace Theatre, 13 September 1957.

rags for the play scene festooned with the blue baldric of the Order of the Elephant, only to be distinguished from the Garter by hanging across from the right shoulder. People weren't quite sure if I was in costume or if I was always going to be dressed like that from now on'.)* For *The Boys from Brazil, A Little Romance, The Jazz Singer,* or *The Jigsaw Man,* which are set in the present day, Olivier wears dapper turn-of-the-century suitings, coloured bow-ties, hats, pearl-grey gloves, and carries a cane – and Denis Quilley once witnessed a Mr Toadish apparition: '[He] was especially fond of a jolly mustard-coloured suit . . . and he had a beige camel-hair overcoat which reached down to his ankles . . . To complete the ensemble, he would sport a deerstalker. After one *Long Day's Journey into Night* performance, I came out of the stage door to find him, dressed in Bookie suit, overcoat and deerstalker, at the wheel of his purple taxi with its purple interior, and something like the Ride of the Valkyries blasting from the car radio. I collapsed against the wall in helpless laughter, and he leaned out of the car window, raised two fingers, shouted, "Piss off, Quilley!", and roared into the night.'

He sounds like a cartoon cardinal, that taxi a tabernacle on wheels. All Saints, Margaret Street, his choir school, was – is – a place of verdigris and terracotta, purple and stained glass. It is over-the-top. 'At All Saints Church there were marvellous vestments, on glorious cloths of gold,' Olivier told the Mobil Showcase Network in 1983. 'I mean real gold. I was brought up in that sort of religion. In a way, it has had its indelible mark on me.' Here Olivier first learned to have his profound belief in the ceremoniousness of his art; he was thrilled by 'the sweet singing and the merry organ and the feeling of a show.' Despite exaggeration or distortion, his characters have a truth about them. You don't laugh at Olivier in silver armour or tights; you don't scoff at his Othello. Anybody else in that Richard III get-up would be a pantomime dame, but as it was Olivier the cast shrank from him in the wings or backstage, especially when he whirled into Vivien's dressing room, to remonstrate with her for making too much noise playing cards ('My darling, you wouldn't hear if you closed the door,' she replied coolly). There is a sincerity to what he does. His innermost soul is there, in his work. (Conscious continuously of how he wished himself to appear to others, the ham actor act, which so amused Quilley, was a contrivance – a comic extension of the tragic Tyrone.) Though private, isolated, or

* Olivier, like his Uncle Sydney, collected honours and decorations galore: the knighthood (1947) and barony (1970), plus five honorary doctorates; the Order of Merit; Commander, Order Dannebrog: Officier Legion d'Honneur; Grande Ufficiale dell' Ordino al Merito della Repubblica; Order of Yugoslav Flag with Golden Wreath; etc.

withdrawn (or, in his voice-overs, for *The World at War, A Queen is Crowned* and Zeffirelli's *Romeo and Juliet*, invisible), he was never furtive. His heroes, and villains, are public figures who have nothing to hide. Richard III confides in us; Archie Rice goes before the audience; Henry V rallies the troops; Astrov seeks company, as does Chebutikin, the old army doctor and hanger-on in *Three Sisters*. Lear squabbles openly with his children in front of the court; Othello enjoys dramatizing his wooing of Desdemona for the Senate. Hamlet communes with the sea – with its beauty, grandeur, freedom; with its movement. Heathcliff proclaims his love to the snow, fire, and rain – into the eternal things.

Often, with Olivier, it's as if he is praying. He propounds and interprets his lines like holy writ; he makes them an address of a concentrated kind. He is petitionary – asking for strength, illumination, forgiveness – and he can have an incantatory force even when not speaking. Look, in *Jesus of Nazareth*, at the way he clutches at the wall, when he is gazing towards Golgotha; at the way he arranges himself, as if he is in a painting. On stage he'd pose against pillars and basalt columns – Oedipus is a monument, in the photograph taken by John Vickers; and Titus Andronicus, as described in Peter Brook's prompt book, deposited in the Shakespeare Birthplace Trust, Stratford, is monolithic: 'Titus offers wine to Lavinia – is tender. Lavinia collapses onto her stool weeping at their misunderstanding her gestures. Titus sits on [opposite prompt] stool in despair.'

The set for *Titus Andronicus* was constructed from interlocking ribbed pillars, which could open to disclose a tangled wood, like exposed nerve endings, or ranks of coffins, for Titus' tombs; or it could close to form an unbroken wall, or descend to become tables for a banquet. It might seem an image of Olivier himself, outwardly strong, full of forbearance, paradoxically private – the bronze horseman, at one with the stones and rocks – but giving us a glimpse, now and then, of his innermost self, of his mental agonies.

It would be possible to argue that the dilemma in Olivier was his fidelity and moral strength doing battle with pagan temptations and amusements: the Church vs. the Theatre; Jehovah vs. Jove. But his family, at least, far from recoiling in puritanical disdain at the idea of drama, actively encouraged Olivier to perceive the theatricality of a religious life. (Sydney Olivier actually wrote three plays, one of which, *Mrs Maxwell's Marriage*, was performed by the Stage Society in 1900.) He remembered Gerard 'smirking a little and putting his thumbs into his waistcoat arm-hole, and saying, mock self-deprecatingly, "Your father wasn't a bad actor."' He was certainly always putting on a performance

– after graduating from Durham he became a schoolmaster at Boxgrove, near Guildford, and had a captive audience in the classroom. Agnes Crookenden was a sister of the headmaster's wife, who recalled Gerard as 'very authoritative in a classroom of young boys'. He tried to spellbind his future wife, too, for careeristic ends: 'I daresay that Gerard's original interest in my sister was mixed – half of masculine attraction and half of concern for his career . . . [He had hopes] to succeed my husband at Boxgrove.'

One thinks of Richard III, intermingling lovemaking with his designs on the throne ('I must be married to my brother's daughter,/Or else my Kingdom stands on brittle glass'). But Gerard, marrying Agnes four years later, on 30 April 1898, at St James' Church, Kidbrooke, decided instead to begin his own establishment, Tower House, in Dorking. No sooner was that organized than he decided to take Holy Orders, being ordained in 1903 and becoming an assistant at the Church of St John the Evangelist in North Holmwood; the following year he was curate at St Martin's. This meant, in 1904, selling the school and dismissing the servants. Agnes did the cooking and cleaning herself – that at a time, don't forget, when the near-Olivier relations were colonels, admirals, canons, or (Sydney) Governor-in-Chief of Jamaica.

Gerard played for Dorking Cricket Club, scoring a century against Reigate Hill in 1902; and though they rationed his bathwater, Olivier's childhood was spent amongst calf-bound books, pony traps, velvet curtains, etchings of Highland cattle, bowls of pot-pourri, fringes and damask, the golf links, and the illkempt tennis court. When he was three, however, the Surrey genteelisms were exchanged for a life in London. As the Revd N. G. T. Stiff commented, in *The Church in Dorking and District*: 'The year 1910 saw . . . Mr Olivier, who was very popular during his several years of persistent and energetic work in the parish, [leave] for the poor district of Notting Hill, West London, where his energies and zeal found ample scope. He went laden with goodwill and affection, and, like most of the assistant clergy who have served at St Martin's, finds occasional visits to Dorking a source of refreshment and pleasure.'

The energy and zeal refer to his delight in splashing incense about. He adopted the High Church rituals of Keble and Pusey and attempted to dress more elaborately than Cardinal Newman. That he was merely the curate of a tin shack, named St James', didn't go overlooked by the ecclesiastical authorities, who sacked him for his theatrical ways. 'Imagine! Sacked! Dismissed! Disgraced! All for a matter of principle!' His melodramatic distress would be echoed by Olivier, in 1948, when he, Ralph

Richardson and John Burrell were dismissed from managing the Old Vic – and again, in 1972, when Olivier was not informed by the National Theatre board that they had appointed Peter Hall to succeed him. 'I've been given the boot – again!' he complained.

Gerard traipsed seaside resorts to conduct services whilst vicars were on holiday, and by Christmas 1912 he had found a new parish, St Saviour's, Pimlico. The family moved to Lupus Street from 86 Elgin Crescent, Notting Hill, and here they remained for six years. Olivier's infant play-acting was facilitated. Gerard knocked him together a toy theatre, complete with footlights, or floats, made from Gold Flake tobacco tins and candles, and this was known as 'St Laurence's Shrine': the toy theatre *as* a church.* (One of Olivier's first assignments at the Birmingham Repertory Theatre, in January 1927, could almost have been about this: J. M. Synge's *The Well of the Saints.* He was an Ancient Celt, Mat Simon, dressed in a fright wig and bearskin breeches, who says of the hermit: 'Isn't it a fine, beautiful voice he has, and he a fine, brave man if it wasn't for the fasting?')

Olivier imitated his father in the pulpit, but his mother attempted to parry the religiosity and (says Sybille) 'deflect him from any youthful ambition to become a clergyman himself'. His mother, instead, 'encouraged Larry to turn his mock-sermonizing into recitations and monologues from well-known plays'. Shakespeare, Marlowe, Jonson. Then, at his choir school, where he enrolled in 1916, at the age of nine, he used to sing the church music of Mozart, Handel, Bach, Beethoven (masses in C and D), Schubert, Mendelssohn, Gounod, Dvořák, Palestrina, Attwood, Tallis, Tinel, Silas, Wesley, Stainer and Stanford: 'masses, evensongs, choral services of every kind, anthems and requiems'.

It was an intense education in discipline and showmanship. ('What matters is whether it's a good show or not' would remain his rubric.) There were only fourteen pupils at the school. They rose at six forty-five; church, then breakfast; choir practice and lessons; lots of Latin. Walks in the afternoon, prior to choral evensong . . . Olivier saw how

* This historical object was still in existence in 1964, when Olivier told an interviewer: 'My sister shelters – cherishes with great love – a large wooden packing box that was my first stage . . . She still keeps it with love up in the trunk room of her little cottage.' Sybille herself had trained briefly to be an actress under Elsie Fogerty, but had abandoned her career and settled for marriage as Mrs Gerald Day. 'She had all the aspirations on earth but was absolutely no good, poor darling,' Olivier said in 1970. Her métier became the Olivier family tree, and she'd bore the tits off guests at Notley with her genealogical lectures. When she met Vivien Leigh she said, 'Oh, you're so young and beautiful and I'm so old and ugly.' Tarquin, witnessing the scene, reports drily: 'True.' Sybille died on 10 April 1989, aged eighty-seven.

the musical measure and lyrical rigour could be adapted for speaking – during the sermon, his father knew when to drop the voice, or bellow, or throw in a quip, or grow sentimental; when 'to turn solemn and pronounce the blessing. The quick changes of mood and manner absorbed me, and I have never forgotten them.' The colour, the texture, the pictures you can create, the mood you can inculcate, with the grain of the voice. One of Olivier's great achievements is the twenty-one-hour narration he provided for Thames Television's documentary, *The World at War*, in 1973. It is the voice of God – not a boom (like Welles), or patrician and pained (like Gielgud), or querulous (like Redgrave), or dotty (like Richardson). Olivier, instead, is brown and resonant, like a cello, or the flavour of muscat wine; and there is something in his tones of a softness that is intensely sad. It's as if, surveying the wreckage of Europe, Olivier is articulating God's awareness and resigned acceptance of sin – of disgraces and defeats.

Olivier's ancestors were religious; he was divine, or could seem as if he were.* For the Technicolor documentary about the coronation, *A*

* In 1983, over dinner at the Midland Hotel in Manchester, Olivier informed his guests (the cast of Granada's *King Lear*) that you can't just go out and *be* a king – there has to be an element of sanctity. 'In the coronation service it would seem that it's God who makes a king. Even Claudius feels it, and he's an [unlawful] king who's only king because he killed his own brother. Watch your popular idols, such as Neil Diamond [*Neil Diamond!*], come out onto the stage at one of those big theatres in Hollywood. He brings on with him this odour of sanctity. As Claudius says, "There's such divinity doth hedge a king." It's the knowledge of what you have to be to an audience. I think a person with a following, with a public, is made aware that his position entails a kind of divinity, or something like it.'

If this was any other actor speaking, I'd gloss it as a vainglorious attempt to define star quality – that aspect of an artist which goes beyond mere technical perfection, and which makes him special. Tynan used to refer to the High Definition Performance: 'the ability . . . to communicate the essence of one's talent to an audience with economy, grace, no apparent effort, and absolute, hard-edged clarity of outline'; and in 1936, Walter Benjamin, trying to explain the uniqueness of a work of art, came up with the concept of an *aura*. Art, he argued, had a 'ritual power'; it is unknowable. 'Unapproachability is . . . a major quality of the cult image. True to its nature, it remains distant, however close it may be' – which could be a description of Olivier, shining in the firmament, and grabbing attention.

When Olivier talks about divineness and the extra-mundane, however, he is both figurative and telling us no more than the truth. For he did indeed levitate out of real life. I was there – I witnessed the Ascension, at noon on Friday 20 October 1989 in Westminster Abbey: the Service of Thanksgiving for the Life and Work of Laurence Olivier OM, Baron Olivier of Brighton, 1907–89. It was a magnificently royal event, with the processions of dolled-up clergy, the crimson-clad chaplains and choirboys, the representatives of the Queen, the Prince and Princess of Wales, Princess Margaret and

Queen is Crowned, made for the cinema in 1953, Olivier is hushed and doting: the Deity tickled pink that Westminster Abbey is housing a dramatic event that is well up to His standards. (He is respectful, rather than regretful.) Christopher Fry's florid commentary is almost a parody of the majestic, and Olivier works hard to avoid sounding obsequious. Shots of Welsh hills, Scottish glens and bustling market towns sweep

---

the Kents; the swelling organ music – Walton, Elgar, Vaughan Williams. Joan Plowright, black-veiled, sat in a place of honour with her handsome children. And who was that in the pew behind? The ghost of Margaret of Anjou, widow to King Henry VI? No – it was Jill Esmond, accompanied by Tarquin. They all looked like a left-over royal faction from the Wars of the Roses.

The Dean informed us that Olivier's ashes were to lie beside those of Irving and Garrick, beneath the bust of Shakespeare, and 'within a stone-throw of the graves of Henry V [the effigy's hands modelled on Olivier's, when the statue was restored after the war] and The Lady Anne, Queen to Richard III.'

Secular and divine, theatre and church, seriously mixed and matched when 'items symbolic of Laurence Olivier's life and work' were shipped to the Sacrarium and laid on the High Altar – the sheer *reverence* put me in mind of those festivals in Mediterranean communities, when holy relics are paraded through the streets. Alleged saints' bones, fragments of the true cross, phials of Christ's blood, the Holy Foreskin, and suchlike bits and bobs. We didn't get to venerate Olivier's prepuce, as no doubt it was long-since lost, or else turned into a set of matching luggage, but the historical artefacts were none the less peculiar – stage props which, owing to Olivier, were rendered religious.

Douglas Fairbanks marched up the aisle carrying Olivier's Order of Merit insignia; Michael Caine (looking as if he felt a bit of a prat) carried Olivier's Lifetime Achievement Oscar; Maggie Smith carried a tea-set – identified as the silver model of the Festival Theatre, Chichester; Paul Scofield carried another silver edifice – a model of the National; Derek Jacobi carried the crown used in the film of *Richard III*; Jean Simmons carried the script used in the film of *Hamlet*; Ian McKellen carried the laurel wreath worn in the Stratford production of *Coriolanus*; Dorothy Tutin carried the crown from Granada's *King Lear*; and Frank Finlay wielded Kean's sword – the one given by Gielgud. Gielgud himself sat alone behind the High Altar, looking pale and frail, peering over his spectacles, and his hair sticking out – a twitchy Clarence. (An effect reinforced by the boom of Walton's *Richard III* fanfares and organ voluntaries.)

Why did these thesps seem so foolish? Perhaps because, whilst ostensibly appearing as themselves, they were actually cast in a play – as Olivier's acolytes. They were having to be dignified, and were conscious only of being *irreverent*, toting those odds and sods, handling the cardboard crowns and bric-à-brac as if it all meant something.

Olivier, one of Hollywood's romantic stars who changed the direction of classical acting, changed the direction of his own memorial service when a recording rang out of the Crispin Crispian speech from *Henry V.* His voice, rattling around the gothic architecture, was like an orchestra – the trumpet, the lute and harp; the well-tuned cymbals, the strings and pipe. It was magnificent – like hearing God speak. The congregation was humbled, many people wept. As Alec Guinness said in his address, 'There were times when it was best to be wary of him' – even after death, it would appear. Olivier didn't upstage, he overwhelmed.

by to uplifting quotations from the classics – 'this royal throne of Kings – this England' . . .

He was similarly patriotic and reassuring – this England being also 'This land of such dear souls' – when King George VI died, and Olivier was asked to deliver a memorial address at the Church of the Transfiguration, East Twenty-Ninth Street, in New York, on 17 February 1952. Here he was again, forty years or so on from St Laurence's Shrine, copying his father – Olivier enjoyed being able to remonstrate with people by saying 'Please, I'm thinking about my sermon!' It was considered a success, and five days later he made a recording for Caedmon;* the text was published as a black-edged booklet. That the King was really a stammering and shy invalid you'd never guess from this laudation – 'He had tremendous industry and a conscientiousness in his work akin to fanaticism . . . We remember the strange beauty which seemed to emanate from him . . .' Olivier's voice, keen and hard, is Henry V's, eulogizing a heroic warrior, a fallen ruler of the world; and he gets mystical, fervid, when depicting the mysteries of kingship, reciting from the scriptures, and saying, a dozen times, with mounting excitement, 'God save the King, long live the King, may the King live for ever. Amen. Hallelujah.' We can almost hear the Walton fanfare – and we are transported to the opening scenes of *Richard III*, though as a matter of fact they weren't to be filmed until a few years hence. The words, to Olivier, evoked 'all the clattering horses' hoofs, the clanging gates, the hurried whispers, the bright shouts, the lights and the darknesses of our island history' – and that he could tabulate this is indicative of his imagination, his vision, his impalpable spiritual dimension.

* *On the Death of King George VI*, the services at Windsor Chapel, written and read by Olivier, recorded in New York on 22 February 1952 (Caedmon Records TC 1003). 'My sermon . . . went down like a dog's dinner, so much so that my congregation besought me to record it . . . My friend Emlyn Williams got someone at home to send a copy to our bereaved young Queen and her consort; I received a kindly message of courteous royal acknowledgement, but I cannot believe that at that time, so fraught with burdensome considerations, either our monarch or her prince could possibly have found time for attending to such a thing,' he commented, in Pooterish mode.

He enjoyed being parsonical – and pedagogic. On 10 August 1950, he proudly sent a copy of Tarquin's essay, entitled 'Sunday Questions' ('my boy's classroom effort'), to Christopher Fry. Olivier has covered the text with his own teacher-style annotations: 'superbly imaginative'; 'most promising'; 'Splendid. This shows very great promise . . .' He's drawn to phrases like 'rays of sun gazed upon the unhappy world of woe'; or passages like 'There came the sound of far-off voices and the heavens came down in the form of a golden wing . . . The glory of Him shone around and an inexplicable peace fell upon the once angry waters.' This is indeed similar to what passes for poetry in *Venus Observed*.

The spirit, however, to be inspired, to be expressed, needs physical equipment, and this Olivier laboured long at, keeping himself fit. He had a gymnasium constructed beneath the Old Vic, where he went to lift sixty-pound weights. 'Almost the prime qualification for an actor,' he stated, 'is physical strength.' Robert Stephens discovered the truth of this when Olivier, as Captain Brazen, made his first entrance in *The Recruiting Officer* and embraced him. 'My dear!' says Brazen. 'My dear!' said Stephens' Captain Plume. The characters were to meet in the centre of the stage and kiss. 'Give me a buss, my dear!' 'Half a score if you will, my dear!'* Olivier clutched his fellow actor round the waist and lifted one leg up behind him, and what Stephens noticed, as he listened to the audience's laughter, was that 'if you put your arms around Larry you could feel his ribs like an enormous steel cage . . . The intercostal muscles between the ribs [had] expanded to provide [him] with lung space, as they do with opera singers. You . . . need that volume of air. You learn to breathe, and your lungs fill, and your ribs expand. And that is how you acquire a voice for the theatre.'

Or for the church. Sybil Thorndike, after describing Olivier's athletic Coriolanus of 1938, claimed, 'Larry has a longer breath than anybody I know. He could do the Matins exhortation "Dearly Beloved Brethren" twice through in one breath. Lewis [Casson] could do it in one and a half, and my father [Canon Thorndike] in one. All of which is pretty good. As children we used to listen fascinated in church to see if Father could get through the collect in one go.' To recite a prayer in this manner – it is like Seamus Heaney's line about the albatross, gliding for days without a single wingbeat. And such dulcet and harmonious breath may be connected with the other aspect of worship, gesticulation and posture. Geoffrey Heald taught the boys how to genuflect, and Olivier's symbolic signs and signals would always have a priestly – papal – solemnity. There's an amazing moment in Tynan's television interview with him, recorded in 1967. Olivier is telling the tale of his audition for the Central School of Speech Training and Dramatic Art, when he was seventeen. He'd given an energetic rendition of 'The Seven Ages of Man' passage from *As You Like It*, when Elsie Fogerty called him down from the stage and 'then she did a marvellous thing, an unforgettable

* Stephens was misremembering his Farquhar. The real joke is that, despite the gleeful greeting, the men don't know each other:

Brazen: My dear boy, how is't? Your name, my dear. If I be not mistaken, I have seen your face.

Plume: I never see yours in my life, my dear. But there's a face well known as the sun's, that shines on all and is by all adored.

thing, she said, "You have a weakness here", and she took her little finger and placed it vertically down the middle of my forehead. It's funny, I must have shown some sort of shyness, and been beetle-browed, and she said, "You have a weakness here and remember that."'

Olivier considered the criticism 'brilliantly illuminating, brilliantly observed' and, taking her advice literally, thought the ridge of his nose, between his eyes, was too shallow, and ever afterwards improved it with putty – handsome, classically beautiful noses for Romeo, Hamlet, Henry V, Oedipus; Roman noses for Caesar, Antony, and Crassus in *Spartacus*; a broken nose for Macbeth; snouts for Richard, Malvolio and the Duke of Wellington in *Lady Caroline Lamb*. But the advice was also figurative – Miss Fogerty was gesturing at what lay inside, behind the eyes, warding him off taciturnity. He never did quite shed an adolescent's rage, though. Heathcliff is an expression of it; Richard an extreme version of it; Henry V an example of how it can be diverted to glorious use; Lear a recurrence of it: '*King Lear* is about an old fool – a selfish, irascible old bastard . . . It's a straight part for me. Absolutely straight,' he said in 1983. 'When you get to my age, you *are* Lear, in every nerve of your body. My family would agree. "No wonder he's all right [in the role]," they would say. "He's just himself, he's got just that sort of ridiculous temper, those sulks, absolutely mad as a hatter sometimes . . ."'

But when Olivier tells Tynan the ridge-of-the-nose/you-have-a-weakness-there story, what holds the attention is the way he leans across to demonstrate, running his finger down the critic's forehead – and it's as if he anoints Tynan – who is tense and veal-faced, nervously tugging his earlobe. Olivier is suddenly a priest – Tynan is mesmerized, terrified, overpowered. This happens in *Rebecca*. When Olivier first kisses Joan Fontaine, who is as scared and timid as a rabbit, he presses his thumb to her forehead – it is done quickly, spontaneously. It is a benediction, and sums up the relationship of the couple: Max, protective, enigmatic, quietly suffering, renewed by his love for a young girl whom, he says, he doesn't want to see grow old. He's fatherly, rather than husbandly.

When he played Van Helsing, in *Dracula*,* the yarn was altered so that Mina became his daughter, who dies after a single suck. The vampire-hunter arrives by steam train – the film is punctuated with train hoots, wolf cries, hoofbeats, heartbeats – and wearing an expression of worry and suspicion he sets about rubbing bulbs of garlic over Dr

---

* Bram Stoker was Henry Irving's business manager. Was the elegant Transylvanian count, with his scarlet-lined opera cloaks and formal evening dress, inspired by the Victorian actor?

Seward's door frames and window latches. Olivier does this ceremoniously – again, he's anointing with his thumb. Anthony Hopkins, when he took the part, couldn't decide how to play Van Helsing. In the recent Coppola film, is the Dutch medicine-man a guru? A crank? He plays it shouting and scruffy; he's determined not to be mystical or magical – but the guffawing, coarse performance never comes together. Olivier, by contrast, sophisticated in his gasolier-era togs, is an avenging angel, trumpet-tongued and hard like marble. One scene, in particular, should have been startling, ominous, poetic. Van Helsing leads a white stallion into the graveyard, so that the hypersensitive animal will detect, and paw at, a vampire's resting place. Yet it doesn't work – it's just an old man with a carthorse hopping around in the dry ice. Undaunted, he returns with a spade, and soon Olivier is digging up Mina's corpse – which isn't there. The coffin has fallen into a mine shaft. Olivier shinnies down after it, wriggling past rats and skulls and the Whitby wildlife, and he is confronted by a ghoul: Jan Francis in green horror make-up. It's her, Mina. They talk in I presume Dutch, a father and a little girl, and as he tries to comfort her she repays his caresses by snarling and trying to bite him on the wrist. The embrace turns into a grisly waltz, brought to a conclusion when Donald Pleasance – how did he get into the mine? Does he have knowledge of a secret tunnel? – scalds her scalp with a crucifix. The languid wraith turns angrily, and is impaled on a stick. This ought to be a replay of Peter Cushing and Christopher Lee in a cinematic nightmare made by Hammer. When Olivier surveys a dead daughter he transforms it into Lear and Cordelia. As Donald Pleasance, breathing hard, finishes off Mina, Olivier lets out one of his great howls, a wail of grief, compounded of high-pitched sobs, which must be reminiscent of his Oedipus cry. A musician could possibly denote it on a stave, like plainchant.

Van Helsing, emboldened now to solve the mystery, to rout the devil and restore order, becomes explicitly priestly. Mina's heart has to be cut out and her body is laid on a trestle table that is draped like an altar. Her father approaches reverently with the autopsy knife. He steals into the Carfax vault, crumbles the host and sprinkles it on the cases of earth. 'If we are beaten then there is no God,' he says. He brandishes the crucifix at Lucy – Kate Nelligan, locked in a padded cell, her dress a bride-of-Dracula peekaboo negligee with cobwebby sleeves – and that face of his when he's intent! His resolve! His dread!

Has a creature ever possessed such eyes before? Or used his black eyes such a lot? The over-arching swoop of the eyebrows, delineating anger, or disdain, or wry amusement, even, though more rarely, tolerance.

Amiably chatting to Joan Plowright ('I'm not denying the existence of inspiration, darling, but I think illuminating feelings can come out of practice more likely than waiting for them to strike you like a flash of lightning'), he'd suddenly alter the temperature by fixing her with a look described by Peter O'Toole as 'that grey-eyed myopic stare that can turn you to stone'. His eyes give him a fiery presence. He rips them out, as Oedipus, and weeps purple gore. As Clifford Mortimer, his eyes swivel backwards into his skull, as his retinas are dislodged. For Titus Andronicus, he'd roll the whites of his eyes up to catch the light, and he'd clutch the pillar, and say in a ringing stage whisper, 'I have not another tear to shed' – which Ian Holm, who played Mutius, one of his many sons, watching night after night, always found a breathtaking moment.

The flash and fury of the pupils; the dazzle of the whites: these are the gleaming eyes of an Inca chieftain; of the plumed serpent that so upsets Sherlock Holmes; they are eyes to gaze an eagle blind. They can be icy and opaque, or else I've seen them exaggerated, painted up and silent-movie-ish, with fluttering lids; and it's the toying with the feminine, the fineness of the lashes (and his all-over nimbleness), which paradoxically leaves us in no doubt of his male energy – of his cockiness, his confident exuberance, which makes audiences tingle. Olivier is a gallant warrior who, if he runs on emotion, ensures it's crystal-clear emotion, and in *Dracula*, the interview between the Count and Van Helsing in the drawing room – with its leopard-skin rugs and vases full of pampas grass – is nothing less than a battle between God and the Devil. 'I'm often told I have a light footstep,' says Frank Langella, who is not as languorous as he thinks (he's lugubrious). He's neither lizardy, nor tragic and prickly, like Gary Oldman, but serious, beseeching, with full, sensual lips. This Dracula is a mesmerist in a high wing collar, with a bat-shaped cloak that tends to have clouds of fog, or flame and smoke, billowing from it. He's a magician, who can slam doors with a glance, ignite a crucifix, do a quick change into a wolf – and Olivier, who in the film he made immediately prior to *Dracula*, had already been an enchanter (you expect doves and ribbons to spring from his clapped hands in *A Little Romance*), opts, instead, to be keen and livid. Bible readings and church services may contain tales of mystery and the exotic, and in *Dracula* Van Helsing consults the sacred texts with a magnifying glass and conducts an exorcism, but Olivier is as scrupulous as any forensic scientist. The intentness is in his eyes, which change colour according to mood and the light reflecting off their delicately textured surface. His eyebrows, white and wintery, in *A Little*

Romance, for a performance of coy winks and leers, are here steel grey and significant.

'Your will is strong,' says Dracula, the hypnotizing of Van Helsing not being the doddle he'd anticipated – and of course nobody can outstare the Olivier eyes, which though narrowed to slits, express outrage and non-capitulation. Langella's eyes throb and protrude like muscat grapes; Olivier's spit fire – he hardly needs to wave his bunch of garlic, sheaf of communion wafers, or gold-leaf crucifixes, all usefully to hand. Drac chucks in the towel and exits through the window in a shower of glass – and with him flee the shades of night.

Peter Hall, a man who can carry himself with a certain assurance, has said that, 'I suspect . . . God is rather like Olivier'; and on another occasion he stated, 'Olivier ran [the National] as a college of cardinals, with himself . . . as Pope.' But it is not his Almightiness which matters; nor his appearance of omnipotence; nor – indeed – his facility with the sacraments and drill – bowing, crossing himself, seeming stately: picture him in April 1922, clad in his rose-coloured cap and cassock, heading the procession of All Saints choirboys at Stratford, and laying the wreath – bay leaves bound with a ribbon of Roman purple – upon Shakespeare's tomb, and singing the choirmaster and organist W. S. Vale's setting of the dirge from *Cymbeline*, 'Fear no more the heat of the sun'; or think of the summer of 1945, when the Old Vic Company toured Europe. Sixty-six people in three coaches; twenty tons of scenery, for *Peer Gynt*, *Richard III* and *Arms and the Man*, in five three-ton trucks. On the last night in Paris, Olivier kissed his finger and imprinted it on the stage: 'I give back the Comédie-Française to its rightful owners,' he intoned. Nor – finally – is it his expert (fuddy-duddy) knowledge of riddel posts, fiddle-back vestments, brass-studded baize, incense, and box pews that concerns me.

What matters is the way High Church ritual and formality, and their associations, related to his sensibility and emotions – to what Philip Larkin calls a 'primitive vivacity'. Virginia Fairweather, his press secretary at Chichester, once asked him outright if he believed in God: 'No – I wish I could,' he replied; and on the one hand, with Olivier, there is his striving and straining ('They well deserve to have/That know the strong'st and surest way to get'*), and on the other, the supposition that gifts are handed down by God, and life has to be spent beseeching and worshipping and being grateful. (A dispute, as it were, between the

* *Richard II*, III, iii: not a play in which Olivier ever appeared, though the words apply to Macbeth or to any over-reacher.

pressures of greed or fear, and providence.) Though Olivier did indeed once say that he owed his talent to being one of those whom 'God had touched on the shoulder', prayer, for him, was not contact with some transcendental being but a communing with his own conscience. (When he was appointed director of the National, a Union Jack flag was pinned to his dressing room door in Chichester with the message 'God Bless Sir!' Olivier read it and was heard to murmur, 'Please, God, help!') Religion wasn't a searching for solace; it was what provided the laws and injunctions by which he lived – laws derived from the authority of those lovely fictions, the gods (Jove, Jupiter, Jehovah); laws, about sensuality and spirituality, remorse and guilt, grief and ecstasy, destruction and creation, which were formulated in wars between angels and demons. ('There does seem to be a race-memory of a lost paradise, a Garden of Eden, that has disappeared,' he stated in 1963. 'I don't accept that with my brain, of course. The emotions are a different thing. Did I ever accept it as real, as actual? . . . Yes I suppose I did believe in the great myths.')

These are the primitive forces, the religious tendencies and sacred themes, which Olivier adapted to theatrical practice. The facts of mortality – of decay – of death's power – conjoin with his sense of moral degradation. What makes Olivier Olivier is that no other actor has been so sensitive to shame, pride, temptation, or – consider Hurstwood's slide in *Carrie,* Archie Rice's anxieties, or the agonies of Richard and Macbeth when they suspect they'll lose the crown – to the fear of ruin. His characters are never passive or pacific; they are never accepting; they are defiant and made strong by opposition. This was so from the start. At the end of the Christmas Term 1917, some years before his success in *The Taming of the Shrew,* he played Brutus at All Saints. Dignitaries and notables took these child productions seriously: here was Shakespeare untrammelled by – unmediated by – a corrupting adult intelligence. The words flowed innocently, it was believed, out of the mouths of babes. 'Oh, don't you love it – don't you love the words?' gushed a trollop, swooping upon Olivier, who turned to his playmates and said, 'Who is she?' It was Ellen Terry, miraculously present (as were Lady Tree and Sybil Thorndike), like a Good Fairy in a pantomime. (It is the subject of a Victorian genre painting, surely: 'The Infant Olivier Receives the Mantle from Our Lady of the Lyceum'.) Later on, in her looping, hectic hand, she confided in her diary that 'The small boy who played Brutus is already a great actor.'

*Julius Caesar** was revived nine months later, and Sir Johnston Forbes-Robertson, the stage partner of both Irving and Dame Terry, told Gerard, 'My dear man, your son *is* Brutus'; and to Father Heald he wrote, 'Brutus delivered his oration to the citizens with a pathetic air of fatalism which was poignantly suggestive – remarkable in one so young.' Olivier was a child actor – 'But this is an actor! Absolutely an actor! Born to it!' said Sybil Thorndike of the same performance† – and *Julius Caesar* is a young play, a schoolboy play, rather in the spirit of *Beau Geste*, in which he appeared in 1929, or *Journey's End*, in which he created the role of Captain Stanhope. It is a play about the creation of a great man – and how worrying this is to the people who know him for what he is, for how he was. Caesar ate the same food as you, was schooled with you, so how is he now more successful and more exalted? 'The fault, dear Brutus, is not in our stars/But in ourselves, that we are underlings.'

Caesar has 'prodigious grown/And fearful.' The conspirators, however, are motivated by spite and envy – the prefecture ganging up on the school swot or genius, and wanting to punish him for getting above his station. He's 'a serpent's egg/which hatched would as his kind grow mischievous'; he's the tyrant who'll 'Soar above the view of men/And keep us all in servile fearfulness.' Brutus, however, takes no part in these paranoid prophecies. His concern is service to the Roman state, to government; to doing good in constructive ways. He is a loner – which is to say he has a distinctive individuality – and his wife, Portia, has difficulty reaching him: 'Dwell I but in the suburbs/Of your good pleasure?' she asks.

It is a play which takes place in darkness. The weather, as in *A*

* Olivier also appeared as Flavius, one of Brutus' officers, in a production for the Lena Ashwell Players, at the Century Theatre (and on tour), in October 1925. Tynan proposed *Julius Caesar* for the National's repertoire in 1965. I found a memorandum amongst his papers in which he argued that such a production 'gets L. O. and J. G. [Gielgud] on the same stage. Valuable to do a *straight* Shakespeare after [Zeffirelli's tutti-fruiti] MUCH ADO and [the all-male] AS YOU [LIKE IT].' Nothing came of the idea.

† 'One day Father Olivier said to my husband and myself: "I wonder if you'd go and see my boy Laurence in a school play and tell me what you think of him" . . . [Afterwards] we went home to . . . Gerard and said "Your boy's born to the stage. You won't keep him off" . . . In fact . . . he was [already] in favour. I think [Olivier's] father would have liked to be an actor himself. He was very dramatic in his sermons.' To another interviewer, Dame Sybil said, 'They asked me to see their son in a choir school show, and I went feeling a little depressed at having to see another wonder-child. But I went and *I knew he had fire*.'

Midsummer Night's Dream, is all mixed up; and the conspirators, crackpots and petty obsessives, meet and mutter like Peter Quince and his troop. (They talk like the rude mechanicals – 'Good gentlemen, look fresh and merrily', etc.) But the main source of darkness is within Brutus, as he wrestles with a sense of sin and evil. 'Brutus with himself at war/Forgets the shows of love to other men' – and this is the angry adolescent Olivier, with his moral sense, his tension between the light and the shadows, his self-involvement. 'No man bears sorrow better,' we are told, when his possible reactions to Portia's death are discussed. It must have been as if, in 1917, Olivier was making ready for the death of his mother three years hence – for the death of Vivien fifty years hence – when night will hang about his eyes. Brutus 'carries anger as the flint bears fire', and Tynan and Joan Plowright concur that 'Larry has this bottled violence, which is what gives him this great authority . . . You quite often feel that with enormous effort he is being civil to people that he would not just like to walk away from, but to kick very hard. That is why, when he is prevailed on to make a speech, he puts on a pose of elaborate humility . . . He pretends to be such a wilting violet, and you know that he would actually quite enjoy seeing all those people blown up.'

Not that he was ever physically violent; he wasn't a bully. His wrath was worse than that. What people feared with Olivier was his disapproval; the loss of his esteem – and you'd want to recover his respect. Thus, Tynan's fate. He presumed to begin a book about his mentor and received the equivalent of that basilisk stare described by O'Toole. His pleading letters, asking for emotional reinstatement, make pathetic reading. 'I cannot imagine why you seem so anxious to avoid being perpetuated in print by a colleague who has written about you with greater admiration than any other living critic,' he argued. Olivier's response, apologizing for his cold attitude, was a masterpiece of hilarious insincerity: 'The fact is that I have sinned by my fault, my own fault and my own most grievous fault, and humbly ask pardon of God and of you, Father, counsel, penance and absolution.' He still (naturally) would not countenance a biography. He functioned almost by black and white principles – he had, like Brutus, an innocent understanding of right and wrong.

Cassius: You love me not.
Brutus: I do not like your faults.
Cassius: A friendly eye could never see such faults.
Brutus: A flatterer's would not, though they do appear
As huge as high Olympus.

But Brutus is an honourable man. He wishes to impose order upon chaos; to discriminate. ('Art thou some god, some angel, or some devil?' he asks of Caesar's ghost, which appears in his tent like Hamlet's father or the pre-Bosworth spectres in *Richard III.*) There is something particular to him. He won't (like Olivier over Tynan) be swayed. If he appears impersonal, unforthcoming, it is not that there's an exclusion of personal feeling, but that, determined to be wholesome, he's refusing to be furtive and collusive. He didn't wish to behave like the people he was around. As Mark Antony says: 'When you do find him, or alive or dead,/He will be found like Brutus, like himself.' Similarly Olivier will be found, like Olivier, like himself, confounding expectations. As an actor, in an astonishingly varied series of parts, witnessed and sponsored by Victorian grandees at one end of the century and given work by up-to-the-minute directors like Derek Jarman (in *War Requiem*) at the other, he never ceased from making himself – as exemplified by the eponymous Julius Caesar – into a great man, a great spirit, the hero who saves his country.

Early in his career, in *Fire Over England* (1937), for example, this meant swashbuckling and dare-devilry, defeating the Queen's enemies with a flash of steel, leaping from burning ships, scaling the rooftops; as Air Chief Marshal Sir Hugh Dowding, in *Battle of Britain* (1969), he simply sits behind a desk, and through the caution of his orders, and by not wanting to be rash and rhetorical, he averts the end of the world, the end of England. He looks out at London burning – at the fires over England – from his office in Bentley Priory, and he has an austerity, and sadness, and a perspicacious nature that's finally lyrical – and the *real* Lord Dowding, watching the shooting at Pinewood, near death and in a wheelchair at the age of eighty-six, wept at the beauty of the interpretation.*

Each role was a renewal, a renovation, an embodiment of the hope of better things to come. Henry V's war cries, which he modelled on Tarquin at Eton ('I hope you will like King Harry. I think of you often while I am trying to play him, he was a fine lad in many ways'); or

---

* Olivier deeply admired Dowding's 'dedicated restraint'. To create his performance, he had visited the old man in Tunbridge Wells, conversed with his wartime colleagues, researched amongst military records, and was determined to portray 'a man who knows his job, wishes to be left alone to do it, and [who] despises the lofty ignorance of officialdom'. He captured it all in a brief scene with the Minister (Anthony Nicholls):

Minister: Churchill puts great faith in radar.
Dowding: It's vital. [Pause] But it doesn't shoot down aircraft.
Minister: So I tell the cabinet you are trusting in radar and praying to God?
Dowding: I'd put it the other way round. I'm trusting in God and praying for radar.

Hamlet flying through the air with his sword ready to strike; or Mr Puff,* flinging snuff and banging his head on the scenery, a character he plunged into immediately after the mutilation of Oedipus, as if he needed a comedy to free himself from, or nullify, the tragedy: what he's doing is exploring the creative process, and Olivier was always, in Welles' words, 'a real fighting star'.

Tireless, with a capacity for work that is a little frightening – 'you think of nothing else day and night' – he had a faithfulness in his calling that was to hold back the pandemonium and fear of what was waiting for him back at home. By which I mean, for instance, that in April 1946 a typical week would contain two performances each of both parts of *Henry IV*; an *Arms and the Man*; an *Uncle Vanya*; and four double bills of *Oedipus* and *The Critic*, when he'd arrive at the theatre at one fifteen, be on stage from half past two until three forty-five; back on as Mr Puff at precisely twelve minutes past four, with a curtain at five thirty. He'd allow himself a twenty-minute rest before making up as Oedipus again for seven forty-five. His eyes would be bloodshot from the glycerine. His head would throb from wearing a wig for nine hours. His ostensible real life did not exist – it was somewhere else: for, meanwhile, sequestered at Notley, Vivien was being ill and mad. ('There is no glamour about an actor when you get to know him,' he said during this period. 'The only glamorous creature left is a racehorse, and that's because the public only see him at his best.')

It's the nineteenth-century work ethic in action ('I get strong feelings of guilt about taking a holiday'). Work whilst ye may – for the night cometh when no man can work. Produce! Produce! Were it but the pitifullest infinitesimal fraction of a product, produce it in God's name! 'Tis the utmost thou hast in thee: out with it then! Blessed is he who has found his work; let him ask no other blessedness . . . He was fully alive when working, and Olivier was always driving himself on. As he explained in 1980, 'It's sort of a yoke, but at times, you know, a yoke is a kind of comfort. And it's always there. It's a bit like climbing the Himalayas, if you get my drift. On the way, you think "This is agonizing – I can't get my breath." And when you scale the top, I suppose you're relieved. "Yes," you say, "it *was* rather nice." But then you have to start thinking how to make your way down. That is the only satisfaction for an artist – the fact you are making a continuous effort. And I suppose as you get on, it gets harder – there's more to lose.' During the inter-

* 'A pert, jaunty, impudent, irresistible coxcomb', according to the *Daily Telegraph*, of 19 October 1945.

missions, or whilst waiting in the wings, he'd be composing letters. 'And now, while Clarence is roaring away in his cell, I hasten to write just one line to welcome you and bring you my love,' he wrote to Tarquin in 1949; 'I am between Acts Two and Three of *Caesar* [*and Cleopatra*],' he tells Christopher Fry, in 1952, 'I must stop [as] I am being called.' Mr Fry informs me that he also received a letter from Olivier, begun when he was 'sitting in his theatre dressing room after Antony had died, and Vivien [as Cleopatra] was left to go on with the play alone'. (Or, as Olivier himself put it, incorporating the flux of his life and art into his text: 'This letter is bound to be a bit jumpy as it has to get written, when and how. I am just dec'd as Antony and Vivien is doing her stuff.')* Whilst actually on stage he'd be monitoring both the other actors ('Get out of my light!' he hissed at Alan Webb in *Titus Andronicus*) and the audience ('I can hear seats tip up . . . and I can also hear the exit doors bang as people go out'), and simultaneously calculating the box-office take. Tom Pate, manager for the National from 1969 to 1979, remembers 'the internal phone would go [between scenes] and it would be Sir Laurence asking for the night's figures . . . in *Long Day's Journey*, say, he'd ring with his American accent, and the next night I'd have Shylock on the end of the line, asking why there were six empty seats in Row O.'

He had an intense practicality. But I must be careful, when spelling out his work ethic, his ideals of duty and service, which occluded the private life, or the recreational life; I must be careful, when discussing the selflessness of his dedication, that I don't make Olivier seem too monkish – anchoritic – spartan – puritan: for what Olivier conjures up isn't the plain and the chaste, but theatre's baroque extravagance – crystal,

---

* Cleopatra spends Act V eulogizing Antony, as Vivien was to spend her latter years fantasizing about Olivier. 'To mention Larry [to her] was like talking to the Virgin Mary about God,' it was alleged.

> His legs bestrid the ocean: his rear'd arm
> Crested the world: his voice was propertied
> As all the tuned spheres, and that to friends;
> But when he meant to quail and shake the orb,
> He was as rattling thunder [. . .]
> Think you there was or might be such a man
> As this I dream'd of?

The impetus for such a speech recurs in *That Hamilton Woman*, when Emma mythologizes Nelson, insisting that he is separate from other people. 'You are not an ordinary man,' Vivien tells Olivier on screen. 'You are a symbol of what is most precious . . . all that beauty – and light – and glory.'

swags, drapes, mirrors, gold leaf; a fountain of colours (which you *don't* find in the South Bank complex, so it is little wonder he seldom went there).* Olivier was compulsive, almost as if he was the one being watched and in danger of attracting censure for laxness – by his father's ghost? (He was continuously aware of his own origins and what he described to Tarquin as 'the cretinous romanticism of the Oliviers'.) By God? (He wrote to Jill Esmond in 1929, of his acting: 'It is my only hope of being of use to God and the world and I think everybody should try to be that.') By, as it were, himself? (He had a reverential sense of his own destiny. 'Don't you realize – I want to be the greatest actor in the world,' he stated in 1920.) The all-consuming nature of his work meant that it was only in his public deeds that his private weaknesses could be examined – hence Straker, in *Potiphar's Wife*, on trial for assaulting Nora Swinburne's Lady Diana Branford, or Captain Ignatoff, gambling beyond his means, in *Moscow Nights*, and accused of spying, or Larry Durrant, in *Twenty-One* Days, accused of murder, or Maxim de Winter, in *Rebecca*, convinced he has killed his wife, or Nelson, in *That Hamilton Woman*, accused of adultery and refused a divorce by Gladys Cooper ('as long as I live I shall be your wife'), or Hurstwood, in *Carrie*, again tyrannized by his first wife (Miriam Hopkins) and accused of embezzlement, or Graham Weir, charged with the molestation of Sarah Miles, in *Term of Trial*, or Chebutikin, in *Three Sisters*, haunted by an operation he botched . . . And so on endlessly. Acting was a projection of his guilt. He has a sensitivity to his characters' thoughts, he so completely inhabits their lives and minds he can, as Chebutikin for example, get beneath a genial surface to suggest self-contempt, the clarity of hideous self-knowledge. The old army doctor has a rolling walk, he kisses and laughs readily, in that overdone way of the lodger, out to please.

Olivier has a candour and (paradoxically) a reluctance, or restraint, and this combination is to be found in Brutus – having personified him as a child he perhaps never deflected from the theme – in Dowding; in Astrov, when he relinquishes the chance of happiness with Ilyena; and in the self-sacrifice of Johnnie, the French-Canadian trapper of *49th Parallel* (the only film in history to mention Winnipeg, the capital city

* At the official gala opening of the National Theatre building, in the presence of the Queen, on 25 October 1976, Olivier made a speech of welcome from the stage – the last words he was to utter in a theatre, as it happens: 'Our very eyes and all happy senses will forever be rewarded by the craft and genius of the actual creator of this situation in which we find ourselves – Sir Denys Lasdun [the architect].' Is it not conceivable that Olivier was taking the piss?

of Manitoba), who is killed when he tries to send a wireless message about the escaped Nazis to the authorities. (Poor Finlay Currie might still be there, tied to his chair in the hut.) With regard to this picture, I have a suspicion that Michael Powell, the director, and a man who was very horribly full of himself,* had an admiration for the Germans – their force and lack of sentiment (though they are superabundantly sentimental – like Powell); their masculinity; their contempt for women and children – for the 'weak' (for humanity?). As Eric Portman and his group commit atrocities across Canada, Powell – the director as autocrat – would like us to admire them for their power and authority; yet he is compelled to plug the script with pro-democracy speeches, which he is embarrassed by and doesn't believe in. Olivier plays against this with a performance of goodness and innocence that is both delicate and emotional. He does, it's true, come out with a Clouseau-esque French-Canadian accent – or it would be atrocious if you'd be wanting phonological exactitude. Like his generic all-purpose Dutch-New-York-Jewish-Mittel-Europa accent, it has a cartoonish musicality. So what holds the attention is Johnnie's sense of obligation, and what differs from one Olivier performance to the next is not the make-up – those noses and plucked eyebrows – or the accent, but the shadings of good and evil, the degree of moral shortcomings; almost, it's the balance he decides to find between the spiritual and the animal, light and shade, that is his pull.

Nowhere is this combination more potent than in *The Power and the Glory*, taped for CBS television in eight days after Olivier had completed the Broadway run of *Becket* in the spring of 1961. The schedule was exhausting. Two studios were booked in Brooklyn, forty sets were constructed – prison yards, jungle clearings, grog shops, various ruined churches – and a hundred and fifty-one actors were clad in bedraggled

* The sadist in *Peeping Tom*? The evil ballet master in *The Red Shoes*? Was he not drawn to these? Powell had a high-flown opinion of his 'art', and yet I can see only the most over-emphatic kitsch. (He didn't have the tolerance and self-deprecation of camp.) The script for *The Life and Death of Colonel Blimp* (1943) was originally developed for Olivier, but the War Office refused to give their support to the film, because 'the thug element in the make-up of the German soldier is ignored and indeed the suggestion is that if we were exactly like the Germans we should be better soldiers' (Ministry of Information memorandum). Olivier, who in any event had reservations of his own about the script ('Surely it should be . . . pointed out how the English constitutional complacence has re-set the English nature time and time again simply by various attitudes to good taste, etc. ever since Drake and his bloody bowls'), was thus not released from service in the Fleet Air Arm. Though he was of course liberated to make the propagandistic *The Demi-Paradise* and *Henry V*.

Mexican costumes and asked to pad and bask amongst the genuine tropical vegetation flown from Florida. Shooting began on 30 May and had to be completed by 4 June, as Olivier was due to record selections from the Old Testament for *The Living Bible* (a twelve-volume set of discs presented by Douglas Fairbanks Jr) and, by 7 June, meet Leslie Evershed-Martin and discuss plans for Chichester. By the end of the week they were working in sustained twenty-four-hour sessions. Olivier was kept awake – alive? – by cold compresses and coffee, and he had to be manhandled on to his donkey. He would similarly fatigue or prostrate himself during the run of *Long Day's Journey into Night*. 'There was a one-minute break between acts, and Larry would sit on a chair in the wings and fall asleep, so exhausted was he,' says Denis Quilley. 'I'd have to tap him gently on the shoulder, remind him which stage of the play we'd reached, and he'd go on as vigorously as ever. He loved hard graft.' The enervation suited Tyrone, a punch-drunk actor whose life is ebbing, whose febrile energies help to block out what his real feelings are for his family. He is a man who'd never dare relax emotionally; indeed, he tranquillizes his emotions by recollecting only platitudes ('The value of the dollar and fear of the poorhouse!' are his motivations), and his despair over Mary, his wife, is that she insists on living in the past: 'For God's sake forget the past,' he howls – an Olivier howl, his face and mouth distorted into a mask of anguish, making us realize that the past (the death of a baby from measles; their son's nightmares quietened with a teaspoonful of whiskey) is as vivid to him as a hallucination.

And in *The Power and the Glory*, too, the actor's exhaustion married with that of the character and Olivier was transported. Filming full pelt, totally drenched in the work, 'in the afternoon run-through the cast took fire; one after another we all caught that rare and inspiring spiritual communion which makes us all living parts of a living whole. It was a wonderful experience and took from us everything that we had. When it was finished we were quite exhausted . . . The going was fantastically tough' – as it had to be, if you crave martyrdom. The priest (who has no name) is a tormented soul, seeking respite and peace by pouring booze down himself and suffering as much as possible at the hands of the police lieutenant (George C. Scott in big shiny black boots: there is always a suggestion of comic exaggeration in his villainy); and the extremity of the suffering was congenial to Olivier, like Oedipus' blinding, or Mr Puff's dangerous stunts, or the public humiliation of Archie Rice, or Othello's debasement by Iago (Olivier made much of the Moor's tearing-off of his crucifix and reverting to savagery), or the pain inflicted upon Titus Andronicus (' . . . with our sighs we'll breathe the welkin dim,/And stain the sun with fog, as sometimes clouds/When they do hug him in their melting bosoms'). It's as if he took pleasure in pain, was revitalized by taking himself to the brink of collapse, and he had a fear of happiness, of contentment. Happy moments have (he wrote to Jill Esmond once) 'just the faintest shadow lurking somewhere near . . . some doubt, or fear – fear perhaps of hurting something, some ideal, God, perhaps the moment itself . . .' (In later life he'd be less lyrical, being of the opinion that happiness was the exclusive province of mental defectives.)

The title of Graham Greene's novel is, I suspect, ironic. The words from the Lord's Prayer refer, here, to no ethereal palaces, to no marble thrones and starry skies, but to a squalid and fly-blown South American township. There is no power; there is no glory – except within the character of the priest. Religion has been outlawed by the Communist revolution; alcohol, also, is prohibited. The fugitive non-celibate holy man who is not averse to a little Scotch pecking at his liver is thus in no place to keep his skin intact. But then, refusing to escape, eager to face tyranny, he seems rather to fancy the idea of the firing squad – and Olivier is back in the moral world of Anouilh's *Becket* (or Eliot's *Murder in the Cathedral*), when to crave sainthood, to know that you are going to qualify for it, disallows you from its graces. If you offer no resistance, isn't that suicide by other means? A sure case of damnation rather than beatification?

Olivier had seen Paul Scofield in *The Power and the Glory*, directed by Peter Brook at the Phoenix Theatre in 1956. 'I think it was the best performance I can remember seeing,' he claimed, twenty years later. 'I was acting at the time in something else in London [*The Entertainer*], and I went to see one matinée, and I went again the next matinée, and I don't often go to see things more than once. I just don't. I was floored by his performance. It was wonderful.' What appealed to Olivier? Scofield's suffering face, which has something of Buster Keaton in it? Scofield's sonorous voice? The overlaps with *Titus Andronicus* ('When will this fearful slumber have an end?'), which Brook had directed at Stratford the previous August, and to which Olivier would return throughout 1957, on a European tour?* Perhaps the activity of mind fascinated him,

* It was seen in Warsaw in June 1957 by Jan Kott, whose book *Shakespeare Our Contemporary* thrilled me as a schoolboy, and in which he reports: 'Watching *Titus Andronicus*, we come to understand – perhaps more than by looking at any other Shakespeare play – the nature of his genius: he gave an inner awareness to passion; cruelty ceased to be merely physical. Shakespeare discovered the moral hell. He discovered heaven as well. But he remained on earth . . . If we were to ask the question who in our time was the first to show the true Shakespeare convincingly, there would be only one answer: Sir Laurence Olivier.'

because this is what he tries to convey in the CBS production. But he is hampered by a coarse black wig, a broad putty nose, contact lenses that gave him an eye infection, and a sombrero. Dressed in a hessian jerkin, its clumsy Stone Age stitching held together with safety pins, Olivier wanders those forty sets and jostles with those hundred and fifty-one actors (amongst whom Roddy McDowall, Keenan Wynn and Cyril Cusack), trying to be humble and determined simultaneously; and we can't believe that, in his peasant garb, he 'looks like any other man', for Olivier positively glows. He tells the villagers that pain and suffering are preparations for the joys and comforts of Heaven (where 'no one ever grows old; the crops never fail'). He searches for a bottle of wine with which to celebrate mass – and Roddy McDowall, the fey wee bounty hunter, and Keenan Wynn, the bootlegger, swig it down, so that Olivier can look on appalled. He tries not to appear upset and to contain his fury, and when he breaks and weeps, such is his suffering, these are Christ's tears over Jerusalem: 'All the hope of the world draining away,' he blubs.

He suffers at the dentist, having an 'old filling which has worked loose and needs attention' (in Greene-land tooth decay = moral decay). He gets spat upon by his daughter. Flung into gaol, he cheers up the inmates by announcing, 'We are all sinners here – all.' If he goes for a walk, there'll be a sudden storm, or an attack of blackwater fever and tsetse fly, or he'll come across an atrocity – e.g. a child killed by the soldiers. ('Light perpetual shine on her,' he says.) *The Power and the Glory* is a piece of such deadly gloom (a fact reinforced by the monochrome murk of the television tape), it amounts, actually, to metaphysical farce. The priest is a masochist, George C. Scott's policeman, on his charger, his equal and opposite number ('I too am dedicated and have little need of women'); and it is a tribute to Olivier that his character becomes heroic. Not because of the struggling and the suffering and the slouched whispery exhaustion; but because he manages not to be pitiable.

The impression we get, when the priest is on the run, sheltering in a banana warehouse or concealing his identity, is that Olivier is acting a man acting abasement. He only pretends to be meek. The shabby, unpressed clothes, the swarthiness, the gutter life: this is alien to him, and Olivier gives the eschatological hokum some zest when he ripples the defiance. 'I am a priest!' he says to the prisoners. 'I'm all you have!' he says to the barefoot villagers. 'Will nobody be my [pause – incredulous] Judas?' In his way, the priest is as confident and proud as Richard III, whom Olivier momentarily becomes when he flinches from the girl's spittle; whom he becomes at length when he crosses the border and enters a church. 'O Lord I love the beauty of thy house,' he says, and falls to his knees. In the next scene he is robed in ornate vestments and conducting services. He is much more alert and dandy – with Richard's sense of being pleased with himself. He pockets the fees for baptisms and sits in a café smoking a cigar. Roddy McDowall turns up and gets him to go into the jungle and take the confession of a dying farmer. Instantly he reverts to being perspiring and anguished – and he's caught by George C. Scott ('Wasn't the trap obvious?'). There is an undertone of menace in the scene, when hunter and prey are waiting for the rains to stop, for the policeman has a compassion which he is suppressing and the priest has a pride that is of the calibre of Coriolanus. When Olivier is at his prayers, his pale, unshaven face picked out in shadow, the squirming has an epic scale: 'I've been useless; I might just as well never have been born,' he says, like the Olivier of *Confessions of an Actor*; then, in the next breath, he sees his death as an atonement and that he's 'at peace with God and with myself'. Up against the wall at dawn he asks, 'Do your men shoot well?' 'Not always.' 'Will you . . . ?' 'I promise' – and the lieutenant does have to add the final bullet, and he is like a matador who has respect – love – for his foe. The camera pulls back, to see Olivier crumpled and slumped at the edge of the prison courtyard. Richard III only masterminds his way to the throne. The priest in *The Power and the Glory*, reliving the trial and execution of Christ under Pontius Pilate, is the Second Coming.

Chapter Five
Friends and Lovers

Olivier could only achieve orgasm if other people were watching him; or perhaps it was that he needed to imagine other people were watching him; or (with Sarah Miles) he'd need a run-down on her previous lovers – and he'd picture himself in competition with them, as if they were watching him. But, in any event, I think this is taking an actor's need for an audience *too far*. Between a player and his public there has to be 'a kind of invisible ray', he once said. 'It's like a string of a bow or a harp or a violin, upon which you can play if you're clever enough.' Olivier wasn't only clever enough: he was a virtuoso, illimitably lingering, abundant, bombastic if he felt like it. He was particularly fascinated by music-hall comedians. They had a direct and tantalizing access to the patrons – an immediate rapport. Sid Field, especially, had 'this marvellous energy bursting out of the pores of his skin and shooting out of his eyes' – which rather makes his star quality seem literally as well as figuratively ejaculatory – and it is the control and receptiveness which Olivier was admiring. The actor has to flirt, tease, dominate, hold the whip hand, and as he told Denholm Elliott, the mask must never slip, otherwise 'the audience will lose faith and it's near impossible to win them back'.

Hence the conception of Archie Rice, a performer who fails in all these departments. But a paradox with *The Entertainer* is that, when the old flop makes his big speech about being 'dead behind the eyes', that's the very last thing Olivier is. (His baleful eyes, like Sid Fields' and Fu Manchu's, spit fire.) Olivier is the confidence man. He's never faded: he'd not rage at his insignificance; he's not indistinct. He's a danger zone. He claimed to have relished Osborne's play because he was bored, 'titled, necessarily self-satisfied, pompous, patronising', and needed a new departure.* In fact, the play is – and he responded to it because it is –

* *The Entertainer* was his first assignment after making *The Prince and the Showgirl* which, though it co-starred Monroe, had originally, as *The Sleeping Prince*, been a vehicle for

a version of his recurrent theme or agitations: his battles with the Christian doctrines of eternal torment, martyrdom, frustration and the feeling of loneliness, of isolation, like Richard before Bosworth, Henry before Agincourt, Hamlet soliloquizing, or the priest, in *The Power and the Glory*, praying fit to bust. The appeal and satisfaction of Archie Rice lay in his absurdity and fastidiousness; he is creepy and poignant (Richard III is creepy and ingenious); he is fearful, and has difficulties with girls: Phoebe, his wife, Jean, his daughter, Tina, a chorine, and Mrs Lapford, Tina's mother, played by Thora Hird – haranguing Olivier as she does as Mrs Taylor, Sarah Miles' mother, in *Term of Trial*.

How did Olivier see himself? And did he believe he was Archie Rice, or is this a ruse? 'It's really me, isn't it? It's what I really am . . . I know that creature. I know him better than he knows himself,' he claimed in the hearing of Osborne, Tony Richardson and William Gaskill. Olivier would have been referring to Archie's persistence; his adherence to his calling come what may. But beyond this, Olivier was conscious of his effect on people – perhaps the first thing any embryonic actor or entertainer learns. After All Saints, he was sent, in the autumn of 1921, to board at St Edward's School, Oxford, which accepted the sons of clergymen at reduced rates – though at £125 per annum still steep, and for which you received sour latrines, buttered toast, and prunes and suet. On 11 December 1923, Mr Wilfrid Cowell, who taught English and Classics, produced *A Midsummer Night's Dream*. Olivier was cast as that shrewd and knavish sprite, Robin Goodfellow, and as he wrote in his diary: 'Played Puck very well – much to everybody's disgust.'* Then, as later, his skills at manipulating an audience were countered by a personal gracelessness over specific individuals; Olivier decided he was friendless.

Vivien Leigh – and it was from the world of gentility and filigree she represented, and which he now saw as fake, that he wished to dissociate himself. He partly achieved this by wondering, 'What would Archie have made of Marilyn Monroe? That would have been a meeting, those two together . . . Wait a minute, perhaps they did meet. They could have been in the same show. Not Monroe – the character. The showgirl. Archie might well have fondled her breasts . . .'

* *Pro*: Robert Cecil Mortimer reported for the school magazine: 'By far the most notable performance was that of Puck. He seemed to put more "go" into it than the others, and succeeded in individualizing his part. To my mind he was a little too robust and jovial for such a quick-footed, light-fingered person, but at any rate he gave a consistent rendering, and showed by his gestures and movements that he has a knowledge of acting and a good mastery of technique.'

Contra: A review in a local paper: 'The entire performance was a cheap burlesque turn. One can only be surprised that the director . . . let the young man . . . get away with such tawdry insolence. Shakespeare has seldom been more ill-served.'

Like many a creative genius, he was essentially solitary – or self-protective, if you prefer. He saw off rivals when they tried to direct him: Gielgud was thrown out of a *Twelfth Night* rehearsal at Stratford in 1955: 'Darling John, please go for a walk along the river and let us get on with it'; and Orson Welles said of their collaboration over Ionesco's *Rhinoceros*: 'He *had* to destroy me in some way . . . He doesn't want anybody else up there . . .'

Olivier had an uneasy awareness of others; he feared their emotions, their whirlpools, and whether he'll go under. He could never entrust his life to anyone (Vivien; Tynan); he was not going to be taken over – and at St Edward's he was convinced 'I just hated school. Without wanting to pull out any violins, I think I can say that I was vastly unpopular.' When this was put to a fellow pupil, Douglas Bader, later a war hero, and later still the man who pushed Dowding's wheelchair around Pinewood when the former Air Chief Marshal came to inspect Olivier's impersonation of him in *Battle of Britain*, he demurred: 'I myself don't think he was unpopular at all, but he was perhaps introspective, lived within himself.' There were reasons enough for this. Eighteen months previously he'd seen his mother for the last time, as she lay upon her bed, completely paralysed down her left side. He was, recalled Sybil Thorndike, to wear a black band on his sleeve for weeks, and if questioned about it would explain he was 'very very sad'. But here's another cause of Olivier's reticence – which made him variously awkward or breezy; another explanation for the shyness or solitude or privacy that lay behind his conformities, and which women (and not only women) often read as helplessness.

One of Olivier's objections against his upbringing was that it confused him about sex. At All Saints, sermons enjoined the congregation that 'Sloth is a sin of the flesh LIKE LUST'; and if heterosexuality couldn't be satisfied outside of holy matrimony – for 'that would have been a mortal sin and I was well and truly steeped in religious thinking' – then there was nothing for it but to dally with what was to hand, and masturbation was a non-starter because during puberty his foreskin had become too tight – a condition known as phimosis. What happened was that the foreskin and head of the penis were imperfectly separated, and when he tried to unsheathe his knob he discovered that fibrous tissue had inflamed and deformed his bits. He eventually had to be circumcised. Then one of his testicles decided to swell up, necessitating more surgical intervention. The upshot, says Tarquin, 'was for him to associate the orb and sceptre of his manhood with humiliation and pain, over and above church-induced guilt'.

By 1964, and the ritual of making up for *Othello*, he could titter about his tackle. 'What a tragedy that such a very great actor should have such a very small cock,' he'd sigh,* as he proceeded to create the illusion he was black ('If I peeled my skin, underneath would be another layer of black skin'), by daubing himself with (a) Max Factor 2880; (b) a lighter brown; (c) Negro No. 2 ('brown on black to give a rich mahogany'); and then he'd polish his body with chiffon, until his epidermis 'gleam[ed] a smooth ebony . . . I was to be beautiful. Quite beautiful . . . Kill with beauty.' He'd always done so. What matters about his early films is that they are not black and white, they are black and silver. Surrounded by shadows, the figures on the celluloid shimmer, the women in close-fitting velvet slacks, the men with wrist watches with an alligator strap. There is a mist of glamour; there is a glow of the flesh. Olivier's pale face has a curious lustre, as if the light shines through him. The silences, the slowness, the nocturnal atmosphere, the glances: it is erotic, just as the way Olivier shapes his phrases is erotic. Desdemona is won, and killed, with speech: 'From year to year – the battles, sieges, fortunes,/ That I have passed/I ran it through, even from my boyish days . . .'

If he'd first been aware that he was a sexual being at school ('Bend more tight! More tight!' he was instructed by the prefects and masters who caned him and ogled his gluteus maximus), then by the time he joined the Birmingham Repertory Company in 1926, 'sex . . . was beginning to obsess me unremittingly' – to the extent that he contemplated a cup of hemlock, or somesuch despatch. 'Not, bless you, because of frustrated art, but because of unrequited love. I wasted valuable glances at passing trams, thinking them good vehicles for suicide.' Amongst his would-be inamoratas during this phase were Angela Baddeley, whom he met at Christmas 1925, when he was First Serving Man, and she was Ann Boleyn, or Bullen, in a production of *Henry VIII* mounted by Lewis Casson and Bronson Albery at the Empire, Leicester Square. (Sybil Thorndike was Queen Katharine.) Baddeley reminded him of his mother, as she had (it was alleged) 'a naturally affectionate way about her with people she liked'. Olivier threw a pass and was politely rebuffed. He worked with her again twenty-five years later at the Shakespeare Memorial Theatre, when she took what we could call his old part of Maria, Olivia's housekeeper, and he was her foil – the madly used Malvolio.† Another idolatrous object was Peggy Ashcroft, who came to Birmingham

* 'There's not a lot you can say to that apart from, "Well, not bad," but you certainly wouldn't offer to swap your own for his,' comments Robert Stephens, our eyewitness.

† Miss Baddeley married Glen Byam Shaw, who directed Olivier in *Macbeth* during the same season.

to play Joan Greenleaf in *Bird in Hand*, in September 1927. Olivier was all set to propose marriage, when the sound of a lavatory flushing down the hall spoilt the moment – which, said Dame Peggy wistfully, 'never recurred'. Then there was Ralph Richardson's wife, Muriel Hewitt, whom he met in the spring of 1926, in *The Marvellous History of Saint Bernard*, at the Kingsway Theatre; or Jane Welsh, who was Molly Byrne to his Mat Simon, in *The Well of the Saints*, Susan Whorlow to his Tom Hardcastle, in *The Third Finger*, a comedy about a false marriage, Ailsa Stroan to his Peter Mannoch, in *The Mannoch Family*, a proleptic soap about star-crossed lovers, and Diana to his Parolles in *All's Well that Ends Well*.

I have examined the prompt book for the latter – all the bawdy puns and sensuous references to sea, sex and moisture were cut, and a thick wax crayon cancelled Parolles' great lascivious come-on speech to Helena about virginity: 'your virginity, your old virginity, is like one of your French withered pears; it looks ill, it eats drily; marry, 'tis a withered pear; it was formerly better; marry, yet 'tis a withered pear. Will you have anything with it?' Instead, Olivier was to enter the Countess of Rousillon's palace carrying his coat, stick, gloves and scarf, and he was given bits of business dropping these, etc., as he shakes hands, etc., and Helena was to help him gather them up. Shakespeare's sinister gallant was made into Bertie Wooster – but Olivier made the part his own in Act IV, scene iii, when Parolles is blindfolded and tricked into believing he's been captured by the enemy. He divulges military secrets – to his own side – and is castigated as a coward and hanger-on. Olivier, however, prowling alone and having what Joan Plowright would call 'a sort of untouchability and unapproachability', gave the character the last quality you'd expect – sincerity: 'Is it possible he should know what he is, and be that he is?' asks an attendant lord, incredulously. With Olivier – certainly. Black tabs descended around him, the set was flown, the furniture concealed, and Olivier faced the audience to explain that he'll live on, and that he knew he had no claims to bravery. To his own self he's been consistently true: 'Simply the thing I am/Shall make me live . . .'*

The thing he was in Birmingham, during that season in 1927, was 'very courtly in manner', says Jane Welsh. 'He was an astonishing mix of boy and man, and many of us wanted to both love him and mother

* 'Mr Lawrence Oliver's [*sic*] fine acting as Parolles was a big factor in the success of the scenes centring round the recovery of the drum, which Mr Bernard Shaw, who was a member of the audience, seemed to enjoy immensely,' reported the *Westminster Gazette*, 18 April 1927.

him.'* Not absolutely everybody. Eileen Beldon, who played Helena, and who'd eventually accompany him on the Old Vic tour of Australia and New Zealand in 1948, considered him bumptious, an upstart, a boorish nuisance: 'Larry Olivier made himself generally obnoxious. Frankly, I couldn't stand him . . . Of course, I realize now that he was just a young boy trying to prove himself, and that much of his behaviour came from the fact that he was so scared and felt so far out of his element. At least, that's what Larry told me recently.'

Call him adorable, puppyish, tiresome or perky; acknowledge that he was appealing to maternal instincts: it remains the case that Olivier, knowing well Parolles' philosophy concerning virginity, lines he was not, however, permitted to speak on the stage – 'There's little can be said for it; 'tis against the rule of nature' – still believed he had to have a wife before he could have it off. 'I was dying to get married so that I might, with the blessings of God, enjoy sex.' It was in this desperate spirit – which I think he understood with hindsight to be by and large objectionable – that he enchanted the ear of Jill Esmond, or Jill Esmond Moore, as she was occasionally billed in the programmes. Educated at Bedales and a graduate of RADA, she'd taken over from Peggy Ashcroft in the London transfer of *Bird in Hand*, at the Royalty Theatre, Dean Street. Olivier himself was in town, also under Sir Barry Jackson's banner, at the Royal Court;† and he'd decided he'd had enough of the provincial apprenticeship: 'I wanted to be a West End actor . . . I wanted money. I wanted violently to get married . . . I think I sort of knew . . . that I

* Later in her career, Miss Welsh would do a regular stint each Christmas at the Scala Theatre as Mrs Darling in *Peter Pan*.

† In April 1925, Sir Barry Jackson had decided to underwrite the costs of running the Birmingham Repertory Theatre by transferring productions to London for longer runs. This 'Metropolitan adventure', as it was called, led to the taking of the Kingsway Theatre, where Olivier appeared in *The Marvellous History of St Bernard* for seventy-six performances (7 April–12 June 1926), and the Royal Court, where *The Farmer's Wife* played for a lucrative one thousand three hundred and twenty-nine nights – though Olivier actually only appeared in this play, as Richard Coaker, on tour and (his début there: December 1926) in Birmingham itself. From January until May 1928, Olivier was at the Royal Court, Sloane Square, with the Birmingham Repertory Theatre Company, to appear in *The Adding Machine*, *Macbeth* (as Malcolm), *Back to Methuselah* (as Martellus), *Harold* (as Harold), and *The Taming of the Shrew* (as a lord). Olivier himself said, 'at Birmingham would be found the absolute foundation of any good that I could ever be in my profession [and] one had a very good chance, if one got on at all, of getting a showing in London, and that was one of the main reasons for wanting to go there, apart from the experience you could pick up at the Rep.'

was going to climb towards something, to reach some heights . . .' Sex and advancement comingled – for Jill was well connected. Eva Moore, her mother, star of *Mary, Mary, Quite Contrary* and *Lights Out*, and heaps of tempestuous dramas that have mysteriously failed to survive, in which women arrange orchids in vases, we have already met, putting Gerard Kerr Olivier into a funereal humour. Her father, H. V. Esmond, who had died of pneumonia and alcoholism in Paris some years before Olivier arrived in Jill's life, was an actor-manager who drew this praise from Max Beerbohm: 'Mr H. V. Esmond – show me the human being who ever cocked an eyebrow so significantly, or smiled with so poignant a sweetness . . . or drew sighs so deep, interspersed with backward glances so piercing.'

Dame Peggy concurs that 'for all practical purposes Larry was finished with Birmingham', and whilst she encouraged him to forge ahead and explain to Jackson that, grateful as he had been for the opportunities he'd been given, London was where he must now try to make a name, she was amazed he wanted to resume his old role, that of Gerald Arnwood, the squire's son who is betrothed to Joan Greenleaf. 'Larry, it's a silly part, no good for your career, no one will know you're in it.' However, when Patrick Susands left the London cast, it was Olivier who joined the company of *Bird in Hand*,* two months into its run, in June 1928.

What was it about the character he found congenial? I think it's that Arnwood was indistinguishable from the way Olivier wished to present himself off-stage at this period. 'Mr Lawrence Olivier [*sic*],' said the *Birmingham Gazette* the previous September, when the play had originally opened, 'showed us Gerald as a thoroughly nice lad; his hatred of fuss, both as an aristocrat and as a lover, and his consequent gaucherie, were beautifully done.' This chimes with remarks and instructions noted by the director and hand-written in the prompt books of other productions. Olivier didn't have much to do in *Quality Street* (June 1927), save rise and kneel and help fainting women into the tent, yet Ensign Blades 'is a callow youth, inviting admiration'. As Tom Hardcastle, in *The Third Finger* (February 1927), set in a vicarage garden on a summer evening, 'He is about twenty, slightly younger than his brother, rather more alert

* John Drinkwater's contract with the company, signed on 4 March 1927, gave Sir Barry Jackson rights to produce *Bird in Hand* for five years from the date of the first performance in both Birmingham and London, and 'the managers shall divide the gross receipts . . . not including the receipts from bars, opera glasses, programmes, or cloakrooms'.

and . . . fresh and healthy';* and as Jack Barthwick, in *The Silver Box* (October 1927), 'His boyish face is freshly coloured and clean-shaven.'

Sepia chromos surviving from the shows almost bear out these descriptions – except that what I note, beyond the hastily painted paper sets, wrinkled canvas, and potted plants, is the thinness of his frame, his heavily made-up eyes and eyebrows (like the early sproutings of Jekyll-into-Hyde), and the way he looks up crossly at people. As Uncle Vanya, chasing the professor with a gun, he froths like Rasputin; in *The Adding Machine* he's hidden under a large cap, but there's no mistaking his scowl; and in *Bird in Hand*, when the young man holds the girl's hand, we see that the arms of his suit are too short. (One of Olivier's own suits, perhaps, a hand-me-down from Uncle Sydney?) Anxious, accusing, aghast or staring into the heavens, Olivier was a volatile lumping of little-boy-lost and grim determination – and this is the man with whom Jill was to spend the seven-month run of *Bird in Hand*, and the ensuing seven years as a wife.

It's an atrocious play, John Drinkwater's. Why did the public love it? And the American public, for Jill went to New York and Chicago with it in 1929? It is like an Agatha Christie without a murder. An assorted group of popinjays are bivouacked at the Bird-in-Hand Inn, Gloucestershire, whilst the wind howls and rain drives against the window: Ambrose Godolphin, KC, the lawyer (played in London by Felix Aylmer); a Cockney commercial traveller, Mr Blanquet, who runs about in a nightgown muttering gibberish to himself; assorted Greenleafs and Arnwoods. Its theme, if it has one, is class-consciousness. Old man Greenleaf, the publican, doesn't want his daughter cavorting with the gentry, because 'People should stick to their own class! . . . We've always known who was who, and which cap fitted which head.' He's angry and bewildered. Peggy Ashcroft's Joan, coping with this, was calm and defiant: 'the swift definition of Joan, speaking in Miss Peggy Ashcroft's every movement and intonation, was a delight,' claimed a reviewer. Jill, in the revival, came off less well. She was more stagey, more actressy. She was out to marry Gerald, and she had a hardness to her. She was also already aristocratic – far too refined to have been born and bred by the publican, who ranted in a broad Cotswolds burr.

This little piece of fluff about pride and prejudice and the disruption of the social scale nevertheless connects with Olivier's conception of himself as an actor; with his suppression of a personal life in favour

* 'I'd just go through fire and water for you. [Crosses to Marion] People are saying all sorts of rotten things about your not living with your husband. I want you to know that if he'll get a divorce I'll marry you – if you'll have me.'

of a pretend life – his full evening dress, full morning dress, plus-fours, sports jacket and blazer, white flannels, shoes, collars and ties which he was expected to buy; his country-house attire, necessary for all those gallants and blades he played. This was all more glamorous than his father's rectory in Letchworth, where the family had moved, from Pimlico, in 1918, or Addington, where Gerard ended up after his remarriage, to Ibo, on 27 January 1924. Gerard had met Ibo, incidentally, when he went on a Mission of Help to Jamaica – where his brother was Governor. It is perhaps to the world of the former lions of his blood, Sydney, Baron Olivier of Ramsden, or Admiral Sir Richard Dacres, or the lords of the manor of Potterne, Wiltshire, or the fact that, before the family were deprived of their wealth and lands in France, after the revocation of the Edict of Nantes in 1685, they held the title 'Sieur d'Olivier', that Olivier aspired. As an actor he could move amongst different social levels with panache – which is what Arnwood, whose forebears have lived in the castle for three hundred years, and Joan, whose ancestors have pulled pints for three hundred years, imply by their wanting to be personally independent of their backgrounds.

Olivier, who every night on stage chastely kissed the shut door of his sweetheart's room, was invited by Eva to spend the weekends with herself and Jill at Appleporch, the Esmond-Moore Edwardian-Jacobean villa near Maidenhead.* Soon, Olivier was calling Eva Mum, and she was forgetting herself and calling Larry Harry, her husband's name. According to her, H. V. 'could put more tenderness, without the least touch of sentimentality, into his words than anyone I've ever heard'; and she tutored Olivier, telling him that acting was, or demanded, 'a humour which was from the heart and spoke to the heart'. Which was interesting and fascinating, but the perspiration mantling his brow during that hot summer had to do with more urgent matters. Instead of romping with Jill, however, he'd go into Hurley church and pray.

Proximity made him propose – and in later life Olivier looked back at his actions with incredulity: 'though not *dazzlingly* attractive, she would most certainly do excellent well for a wife.† I wasn't going to wait for anyone better to come along . . . and I wasn't likely to do any better . . . so I promptly fell in love with her. Being nobody's fool, she did not respond automatically. In fact, she took two years to agree to it and never did really respond at all.' If, in his memoirs, he wanted to make it clear he never loved Jill, and that it had been nothing but an extension

† Telephone number: Hurley 234.
* The sarcastic italics are Olivier's; the line is Petruchio's.

of the role-playing of his Birmingham parts, he appeared to behave sincerely, if impetuously, at the time; and to dismiss Jill as indifferent and cold, and his own devotion as something he'd made up, is simply cruel. (Nauseating and infuriating are other words that spring to mind.) But then, Olivier is not interested in our complicity. What happened is that, such was the effect of Vivien on his life, Olivier couldn't believe his first marriage was of any lasting consequence. He attempted to dismiss it – as, in 1935, he dismissed Jill herself to resettle with Vivien. (In her turn, Vivien would be usurped when he wanted to possess Joan. Olivier's life is a saga of the successive abandonment of women.)

The facts of the matter are that when Jill left for New York in April 1929 – *Bird in Hand* opening at the Booth Theatre or the Ethel Barrymore, sources differ – Oliver wrote to her, and to her mother, virtually hourly ('I'm loving you Jilli darling much better now, and at the moment so oh so much . . .'); and after appearing in a number of West End flops – *Beau Geste, The Circle of Chalk,* and *The Stranger Within* ('Mr Olivier gets out of bad parts all the charm there is in them': Agate) – he on 10 August, and wearing one of his white linen suits, boarded the transatlantic liner *Aquitania,* with the intention of making his Broadway début in *Murder on the Second Floor,* a piece of flapdoodle at the Eltinge that sounds like Drinkwater's play with a plot: Olivier was cast as Hugh Bromilow, a detective novelist who imagines that the guests at his mother's inn are involved in nefarious deeds. He was guaranteed five hundred dollars a week for ten weeks; the curtain was ordered down for good after only a month. What's curious is that he didn't inform Jill that he was on his way or what he was up to. 'I'm awfully glad Larry has another job,' she wrote to Eva, assuming he was in London. Suddenly, there he was, in her dressing room, importunate, calf-eyed. He proposed marriage again; she accepted, so long as she was given plenty of time to mull over the implications. They went out to dinner, exchanged gifts from Tiffany's, and couldn't pay their bill.

Olivier's terseness later, the reason why she became associated in his mind with release and escape (he was released from childhood by marrying her; he escaped into greatness by divorcing her), was because, when they were first associated, Jill was the more successful and authoritative. Indeed, she was bossy; her nickname was 'The Colonel'. 'Larry, this is something you simply must do,' she'd urge – for example, passing him the script of *Journey's End,* which was presented as a one-off by the Stage Society on 10 December 1928. 'You'd be a fool to play Romeo in Gielgud's company. You're all wrong for it,' she barked in 1935. Witnesses describe her as being frank, straightforward, direct, independent – she was not cloying and affected or cunning and charming (like Vivien). 'She had many of his mother's personality qualities,' it was claimed. (A dangerous sign? Was it not her death when he was twelve that maimed him? Was his mother therefore not linked with a *withdrawal* or *loss* of love, respect, and affection?) She had a knowledge of theatre and literature, of the technical aspects of acting; and perhaps she was too much the teacher? Jill was practical and sensible – and brisk – and he resented this. She was slightly superior to him – and the qualities he admired, and needed, in his early twenties, were the ones that drove him from her, when he was no longer faltering sexually, and in charge of himself, and ready to try out Vivien's volubility. (Compared with Jill's eager earnestness, her sceptical and scoffing ways, Vivien, gleaming at him with green eyes, seemed a fascinating free spirit.)

American Equity disallowed any English actor from playing more than one part in any six-month period, so after the closure of *Murder on the Second Floor,* and debarred from joining *Bird in Hand* on its tour to Chicago, Olivier returned to London. '[It was] lovely just standing there, with no one but God and you,' he wrote to Jill from aboard the *Lancastria,* recounting a Romeo-ish moment, leaning over the ship's rail and gazing at the sea. Jill, meantime, was whooping it up in the speak-easies, gushing to Eva that 'all you have to do is to have a white face, full red lips, long earrings and a sad expression and men think you are marvellous'. She was high-spirited; he was melancholy, and played a shell-shocked Royal Flying Corps officer in *The Last Enemy,* opening on 19 December and closing on 15 March 1930. The play 'brought me friendly and timely establishment as a leading character-juvenile,' he said.

It is at this juncture he made a foray into the flicks: *The Temporary Widow,* about an artist who is presumed to have been killed in a faked boating accident by his wife – a ruse to inflate the value of his paintings – and *Too Many Crooks,* in which Olivier appears to be a raffish burglar, but is actually the owner of the house; and it's his tenant, impersonated by A. Bromley Davenport, who is really a spy, that the police are out to snare . . . The picture was shot in four days; the story takes longer than that to explicate. Then there's *Potiphar's Wife,* which was retitled *Her Strange Desire* for the American distribution in 1932. The first two films are capers, wheezes, boffs, which, if I took their minutiae seriously, would set back the art of criticism a hundred years* – but in this latter photoplay his child's vulnerability and tentativeness take on a sexual glow. It is a film about awakenings.

Olivier is Straker, Lady Diana's new chauffeur. His skin has such a softness and delicacy, there's no blood circulating in it. His eyes are made up like a girl's, and his moustache is the narrowest black wisp; but there's no mistaking his masculinity, nor his dignity. He has a self-sufficiency, a vividness, that's out of key with the other inmates of the servants' hall – Matthew Boulton's supercilious butler, genteelly misconstruing his vowels, or Elsa Lanchester as the face-pulling French maid. Olivier looks at his colleagues and employers with amusement and slight disdain. The only things he seems to trust unconditionally are motor cars – and there are many adoring shots of purring engines, spinning chromium spokes, revolving white-wall tyres, El Morocco upholstery, and gleaming black coachwork with silver handles. As in *The Betsy*, here's a homage to grace and power – Olivier's, which limousines, technically perfect and lustrous, symbolize.

Lady Diana is one of those bejewelled cat-lady vamps that survived from the silent-movie era, and who were inspired by the pseudo-biblical bitches of the nineties: Salome, Delilah, Bathsheba. (Scarlett O'Hara is of their kind.) Nora Swinburne, who plays her, like those other pyrogenic vamps who ignited the silver nitrate, Theda Bara, say, or Gloria Swanson, has swept in from a Beardsley drawing or a Conder painting, and her intentions are gorgeous and dishonourable. She exists for her own pleasure, and Lord Branford, her elderly husband, perhaps knowing you'll not chain down Catherine the Great, tacitly condones her flings. She justifies her adulteries by claiming, 'I've kept my side of the bargain – I've entertained his friends, agreed with his politics'; and this could all make for a silly farce, except that you do feel her loneliness and boredom – the anxious sensations she has about her behaviour. We sympathize with her because Olivier does; we are pitying because he is. 'The more I see of her the more I like her,' he murmurs, guilelessly heeding her nocturnal call to fix a lamp.

The film sets out to be a comedy; and it has the trappings of a

* Olivier, whose family came from France, is the century's greatest Englishman (next to Churchill), and it is mildly ironic that his first film was therefore made in Berlin. *The Temporary Widow* was simultaneously shot as *Hokuspokus*, with Willi Fritsch, Gustav Grundgens, and Oscar Homolka doubling for Olivier, Felix Aylmer, and Athole Stewart. Lilian Harvey was the wife in both English and German versions. Making the picture bred one nice anecdote: Olivier was meant to meet Jill at the *Kunsthalle*, and for some reason he asked his driver to take him to the *Fuchshalle* by mistake.

comedy. Events unfold in a jazz-moderne mansion where thin women smoke cigarettes and chumpish chaps mix drinks in cocktail shakers. 'They got the morals of monkeys,' the butler says, and soon Straker knows what's meant. He's at the wheel whilst milady cavorts in the back seat with a potential lover – and later, both her husband and the lover being absent (possibly, bedevilled relentlessly, they've slipped off to join a circus), she summons the chauffeur ('Quite an attractive fellow') to her boudoir. 'I hope it doesn't make you feel embarrassed, my being here,' she says, swishing in satin up and down the carpet, wearing out the pile. She puffs at her monogrammed cigarette holder; she sprays herself with musk; she ogles and sways orgiastically. Straker gives polite, noncommittal replies to her questions. He refuses to meet her gaze – he knows he is being watched, fancied, ravished by her glare. 'Why are you always so reserved, Straker?' she asks, breathing hard. 'Reserved?' 'There's a queer fascination about you, Straker.'

If ever a lad received the come-on, it's here and now. Lady Diana is like Lady Chatterley, choking for a rub-down and service, and Straker won't glimpse her bloomers or succumb to kissing her for ages. When he does do so, she drops her cigarette case and the slim white tubes spill across the floor. 'Oh my dear, we live in such different worlds,' he says – like the mismatched barmaid and squire in *Bird in Hand*, or Heathcliff and Cathy, or Darcy and Elizabeth, or the parson's son and ex-chorister at Appleporch. When Lady Diana retorts that class and social station is not at issue, he sees it's only sex, and he's being used, and he wants to walk out – and she won't let him. 'It'll be your word against mine,' she hisses. She accuses *him* of having a dash at *her*.

It's at this point that the narrative sours ('This man forced his way in here!'), and whilst Straker is getting arrested on a charge of criminal assault and Lady Diana is (a) remorseful and wanting to deny her accusations, except (b) how can she go back on what she told the police, so (c) she squares her false alibis with the French maid and a house-guest, I had leisure to reflect on the qualities of the foregoing sequence, its crackle of sexual frustration. When he is summoned to re-fix the lamp, this time Straker scowls at her. He knows her mind, and he won't be possessed or kept. Nora Swinburne languishing on the bed amongst furs white enough to give you snow blindness; Olivier intent with the cables and plugs on the other side of the room: it is a long, silent scene, in which the man is keeping the woman at bay. Olivier has a reticence, a soft luxuriance; but it's not passivity. His eyes always burn with a hard, gem-like flame. His brain was tireless – and what's registering here is his very own attitude to romantic love, which he sustained with Jill. For whilst Jill was trying to enjoy herself and be social, Oliver cultivated a posture of exclusion, fretting about his 'mental battles' over wanting to marry her; and he writes to her from the Green Room Club that 'I'm a bloody fool ever to have them, but they just happen like a very well laid plan before I know where I am . . . Still I'm getting better – and happier than I was.' Olivier takes refuge in religious qualms; he can't abide the idea of pre-marital sex, but he's tormented by the knowledge that he's missing out.

The last reel of *Potiphar's Wife* contains the trial. Lady Diana perjures herself, saying she made no overtures, and Straker is silent in the dock – an image of suffering, wronged innocence. Surrounded by shuffling, muttering barristers, he's bewildered, as a child might be, by the world's nuances, subtlety, slyness. But most of all, what shows in his face (he has no dialogue – he's as silent as a painting) is that he doesn't like his accuser's humiliations – what she is doing to herself with her lies. (Olivier makes the scene poignant.) Straker's defence hangs on why the chambermaid was not present on the fateful evening; did Lady Diana pack Elsa Lanchester off to look after the house-guest? 'You deliberately got your maid out of the way that night so that you could be alone with my client . . .' She breaks down and confesses; it is a front-page sensation, a society scandal – though we don't go on to see the effects of any disgrace. Nor do we hear from the chauffeur again. He drifts out through the crowds surging from the public gallery – and that sexual allure, which will infatuate the heroines of *As You Like It, Fire Over England, Wuthering Heights, Pride and Prejudice, Rebecca, That Hamilton Woman* . . . goes with him.

Olivier was a thing of beauty who became a thing of power. Erotic when arresting his eroticism, his kings, generals, princes, often hold themselves back; they are reserved; they are firm and commanding and self-possessed. They have set purposes, as he did: 'I want to get out, I'm going to get out, when I get out of this . . . I'm going to be a simply smashing actor' – by conquering Hollywood; conquering the London and New York stage; conquering television; by founding and running the National Theatre ('I looked around as honestly as I could and thought I was the fellow with the best sort of experience to start the thing going'). What humiliated him about his first marriage was his uncharacteristic confusion of motives: 'I had insisted on getting married from a pathetic mixture of religious and animal promptings.' He felt the self-disgust, the wretchedness, that Straker had avoided. But worse than this, in requiring Jill and Eva for his career, in marrying out of expedience, he was exposing the nature and scope of his ambition and need for supremacy; and on his wedding day he was the least distinguished person present.

The plan had been to hold the service at the Chapel Royal of the Savoy, where Eva and H. V. had been hitched. ('This did not strike me as being the most felicitous of omens,' said Olivier later.) Gerard, however, with comic high-handedness, and maximizing his son's embarrassment, vetoed the scheme – 'it is known that divorced people are able to be married there' – and the nuptials were rescheduled at All Saints, taking place on 25 July 1930. Father Mackay officiated; Olivier's former choir did the singing – and it was quite a society function. Photographers were present from the *Tatler* and the guests included Jack Hawkins, Ralph Richardson, Sybil Thorndike, C. Aubrey Smith, Ivor Novello, Gladys Cooper and Nöel Coward. A gift of black pearls was received from Princess Marie-Louise, grand-daughter of Queen Victoria. Olivier gave his bride a green octagonal bloodstone ring, mounted on a gold girdle-effect band, inscribed *Sicut Oliva Virens*: as flourishing as the olive tree – the family motto.* Jill continued to wear it until her dying day.

The honeymoon, at Lulworth Cove, was a catastrophe. They had been loaned a house by a friend of Eva's; and Eva's friends were still stubbornly in residence. The newly-weds made up a foursome for card games. 'We all four sort of hummed and hawed and didn't know what to say,' reported the groom, who slithered away to write letters to – of all people – his mother-in-law: 'Hello Darling Mum . . . Mum darling . . . O Mum darling . . .'; and of Jill he commented 'I think she is fairly happy.' She was not. She had an ovarian cyst which put her off hanky-panky. Olivier, misunderstanding her coolness, ever afterwards believed that this was a tacit confession that she didn't love him particularly. As his hopes of marriage were 'nothing more commendable than a convenient passport for a rush into bed', he was at a crisis point in his young life. He recalls that on their wedding night, after a few clumsy fondles, they turned their backs on each other in disgust.

It was the end of innocence. The shock of real sexual experience had been exacerbated by his fear of failure – or, as he'd see it, his desire to be perfect. His anxieties killed off religion for him. He'd stayed within its tenets, and it had let him down; nor could he now document himself, look at himself (literally: he accidentally shaved off half his moustache by not squinting in the mirror). 'From this wedding day I kept no diary

* From Psalm 52, verse 8: *Sicut oliva virens laetor in aede Dei*: just as the flourishing olive tree, so do I rejoice in the house of God.

for ten years, and did not pursue my religious practices ever again.' The consequences of his bungled marital consummation are connected. He didn't wish to record events – or to be accountable, by logging his deeds and perceptions; he didn't want any reckoning. He required invisibility. An emptiness had overtaken him – a desire for oblivion – and henceforward there'd be an eradication of a private life – a real life – and art would come first. There'd be a single-minded devotion to work (at the expense, eventually, of family).* He recoiled from intimacy in his relationships, and in a sense he compensated for this by being erotic in his acting. 'He did not exude sex appeal, at least not to me,' says Lauren Bacall. 'Privately, he was not the imposing figure of grandeur that he was in the theatre . . . He was a somewhat shy and serious man. It's a funny thing about sex appeal. When I see Larry now in *Wuthering Heights, Rebecca, Pride and Prejudice* . . . he exudes sex, passion, romance. Knowing him, I never saw it. I saw other things. He clearly saved that other side for work.' He had a sexuality and attractiveness when performing – but that power was not there in reality: the small penis, the knotted prepuce, the sterile testicle, the premature ejaculation ('dreaded weakness').

Olivier claimed, 'I married badly'; in fact, he'd married unrealistically. His courtship rituals were like a continuation of childhood – he was conducting a pure, idealized romance, like Peter Pan and Wendy; and he was still dependent on a mother figure (Eva – who organized the furnishings and décor at the matrimonial home, 13 Roland Gardens, SW7). Jill was more practical. Two months prior to the off at All Saints, she'd offered her opinions on 'What I Think of Marriage' to a newspaper:† 'Victorian girls must have looked forward to marriage as a partial escape from a domestic cage,' she said. 'Today marriage is in some ways more like an entrance into a cage.' Any prospective bridegroom reading this – but especially the high-strung Olivier – would at the very least have felt crestfallen. But it wasn't that Jill was expecting marriage to be (as it turned out to be with Vivien) a battle of the sexes that alarmed him; nor that she hoped to avoid (as Vivien did not) the submission and/or dominance imbalance of most matches. What alarmed him is that she wanted marriage to be a partnership, with the husband and wife treating each other as equals – treating each other with courteous respect and distance. 'I should certainly have secrets and

* 'I now make a big effort to spend time with my son,' Richard Olivier told *The Independent* on 29 April 1996. 'When I can't see him I tell him I miss him. My father never said that so in the void I heard: "I prefer my work to you."'

† *Daily Herald*, 30 May 1930.

friends unknown to a husband of mine, and I should sometimes have a holiday from him as well as from work.'

It is a modern attitude: marriage as a social contract; and in the face of Olivier's pleadings and beseechings and prayers, she was attempting not to be expected to dissolve her identity and forsake her independence. She didn't want marriage to be a clinging, a leeching; nor did she expect or want to subjugate her ego to his.* She'd even answer her future husband back. If he rebuked her she'd say, 'Oh, pack it up, mate. I've heard enough of your rot.' Jill was more famous than he was; she was earning more than he was (in a play called *Nine Till Six*); he resented this and, two months after the wedding, he, too, spoke out publicly: 'Only fools are happy. I suppose it is because they don't really know what they want in life, and so every little pleasure that comes along they regard as a paradise of happiness. I somehow can't get away with that. I always examine things so very closely that immediate pleasures are dwarfed by my insistence on ultimate benefits.'†

The ultimate benefit of holy matrimony, instituted of God to signify the mystical union that is betwixt Christ and his Church, having left him distraught, Olivier took umbrage at his first alliance; at the disappointments of heterosexuality. 'You see how soon the day o'er cast,' he sighed archly.‡ Yet a saviour was set to appear, in a puff of hand-sewn genuine Chinese shantung silk: 'The Great God Coward!' (as he'd signed himself in Jill's first edition of *Hay Fever*). He was an Esmond/Moore family friend, and it was at Jill's insistence that Olivier put himself forward as a potential Victor Prynne in the première of *Private Lives*. 'The part's no good . . . [and] Noël's offer smacks too much of charity,' he complained. 'Rubbish,' said Jill. 'Noël wants you for it. You're an actor aren't you? How can you pass up an opportunity to work with Noël? It's sure to be a success. You'll learn so much from Noël.'

---

* Jill's matrimonial philosophy was further adumbrated in *The New Movie Magazine*, September 1932: 'I know that we will never be divorced. Because we've talked about it, about everything. We know that we'll be attracted to other men and women, respectively. But we have determined that, no matter what happens, no matter what the difficulty or what the temptation, we won't let it break us. *We're too good for that* – that's our slogan. I don't mean that we're too good morally, or too good as individuals. I mean that we are too good *together*. We mean too much together. We have too much value together and too much to do.'

Exhume Jill, and you'd find these words engraved on her heart. It is precisely the presumption of *togetherness* that Olivier would flinch from.

† *Evening Chronicle*, 13 September 1930.

‡ *Richard III*, III, ii – a reference to the lords who journeyed heedlessly to Pomfret Castle, without knowing the chop lay in store for them.

Coward entered Olivier's orbit as a parody of paternalism. He insisted he should appear in *Private Lives* ('Look, young man, you'd better be in a success for a change'); he cured him of corpsing ('much the same dreaded weakness as premature ejaculation'); he advised him to go to Hollywood ('you could make millions'); and Olivier was still deferring to him a quarter of a century later, as for example after the first night of *Titus Andronicus* at Stratford. There was a reception at Michael Denison's house, attended by John and Mary Mills, Mr and Mrs Ernest Hartley (Vivien's parents), and Emlyn Williams. Olivier told a long-winded anecdote and kept looking at Coward, playing to Coward, and he was relieved and pleased at getting his laughter. 'Larry,' said Dulcie Gray, 'you were watching Noël all the time you were telling that story. Does it really matter to you if Noël laughs or not?' 'Certainly, Noël was my first leading man and the gap never lessens.'

Indeed, Coward would always be seven years Olivier's senior; he would always be the tutelary genius who 'took hold of me and made me think; he made me use my silly little brain. He taxed me with his sharpness and shrewdness and his brilliance; he used to point out when I was talking nonsense, which nobody else had done before.' He was like a father – and he was like a wife. 'If one of these is intercepted,' commented Joan Plowright, of the effusive letters and wires which continued to flow back and forth, 'you will both be arrested.' Coward consolidated what Jill, and her social connections, had begun, introducing him into a glamorous world of luncheons, first nights and supper parties, where he'd mix with Dickie and Edwina, Rex and Lilli, Charlie and Oona. 'You can never live too well, my dears,' Coward announced. 'When you live well people want to know you.' He gave Olivier and Jill a sofa for Roland Gardens; he was instrumental in their move to 74 Cheyne Walk, with its sixty-foot-long drawing room rising to the second storey; the white furnishings; the – nice decadent touch – ring-tailed lemur on a golden chain. Here the Oliviers entertained Shaw and Barrie.

Manners and control: these were the virtues Coward imparted, the examples he set. (Though this didn't stop the master and the boy he was mad about pelting each other with chocolate mousse in the dining car of the London North-Eastern Pullman, bound for Edinburgh, in August 1930.) The actor Robert Harris, who had been a fellow understudy nonentity in *The Marvellous History of St Bernard*, four years previously, recalls seeing Olivier walking along the Haymarket, and suddenly here was this elegant, manicured, groomed West End star, 'obviously very much influenced by Noël Coward'. The apparition also appeared to

Anthony Quayle in Chelsea – this time Olivier was accompanied by a pair of schnauzers on leads.

It's frightfully camp, all this. Homosexuals were always to be ambivalent about Olivier. Kenneth Williams made the effort to write to Joe Orton in Tangier and tell him, 'Olivier has prostate trouble. All this taking up fucking at such an advanced age, I expect!'* He himself found the subject, or the tendencies rippling and flexing within himself, the source of profound guilt and dread: 'I felt that the homosexual act would be a step darkly destructive to my soul.' Does this mean he stopped short of the full monty, i.e. sodomy? That he'd go as far as winky-wanky-woo? That he'd have none of it – not any of it? His memoirs are mind-crunchingly obscure on the subject: 'I had got over like a spendthrift sigh my nearly passionate involvement with the one male with whom some sexual dalliance had not been loathsome for me to contemplate.' The reference is to Coward, who insisted on nude bathing when Olivier and Jill accompanied him on holiday; and on one occasion Noëlie held Larry-boy down and shaved his pubes: 'That's much better, don't you think?' Coward was Tarquin's godfather, and was disappointed that his charge was not queer – 'Not even a little bit?' Olivier, hearing of this interrogation, which took place at Notley, cross-examined his son. 'Are you sure you said no?' 'Yes, of course. Why?' 'He can be very persuasive.' 'Did he persuade you?' 'Christ, no. But he tried, when I was much younger. I've never been queer.'†

---

* 'I'm glad he's had something wrong with his prostate ... Perhaps now he'll release Plowright from childbearing. She's going to be a great actress one day.' (Orton in his diary, for 3 July 1967.)

I'm not certain she's a *great* actress; but it is a shame Orton did not live to see her become a camp one – e.g. the Yugoslav accent in *I Love You to Death*; or the way she mocks Olivier's legend in *Last Action Hero* – where she's a schoolmarm teaching *Hamlet*. She shows a clip from Olivier's film, and explains that Olivier will be known to her class as the star of the Polaroid commercials and as Zeus in *Clash of the Titans*. We see the scene where Hamlet fails to stab Claudius because he's at prayer, and suddenly Arnold Schwarzenegger bursts through a stained-glass window. The spoof of the Olivier *Hamlet* is, in fact, expensively, stylishly, done: Furse's sets; the silvery costumes. It is snappily edited. The joke, really, is not Arnie's gung-ho Dane, hurling Claudius off the battlements, and Elsinore exploding; it's that Olivier's prince should have done these violent things. Olivier was *not* Prince Hamlet; nor was he ever meant to be.

† Everybody asks me: What about Danny Kaye? An ingenious homuncule, an American academic in all probability, examined the guest register at Notley, travel plans, engagement books, cast lists for charity concerts, etc., and bruited it abroad that, because Olivier and the star of The *Secret Life of Walter Mitty* had, over the years, shared the same table or dressing room, they were therefore/thus/hence clandestine lovers. This is what we might call the Falconer Syndrome, after a dotty scholar who once picked his way through the

Olivier transmitted signals, only to cancel them, with his hard, masculine, derisive power; his hard, cold fury; his cold, hard mouth. Coward said of *Richard III* that it was 'the greatest male performance I have ever seen in the theatre'; and his praise, in his diaries, was consistent and selfless. 'He is a superb actor and I suspect the greatest I shall ever see' (11 October 1946, on Lear); 'it was one of those rare magical evenings in the theatre when the throat contracts, the eyes fill with sudden tears, and there is nothing to say afterwards but abandoned, superlative praise ... Larry rose and shone and dominated and swept the whole evening into another realm' (7 August 1955, on Macbeth).

Olivier told Robert Helpmann, who told Kenneth Williams (who put it in *his* diary), 'I'm sorry to say this in front of you, Cocky, but I don't think there is any place in the theatre for queers.'* I can see what he means. The point of Olivier's art is his fertility; his ecstasy. The point of his performances is their moral bearing. He went in for a good deal of feyness, kissing, mincing, and luvvy self-obsession – 'perhaps I should tell you that his epistolary style was not given to understatement, either in saying what he felt or in the affectionate warmth with which he addressed his friends,' said Christopher Fry, handing over a bundle

---

complete works of Shakespeare, underlining words, images, references, what have you, related to the sea – water, raft, fish, mast, etc. – and wrote a tome, for which he received tenure, at the University of St Andrews, arguing conclusively that the bard was a fully qualified professional sailor, up there with Nelson and Mr Midshipman Hornblower. (*A Glossary of Shakespeare's Sea and Naval Terms including Gunnery*, by A. F. Falconer, Constable & Co., London, 1965.) Nonsense, of course. Having fine-tooth-combed the texts myself, I can inform you that, such is the profusion of information on crowns, sceptres, majesty, coronations and the problems of succession, Shakespeare was actually a king – or, more to the purpose, a queen.

* Helpmann took his revenge by spreading the rumour that he'd slept with both Olivier *and* Vivien, and 'Of course, you know, Larry's got a *very* small cock.' Yet, in being a trifle high-minded about all this, I can't help wondering: to what extent was Olivier ever really *pretending* to be an *iron hoof*? Because let's face it, in the acting profession, and in the arts in England (and in politics: there are over eighty homosexual Members of Partliament), it is practically impossible to become successful, or to garner honours, if you are too exclusively heterosexual. (Helpmann was knighted in 1968.) It is a conspiracy – as bad as anti-Semitism. Literary editors, television producers, theatre critics, publishers, opera, ballet, museum curating: domains all controlled by the 'hoofs. (Ackerley, Acton, Agate, Albee, Ashton, Auden, at the front of the alphabet alone.) And it is the case that Olivier's career and legend impinge on not only the theatrical but the social history of our century; and this, together with the distinction between sincerity and authenticity, is a subject in itself: think of All Souls; the influence of Sparrow; the hard-to-credit immunity from prosecution of Driberg; the business of Blunt and Burgess, where homosexuality, the arts of concealment and the thrill of espionage overlap. You can see that there are moral principles at work, pertaining to the masks of vice and virtue.

of his letters* – but this was part of his physicality and flirtatiousness; the way he wanted people to respond to him at once. The pretence of intimacy is related to his suits and spectacles, his deathly pale face, when he was running the National: it's a carapace; Olivier is playing possum, like T. S. Eliot, who'd disguise himself as an accountant or a Faber & Faber grandee. We must remember the extent of theatre's homosexual mafia – H. M. Tennent; Hugh ('Binkie') Beaumont; the Ivy restaurant; Rattigan, with his beautiful clothes, a Rolls, exquisite courteousness (and behind that the emotional distress); the Royal Court – Tony Richardson: 'I'm looking for a new rough theatre.' John Dexter: 'What you're looking for, Tony, is new rough trade.' In the theatre, the bounds of what is sexually accepted are further off than for the rest of the world, though Vivien, too, seems created by homosexual tastes. Her carefully applied make-up and locks of hair – primped and tonged and lacquered and flossed and teased and frizzed – provoke no lust. When I watch *Gone with the Wind*, she's like a parody of a great beauty: the over-sculpted profile, the clenched buttocks, the waist which is too trim, and her voice! Shrill and elocutionary, and faintly patronizing, like an old-fashioned presenter of children's programmes. Her exaggerations; her crystalline image: was she aware of having to send herself up? It's like female impersonation, belonging in the homosexual hall of fame alongside Marlene, Judy, Mae, Bette, Greta; and it is no surprise Olivier didn't want her for Ophelia, Cathy, Lady Anne, Princess Katherine, or the second Mrs de Winter; nor that in the end he'd find Joan Plowright, forthright and downright, and with haymaker's arms, more appealing and natural.

Homosexuality is a mockery of nature; Olivier's duty was through acting to try and control nature. Though he infiltrated a web of abnormality and nonconformity – rousing and flattering and making people think of him as their fantasy lover – he was actually withdrawing, displacing, disappearing; and the powers he always had to change himself made him a warlock. John Gielgud has confessed that 'Larry was rather frightening at times. He had a very dark side'; and Cecil Beaton, commissioned in the winter of 1947 to design the sets and hats and frocks for *The School for Scandal*, claimed that 'The Oliviers [were] rather grudging in their generosity and I fear they are not good friends behind my back.' (To Garbo he waspishly maintained, in November 1950, 'They aren't real friends of mine though they may now pretend to be.') Charles

* 'Dearest Kit . . . oh, my darling boy . . . My dearest Kit, Forgive, please, my wicked silence . . . and take my throbbing New Year's love . . .' etc.

Laughton was similarly disparaged by Olivier – though to his face, not behind his back. 'We got on quite splendidly,' Olivier is quoted as saying, about *Spartacus*, in Simon Callow's biography, 'though I was a bit distressed at what I considered to be his discourtesies on the set [i.e. Laughton's clandestine improvements of the script with Ustinov], and told him so.' In the event, Olivier could only master his own dialogue if Laughton was not present – he genuinely couldn't bear the sight of him. It was a clash of temperaments – and it is little wonder that Olivier refused to direct him as Lear at Stratford in 1959: 'I really did not believe that he and I would get on . . . I never felt on quite the same level as he.'

Michael Redgrave, who was only sporadically in the vagina business, was another object of pity and terror, whose sexuality traduced the classics. 'I once saw Michael Redgrave have the courage to do Richard II as an out-and-out pussy queer, with mincing gestures to match. But there comes a time when Shakespeare says . . . "You can drop all that and become St George like everybody else, can't you." And that's what you have to do.' Olivier – teased? perplexed? tormented? – Redgrave by making appointments for him at colonic irrigation clinics. When Redgrave joined the National, Olivier was an outright bully, accusing him of alcoholism when Redgrave's forgetfulness was in fact the onset of Parkinson's Disease. 'As the taxi crossed Waterloo Bridge I would begin to tremble,' he recalled, terrified that each evening he'd dry as Solness – a role Olivier took over with ill grace. (Redgrave couldn't bring himself to go and see his replacement.) Olivier was particularly dismissive during the rehearsals for *Hamlet* in 1963 – 'When you came on as Macbeth, it was as if you were saying, "Fuck you, I am Macbeth." As Claudius you are *dim*' – and his very worst insult was to say a performance reminded him of Gielgud: 'Very good, Michael. But loud echoes of Sir John. Very loud echoes.'

As Olivier told Tynan, 'I've never thought of myself as quite the same actor as he is, not the same sort of actor . . . John, all spiritual, all spirituality . . . and myself . . . all earth, blood, humanity.' Gielgud: airy-fairy; Olivier: reality – or, what is actually meant by the discrimination: Olivier is a heterosexual artist. He was to acting what William Walton, who scored his Shakespeare films, was to music. They share the same force, power, lyricism, fire, suspense – they assault the senses, to produce (as Olivier said of the tunes for *As You Like It*) 'the most gutsy bash and crash and bang you have ever heard in your life'.

Walton was the protégé of the homosexual Sitwells; they championed him as Coward did Olivier.* It was Coward who suggested Olivier and his wife to Gertrude Lawrence, his *Private Lives* co-star, as supporting players in *No Funny Business* – a photoplay so rare, no mention of it is made in many of the reference books and memoirs of the period. It's like a Noël Coward play without Noël Coward: the Côte d'Azur locale, with the obligatory moonlight on the patio; the sumptuous Art Deco hotel suites; those shape-clinging period cocktail gowns, which emphasize curves (especially the women's boyish bottoms); compartments in a steam train racing across Europe; bittersweet songs at the white baby grand – 'No funny business – or else – we'll say good-byee!' – and brittle dialogue like this: 'Oh darling, I've been a little beast to you, haven't I?' 'No. [Squeeze-kiss-pause] Go on being a little beast.' Olivier and Jill, as Clive Dering and Ann Moore, are employees of a shady agency that provides professional co-respondents for couples seeking a divorce. There's an atmosphere of prostitution – of a gigolo or hustler's despair – about the proceedings. Ann puts an ad in the paper: 'Young lady urgently requires work. Will go anywhere – do anything. No funny business.' Clive, too, like Hurstwood in *Carrie,* is down on his uppers: 'I'll do anything, so long as it's decent.' Olivier gives a quick, sharp emphasis to that last word, ever so slightly spitting it out with contempt – and it's a self-contempt he is registering, for here are characters asking to be used, to be abased.

A number of Olivier's early films, dealing with adultery, lust and lechery, are surprisingly amoral; or, shall we say, not conspicuously didactic or preachy. In *The Divorce of Lady X,* he gives one of his capering performances, and in court as a barrister, his wig seems curiously fluffy: he's an eighteenth-century fop, teletransported to modern London. Relishing the rhetoric of his closing speeches to judge and jury, he's sure of himself and cocky; and the joy of the film is seeing Olivier trip himself up – lapse – over a woman. His knight-errantry – his purity – comes under attack when Merle Oberon's Leslie Steele flirts with and tries to seduce him. The town is fog-bound, hotels are full, and Merle wants Olivier's suite – but her exploitation seems more comprehensive than that. This is a film about honour, betrayal, and innocence traduced – it's a medieval tale – and Olivier, immaculately dressed, beguiling and agile, shows the dilemma of a man who wants to follow his natural instincts (for fucky-fucky), yet he must obey the letter of the law, with its cunning and retribution. (He mistakenly believes that Leslie is Lady

* To Coward, Edith, Osbert and Sacheverell were known as Hernia, Gob and Sago Whittlebot.

Mere, i.e. his client's unfaithful wife. Owing to the hotel room confusion, he, the barrister, might be named as co-respondent.)

Olivier is clenched and mannered – an ideal combination for farce. But as we watch his character's increasing impatience and discomfiture, little can assuage our difficulty with the ugliness – the pulpy face, the plucked eyebrows, the simpering and boring pop-eyed girlishness – of Merle Oberon, who is similarly hopeless as Cathy, in *Wuthering Heights*. Olivier, as when he is Heathcliff, has a courtliness that is self-contained; he's on his own with his romantic agony. So perhaps it isn't actually Merle Oberon's fault or lack? Perhaps no one could counter Olivier's need to be solitary? His independence was such, he was not really wanting to be bound by any permanent relationship.

Like *Carrie*, or *That Hamilton Woman*, *The Divorce of Lady X* and *No Funny Business* are about sexual conflicts and the pleasures of transgression – with Olivier, the man, as the object of desire being pursued. My problems with Merle are anticipated by reservations about Jill – who, in *No Funny Business* (or *Professional Co-Respondents*, as it was baldly retitled for the American market in 1934), has a curious grin and a toothy way of talking. She also has no neck, flat black hair, and a scolding delivery that is meant (I assume) to be breezily confident. She and Olivier arrive in Cannes, as clients of Gertie Lawrence and her cumbersome fool of a husband, identified in the credits as one Edmond Breon. Gertie and Edmond aren't aware that they have set traps to monitor each other's peccadilloes; they aren't aware of their mutual mistrust, or that they each want a divorce. Meantime, Jill and Olivier mistake themselves for their employers, who are anxious to plant 'proof' of adultery, and they have dinner in their regal hotel room and put on shows of affection before the waiters – and of course it starts not to be the staged affair they assume they are being paid to give. 'I was sincere,' says Olivier, with a snap of surprise, as they dance on the terrace, stroll hand in hand, and kiss just prior to a discreet fast-fade.

Is this like the real Jill (or Vivien, or Joan), who couldn't quite trust Olivier, or know when his acting began and ended? For, the next morning, at the breakfast table, Ann is a bit shrewish, accusing Clive of giving a 'convincing performance' the previous evening; and he tries to say it began as a performance, but as the shadows lengthened, the champagne was drunk, and the music played on, 'things were entirely different'. They declare undying love, though Ann remains sceptical: 'Still if it wasn't real, it was quite entertaining.' She's never certain about where she stands with him; there's an element of fakery in his spotless courtesy and charm – and when he rushes through a door, expecting to embrace her, and it's Gertie, for a moment he *doesn't notice.* 'There's been a slight misunderstanding,' murmurs Miss Lawrence's Yvonne Kane, and he's attractive to her. Olivier interests women – Jill's Ann can't stop glancing at him, he's so lovely – and yet there's a part of himself inside, suggested by the reticence, which nobody can get at, which he won't yield. This is very important. Not even Olivier's wives could ever lay claim to it. He found it essential to protect his privacy in the end – Vivien was desperate to penetrate it, and it drove her mad. Olivier was like Othello, who pleads with Desdemona to 'leave me but a little to myself', and there was an element of domination in his apparent submissiveness. In the spring of 1931, for example, Coward and Jill arranged Olivier's contract with RKO, for seven hundred dollars a week; but it was Olivier who eventually insisted on returning to England, ruining Jill's chances of stardom in *Bill of Divorcement.* As Olivier told it later, Selznick all along had planned to give the role, of the ambidextrously named Sydney Fairchild, to Katharine Hepburn; he was saving Jill from disgrace and disappointment, by not allowing her to linger in Hollywood failing to land a role she felt she'd been promised. Other sources suggest Selznick genuinely intended Jill to 'hit it big'. Did Olivier not want his wife to succeed? Or did he want her beside him in London, when he returned to the stage? Eva, his mother-in-law, never forgave him for encouraging Jill to give up her hope for the film – though was it a backhanded compliment, if he deemed her a rival? We should remember how he reacted when Vivien won the Academy Award for *Gone With the Wind.* He looked at her, at the statuette, and 'it was all I could do to restrain myself from hitting her with it. I was insane with jealousy.' Or his remark to Michael Redgrave, when he and Joan Plowright were to receive prizes from the *Evening Standard,** which Olivier decreed should be handed over in their dressing rooms and not at a grand reception: 'I don't really approve of awards for actors unless I'm receiving them.'

Olivier would bend the world to his will. As *Private Lives* closed in New York (Jill having replaced Adrianne Allen as Sybil), after thirty-two weeks in Times Square, it was that transitional period when the silents were becoming the talkies, and English voices were recruited from Broadway to work in California: Laughton, Claude Raines, Cary Grant, Basil Rathbone. Olivier and Jill lived sybaritically at 8856 and 8945

* 1963: Best Performance by an Actor – Michael Redgrave in *Uncle Vanya.* A National Theatre Production at the Old Vic Theatre. Best Performance by an Actress – Joan Plowright in *St Joan.*

Appian Way, in Santa Monica – palazzos built into the cliff, from which they could view the grid map on the Los Angeles streets disappearing way into the distant plain, like fields neatly subdivided by twinkling rivers – and he made a series of films which have been overtaken by the ravages of time – *The Yellow Ticket, Friends and Lovers, Westward Passage* – and worked with twilit legends like Lili Damita, Elissa Landi, Adolphe Menjou and Erich von Stroheim, of whom Olivier said: 'To appear ultra-sinister, he was to wear a black patch over one eye and a monocle over the other . . . Years later when I saw him in *Sunset Boulevard,* it occurred to me that he was very much like that in real life – the fallen giant of the silent era, dazed by his fall.'

Olivier, however, was in no mood to enjoy the crepuscular gothic – the camp – of vintage Hollywood. He hated the inactivity;* he grew bored with the parties and practical jokes ('a wild, wild place in those days', he said in 1976 of Hollywood in the thirties – though, in retrospect, Olivier seems to have been the victim of the tomfoolery: his seriousness asked to be sent up and he was not naturally a member of a gang); and in what I've seen of his work from this era, Olivier is a variation of Victor Prynne, from *Private Lives.* He has a frivolity, with a sombre inside. He is scamping around, in a panic – though he is still sharp – and then there are the quiet moments, when he holds a line or a glance, which are almost out of key, but which suggest the actor he was to become. Why, then, did Garbo remove Olivier from *Queen Christina,* and humiliate him publicly by recasting the role (of Don Antonio de la Prada, the dashing Spanish ambassador) with John Gilbert, her partner from the silent days? Olivier tried to tell it as a funny story:

* The doldrums are recorded in a home movie, and given that Olivier would win Oscars for Best Actor, Best Picture, and in 1979, a special Academy Award for 'his unique achievement and for a lifetime contribution to the art of film', it is heartening to note that his Standard-8s are as tedious and amateurish – camera jerks, jump cuts, people mugging and being self-conscious and boring – as any perpetrated by the rest of us: Olivier himself diving again and again into a pool and swimming underwater, like a Hockney model; Olivier and Jill on the promenade deck of a ship; Noël Coward mouthing an expletive and flashing the V-sign; Raymond Massey in striped dressing gown; Douglas Fairbanks Jr twirling his moustache, etc. For all that they are actors they smirk into the lens like ordinary people do. There's even a holiday home movie extant, the scenes interspersed with typed captions: *Nassau Bound* – 'Our boat', 'Captain Brown', 'Hogg Island', 'Noël and Jack', 'A barracuda!', 'A strike! and it's a marlin!' – this followed by close-ups of Olivier winding the fish in, his muscles taut as it struggles. He then ropes his quarry down on the deck, and we notice its huge sad eye as the carcass is winched aloft and Olivier poses next to it. Bronzed, with black curly hair, Olivier is a pirate boy, whom we also see in a white shirt and black shorts building a fire on a beach (the last caption: 'Farewell Nassau').

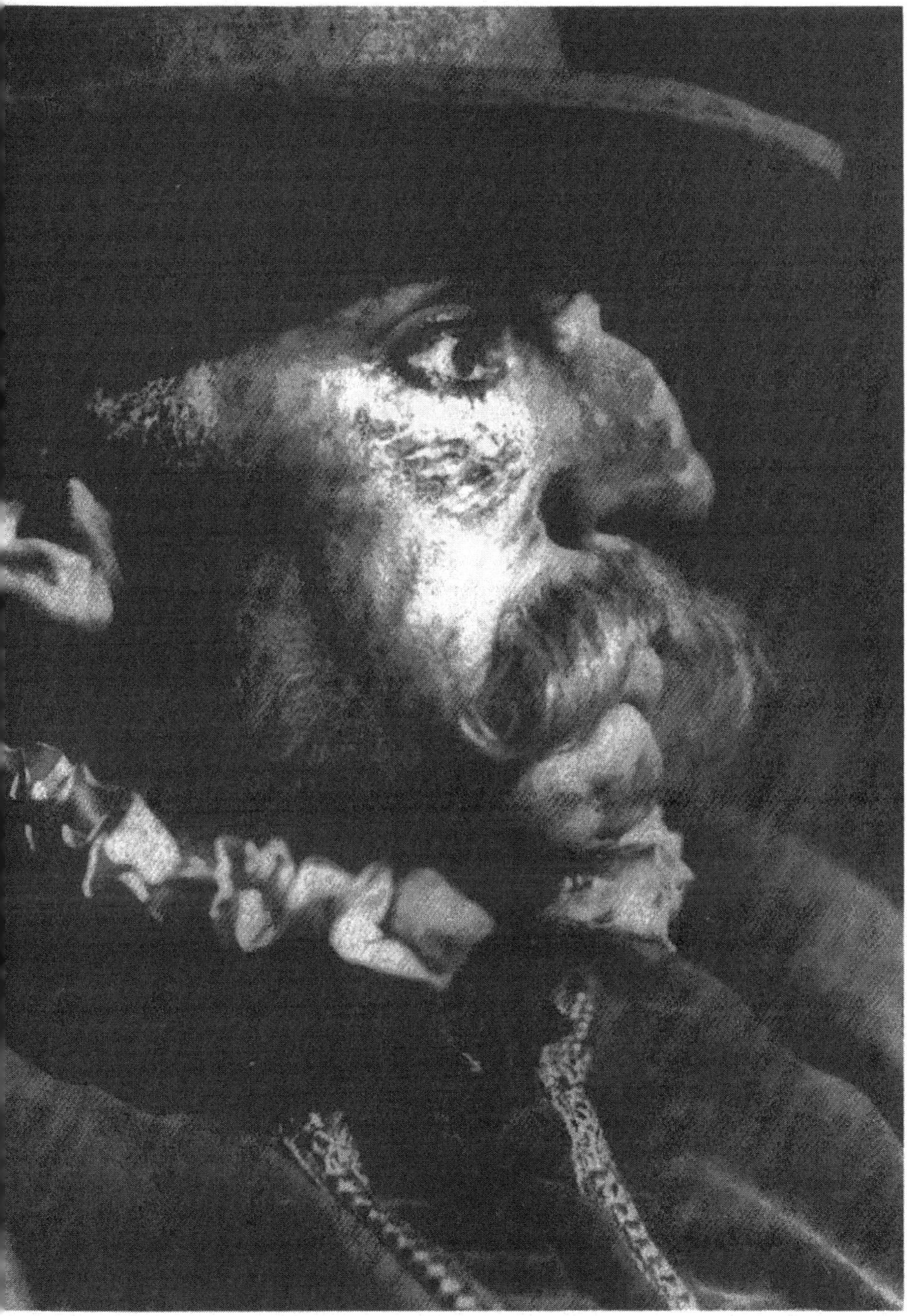

1. Sellers or Olivier? Sir Toby Belch in *Twelfth Night* (Old Vic Theatre, 1937).

2. A love of wigs and false noses: Justice Shallow in *Henry IV Part II* (New Theatre, 1945).

3. The Goons? No – Olivier as The Mahdi in *Khartoum* (1966).

4. Olivier or Sellers? Peter Sellers, with Richard III's snout and glint, as Old Sam the busker in *The Optimists of Nine Elms* (1974).

5. Zeus in *Clash of the Titans* (1981) – though Olivier was rather more Roman than Greek.

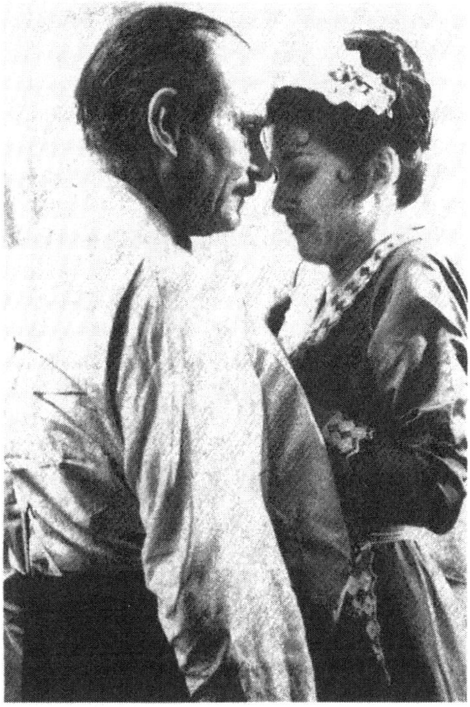

6. As Grail Knight who has survived into the modern era: Olivier in *The Betsy*, being led into temptation with the French maid, Roxanne, played by Carol Williard.

7. The Black Whirlwind: Richard III (on stage from 1944; on film in 1955).

8. "I suspect that God is rather like Olivier" (Peter Hall) – King Lear (New Theatre, 1946).

9. The Lost Boy: Olivier as Oedipus Rex (New Theatre, 1945).

10. ABOVE LEFT
Transformed into his mother: Katharina in *The Taming of the Shrew* (All Saints School, 1920; Memorial Theatre, Stratford-upon-Avon, 1922).

11. TOP RIGHT His real mother: Agnes Louise Crookenden.

12. RIGHT "My mother should really be around with slipper or hairbrush": Eileen Herlie, who played Gertrude in the film of *Hamlet* (1948), was a dozen years Olivier's junior – yet he peculiarly insisted on being her son.

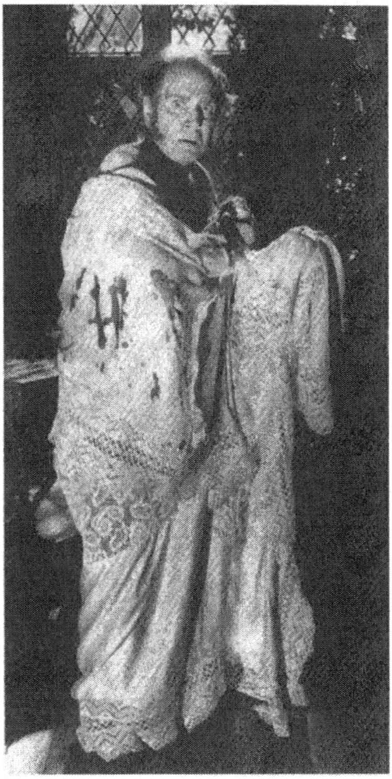

13. ABOVE His real father: The Rev. Gerard Kerr Olivier, B.A., M.A. (*Dunelm*).

14. ABOVE RIGHT Transformed into Farve: Professor Moriarty in *The Seven Per Cent Solution* (1977).

15. BELOW Fathers and Sons: *The Jazz Singer* (1981).

16. The Second Coming: *The Power and the Glory* (1961).

17. Olivier with his first wife, Jill Esmond, in *The Green Bay Tree* (Cort Theater, New York, 1933).

18. "I felt that the homosexual act would be a step darkly destructive to my soul." Olivier and Noel Coward in *Private Lives* (Phoenix Theatre, 1930).

19. Portrait of a Marriage: Larry and Viv as the Macbeths (Memorial Theatre, Stratford-upon-Avon, 1955).

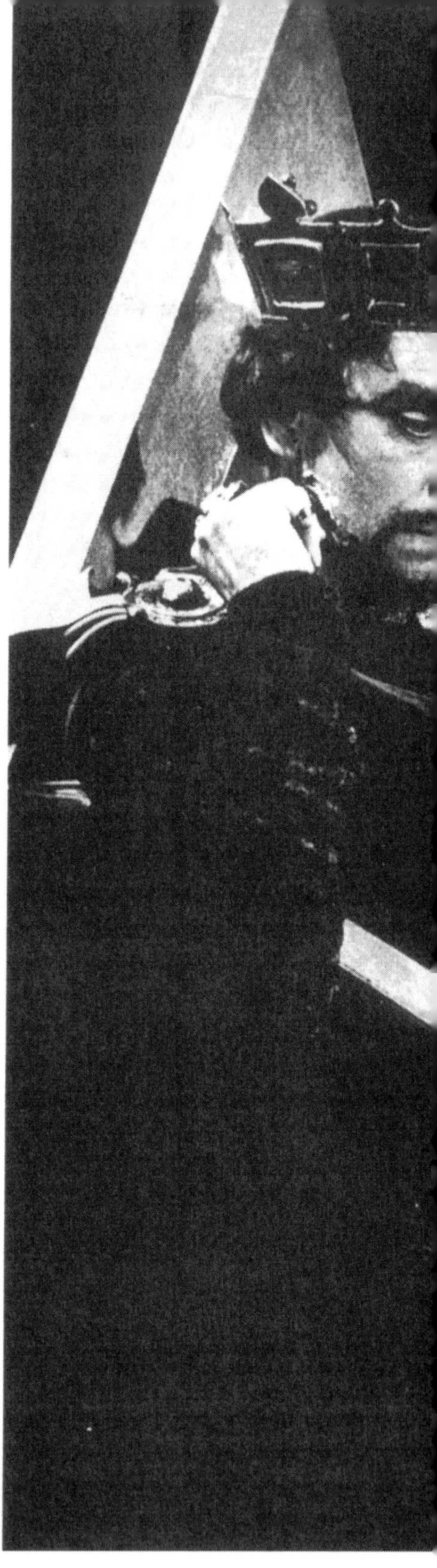

20. "In loving thou dost well, in passion not" (Milton): *Fire Over England* (1936), with Olivier as Michael Ingolby and Vivien Leigh as Cynthia.

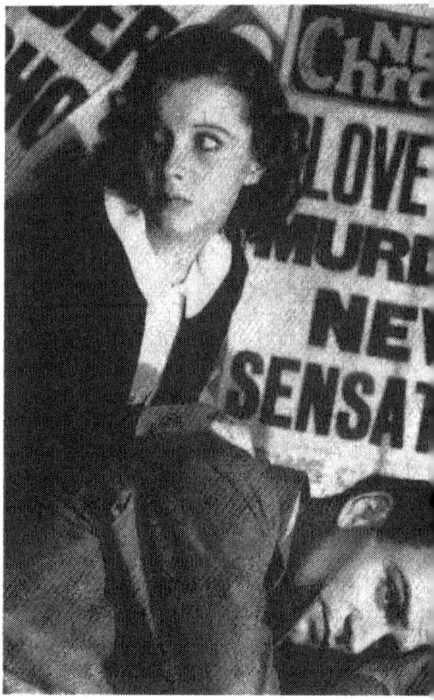

21. *Twenty-One Days* (1939).

22. *Romeo and Juliet* (Fifty-First Street Theater, New York, 1940).

23. Sir Peter and Lady Teazle, in *The School for Scandal* (Australasian Tour, 1948).

24. The Man Born to Play Kings: Henry V (1944).

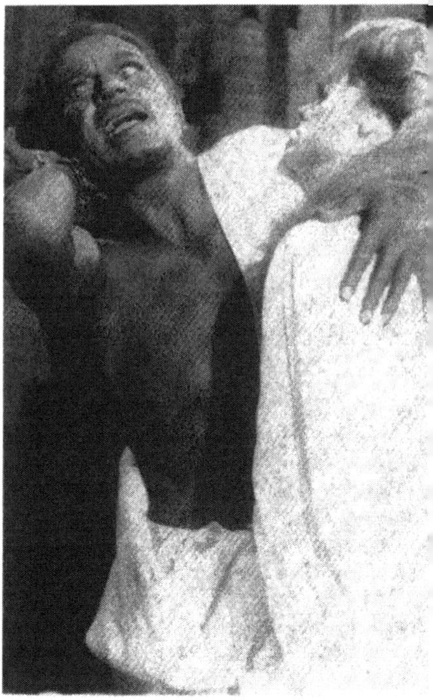

25. ABOVE LEFT The Duke of Wellington – about to meet his Waterloo: *Lady Caroline Lamb* (1972).

26. ABOVE RIGHT "[Maggie Smith] made him look like a complete monkey and not many people ever did that to Larry and lived to tell the tale" (Robert Stephens). Olivier as Othello and Maggie Smith as Desdemona (The National Theatre Company, 1964).

27. BELOW Soft Beds and Hard Battles: Vivien as Lady Hamilton and Olivier as Lord Nelson, in *That Hamilton Woman* (1941).

28. ABOVE Joan Plowright, the next Lady Olivier, as Archie Rice's daughter Jean, in *The Entertainer* (1960), confronting her husband/father.

29. BELOW LEFT "Larry and I regard the play as a wholly realistic study of marriage red in tooth and claw. In fact, there are whole passages that take me back to dear old Notley" (Kenneth Tynan to Alan Dent, March 9th 1967). Olivier as Captain Edgar with his wife Alice (Geraldine McEwan) and her cousin, Kurt, played by Robert Stephens (The National Theatre Company, 1967).

30. RIGHT Frailty as strength: the blind Clifford Mortimer, in *A Voyage Round My Father* (1982), with Elizabeth Sellars.

31. Scenting the air for danger: Laurence Olivier 1907–1989.

the ambitious young blood receiving his comeuppance. 'Before work had started one morning, I found [Garbo] sitting on an old chest on the set. I went boldly up to her and said the three or four sentences that I had made up and practised: but no utterance from her. I began to flounder and grab at anything that came into my head: some sayings of . . . Noël – anybody – anything at all . . . After a breathless pause, she slid herself off the chest sideways saying "Oh vell, live'sh a pain, anyway." I knew then that the end was not far off.'

The experience rankled, especially as Gilbert himself proceeded to create chaos. 'His performance in *Queen Christina* was catastrophic,' Garbo vouchsafed. 'He began drinking more and more. He lost his money and his house . . . He tried to commit suicide several times . . .' Yet this was the personage she preferred to Olivier? What was going on? It wasn't that Olivier was bad, or even too good; it's that, stroking Garbo on the screen, his disgrace lay in being too much the same. When with women, Olivier could become feminine: exquisite, dignified and with an awkwardness, a girlishness – though there's still an intensity and directness that'll remind us of his real identity. Crossed, made a fool of, or set up (as for instance in *The Divorce of Lady X*), his looks grow dark and there's fire there, suggested paradoxically by the way he maintains a coolness. He had, like Garbo, an androgynousness ('I shall die a bachelor!' says Queen Christina enigmatically); and to try and label them gay, straight or bi is hopeless – they transcend gender (like the gods), and in *Queen Christina*, Olivier and Garbo might have been twins – or, in the scenes where Garbo is dressed as a man, in breeches and jerkin, doubles.

I don't mean physical appearance particularly. I'm referring to their manners and sensuality. Olivier was neither soft nor pliable – he's always aflame – and when he was young, for all the gaiety, there's a gloom. Hence, Garbo. What's afoot in her acting? What is her appeal? As with Olivier, she has perceived what Wordsworth called the intimations of immortality, or what Virginia Woolf, or was it Hardy, called a well of tears. It is as if, looking at the outer world, what registers with them is what life – fate – has in store; the ending of innocence and the coming of sorrow.* Later, in *The Ebony Tower*, say, or *A Voyage Round My*

* Hence in a season of calm weather
Though inland far we be,
Our souls have sight of that immortal sea
Which brought us hither,
Can in a moment travel thither,
And see the children sport upon the shore,
And hear the mighty waters rolling evermore.

Father, there is this same mood, in reverse. In old age, Olivier retained a bloom, and his face was unblemished. (Afraid that the processes of age and disillusionment would overtake her, Garbo retired from acting and the public's gaze at the age of thirty-six.) He retained that strength which in old days moved earth and heaven; that which he was, he remained, with a sunset glow. I'm not saying that Olivier was nostalgic – he wasn't backward-reaching or sentimental. As Lord Marchmain, for example, or any of these Lears and Prosperos, he wasn't hankering for a lost golden age: it's reminiscence. He was there – he comes from that era. Consider the death-bed speech in *Brideshead Revisited* – a whisper, but an Olivier whisper, full of resonance and deep tones. He talks about the old house; how it is possible to see traces of its original site, the dips in the ploughed fields, the hollows and the nettles, and the yews and the flights of crows. He says how the Marchmains were once chivalric knights, and we go back with Olivier to the Middle Ages – to Merry England. We can see the armour and the frost; the snow blowing across the landscape; the wild deer and field sports; the Christmas gambols; the flowering hawthorns. As when Astrov shows his maps and charts of the forest in *Uncle Vanya*, Olivier conveys a sense of living history – of being connected to it. The actor is himself an old grail Knight who has survived; this is not a fantasticated, fake looking-back. Olivier is a sentinel, with nothing defeated in his voice.

Lord Marchmain, Henry Breasley, Clifford Mortimer, Sir Arthur Granville-Jones, in *Love Among the Ruins*, who had a brief affair with Katharine Hepburn's Jessica Medlicott fifty years earlier (which has haunted him but slipped her mind), or Gaius, the retired Roman senator in *The Last Days of Pompeii*, who recollects his days in Nero's court ('How I miss the power I had then! The glory of it all!'): Olivier moves from death to spiritual regeneration, from age to youth. Playing men who are highly self-aware, who are manipulative and insinuating – who know that they act, that they show off, that they are getting away with things – Olivier takes them over, giving added meaning. They are not only the characters he is playing; they are aspects of his own personality, of his great presence, of Camelot. Olivier understands people better than they know themselves – he is miles ahead in his understanding – and, as his sexuality is not centred on the genitalia or libido, what counts with him is the eroticism of a life force, a joy of living, which transcends age, and the body. He draws this essence out of his characters – not only obvious examples, like Henry V, whose attitude to war is medieval and picturesque and heroically vivid. (The patriotic stage production of 1937, the radio adaptation of 1942, and the cinema version of 1945 quite ignore the lessons of modern combat: no cold, no trenches, no deaths of multitudes. Olivier's vision of England is untouched by what the Great War did to it, or what the Second World War was doing to it.) But Olivier's saturation and intensification and being on the grand scale is also evident when he got around to playing victims (e.g. Archie Rice), whom he transforms into victors; and the demeaned and the excluded, i.e. homosexuals. You should see the way he delivers the slum-slug torrent in Harold Pinter's *The Collection*, recorded for television in 1976. Olivier is Harry Kane, a dress designer, whose catamite, Bill, impersonated by Malcolm McDowell, may well be playing away:

> There's something faintly putrid about him, don't you find? Like a slug. There's nothing wrong with slugs in their place, but he's a slum slug; there's nothing wrong with slum slugs in their place, but this one won't keep his place – he crawls all over the walls of nice houses, leaving slime, don't you, boy?

This is intended as an insult – it is calculated to hurt – yet Olivier gets Kane's thwarted love across as well. As he performs it, it is a love lyric, contained, courteous, menacing and desperate – with all the isolation and grief that romance involves. It is spirited and Olivier crackles with energy. As Kane, Olivier isn't giving himself a counter-existence as a homosexual; he is giving a homosexual character his own dark-minded acumen.

Hence *The Green Bay Tree*, by Mordaunt Shairp, which opened at the Cort Theater, New York, on 20 October 1933. It was to this production that Olivier (and Jill) fled after the *Queen Christina* embarrassment, and the play's theme is homosexual lust – an oldish man, his adopted 'son' (Olivier), and the girl (Jill) who wants to claim or save him. Might this have been a configuration of the triangular friendship with Coward? It was Jill, by the way, who had to chase Coward away – with a broken bottle? and electric cattle prod? – after the pube-shaving incident; and Coward is much in evidence in the home movies, always on the premises and he was clearly after Olivier. When *The Green Bay Tree* was revived in 1951, Denholm Elliott played Julian Dulcimer, and the torment of the bisexual, seduced by the high life, was a suitable matching of actor and material. But Olivier? He told his sister Sybille, 'It's a terrible thing for an actor to say, but honestly I've never hated playing any part so much before.'* He hated the perversions and his character for succumbing to them; and it is Dulcimer's faltering resolve or moral weakness which he was to focus upon, not (as with Elliott), Dulcimer's indecisions, whom to follow to bed, the man or the woman? Critics were to praise his virtuosic writhings, his physical representations of remorse and conscience. Florence Fisher Parry in the *Pittsburg Press*:

> In the horrifying scene where he is beaten into slavish submission by his benefactor's abnormal attraction for him, his acting becomes not acting, but an exhibition of emotional collapse so painful to witness that the eyes of the audience are torn away; the spectacle of his ignominy actually becomes too terrible to bear.

Hotspur, mortally wounded at the Battle of Shrewsbury, laughing not at death but his own life; Oedipus' yells; Richard's dying spasms; Clifford Mortimer, in the potting shed, where his laughter at one of his stories turns to choking and gasping for breath (he's breathless, but it's breathtaking): Olivier finds ways of making his feelings or emotional response to a character visual, dramatic, dynamic. In *The Ringmaster*, a play by Keith Winter to which Olivier acquired the rights in 1935, and which closed at the Shaftesbury Theatre after only eight performances, he took the role of the wheelchair-bound meddler, who amuses himself by disrupting the lives of the guests at the country hotel, and his twisted nature was revealed when he threw off his blanket, toppled to the floor,

* Another reason for the discomfort: Olivier's loathing of the director, Jed Harris. The antipathy he felt for him he channelled into the performance. 'I hate Jed so, I have to get rid of all the drive to kill him,' he said. That Harris was indeed truly awful is demonstrated in the remarks he made to Thomas Kiernan in 1980 (through a ouija-board? Or was the copy-editor simply inattentive? Halliwell gives Jed Harris' dates as 1906–79): 'All actors are over-rated, and Olivier is a prime example. Actors are . . . self-indulgent, petulant children who think only of themselves. In order to function at all in the theatre, they need strong directors to be their parents and show them the way. I've heard Olivier complain about me as a director. But I'll tell you, he and all these other actors who get anywhere labour under the delusion that they are responsible for their success. That's horse shit. The reason Olivier was halfway good in *The Green Bay Tree* was because I made him good . . . I just told him to read his lines my way, and if he didn't like it to get the hell out of the play – I'd get somebody else. Actually he was plenty scared and he wouldn't have dared challenge me . . . His performance in that play was all my doing – he just supplied the body and voice. That's all any actor does . . . Look at Olivier's career. You'll see that his best performances always came when he had a strong director, like me.' 'His own worst enemy,' decided Olivier. 'Not while I'm alive,' responded George S. Kaufman. We can see how such an unrepentant swine inspired Richard III. Olivier was fascinated as well as repulsed.

and squirmed on the carpet – one thinks of Dr Strangelove: 'Mein Führer – I can walk!'*

Olivier's reliance on physicality and acrobatics in his acting may be traced to his childhood. His father was a cricketer; his brother was sporty – Olivier was not. He hated not being good at games and overcompensated later. All those vertiginous leaps and tumbles, hanging on to the tabs, diving off parapets, and so on; those death scenes, as Coriolanus, Hamlet or Richard III, which I said were paradoxically full of life: it was as if Olivier wished to connect himself with the circus, with a stuntman, fairground element. The animality of his acting toughened and seasoned him. All that physical risk – horse-riding for *Henry V* and *Richard III*, for instance – all that danger: why did he put himself through it? Punishment? (For what?) They were ordeals, like moral trials, and he needed to prove to himself he could survive unharmed; that he was virtuous and upstanding.

The athleticism – the fighting fitness – conceals, or utilizes, aggression. He was famously dangerous and full-blooded in his sword play with Redgrave or Richardson. As Macbeth he'd have to be reminded he was meant to lose. *Sleuth*, with Michael Caine, or *The Prince and the Showgirl*, with Monroe, are also duels: Olivier has to win. He could be perilous, too, when at rest, or ostensibly enfeebled. Even when still he expresses motion – or emotion – and after having under-used him in *Private Lives*, misused him as gabby magazine editor in S. N. Behrman's *Biography*, at the Globe Theatre in 1934, Coward found the perfect outlet for Olivier's talents in Ferber and Kaufman's *Theatre Royal*. He was to be Anthony Cavendish, a role based on the antic John Barrymore. 'This was a new Larry – it was the first time anyone had seen him so obsessed with a part,' claimed Jack Wilson, Coward's business manager. Olivier claimed, 'I've caught the essence of Barrymore' – but what he really meant (says Wilson) was 'No one else can play this part, damn it! It's mine!' And it was.

Barrymore had been Olivier's favourite Hamlet, and in *On Acting*, like a dotty genealogist, he is anxious to make the incorrigible Jack part of the Great Tradition – of the family tree that began with Shakespeare and ended with himself. 'Barrymore was the top man in the American theatre . . . perhaps a little too leeched on by Hollywood, but then . . . if Beverly Hills had been around for Burbage, Garrick, Kean and Irving,

* 'Mr Laurence Olivier, as the dark, ferocious Hammond, continually lit up his part with baleful flashes, and easily had the house cheering with his ultimate contortions on the floor' (*Observer*).

they would have found themselves on a fast boat to the New World before breakfast. It would seem to me that Barrymore was the direct link with Edwin Booth . . . Booth's father, Junius Brutus Booth, was a contemporary of Kean, so it's easy to see how things slowly match up, like a detective story. The hand stretching down from Burbage finally crossed the Atlantic.' Barrymore, who died of cirrhosis of the liver, kidney failure, chronic gastritis, ulceration of the oesophagus, hardening of the arteries, and chronic eczema – i.e. booze – in 1942, wasn't much of a peasant, nor anybody's slave, but he was certainly a rogue. Found peeing in the wrong lavatory – 'Mr Barrymore! This is for ladies!' – he swung around and declared, 'So, madam, is this!' He was shiny-eyed and audacious, ideally cast as Mercutio, Sherlock Holmes, Raffles, Rasputin or Captain Ahab. He wore an astrakhan coat and a fedora – he had an air of magnificence (like Oscar Jaffe, the impresario in *Twentieth Century*) – but what really matters is that he knew he could appear ridiculous. He had (like Olivier) a comic genius, a childlike glee. (When he came to London he loved to wander in the fogs, feeling they were full of romance and adventure.) He was excessive, restless, and his acting suggested virility, glamour, lusciousness. He was a man to stir things up – and he was seen by the thirteen-year-old Olivier at the Haymarket. 'Everything about him was exciting . . . My Hamlets in later years owed a great deal to Jack Barrymore . . . [He] breathed life into the characters, which, since Irving, had been lulled into arias and false inflections, all very beautiful and poetic, but castrated. Barrymore put the balls back.'

This is the testosterone tycoon – and the heterosexual camp – of *Theatre Royal*. Olivier was in constant motion: fingers flicking his hat brim, the light glinting on his roving eyes, his thick black hair falling across his forehead, his body, in those thirties suits, generally quivering; and then the jerks in his voice. Coward had originally only wanted Olivier to play Anthony Cavendish in the provinces. Brian Aherne was to take over for the West End. Olivier decided to be so impressive and high-spirited – to the point of foolhardiness – in the role, Aherne would tactfully withdraw, being of the opinion that you could only follow Olivier (as they'd say of a show-stopping turn in music hall) with acrobats. So it proved. Olivier leapt over balconies, scaled the set, wore the Barrymore clothes with aplomb, sent himself up as a Hollywood star – a movie-era version of the grandiloquent Rover, gesticulating and declaiming and wearing feathery hats, in *Wild Oats* – and, one night, he misjudged a stunt and broke an ankle. Brian Aherne having fled the country to work with Katharine Cornell in New York, Olivier was replaced by Robert Douglas – who was shortly to marry Dorothy

Hyson, a friend of Vivien Leigh's. The wedding took place at Chelsea Old Church, Olivier was an usher, and the reception was held at his and Jill's house in Cheyne Walk. Vivien was of course present, with her husband, Herbert Leigh Holman, 'a dull man, dry, cerebral, without sparkle', judged Olivier, his cuckolder. Owing to the success of *Theatre Royal*, and the money they had earned in America, Olivier and Jill had also taken a country retreat – the Dower House, Burchett's Green, Maidenhead. The Leigh Holmans were invited for a weekend. Vivien switched on her charm with Jill, trying to befriend her, extracting intelligence about Olivier's quirks and quiddities. Olivier capered and pranced – a real life Cavendish/Barrymore, 'effusive, grandiose, excessively talkative, full of jokes, reciting speeches from this or that play . . . showing off for Vivien,' said an observer. He enjoyed spellbinding her. He saw *The Mask of Virtue*, at the Ambassadors Theatre, in which she played Henriette Duquesnoy, a prostitute masquerading as an innocent virgin, and said he had an instant desire to know her. He was twenty-eight. She was twenty-one. She came to see *Theatre Royal* eight or nine times, she dropped by at his dressing room during *Romeo and Juliet*, and tentatively kissed his shoulder, and Olivier responded to her eagerness, to her devotion – which contrasted with Jill's would-be pedagogic hold over him; and, indeed, it was Jill who could see that 'she no longer had a hold over Larry as an actor,' said a family friend. 'She saw that he was going to be a big star with or without her . . . He'd made it clear to Jill by his attitude that there was no need for her in his rocket ride to the top.'

Vivien fell into his life like a wounded bird. When I watch her films, despite the prettiness, the glitter, the gaiety, the effect (for me) is elegiac, because I know she is going to die. Vivien was Olivier's tragic empress. She plotted and schemed to get him; and then she had to plot and scheme to try and keep him. If his art and emotional textures changed as his women did – callow with Jill; patriarchal with Joan – then with Vivien, and in his prime, he was a hero, beset by sin, and a demi-god, afflicted by fallibility. They never got over each other. Vivien was destroyed by the extent of her passion for him; Olivier was cast into a frenzy of guilt and disillusion – which he embodied in his portrayal of the marriages of Archie Rice, the Macbeths, Strindberg's Captain Edgar and James Tyrone. They missed so much what they thought they had; and they grieved for a world of lost innocence and happiness – which had never, in fact, existed. Jill, who almost encouraged the alliance – half wanting to relinquish him; half certain that he'd not betray her trust and investment ('I was always conscious that his potential was enormous.

I always knew he was the much more important person,' she said in 1961) – was bold enough to be direct. 'Do you mean to marry Larry?' she asked the woman who was to quite eclipse her. 'I do – and he intends to marry me. One day, when all the hatred and resentment is finished, we will marry.'

Chapter Six
Cat Woman

What *is* a person? How *do* they come about? For all that I can trace Olivier back to the Pyrenees, and to the rectors in *Crockford*, and shadow him with his sister Sybille's genealogical expertise; or given that I can discuss the influence of his family – those artists, statesmen and divines – and contemplate his intense religious and choral education; and for all that I may discover about his days as an indigent drama student and as an apprentice at the Birmingham Rep; or divulge about his disastrous first marriage; or depict what it was like, being a pseudo-camp cohort of Coward – the fact remains, do I really know what dislocations and adjustments created him? I have argued that his determination, embarrassments, eagerness and persistence relates to his understanding of the gods – that he was Jupiter; and I took Olivier quite out of history and saw him in terms of pre-history and myth. But the two dominant external forces directing his life – which made Olivier Olivier – were actually the war, and Vivien.

They are of course connected. Look at Othello and Desdemona, Oberon and Titania, Romeo and Juliet, Troilus and Cressida; the matches in *Henry V* or *Richard III*: the classics teach us that love isn't peaceable; it is promulgated by conflict and pain, adversity and strife. Love scenes, in Shakespeare, don't contrast with the battles and the blood-lettings – they are continuations of them. In *Antony and Cleopatra*, which Olivier and Vivien presented in London and New York in 1951 and 1952, love itself is a mode of combat, deconstructing the emotions; a seizure, an attack. Political dissension, skirmishes, intrigue, amongst the Romans and the Egyptians, are an extension of, or a version of, the sexual rivalry. Love is an appetite – it's greed – with people hungering for each other, devouring each other, making conquests. *Henry V*, in which the arrows at Agincourt fly like Cupid's darts, and which might have been thought safely and exclusively militaristic – being to do with honour and glory, steeds and foes, the field and the fallen, and the sporting spirit – is an audacious alignment of the marital and the martial. Olivier, in cream tights and a velvet doublet woven with gold, concludes his imperial designs by annexing the Princess of France – Renée Asherson, moon-faced in a wimple:

Katherine:	Is it possible dat I sould love de enemy of France?
King Henry:	No, it is not possible you should . . . Kate; but, in loving me, you should love the friend of France, for I love France so well . . . I will have it all mine; and, Kate, when France is mine and I am yours, then yours is France and you are mine.

Like Richard III ('one of the most sexually attractive characters ever to disgrace the stage': Rattigan), who woos with his sword and wins Lady Anne's love doing her injuries (she was played on the Australian tour by Vivien and in the film by Claire Bloom – later Lady Marchmain), the word play is nimble. The opponent is outmanoeuvred. Sex and violence become not opposites – they are inseparable. This is Olivier as an actor, too, seizing his roles, subjecting them, altering and redesigning them. The erotics of his acting involve a swooning, a languorousness, as he transmits himself and flows into a new role, laying bare his energy and evidence of his strength.

This is the meaning behind the Tyrone Guthrie/Sergius Saranoff *Arms and the Man* story, which Olivier often told: Guthrie 'gave me the most priceless bit of advice I've ever had from anybody . . . Ralph Richardson and I opened . . . *Arms and the Man*, at the Opera House, Manchester [on 7 August 1944]. Ralph and I had been got out of the Navy in order to do this work, and we opened . . . [and] the next day Ralph . . . bought a paper and . . . I remember seeing "Mr Ralph Richardson was a brilliant Bluntschli. Mr Laurence Olivier, on the other hand . . ." and I thought, "That's it. That's it . . . I'm going back to the Navy. I can't stand it . . . I cannot stand criticism, I can't bear it any more." Well, that night Tony Guthrie came to see the performance, and as we came out of the stage door . . . Tony said, "Liked your Sergius very much." And I snarled and said, "Oh, thank you very much, too kind, I'm sure." And he said, "No, no. Why, what's the matter?" And I said, "Well, really, don't ask . . . no, please." And he said, "But don't you love Sergius?" And I said, "Look, if you weren't so tall, I'd hit you. How do you mean, how can you love a part like that, a stupid, idiot part?" . . . And he said, "Well, of course, if you can't love Sergius, you'll never be any good in him, will you?" Well, it clicked, and something happened, I suppose, that gave me a new attitude . . . towards the entire work of acting.'

It's not just that Olivier must love his characters particularly; it's that the process of acting itself is like falling in love. The newness, the excitement, a relationship that has no constraints; in a love affair, the participants may be purely themselves and unencumbered. It's what life should be for, this joy and happiness. It's a rediscovery of life, romantic love; and, by the same token, it is an interlude from real life, and it makes returning to normality like relapsing to something pale and insignificant. Was this why Olivier worked so hard? Was this the purpose of his self-expenditure? He didn't live a real life; he only visited it – and then, back to the theatre. Olivier's life was lived in the roles he created. He expressed his nature and inhibitions through the plays – which then formulated for him a personality, a character. The Roman plays, for example: they were who he was, who he wanted to be. He was all these heroes, at one time or another. Brutus' idealism, in *Julius Caesar*, blinding him to justice; in *Antony and Cleopatra*, Antony's love, blinding him to sense; and Coriolanus' inability to make allowances for the weakness of other people is related to Olivier's impatience and briskness – I wouldn't have wished to have been one of the students at the Central School, in 1933, when Olivier came to adjudicate a performance and was, allegedly, cross and contemptuous about the standard of make-up; nor should I want to have been the critic who gushed that he'd long admired him but never met him and Olivier said, 'We can leave it like that if you like,' and stalked off. And what about Joan Fontaine? Informed that she'd just married Brian Aherne, Olivier, his voice carrying across the *Rebecca* set, stated, 'Couldn't she have done better than that?'

Outrageous? Heartless? No: it's more accurate to say – as when he told Denys Blakelock, who was self-conscious about his funny stumpy little hands, 'Funny stumpy little hands, aren't they?' – that he refused to lie, to dissemble. The key to understanding Olivier is that he wouldn't simplify life; he's truthful and meticulous, like a child. (When he claimed that lying was his besetting sin as a child – perhaps he was lying even about that?) Coriolanus, indeed, is mocked as a 'boy of tears', and Volumnia, his mother (Sybil Thorndike in 1938, Edith Evans in 1959),*

* Olivier played Coriolanus first at the Old Vic in April 1938, in a production directed by Lewis Casson. True to its era, the play allowed opportunities for Coriolanus to be the disdainful fascist dictator – the military commander, loathing the people, the mob, who dare to assume that his wounds are 'received . . . for the hire of their breath only'. He's elected consul, but the other politicians know that the people 'have chose a consul that will from them take/Their liberties'. In the domestic scenes, he continued to have a violent temper, upsetting the people he depends on with his insolence.

By 1959, Olivier didn't need to allude to Hitler, Franco or Mussolini – except he died like Mussolini, suspended by his ankles. Though still believing in social hierarchies

is a strong-willed woman who still treats her son as an adored and invincible infant; he's sent into battle to 'prove himself a man' and Volumnia relishes the picture of 'his bloody brow/with his mailed hand then wiping'. She's proud of his wounds. Maternal love is connected to war – even to sex (for Volumnia day-dreams, 'if my son were my husband') – and Coriolanus' mother exists to give him reassurance. He's a man of action – he doesn't need to be contemplative. His sword speaks for him – and 'he moves like an engine and the ground shrinks before his treading'.

Could this be an image of Olivier, the supreme contriver, pure of technique, keeping the mess of emotion and sensation at bay? No – though he's often misunderstood like this. It's his gift to be brave, and unsentimental, and fortifying, and to make us, his audience, face things without weeping. Similarly, his Coriolanus was not full of petulance and pride; he was full of confidence. He didn't dilly-dally, like Hamlet, unlawfully murder, like Macbeth, go mad, like Lear and Othello; Coriolanus is beset by sincerity: 'Would you have me/False to my nature? Rather say I play/The man I am.' (He's like Olivier's Brutus, at school, or Parolles, in Birmingham.) Indeed, far from being proud, he's modest – though informed ''twere a concealment worse than a theft to hide your doings', he doesn't want the tedium of ceremony and praise; he wants new challenges. It's enough that he's a survivor, 'unbruised' by his escapades. (After taking Corioli, he says, 'My work hath yet/Not warmed me': our man is a joker.)

Aspects of Olivier's nature underlie Coriolanus'. For the latter's inability to keep a constant good temper, we have the former's fierceness and sensitivity; for Coriolanus' tyranny, we have Olivier's power; and where Coriolanus was an egoist, Olivier was an individualist. In shaping his own life, Olivier allowed art to transform it. His nobility is matched by his character's sovereignty; both have a strange delicacy and an instinct

---

– in order – this older Coriolanus mistrusted democracy because he was personally frightened of the mob – of their 'general ignorance'. He warns the Roman Senate of the example of Greece – 'Though there the people had absolute power, I say they nourished disobedience, fed/The ruin of the state.' Olivier's Coriolanus was a patriot. Making his first entrance on a raised platform, walking slowly through a crowd and down flights of steps, he was also an actor amongst his audience – and he was deriding them, like Archie Rice who likewise, though figuratively, bares his scars to the public. (During the day Olivier was filming *The Entertainer*, and he commuted between the locations in the north of England and Stratford in an ambulance.)

An incomplete bootleg according to the Shakespeare Memorial Theatre production, directed by Peter Hall, is housed in the National Sound Archive, a subdivision of the British Library.

for survival. I am aware always with Olivier of a restraint, even of a withdrawal – of civilized qualities which contain his savagery – his desire to be loose and irrational: Mr Puff climbing the curtains; Hamlet's swallow dive ('I wanted to leap off the top platform, bounce on to something, catch hold of the pole that was to cross this sort of proscenium arch, swing twice round the pole . . . leap towards the astonished audience and land in the footlights before their blanched faces'); or Macheath, in *The Beggar's Opera*, racing on horseback across moors and fens, singing lustily and wearing a scarlet coat, or in triumphal procession to the gallows, lolling astride his coffin, idle and happy, like it is a couch or divan. Macheath is so full of life, he is continuously made to face death: warrants are forged for his arrest; he's locked in condemned cells; he fights duels, attends and disrupts balls, scatters the farmyard animals during hayloft seductions, when scythes and pitchforks threaten to fall on him. Olivier is the highwayman – the villain – whom all women love. He has a lurking danger, and his midnight brows and curls are related to Richard III's. Olivier, his face alert, smiling and gleaming, is always on the look-out, for Polly and Lucy, who'd settle marriage on him, or creditors and soldiers, who'd similarly box him in and call him to account. He has a maleness, a boisterousness; he's dark and fast – and he could say to his critics, as Coriolanus does, as Olivier could: 'Why did you wish me milder?'

This is the maleness of *Theatre Royal*, which set Vivien's juices flowing; here was an actor, and a man, to take her to the sky. After that weekend at the Dower House, Burchett's Green, they discovered each other waiting for a taxi outside the Savoy. They began lunching together at the Ivy, the Café Royal, and Quaglino's (Vivien was already well known about town for her exquisite frocks and expensive perfume); and on the pretext of nursing her through a cold, Olivier stayed long hours at her house in Little Stanhope Street. 'Like any first act of the period, isn't it,' commented Olivier years later. He soon began to feel pity for Jill, 'to feel pain for her and, of course, guilt. But this thing was as fatefully irresistible for us as for any other couple from Siegmund and Sieglinde to Windsor and Simpson.' It is interesting that Olivier should compare his liaison with pairs of forbidden lovers – Wagner's brother and sister, or the royal family's crypto-fascist and the American divorcee. But at the time, discretion in his adulterous affair would have nullified what they were doing. They enjoyed being seen to be wanted and desired – they enjoyed the attention; they loved being loved. Vivien looked back on their encounters and courtship with glee – 'I don't think I have ever lived quite as intensely ever since' – whereas Olivier, typically, recalled it as a moral lapse. 'We could not keep from touching each other, making love almost within Jill's vision. This welding closeness tripped the obvious decision, and two marriages were severed. I suspect this . . . may not be pleasant to read. It is, to be honest, a little nauseating to set down.'

Vivien was a tricksy spirit and Olivier was drawn to the appeal of her artificiality (which contrasted with Jill's practicality) – to that ideal of beauty that is now out of fashion. The bows and ribbons, the tiny wasp waist, the make-up, the hair: the 'poetry', the 'perfection'. She never left the stage door unless impeccably dressed. But where's the carnality, the ferocity, in maintaining such a tone? Perhaps the sexual thrill lay in imagining taking it all apart – getting inside that contraption – loosening it? She looks like she's ready to snap, I feel, in those period portraits by Norman Parkinson, Cecil Beaton, and Angus McBean.* Indeed, she'd go from hilarity and enjoyment to derangement in no time at all. She was compulsive, writing letters, cutting flowers, chain-smoking, organizing parties and deploying teams of gardeners and interior decorators to tart up her homes. She was an insomniac – 'she is not a sleepy baby', the doctors declared early on – and (if only she could have suggested this in her chilly acting) she was insatiable in the sack. Told he was looking wan, Olivier said, 'It's Vivien. It's every day, two, three times. She's bloody wearing me out.'

I've argued that Olivier wasn't a modern man; that his origins or the source of his strength are in the nineteenth century and that the scale of his acting is for the Victorian stage. Vivien, likewise, never seems quite a modern woman. Despatching bouquets, trinkets, birthday cards and get-well messages galore, pampering her guests at Notley, laughing at their jokes, making each person seem special, enslaving herself to Olivier – 'constantly adoring of Larry, constantly deferring to him, constantly flattering him and making him feel like the greatest, most attractive and brilliant man under the sun. She always made herself look perfect to him, she worked hard to make their surroundings perfect. There was no end to what she did to try to create a perfect fantasy life for them' (says Margaret Leighton) – Vivien's devotion and loyalty and formality suggest incredible anxiety. She's like the Victorian paragon or good fairy who ministers to other people's tribulations, who has a sense

* McBean's sepulchral pictures are collected in a handsome volume, *Vivien: A Love Affair in Camera* (Oxford, 1989). He first photographed her in 1936 and she posed for him regularly, the final sitting being just three weeks before her death. For thirty years she came before his lens as a marble angel with clasped hands, her face covered with funereal veils.

of responsibility, of compassion, and yet who is not confident about who or what she herself might be. (She was nothing because Olivier was everything: she lost a sense of herself.) Her precision and observance of good form – her punctiliousness and wanting things to be just so – suggest not solidity but a fear of chaos, not rectitude or brightness or poise, but those things which are on the other side of sanity. Dulcie Gray remembers being invited to Notley after a Friday performance of *Macbeth*. Vivien, embroiled in the mood of Lady Macbeth's griefs, worked herself up into such a mood of rage and despair, she refused to let any guest retire to bed. Then she went down with a bout of pleurisy. Olivier, along with Dulcie and Michael Denison, escaped for a walk – only to return and find Vivien button-cute and rapier-keen, organizing an impromptu party for fifty people she'd telephoned. 'My God! It can't be!' said Olivier, seeing the cars arrive. The party went on until five a.m. Monday. Vivien was 'radiant'; Olivier, 'paste-white with exhaustion', trying to work on his film version of *Richard III*, and with Malvolio to play that evening. If he dropped off asleep, Vivien would slap his face with a wet flannel – she could be pounding a rock to incite sparks.

Her appetite – for famous people, exquisite food, non-stop revelling – was not a life force. She wasn't subjugated to pleasure, to joy. It's more like a search for oblivion, for extinction. The formality – the place settings, engraved invitations, flower arrangements – concealed impetuosity. If she kept still, she'd drop dead. I realize I'm describing a character we never see, but whom we hear a lot about – Rebecca.* Indeed, the conceit of Hitchcock's film† is that it is permeated by a fretful and fractious character who never appears – yet the film we recall afterwards, which is not the actual one which was made, is crammed with her image: Rebecca in her boudoir, pacing the floor in a négligée, or ordering the servants about, or at the ball in that dress, or canoodling with George Sanders in the boathouse, or her body under the sea, her hair streaming and undulating in the current. Mrs Danvers keeps the first Mrs de Winter's boudoir as a shrine, and full of flowers. The silver-backed hairbrush, the hand mirror, the gowns in the wardrobe, the furs ('Feel this!' purrs Danvers the dyke – Rebecca was Venus in furs): these are

* Also, Marguerite, in *Sleuth*, over whom Olivier and Michael Caine do battle. (It's also a duel of acting styles: Olivier, theatrical, deliberate; Caine's Milo Tindle, weeping, dissolving and shouting.) Marguerite has profligate tastes, and Olivier taunts Caine with this, and how can he afford her, satisfy her? On the wall are celebrity stills of Olivier – as Andrew Wyke – as a young man – and is that Vivien, as his wife?

† Olivier was working on costume fittings for *Rebecca* when Britain declared war on Germany, on 3 September 1939.

fetishistic objects. Everything is monogrammed – like a cattle brand – from Rebecca's nightdress to the large photograph of Max – i.e. Olivier – in a silver frame. And I imagine Vivien's bedchamber was like this: red chintz hanging in soft folds to cover the walls, rose-patterned upholstery and quilts, a green carpet to match the telephones and water jugs. As the *Ladies Journal* gushed in June 1951, 'everywhere there is evidence of the loving accumulation of a woman who finds happiness in her home and takes joy in discovering beautiful pieces for its adornment'. What particularly struck the reporter were the flowers: 'Flowers are everywhere – great baskets of them, widely spreading bowls, delicate vases with a single perfect spray. Lady Olivier loves white flowers best of all – lilacs, camellias, freesias, hyacinths, lilies-of-the-valley . . .' It must have been like a funeral parlour.

As Mrs Danvers caresses and touches the materials, the fabrics, we realize Rebecca is not allowed to be dead. Vivien, despite the fun (which would switch in an instant to anger), despite the signs of a high life – the limousines, Château Lafite, and jars of beluga, sent over from the Caprice – was dying from the first. 'We didn't know it then, but then how could we? It was there, though,' remembered a schoolfriend. 'Vivien would get along fine for a few weeks – then, suddenly . . . we'd see a completely different girl, moody, silent, petulant, rude, often hysterical. None of us understood it, not even the schoolmistresses . . . She definitely suffered from some mental peculiarity that on occasion put her severely out of sorts.' She was emotionally volatile – and what the need for luxuries and manic order suggests is a fear of boredom. She was drawn to self-destruction, symbolized not, as for Rebecca, by a cancer brewing inside her ('Why can't I have a nice respectable illness like cancer?' Vivien used to complain), but by chronic pulmonary tuberculosis – an old-fashioned and picturesque ailment to expire from in 1967.*

Did Vivien come out with the turbulence Olivier felt, but which he controlled? Were her breakdowns and disruptions a product of his own ambition and rise? With Olivier, it wasn't that he succeeded, but that others must fail (Jill's lost chance with *Bill of Divorcement*; the jealous rage over Vivien's Scarlett O'Hara fame); and his life was most of all a battle with himself. Others (wives, children, colleagues) can't hope to win, or to come out evens, because the battle is going on in his head. He

* I wonder? Was it really consumption? The way she died, suddenly, coughing up blood, haemorrhaging all over the bedroom carpet at 54 Eaton Square, suggests cirrhosis. Peter Evans, who sat next to her at a dinner party at John Mills' house in the mid-sixties, tells me she was pretty well gaga from a heavy intake of booze, and had become in real life the elderly alcoholic Lady Hamilton.

attended a rehearsal of *The Tempest* simply to disconcert the Prospero: 'Gielgud obviously is disturbed by Larry, and Larry knows it,' noted the director, Peter Hall. He'd say one thing, and his body language would say another. This 'curious duality' drove Peter Hall to distraction. Olivier would claim he was anxious to resign from the National, then he'd retract and stubbornly cling to power. Hall would be assured he 'is fed up with the load and the worry and the burden and wants to leave at the end of this year and relax', and yet then, at a board meeting, Olivier will be 'in a devilish mood and was changing ground on everything that had been said previously'.

Hall never seemed to understand that Olivier was playing a game with him, that 'Larry's contortions', 'vacillations', were a deliberate imposture. Hall is like a nurse humouring a cunning and senile old fart ('He loves being naughty'); but it is Hall's sobriety which is comical. He can't quite decide on the level of Olivier's skulduggery and guile, and so settles for thinking him an irresponsible fool; whereas it is plain to anybody that Hall was dealing with King Lear, who wanted to keep the National until his death, and who was only pretending to dispose of his kingdom. And in a way, this is what being married or in love with him must have been like: he was unknowable, impenetrable, and your life – or Vivien's life – was defined by the suffering or pleasure Olivier afforded her. You'd realize, if pulled into his orbit, that you were not quite in charge of yourself.

I've said that Olivier was Kipling's Kim. Vivian [Vivien came later] Mary Hartley was actually born in India, at the hill station of Darjeeling, on 5 November 1913. In those greenish eyes there lingered her childhood amongst the tropical birds, swamps and storms; and though her father, Ernest Richard Hartley, an exchange broker and later the senior partner in the firm of Pigott, Chapman & Co., was from Bridlington, Yorkshire, her mother, Gertrude Yackjee, who was born in India in 1888, had Armenian blood, which would account for her daughter's oriental features. Such was the racism of those days, Gertrude didn't demur when people said she was Irish – and in the publicity material for *Gone With the Wind*, Vivien was described as Scots-Irish. Perhaps in deference to this, Vivien was at any rate educated at Catholic schools and seminaries, chiefly the Convent of the Sacred Heart at Roehampton, where she enrolled at the age of six and a half. Olivier's religious upbringing, in the choir, educated him in music and drama. Vivien's nurturing by the nuns was to make her later morbidity and madness not wholly unexpected. The girls had to bathe under heavy smocks, so that they'd not glimpse their own nakedness; food would be spoilt with too much salt, so that eating would not be enjoyable (the flesh had to be mortified); friendships were discouraged; and clothes had to be fanatically neatly folded, with stockings arranged in the shape of the cross. Soiled undergarments were concealed under special woven fabrics: Satan's gussets, like nipples or pubic hair, were to be spurned. When the clock struck or chimed, the girls were to murmur – with St Thérèse of Lisieux – 'An hour nearer to death. An hour nearer to heaven or hell.'*

Given the rules and rituals, the spiritual death wishes, of such an institution, it's a wonder there aren't more serial killers and schizophrenics making havoc in the community. (In a rare flexing of the regulations, Vivien was allowed a white kitten: a witch's familiar.) For such a one as Vivien, with her combination of frailty and nervous strength, it was an upbringing calculated to send her round the twist. Olivier was to say that, when mad and dazed, tottering around the house believing herself to be Scarlett O'Hara or Blanche Du Bois, she wore on her face the blank 'wonderment' of a communicant. She was the angel with glass eyes (photographed by McBean) staring upward. She was lucky (or did it divide her further?) to have wealthy parents who'd make the vacations festive. Fishing trips to Ireland and the Scottish Highlands; summers in Biarritz or winters in Switzerland. She was an indulged only child – and so she remained. Only one person has dared to go on the record and say this (everybody else is taken in by the feline charm: 'She was very like a cat. She would purr and scratch, and looked divinely pretty doing either,' said Rex Harrison)†; Kenneth More, Freddie Page to her Hester Collyer, in *The Deep Blue Sea* (1955), thought her suspiciously too sure of herself. 'I could never really trust her and I suspected her almost

* Born in Alençon in 1873, Thérèse Martin died of TB at the Carmelite convent in Lisieux, aged twenty-four. Her off-putting belief that personal suffering was a worthwhile offering to God proved a popular philosophy during the Great War; and she was made one of France's patron saints after the Second World War. Her obsessional crush on Christ, her bridegroom, interestingly prefigures Vivien's pure love for Olivier.

† Eulogies of Vivien form a cattery: she had 'the smoky-blue eyes of a Siamese cat' (Godfrey Winn); 'quicksilver elegance and composure, like a small Siamese cat' (Olivia de Havilland); 'those Siamese cat's eyes blazing, those exquisite nostrils quivering' (Terence Rattigan); 'she wore a green chiffon dress – just the colour of her eyes – and she was as beautiful as a cat . . . Incidentally there were many cats [in her house], live ones, china ones, painted ones' (Toby Rowland); 'She was very fond of cats and . . . made a great fuss of a beautiful and highly born British Blue kitten which we had just acquired. Suddenly she put on an act. Her face became contorted with tigerish jealousy, and, in a hoarse, stagey voice she snarled, "How dare you be so beautiful!"' (Christopher Sykes).

overwhelming friendliness. I thought she was petulant, spoilt, overpraised, and overloved.'

Did Olivier himself come to hold this view? There was a tremendous egoism to their love, to the secret or private images they had of each other; and Vivien was to weigh him down, when she was near, as she clung to the 'romance'. He grew to be irked by her presence, exasperated by her cycles of excitement and lassitude; she was unadjustable, believing if she couldn't have his love exclusively, she'd think of death, of annihilation, and she couldn't cope with the danger of disillusionment. When we are taught that life is life and poetry is poetry, this isn't so necessarily, not when you have a transfiguring experience – a sexual love affair, like this. Suddenly, Vivien and Olivier were coping with opera-size emotions (asked if she'd spent a pleasant break from filming *Gone With the Wind*, Vivien replied, 'Larry met me in the hotel lobby and we went upstairs and we fucked and we fucked and we fucked the whole weekend'). But it's an idyll. Sooner or later you have to get out of bed. There's no real life in these relationships. Romeo and Juliet, Tristan and Isolde: look what happens to them! This was all exacerbated for Olivier and Vivien because they were actors, playing opposite each other, playing lovers. Their reality was a make-believe. They didn't have what they thought they were going into – and all the fixtures and fittings of Notley or Durham Cottage, Chelsea, couldn't conceal this fact, that they'd deceived themselves it was a perfect set-up.

Vivien had had a peripatetic youth – a rootless, shiftless existence at finishing schools in France, Italy and Bavaria. She resided in hotels, lodged with rich friends, and her address would be given as the Empress Club, Dover Street. She moved in and out of different languages, went to the theatre in different countries, made yards of acquaintances; she had everything, except security. Though she was quite right to look on the bright side – her upbringing had given her 'that flexibility of mind which is so necessary to an artist and taught me, I hope, understanding' – the flexibility, fluidity and plasticity, combined with the Catholic rigour and having things her own way – raised amongst bare-footed Indian servants, Vivien was accustomed to ordering people around – meant she was literally *all over the place*. In this respect, her retreats into madness, those bouts of mania when Olivier had to kneel on her chest and pump in the drugs, seem like self-defence – a retreat deep inside, an implosion. Once, in New Zealand, she stripped to the buff at midnight and dived into the sea and swam towards the horizon, no doubt intent on reaching Europe, or possibly the moon. She was strong and fearless, even when otherwise ill. The cold water challenged her blood – as did narcotics. 'She exercised an extraordinary will-power in her resistance to succumbing to even the strongest advisable drugs,' Olivier has explained. 'If there was one thing of which Vivien was terrified it was needles, hypodermics of any sort. Our new nurse appeared with what seemed . . . a hefty container filled with liquid . . . Vivien screamed appalling abuse . . . with particular attention to my erotic impulses.' Nothing short of electro-convulsive shock therapy could sedate her, and gradually her disturbances burned Olivier's tenderness away.

At school she was popular with the pupils, and a creep with the nuns. She had a highly developed repertoire of simpers and smiles, which she could switch on and off, and which she'd deploy to appease, win favours and get her own way. She'd consciously set out to charm, to seduce – especially when a screen test was coming up, or if there was a producer to impress. Determined to win the role of Scarlett O'Hara, she stage-managed her introduction to David O. Selznick – what dress to wear, what expression to put on. She and Olivier went to watch the burning of Atlanta sequence, and 'Viv looked lovely that night. Her eyes were dancing in the light of that tremendous blaze. When I saw her like that, I knew she would get the part.' Vivien had decided she'd play Scarlett because she *was* Scarlett ('*I* shall play Scarlett O'Hara, wait and see,' she'd prophesied in London, when every star in Hollywood was under consideration); and she professed similar affinities with Ophelia, Anna Karenina, Lady Hamilton, Blanche and Cleopatra – all of them you'll note, women with that brand of beauty which begs to be destroyed.

Herbert Leigh Holman – whose middle name became her stage name – was no Rhett, no Vronsky, no Stanley Kowalski; he was not going to contribute to her deterioration and death. The security which he represented, and which, at the age of nineteen, in 1932, she decided she wanted, was what quite quickly made Vivien's wild nature rebel. Holman, who was born on 3 November 1900, and educated at Harrow and Jesus College, Cambridge, had blond curly hair, enjoyed sailing, riding and tennis, and was a distinguished lawyer at the Admiralty bar – his family had for centuries been in the shipbuilding business and marine insurance. Vivien met him – he's Ashley Wilkes – at the Dartmouth Hunt Ball, and the dozen-year gap in their ages allowed her to play at being the child, pretending that Holman was her secret father. Everybody assured him that 'the Vivling' was 'indescribably lovely, gentle, sweet and friendly' and by 7 July, Vivien was able to tell her friends, 'great thrilldom, Leigh and I are engaged. It was officially announced this morning.' They were married at St James's, Spanish Place, the following Christmas, on 20 December 1932, and the honeymoon was spent touring Bad Reichenhall,

Kitzbühel, Munich, Leipzig and Dresden. 'It is very lovely here with quantities of snow and hot sun,' Vivien informed her parents.

Had she not been off her rocker, had she not decided to be an actress, had she not seen Olivier soon afterwards and declared, 'That's the man I'm going to marry,' Vivien and Holman would have made the happiest of husband-and-wife teams – he the successful barrister, pottering off to the Temple; she the pretty young wife, looking after the home, raising a family, involving herself with charity work and the Women's Institute – ageing into the kind of English country goddess you'd find out in the garden with a trug and secateurs, pruning the honeysuckle. Actually, this is a role she continued intermittently to play right up until her death. She never stopped writing to Holman ('Goodnight my darling . . . Don't be lonely and take care of yourself') or going to stay with him at Zeals, his manor house in Wiltshire. They even went abroad together, which provoked Jean Mann, MP, to complain on the *Tonight* programme: 'When a woman finds her ex-husband so easy to get on with that she can spend a holiday with him she should have thought a little longer before she cut the knot.' Which elicited a terse telegram from San Vigilio: 'Criticism ill-considered and unmannerly. Presence our daughter gives explanation holiday to any reasonable person.'

Suzanne Holman was born at the Rahere Nursing Home, Bulstrode Street, on 10 October 1933 – Vivien was not yet twenty; she'd been married less than a year. In the summer before her wedding she'd begun studying at RADA (and learning rather too much about acting being an actress), and it was into the theatre, rather than domesticity, that she wished to plunge. 'Some force within myself would not be denied expression,' she said. A nanny was sought for the baby – and quite soon maternal duties were assumed by Gertrude Hartley. (Attention psychoanalysts: during one of her spasms, Vivien attacked her mother and tried to rip her tits off – 'Gertrude forgave her at once and never mentioned it again,' reported Olivier, straight-faced.) In between decorating the marital home at Little Stanhope Street – her first web to be done out in a Frenchified clutter (the effect is false – like a film set) – and perfecting her off-putting precision at drama school, Vivien acquired an agent and made walk-ons as a pertinacious schoolgirl sticking out her tongue in *Things Are Looking Up*, *The Village Squire*, *Gentlemen's Agreement*, and *Look Up and Laugh* – the latter with Gracie Fields, who said, 'Don't worry, love, you've got something.'

Holman and his circle never took the Vivling's ambitions seriously; she didn't need the money after all (she had no poverty, genteel or genuine, to escape), and he'd write her admonishing letters: 'Really if this film business is going to take you away too much I shall be wanting you to stop it.' But rushes from her pictures had been seen by Sydney Carroll, who cast her in his play *The Mask of Virtue*, which opened on 15 May 1935, and as Vivien said to her friend Hamish Hamilton the following morning, 'Don't you ever read the papers? I'm a STAR!' And so she was. Olivier saw the production, as did Coward ('I loved her instantly'), as did Alexander Korda,* who arranged for her to have a screen test at the recently constructed Denham Studios. She was offered a contract worth £50,000 over a five-year period. Holman began taking sailing holidays in Scandinavia on his own. Vivien began to gallivant, though she was always scribbling messages to her husband, saying she missed him and passing on items of news – simultaneously affectionate and fending him off: 'I think I'd almost rather you stayed on sailing my love. That isn't because I'm not longing to see you and be with you but I feel so mean when you're waiting for me all the time.'

She danced and dined out with David Collet, John Freemantle (later Lord Cottesloe), John Buckmaster (Gladys Cooper's son) and Carl Harbord, who was in the cast of *The Happy Hypocrite* with her, and who expostulated, 'Even when she was sleeping with *me*, she was talking of Olivier.' It has been rumoured that she also agreed to play the Bedspring Sonata with Korda himself, so long as he cast her in *Fire Over England* (biographies euphemistically call him her 'father-confessor'); and as it is the case that Korda found Merle Oberon attractive enough to marry, I suppose anything is possible. Korda considered Vivien his discovery. Born in 1893, as Sandor Laszlo Kellner, he worked in Vienna, Berlin and Hollywood, before creating London Films in 1932. One brother, Zoltan, was his chief director; another, Vincent, was in charge of the art department. Gummo and Zeppo Korda were no doubt assigned useful tasks as well. Out at Denham they built seven sound stages, with fifteen star dressing rooms, cutting rooms, suites for writers, and with a private electricity plant that could've powered a small city. Buildings were spaced so far apart, staff moved between them on bicycles – not Korda, of course, who had a limo, and a flat complete with butler and chef. He was a benign despot, the father of his people, who dealt with

* As did Isabel Jeans ('she was the loveliest thing I had ever seen on the stage'); Douglas Fairbanks Jr ('I . . . shared the general enthusiasm for her staggering beauty, engaging personality, unique quality of voice, remarkable talent and for her undeniable possession of what Noël Coward has called "star quality"'); Athene Sayler, who was a little more realistic ('I thought her exquisite to look at, but no actress') and Roger Furse, who to the usual eulogies added, 'I don't suppose that up to the sad break-up with L[arry] she had ever had a serious "No" said to her since she was born.'

industrial disputes by saying, 'You are my children and I've looked after you, and all I will say is that if you are not back inside the studio by midday you will never work for me again.'

Their first success was Charles Laughton's *The Private Life of Henry VIII*, and this was followed by *The Scarlet Pimpernel*, *The Ghost Goes West*, *Things to Come*, and *Rembrandt* – that is to say, Korda's speciality was the sophisticated and romantic costume picture. When he died, in 1956, it was Olivier* who appeared on television to give the oration – which he did by facing the camera and speaking in a low, muffled voice, and by glancing away slightly now and then, he showed how moving and emotional he found the occasion. It is a reverent performance – apt for the sad story of the death of kings: 'We give thanks for his vision, his wisdom. [Pause] He was generous – he was gentle and strong, and managed to be that rare mixture, an artist who was also a man of business – extraordinary virtuosity; a joyous humour and an enchanting imagination. Great company – with his shrewd wit. [Pause] We loved

---

* Korda produced the following Olivier films: *Moscow Nights* (1936), *Fire Over England* (1937), *The Divorce of Lady X* (1938), *Q Planes* (1939), *Twenty-One Days* (1940 – made 1937), *Conquest of the Air* (1940), *That Hamilton Woman* (also directed – 1941), and his death caused the collapse of the financing for a film of *Macbeth*. Korda had wanted Olivier for *Anna Karenina* (1948), but in the event Vivien's Vronsky was Kieron Moore.

In 1949, London Films bought a shareholding in Laurence Olivier Productions – LOP – and Korda joined the board, along with Cecil Tennant, Anthony Bushnell, Roger Furse, Lovat Fraser, David Kentish and Herbert Menges, who'd worked for Sir Barry Jackson, and who since 1931 had been musical director to the Old Vic. It was an attempt by Olivier, pre-Chichester, pre-the National, to be Irving at the Lyceum. A lease was taken on the St James's Theatre, though nearly a dozen other addresses were also used, and these were the productions they presented: (a) in which Olivier also appeared: *Venus Observed* by Christopher Fry (1950); *Caesar and Cleopatra* by Bernard Shaw, and Shakespeare's *Antony and Cleopatra* (1951); (b) which Olivier also directed (but in which he did not appear): *A Streetcar Named Desire* by Tennessee Williams (1949); *The Damascus Blade* by Bridget Boland (1950); *Captain Carvallo* by Denis Cannan (1950); and (c) which Olivier merely managed: *Daphne Laureola* by James Bridie (1949); *Fading Mansions* by Jean Anouilh (1949); *Top of the Ladder* by Tyrone Guthrie (1950); *The Consul* by Gian Carlo Menotti (1951); Orson Welles' *Othello* (1951); *The Happy Times* by Samuel Taylor (1952); *Anastasia* by Marcelle Maurette (1953); *Waiting for Gillian* by Ronald Millar (1954); *Double Image* by Roger MacDougall and Ted Allan (1956); *Summer of the Seventeenth Doll* by Ray Lawler (1957); *The Shifting Heart* by Richard Beynon (1959); *One More River* by Beverley Cross (1959); *A Lodging for the Bride* by Patrick Kirwan (1960); and *Over the Bridge* by Sam Thompson (1960).

In 1957, LOP and Marilyn Monroe's film company co-produced *The Prince and the Showgirl*. When *The Sleeping Prince* had been originally staged, in 1953, Olivier had asked Korda to read out the Regent of Carpathia's lines so that he could copy the thick Hungarian accent.

him, as artists and craftsmen, because he loved us. [Pause] Warm radiance of his friendships. [Pause] He lived life in beautiful and enviable style. [Pause] We shall not look upon his like again' – as Hamlet says of his late father, up on the battlements, ghost-hunting with Horatio.

Fire Over England, Olivier and Vivien's first outing together, perhaps represents their sole period of pure happiness, before the shadows of practicality, the dreary tasks of everyday life, the complex set of problems to do with offspring, housing, maintenance, custody and alimony, closed in on them. (What was ahead of them, if happiness was behind them?) The film might actually be about beauty and its ebbing. Flora Robson's Gloriana, imperious in a huge ruff (like gigantic insects' wings), is a tragic Titania, who decides to have 'no more mirrors in any room of mine'. She's angrily aware of age and the destruction of loveliness; and in her peremptoriness it's almost like she's blaming her loyal subjects or even the world itself for making her old. Though the Queen is vain, flirtatious and cruel, Dame Flora's performance is majestic and selfless – she never appeals for sympathy; she doesn't soften her character's viciousness, and yet you know how much she is hurting when, in the privacy of her bedchamber, she takes off her shoes, unbuckles her collar, removes her jewels (she dismantles herself), whips off her wig and murmurs to her lady-in-waiting, Vivien: 'Do you like what you see in the glass?' Dame Flora doesn't sentimentalize – nor is she grotesque. The moment is more like Hamlet looking at the skull: to this favour, of illness or injury, she must come. I'm reminded of Picasso, who took a new mistress, Françoise Gilot, to see one of her predecessors, Germaine Pichot: 'She's old and toothless and poor and unfortunate now. But when she was young she was very pretty. She turned a lot of heads. Now look at her.' This horror of time's ravages was echoed by Olivier, too, when he was with Tarquin scouting for locations for *Macbeth* in Scotland, and their car stopped to allow an old lady to cross the road: 'See her? That woman? She's my age to the very day. Fifty – and who wants her? What has she got to look forward to? Where's the sex in her, and who the fuck wants to be touched by her?'

This is the weary self-disgust – an awareness of death behind the surface of life – which Dame Flora embodies; and in *Fire Over England* the melancholia, which is a strange compound of sex, fear and thwarted desire, is particularly apparent in her scenes with a young Olivier, which are not merely twisted courtship scenes – they are perverted sex scenes. The Queen relishes the news of English pirates captured and burned by the Spanish Inquisition; she's thrilled by the danger they face, the torture they know they'll endure – and all of it for her, she believes: 'That does not stop them from dying for me,' she says, with lips parted. She yearns for young bloods to sacrifice themselves – it's a sado-masochistic exercise; death and patriotism rendered erotic. Olivier's Michael Ingolby, a brave buccaneer, flying from ropes, his sword flashing, leaping aboard a ship as its sails burst into flame, is exactly the kind of dark, slim hero, full of energy and attractiveness – full of fire – that spices up her dreams. He's the pure soul who'll commingle, like a Christian martyr, love and death. The more daring his deeds, the more impossible are the missions she sends him on. 'I love her,' he says of Vivien's Cynthia, 'but I will not ask any girl's leave to do what I must' – i.e. serve the Queen, give his life for her. There is a sexual undercurrent to his obedience; a strange enslavement suggested by his need to do his duty.

War and courage is man's work; it is stirring, adolescent stuff. So where does that leave Michael's relationship with Cynthia? Back in the nursery. Olivier and Vivien scamper through the film as children, stealing kisses. Swishing along the corridors like the white peacock at Tara, the Queen's lady-in-waiting arranges flowers, hunts for a lost pearl, plays the spinet; and when she embraces Olivier, Dame Flora slinks off, looking back at the couple with envy: they belong to a romantic world she's never known. No wonder – for James Wong Howe, the cinematographer, lights them as Romeo and Juliet. Olivier is actually posed on a balcony at one point, and he has dark eyes, and a luminous complexion; and he and Vivien, if we can close our ears to their prattle ('I had forgotten that you were so beautiful' – 'I had forgotten that you were so tall [pause] and haunted' – 'Spain is a land of ghosts'), belong in an Old Master, Vermeer, perhaps, or – apt for Korda – Rembrandt. They are positioned in silhouette, with the light almost tawny, despite the black and white. Sunshine, shafting through the mullion windows, glints off an hourglass. A single silver candlestick decorates the room. They debate whether they have a right to be so happy.

Vivien is dressed in white gowns and the buildings have white plasterwork that suggest the elegant eighteenth century rather than the Tudor period – but what does this matter? We are really nowhere other than England in the thirties, and the invective about Spain ('which rules by force and fear') is directed at Nazi Germany. When he's not playing Gloriana's S & M games, or chasing Vivien in the palace, Olivier is spying for England as a resourceful secret agent. 'I *am* England,' says the Queen; 'How small we are,' sighs Cynthia, studying a globe. Nobody has seen the connection before, but it is to Dame Flora's line that Charles Laughton was alluding – ironically? whimsically? – when he called backstage after *Henry V* at the Old Vic and said, 'Larry, you *are*

England!' Elizabeth I, indeed, becomes a warrior-queen. When the Armada has been sighted, and the beacons lit on every hilltop, and the call to arms sweeps across the country – accompanied by a montage of drums and activity and horsemen carrying torches – Dame Flora, resplendent in a huge hat, is amongst her troops at Tilbury, informing them that 'I have the heart and valour of a king.' She's a female Henry V; and by the amount of mascara and lip gloss he's wearing in souvenir stills of the Old Vic show, so was Olivier.

Olivier represented the English consciousness in the same way that John Wayne symbolized the American ideal of gun-slinging frontier heroics. As we'll see, he played Nelson as a mouthpiece for Churchillian propaganda ('I would not for the sake of any peace, however fortunate, consent to sacrifice one jot of England's honour'), and *Henry V* (unlike the stage production) was a contemporary war film in fancy dress. Olivier gave speeches at the Albert Hall, ostensibly as himself, but he was still the King: Lieutenant Laurence Olivier of the Fleet Air Arm, ends the 'Battle for Freedom' pageant with quite the most declamatory performance he ever gave – he contorts his body, writhes, yelps, and throws himself about like a lunatic: 'We will go forward, heart, nerve, and spirit steeled; we will attack; we will smite our foes; we will conquer. And from this hour on our watchwords will be urgency, in all our decisions, speed, in the execution of our plans, courage, in the face of all our enemies. And may God bless our cause!'*

In *Fire Over England*, his superior sense of Englishness is conveyed by the way he decides to sail single-handed from Lisbon in a fishing smack to tell the Queen personally that 'Spain is the prison of all freedom'; and, kneeling, then lounging, at the foot of the throne, 'Spain is horror.' The Queen is so transfixed by this intelligence, she sends him back. In her robes and strings of black pearls, she's an angel of death – quite as forbidding as Raymond Massey's King Philip, who sits in the Escorial dressed in a black tunic, with black collars and black cuffs, like Mephistopheles. 'Only by fear can the people be made to do their duty,' he opines. So how is it the English do their duty? Out of gallantry? ('I had no idea that Englishmen were so gallant,' Michael is informed by Elena,

* As if this wasn't stirring enough, 'British News No. 100: *The Freedom Pageant*', which also includes, in the newsreel, reports on the Allies in Burma, Stafford Cripps returning from India, the enthronement of the Archbishop of Canterbury, and an inspection conducted by the Colonel-in-Chief of the Grenadier Guards, the sixteen-year-old Princess Elizabeth, exists only on inflammable nitrate stock, and I had to view it in a refrigerated shed situated on the roof of the British Film Institute. Much more of Olivier's incendiary acting and I'd have been bouncing off Big Ben in my charred undergarments.

played by Tamara Desni, who in the shadows of the Spanish garden resembles Vivien – as women in Olivier's films often tend to: Jean Simmons in *Hamlet* and *Spartacus*, Dorothy Tutin in *The Beggar's Opera*, Sarah Miles in *Lady Caroline Lamb*.) Out of a love for their country which is distinguished by a contempt for everybody who lives abroad – who have different habits and eat funny foreign food? Olivier, disguised as a spy (he turns up in a pointy beard), attends a dinner party in Madrid, but gives the game away when he refuses to raise his goblet and toast the Armada; despite his banter during the meal, including the singing of a song to lute accompaniment ('Love often turns to hate/Does it not, madame . . .'), the alert observer will have already noted the power and resolve in his fierce hazel eyes. His slight pout protests his patriotism. In a trice, he's barricading the door and setting light to the curtains – *Fire Over England* is a pyromaniac's dream: it begins with heretics being burned at the stake, the monks chanting spookily as smoke spirals into the sky; it concludes with the defeat of the Spanish fleet at night, the ships on fire, the masts and rigging exploding in showers of sparks.

It's a mystery how Olivier gets a blaze going at the Escorial; it has huge empty rooms, the only kindling being an ebony crucifix. Perhaps Michael Ingolby brought a canister of petrol with him in the fishing smack? In no time at all, he's leaping off the roof and banisters, clattering across the roof tiles – flames shooting everywhere – and, dramatically dishevelled, he's teletransported to another private audience with Dame Flora in order to say, 'When the Armada sails there will be fire over England!' What's more arresting is the fire in his voice. Olivier was on the brink of thirty when he made this film. He looks at least ten years younger, and plays it as pert, cocky, strong and gentle: Ingolby is an innocent. (Dubbed a knight at the end he mutters, 'Your grace, your grace,' much moved – he'd have settled for election to Pop.) It is a hyper-romantic performance, allowing us to imagine what his stage presence must have been like at this period: direct and physical, more alive than anybody else; and when the camera was not rolling he was toning himself up behind closed doors with Vivien. 'I knew what was going on. I felt sad for Jill,' said Raymond Massey, '[because] she was ignorant of the whole business. In a way I was happy for Larry, for I could see that Vivien was making a new man out of him. On balance, though, I had a feeling of foreboding for all of them . . . But then I talked with Larry. It was about a month after his son was born. He was consumed with guilt. He was putting an end to it, he said. He loved Jill and he'd been a fool. With Vivien – well, it was just a wild infatuation, but it was to Jill he owed his loyalty, and the child. And that, I thought, would be the end of it.'

Did Jill become pregnant at the end of 1935 to try and bind herself to him? (By remaining at Burchett's Green for the duration, growing fat and letting her complexion go, Jill in fact, though inadvertently, gave Olivier his liberty to be in London.) Simon Tarquin Olivier – '[the name] came to me in a mad moment. It has such dramatic overtones!' I'll say: Tarquin is Lucrece's rapist* – was born on 21 August 1936. Olivier rushed from Denham to the hospital to view mother and child, still smelling of Vivien's perfume. Vivien accompanied him in person on a subsequent visit, and she wrote and told her husband: 'Jill had her baby and I saw it last night . . . Larry says it is like Edward G. Robinson which is a little cruel. He has already started reciting Shakespeare to it.' Was Olivier trying to be open about his adultery? Was he confronting his guilt? Or was he like a child, mesmerized by his own misdeeds? (He arrived late at Tarquin's christening – with Vivien.) What a scene: a wife, a mistress, a new-born son! It is at precisely this moment, I think, that he started to become stiff and withdrawn. What these people meant to him in the long run was not love (with its involuntariness), but that he couldn't love; he couldn't be happy in the settled state of marriage; its day-to-day basis – he didn't feel part of such things. What is significant with Olivier is not love, but the fact of his inability to feel it, to need it. Or – to look at this from another angle – he could love, but he didn't want to be loved back. It gets in the way. The intensity of Vivien's love, the position she put him in, was a humiliation – as he said to James Wong Howe, 'I've got to give her up, Jimmy. I don't want to, God knows. But I must. And I can't.' She was new and disruptive; and with Joan Plowright, who was his comforter or nurse, Olivier was quickly adulterous again, with Sarah Miles. His preference was for transgression; for uncertainties and hazards – and it's no surprise that he confided to Tyrone Guthrie at this time, 'I already know what it feels like to be a Hamlet in real life.' As Guthrie glossed: 'Larry was profoundly unhappy. It all had to do with the conflict between his violent, immature love for Vivien Leigh and his more mature, subdued attachment to Jill Esmond. He was . . . in a quandary about what to do.'

What Guthrie convinced him he had to do was go ahead and play Hamlet on the stage. But though the problems did indeed concern

---

* His 'ravishing strides', according to Macbeth, are like a wolf's, padding about his murderous business; and Iachimo, sneaking into Imogen's bedchamber, talks to himself as 'Our Tarquin [who] thus/Did softly press the rushes ere he waken'd/The chastity he wounded.' To Shakespeare, he's an image of stealth and mercilessness.

and were provoked by Vivien and Jill, and their respective children and commitments, I don't think maturity or the lack of it is at issue; and in psychological terms we could reach back to Olivier's childhood and argue that, after the loss of his mother, he would never get possessive again: that would be to expose himself to hurt, should he be betrayed or abandoned again. What interests me is that compared with how he could be towards Vivien as Michael Ingolby, Nelson, Hamlet, Antony, and so on, in real life he was paradoxically impersonal; Jill had felt this after *Bird in Hand* and *No Funny Business.* (Did Joan, in relation to *The Entertainer, Uncle Vanya, Three Sisters* or *The Merchant of Venice*?) Olivier can imagine being in love – as with Vivien in their films and plays together – but because of his separateness, his sense of isolation, actually being in love is an impossibility; and he can make use of this.*

Guthrie had admired Olivier in *Romeo and Juliet*; he particularly noted those qualities I drew out of *Fire Over England*, and informed the star that 'your performance had such terrific vitality – speed and intelligence and muscularity – a lyric quality pictorially, if not musically'. Guthrie† first met Olivier at Eva Moore's place, Appleporch, and had invited him to join the Old Vic for the next season, 1937/38, to play the Prince of Denmark, Sir Toby Belch, Henry V, Macbeth, Iago and Coriolanus. When I look at photographs of him in these roles, what strikes me is the heaviness, the ornateness, of the make-up: a great freight of silvery crêpe-hair, highlighted creases and crevasses on the skin, greasepaint whorls, green and white and black. This isn't disguise, it's sculpture. Olivier's head belongs with Jacob Epstein or Michael Ayrton – with the constructions, masks and busts with bits added on of the thirties and forties. (The style lingered, of course. As Sir John French, in *Oh! What a Lovely War*, his moustache gives the performance.) There was also to

* Picasso said of Chaplin – and we could substitute Olivier: 'He's a man who, like me, has suffered a great deal at the hands of women'. It's absurd, these powerful males, seeing themselves as victims.

† Sir (William) Tyrone Guthrie (1900–71), the cousin of Tyrone Power, the actor, educated at Wellington and St John's College, Oxford, was Lilian Baylis' senior director at the Old Vic and Sadler's Wells; and he succeeded Baylis as the chief administrator after her death on the opening night of Olivier's *Macbeth* in 1937. He resigned ten years later and moved to the Edinburgh Festival, where he placed the audience around three sides of the stage at the Assembly Hall – thus developing the principles of his non-proscenium-arch theatre, which was first seen at the improvised ballroom setting of Olivier's *Hamlet* in the Merienlyst Hotel, Denmark, in 1937. The techniques were refined at Stratford, Ontario, in 1952, and at Minneapolis, in 1963. Guthrie was consulted over the design for Chichester and the National's Olivier Theatre. He retired to Ireland to run a jam factory.

be a modern piece, *The King of Nowhere*, by James Bridie, in which Olivier played an actor who has escaped from a lunatic asylum – and to quote from the review in the *Times*, 'Mr Laurence Olivier's is . . . a shrewd portrait of this man whose tragedy is that, except in the parts he plays, he is without identity.' The role of Vivaldi, as he was called, the blank, the cipher, must have seemed wish-fulfillingly ideal to Olivier – who was beset. In a photograph from the production, he's dressed in a tweed coat and a homberg hat, and on his face he's wearing the saddest clown motley, frightened eyes, a down-turned mouth, outside of Picasso's harlequin phase. He's a man who does not respond; who cannot understand.

How could Olivier recover himself? Regain himself? By an immersion in work; and henceforward there'd always be a definite presence – an inescapable solid force – within his roles. Vivien, meantime, was acting out her emotions and telling Korda, 'Alex, we must tell you our great secret – we're in love and we're going to be married.' The moghul reputedly smiled and said, 'Don't be silly – everybody knows that. I've known that for weeks and weeks.' Long enough, therefore, to set up a project for the pair of them: *Twenty-One Days*, directed by Basil Dean, with a script by Graham Greene,* who slighted the assignment: 'a terrible affair and typical in one way of the cinema-world. I had to adapt a story of John Galsworthy – a sensational tale of a murderer who killed himself and an innocent man who was hanged for the suicide's crime. If the story had any force, it lay in its extreme sensationalism; but as sensationalism was impossible under the rules of the British Board of Film Censors, who forbade suicide and forbade a failure of British justice, there was little left of Galsworthy's plot when I had finished.' The film is difficult to find; and those who claim to have seen it or even to have heard of it follow the example of its stars, who walked out of the screening before the end. 'The Oliviers forbade me ever to see this film and I never did,' states Alan Dent.† 'They themselves only saw

* Greene met Olivier and Vivien on board Korda's yacht, sailing to Istanbul: 'I quite like the Oliviers – he is nicer, but she has more brains.'

† Alan Dent, known as Jock, was the theatre and film critic of the *Manchester Guardian*. He it was who carried the *Richard III* sword from the Haymarket, where Gielgud was appearing, to the New Theatre, for the presentation to Olivier. In 1947, Dent was Olivier's textual adviser on the script for the *Hamlet* film, and he joined the team in the sunshine of Santa Marguerita Ligure, where the gloomy Nordic production was planned. Vivien had insisted on a five-room suite at the Hotel Miramare filled with specially hired antiques. Also present, in addition to Dent and the Oliviers, were Filippo Del Giudice, the producer, Roger Furse and Carmen Dillon, the designers, and Reginald Beck and Desmond Dickinson, the associate producer and cinematographer. The

"about a third of it" at a public showing in New York.' Felix Barker, another critic they befriended, concurs, and consigns the photoplay to a footnote: 'To this day, they have never seen the film right through.'

It's not that the film is bad (though Korda cannily didn't release it until three years later – 1940, when Olivier and Leigh were famous); it's that it's disconcerting. Disallowed from reproducing Galsworthy, Greene introduces Greene – it's a film about sin and redemption, rather than crime and punishment. The sordid sense of religion; guilt and suffering; the wallowing in a sense of unworthiness: the sado- masochistic squirming of *The Power and the Glory* is here, and not only in the character of the priest, John Aloysius Evans, who is wrongly arrested for the murder, yet who wants to be executed, because he believes he is damned anyway. Olivier, as a man who can't be false to himself, is the one wrestling with his conscience – just as he was doing so in his private domestic life – and it is wonderful that his character is called Larry (Larry Durrant), and that Vivien runs towards him and embraces him, exclaiming, 'Larry!' (The way she pronounces it, he's in fact 'Lerry!')

There is a moral ambiguousness at the centre of *Twenty-One Days*. It concerns the cover-up for a murder, yet the victim would seem to have deserved his fate. But who has the right to make such judgements? What happens is that Larry goes to visit his mistress, Wanda Walenn (Vivien), and discovers her in a dispute with a plump little villain, played by Esmé Percy, who is demanding money and threatening blackmail. He turns out to be Wanda's husband, who'd captured her in Paris three years previously, and who abandoned her soon after using her. Wanda never informs us precisely what was involved – except that she says she was a Russian refugee and starving – but prostitution and pimping are implied. Esmé and Larry get into a tussle; the former clonks his noodle on the fender, and so Larry drags the body out into the foggy night, abandoning it in the alley – where the drunk priest lays claim to it. Larry then visits his brother, a barrister played by Leslie Banks, the

---

screenplay was completed, in fine detail, after a month. Olivier handed the document reverently to Del Giudice, who recalled, 'I was moved to see a great man like Larry make such a gesture, and, excited by the marginal notes and corrections in Larry's own hand, I was kept awake by the script all night.' The hotel bill came to £7,000.

Dent worked in a similar editorial capacity for Olivier (and Shakespeare) on *Henry V* and *Richard III*. He was doolally about Vivien, and after her 'untimely death at the height of her career', produced *Vivien Leigh: A Bouquet* (London, 1969): not 'a formal biography but shows his friend as he knew her' – i.e., out in the garden mostly, snipping off buds for her flower arrangements, subduing, taming nature. I attempted to reach Dent's family, using the address in *Who Was Who*, but Chilterns Manor, Bourne End, Buckinghamshire, is now a 'Private Residential Home for the Retired and Elderly'.

Chorus in *Henry V*, who helps destroy the evidence and invents an alibi. The priest is arrested and remanded in custody for twenty-one days. Larry marries Wanda, frets and emotes, and decides to confess – but there's no need to do so. The priest dies of a heart attack and the case is dropped. Leslie Banks, meantime, conveying intelligence and anxiety by smiting his forehead, and who becomes implicated, trying to help his brother and taking charge, gradually loses his grip – and, at the end, does he go off to commit suicide? The last shot is of him gazing through the window as Larry disappears into the throng of a street market. Perhaps Larry is about to top himself, too, distressed that Keith Durrant, KC, destined for the Bench, has offered to bribe him to go abroad, to avoid scandal?

The bodies might pile up, as in *Hamlet*; and this is a version of *Hamlet*. Murder most foul; an unnatural love affair; vengeance; a self-involved hero. Olivier is meant to be a wastrel, whose farming schemes have failed in Rhodesia or Brazil (each time he's on a ship he's 'the first man in the bar'); but Olivier doesn't play young Durrant as the ravaged, penniless ne'er-do-well. Though he is tense and neurotic, he is vigorous. His fedora is at a rakish tilt (he flicks the brim); he is natty in his gloves (which play a part in the murder enquiry); and we are treated to long, lingering close-ups of the planes and angles of his cheekbones – he's made up to look like Vivien's twin, or the Old Vic Hamlet photographed by Angus McBean, and we can picture him as being down from Wittenberg for the vacation, comparing and contrasting the mess and muddle of the plot he's pitched headlong into with the higher truths he's been contemplating at university. He has an essential decency: he knows he'll have to go to the police and confess, after the 'reprieve' of twenty-one days; Olivier's Larry has got drive and purpose – he's unable to be fully furtive. He *is* Hamlet. Young and smart and with a nobleness that shines through in a world of death and intrigue, his initial fecklessness disappears and he smiles sadly – ironically – on learning of the timely collapse of the priest. This news doesn't make him happier; he's still uncomfortable with his conscience. His humour is that of a Hamlet who is not taken in by the artificiality of the twenty-one-day idyll: 'If it be now, 'tis not to come. If it be not to come, it will be now. If it be not now, yet it will come . . .' – that is to say, the moment of dying and accountability.

He and Wanda go shopping and we see them reflected in plate glass; they traipse to Southend on a paddle-steamer – a Pearly King and Queen are on board, laughing and carousing, and the London scenes have a documentary realism: lots of exotic foreigners in Soho cafés; a noisy funfair, where Larry wins a doll in a shooting gallery, which needless to say gets trampled underfoot. We have shots of the Thames, of the City: it is a world and a way of life that is about to come to an end, for the characters, who can't have happiness on false pretences, for the Londoners themselves, with the war, and for Olivier and Vivien. The journey down the river, which contains no dialogue (it is a travelogue), also gives us a moment to differentiate between Olivier's first Hamlet and, across an interval of years, the blond-rinse version which he put on film, and where he seems dulled, docile. In 1948, the camera records his absorption in being a private person; his cynicism. He knows what life is demanding of him – whereas in 1937, when turning thirty, he was only finding out. His first Hamlet has more energy – he's all nerves and feeling; more edge as, off-stage, as we know, he was carrying on with Vivien and abandoning his obligations. He was quite candid to Tynan about this. Olivier admitted to him that 'his Hamlet was done primarily for Vivien. With all its physical virility and acrobatic flash, it was his way of wooing her.' Vivien, as we also know, attended most of the performances,* so that (says Tynan) 'she could be near Larry during a time when she was supposed to be staying away from him. Larry's performance was his long-distance valentine to her.'

If *Hamlet* was a love letter, it was also a confession of guilt: in the play, as Olivier understood it in 1937 ('although I now think there are many more things in *Hamlet* than that', he admitted in 1967), the prince was irresolute because he felt subconsciously guilty himself. He can't kill Claudius, because Claudius has only done what he, Hamlet, secretly desired – a removal of his father so as to have unimpeded access to his mother. Translating this directly to Olivier's experience: how badly are you going to behave? Are you really going to risk purchasing happiness at the cost of your soul? And if Vivien was separated from him, out in the auditorium, she's similarly faint in *Twenty-One Days*. She doesn't register; she simply does not register. Ostensibly the Russian refugee, we know nothing of her deprivations or her strength; nor how she's currently supporting herself; or what she feels about Larry's accidental crime and his pangs of conscience. (Let alone what she got up to with her first husband – Esmeé Percy, incidentally, had a glass eye, which once plopped out on the stage: 'Don't step on it, for God's sake,' he yelped, to the consternation of his fellow actors and the audience. 'They're so expensive.') Vivien is neither shrill, nor abusive, nor noble – the gamut

* He gave forty-two performances, between 5 January and 20 February 1937. Vivien saw a minimum of fourteen of them.

she essays as Scarlett O'Hara; she's blank. There's no enterprise between Larry and Wanda – which is to say, Vivien has no inner access to Olivier. What we are watching is their doomed love.

Before filming began, and whilst Olivier was preparing for the Old Vic season – after *Fire Over England* – there'd been an ugly, clumsy private drama. In October 1936, Olivier and Jill went on holiday to Capri, in an attempt to patch up the marriage. Vivien and a friend of Leigh Holman's, Oswald Frewen, suddenly turned up out of the proverbial blue – as Vivien wrote mock-disingenuously to her husband: 'They [Larry and Jill] were thrilled to see us, as they haven't spoken English to anyone for two weeks they said! and we got an avalanche.' The foursome traipsed to Naples and Pompeii. Jill was justifiably outraged at the encounter; she was humiliated, especially when Olivier came out with his prepared speech. 'He told Viv he was finished with Jill,' Frewen wrote in his diary. 'He was all set to send Jill back to London on her own, and he wanted Viv to go back to Capri with him.'

Jill appeared resigned – she'd seen it coming. 'Real passion – I've only seen it that once. If you are ever hit by it, God help you. There's nothing you can do.' But was it real? Isn't there an element of play-acting, suggested by their nursery-room endearments – Vivien called Olivier Ba or Baba; he called her Puss or Pussy; sometimes they referred to each other as Boy? Hollywood columnists were soon to gush, of the alliance of Scarlett and Heathcliff, 'Their love is the most beautiful thing I have ever known' – but it was an artificial construct, a painted paradise, less substantial than the scenes from a marriage in *Rebecca*, when Max forgets the certificate, and it is dropped from the window of the *mairie*, and he catches it in his hat; and a French wedding party goes by – a jolly procession – and it's all captured in a home movie; and we see Joan Fontaine and Max's happy faces on the screen – Max forgetting his bitterness – and this contrasts with the gloom of the Manderley library, where they are sitting now.

Twenty-One Days, the contracts for which were signed in March 1937, and which began shooting in May, was halted for a week in June, so that Olivier could lead the Old Vic Company's *Hamlet* to Denmark – to Kronsborg Castle, to Elsinore itself. Guthrie had offered the part of Ophelia to Jill, but Olivier was insistent on having Vivien in the cast. 'But I've already asked Jill' – 'I don't care . . . Vivien plays it or I don't go.' The production was to celebrate the Silver Jubilee of King Christian X; and as an official ceremonial occasion, Jill was expected to accompany Olivier in a civilian capacity as his wife. It was worse than Capri. Alec Guinness, playing Osric, took Jill boating on the lake, as a diversion away from the public lovers. The show itself was rained off, so performances were given in the ballroom of the Merienlyst Hotel – as virtually and perforce theatre-in-the-round, the thrust staging was a forerunner of Chichester. 'Larry conducted a lightning rehearsal with the company, improvising exits and entrances, and rearranging business,' remembers Guthrie, who gave himself the job of setting out the chairs. Vivien, meantime, having posted cheerful holiday postcards to her husband, and perhaps preparing herself for Ophelia, went mad: 'She sort of disappeared inside herself,' said an observer, 'at first she wouldn't talk to anyone, then she wouldn't stop talking – yelling, really.' Olivier bundled her into a dressing room, from which she emerged made-up and in costume – but 'not a word to anyone, just staring blankly into space'. She dutifully recited her lines ('her talent fell short of her beauty', claimed Anthony Quayle, her Laertes) and returned to her dressing room, without explanation or apology.

Within ten days of their return to England, Vivien and Olivier officially separated from their spouses. Two decades later, Holman still felt the need to explain to Gertrude Hartley why he didn't cling to her daughter: 'I felt utterly hopeless but I did not badger and beseech her to change her mind and had I done so I would only have got something equivalent to no flowers or cable on a first night' – i.e., Vivien would have turned on him, an actress in a snit. His only weapon, and defence, was to refuse her a divorce. He wanted to be quite sure it wasn't a crazy elopement, an infatuation that would run its course; and he told his friends, 'she can come back whenever she wants'. Jill sought solace in Tarquin – in motherhood. 'I made it seem as though we were just another family separated by the war,' she told Herbert Kretzmer in 1961. 'That helped a lot . . . All the time Tarquin was growing up, he had a picture in his bedroom of Larry in his Fleet Air Arm uniform. He was brought up to be proud of his father.'* Of his father the actor, or the man?

---

* The interview continued: 'I still see Larry often when he is in England, and we correspond regularly . . . I sent Larry a telegram of congratulation when he married Joan Plowright, and I had such a charming letter back from Joan. I've never met her. I admire her tremendously as an actress, of course. Yes, I'm awfully pleased about Larry and Joan Plowright. Awfully pleased about the whole thing. Really I am. Of course, I wasn't *quite* so pleased when it happened with Vivien. But there you are.'

After the divorce, Jill and Olivier met four times to my certain knowledge. Tarquin's twenty-first birthday party was held at Notley; Olivier escorted Jill to Tarquin's wedding at St Mary's, Cadogan Square, in 1965; and at the beginning of the fifties, in what Tarquin accurately calls 'a curious pot-pourri of past betrayals, divided loyalties and

Prior to the Denmark trip, Olivier and Vivien had pooled their Korda earnings to purchase and decorate Durham Cottage, in Christchurch Street, Chelsea. Two up, two down, and soon smeared with striped primrose wallpaper, moss-green carpets, and curtains with blue bows and white frills, bobble fringes and pleated edges. Vivien imparted her household hints to *Woman's Own*: (a) use orange-red and purple-red together for a striking effect, (b) pale tones give a sense of space. Keep the lightest for ceiling, darkest for floor, and (c) make bathroom or kitchen pretty with the new steam-proof floral papers. 'Everything matches in this exciting kitchen,' readers were informed. 'The gay blue and white wallpaper has been cellulosed to withstand condensation . . . Chairs and table legs have been painted powder blue . . . Manufacturers are making kitchen equipment now in this lovely blue shade so that everything from pan handles to canisters, casseroles and pedal dustbin has been bought in the same colour . . . To warm the gay blue and white scheme, Vivien Leigh chose a cosy red for the lino flooring and there's always a touch of red on the mantelpiece in candles and a vase full of flowers or berries.' What are the words I'm looking for? Migraine-inducing?

They were installed in this house of horrors by November 1937. Vivien read and reread *Gone With the Wind*, telling a reporter, 'I've cast myself as Scarlett O'Hara, what do you think?' Olivier made *The Divorce of Lady X*, converting into farce his experiences of flirtation and courtship; his knowledge of what happens to people who freely follow their natures. His adversary is Ralph Richardson who, as the cuckolded and addle-pated Lord Mere, has that weird clarity – or clairvoyance – which at the Old Vic he'd bring to Falstaff and Peer Gynt. He telephones Logan, the lawyer, in the small hours, so that we can see Olivier in a chaste, narrow single bed; and when he comes for a confrontation, there's real danger and malice crackling in the air. Richardson is the 'deep-revolving, witty' Buckingham of *Richard III*; and what a lost opportunity, Olivier's not being Vronsky to Richardson's shamed and inscrutable

present laughter', Vivien, Olivier, Holman, Suzanne, Jill and Tarquin went on holiday together to stay at a villa called L'Oulivette, near Cannes, which belonged to Leigh Holman's sister, Joyce. Vivien, in between the bathing and picnics, read Williams' new play, *A Streetcar Named Desire*.

The last encounter is poignant. Jill went to Vivien's memorial service. 'I wanted to go for myself. I don't quite know why, but I felt an urge. Viv had been part of my life for so long, over thirty years . . . When I turned to leave I found Larry standing right behind me. In that very large church full of hundreds of people, wasn't it extraordinary that we should find ourselves together . . .' More extraordinarily sad is that he hadn't recognized her.

Karenin in *Anna Karenina*; for even here, in a light comedy, he and Richardson are sexual rivals – which is a version of their being acting rivals. They'd first met at the Birmingham Rep, Olivier amusing Richardson by downing a glass of gin and peppermint and proclaiming it 'good for the ovaries'. It was to be a curious friendship, marked by the number of times they attempted to kill each other. Olivier, driving the two of them to Brighton, went bang over a crossroads at Croydon without slowing up – indeed, he accelerated. 'It is a well-known thing, Ralphie, that when you get to a point of danger, get over it as quick as you can.' To which Richardson, who'd practically shat himself, replied, 'Laurence, never, never, as long as I do live, will I forgive you for that.'

Was it recklessness or courage? Olivier, as with his death-defying physical stunts in his work, and the liveliness of his actual death scenes, was simply trying to cheat death; and he had another opportunity to count his lucky stars in Paris, in 1945, when after a performance of *Richard III*, at the Comédie-Française, a drunk Richardson entered Olivier's bedroom, picked him up and dangled him out of the window by his legs. The reasons behind the assault emerged years later, in a conversation Richardson had with Peter Hall. They were discussing their ambivalent attitude to Olivier; how, in his absence, you could decide in your mind not to like him, and yet then, 'Ralph said . . . as soon as he saw him, the charisma, the size of the man, took over, and he loved him again.' The actors were professionally jealous of each other. Richardson was stung with envy when Olivier was greeted at the Glasgow Arts Club and told he had 'the eyes of a poet' – i.e. glamour. Olivier, as Shallow, tried to steal the Gloucestershire orchard scenes from Richardson's Falstaff by swatting bees in an elaborate interpolated pantomime; and, as Hotspur or Richard, he'd really go for him in the fight scenes: 'Steady boy now, easy fellow, merely venture to submit,' Richardson would murmur. Yet it is as a critic of Olivier and Vivien's interior decoration – of their taste; of the celestial conditions they made for themselves – that Richardson proved to be most assertive. He brought fireworks for a party at Durham Cottage; they went off backwards, burnt the curtains and ignited the dining room. His violent comment on his friends' display and grandeur didn't stop there. 'At Notley, while admiring the ancient paintings on the ceiling, which is now the loft, I stepped backwards and came through the ceiling to the best bedroom.' According to Olivier, Richardson had whirled around 'in pure wonderment' and toppled off the beam. Richardson's account is more sinister: 'Larry said to me, "Why don't you take a step back to see the pictures better?"' Whatever the complete truth, after the rocket incident Vivien emerged from behind the sofa, blackened with soot like G. H. Elliott, The White-Faced Coon; and after the second affair Richardson made the Confucian prognostication: 'If you prod a tigress twice in her lair, you must not expect her to purr.'

Olivier and Vivien, for all their apparent happiness and cold perfection, struck a friend as 'two exquisite pieces of china teetering on the edge of a shelf'. Their former partners were growing truculent. After a gourmandizing trip to France, the route from restaurant to restaurant devised by Charles Laughton (with whom Vivien had recently made *St Martin's Lane*), and which took in St Paul de Vence, La Dramon-Plage, Vonnas, Grenoble, Sauveterre and Nay – where the Oliviers came from – Vivien appealed to her husband: ' . . . perhaps, Leigh darling, it might be easier for you . . . if things were clear and definite . . . the last months have been full of pain and unhappiness, not only for you and Jill, and don't you think this might be remedied . . . if you think you possibly can . . . divorce me[?]' He did not relent. Jill was delaying the divorce, as if waiting for Olivier to become rich and famous in Hollywood before settling the level of alimony. ('For Christ's sake, Larry, pay her what she wants,' snapped Vivien.) Indeed, she never really worked again, retreating into obscurity at the age of thirty. One of Olivier's principal grouches, in old age, was that 'Jill saw me as a meal ticket for life', which might explain why he is hard on her in his memoirs.* Jill was determined to get money out of him ('I have no need to worry for at least two years,' she stated in 1940, whilst her flatmate, Jessica Tandy, had to augment her earnings by taking a job as a clerk at the British Consulate); it was her revenge for betraying her trust, for turning his back on the help the Esmond family had given him at the beginning of his career, for succeeding in the Shakespeare roles he'd been discussing and planning with her for years. They last worked together in Guthrie's *Twelfth Night* at the Old Vic, in the spring of 1937, when Olivier was Sir Toby; she was Olivia, to Jessica Tandy's Viola, who exclaims: 'I hate ingratitude more in a man/Than lying, vainness, babbling, drunkenness,/Or any taint of vice whose strong corruption/Inhabits our frail blood.'

Jill's hair went white; her voice dropped an octave; she forswore men and lived in St John's Wood with a succession of lady companions. Her view of events – congruent with what we know of her temperament, and how she always treated him, i.e. as if he was back at school – was that Olivier, an inherently weak-willed man, was in thrall to a hell-cat.

* 'Was Jill really ever that good?' he asked David O. Selznick in later years, fully expecting him to collude and be dismissive.

'I still think he is a nice person. He was just *very* weak and still is,' she told her mother in 1941. With due allowance for personal animus, she was perceptive about Vivien: 'her face is just a mask and her eyes hard and cruel . . . We were *so* charming to each other and so insincere,' she said of their courtesy calls. But Olivier wasn't weak. There was a determined toughness in all he did; and it was her belief that he needed to be directed which made him swerve away. He wanted to do good; he was never facile, and the love he had for his art came first. If he'd eclipsed Jill, in terms of fame and accomplishment, he tried not to let this happen with Vivien, with the result that as she lost him, and grieved for him, and faltered, the process went on in public. (The Oliviers must be judged by appearances.) *The School for Scandal*, for example, on the Australian tour, in 1948,* laid emphasis on Sir Peter Teazle's marital relations and not, as is usual, on Joseph Surface's hypocrisy or the comic gossips. Sir Peter, gouty and fruity and ruefully wise, had a new young wife of whom he says, 'How happy I should be if I could tease her into loving me.' Off-stage (only slightly off-stage) Olivier was less wistful with his Lady Teazle. Vivien, her cue approaching, had mislaid her red shoes. 'Put on any shoes, and just get up there!' yelled Olivier. She wouldn't budge. 'Get up on that stage, you little bitch,' he insisted, and slapped her face. 'Don't you dare hit me, you bastard' – 'And don't *you* dare to call me a bastard, because *we* know who is one, don't *we*' . . .

Three years later, Shaw's *Caesar and Cleopatra* and Shakespeare's *Antony and Cleopatra* again probed their combative personalities. In the former play, Caesar teaches Cleopatra how to rule; how to deploy her greatness and power wisely. In Shakespeare's account, we see how she's not bothered to learn these lessons. Caesar's advice on clemency has gone for nothing – and Olivier played him as a worn-out conqueror, who clings to imperial rank and self-command. He kept his energies for Antony, whose emotional squandering, waywardness and sexual infatuation ran up costs he could comprehend: 'I mean really he's an absolute twerp, isn't he? A stupid man . . . Not a lot between the ears has Antony. Now Cleopatra, she's the one. She has wit, style and sophistication . . . It was a purely physical relationship. Two very attractive human beings determined to do wonderful things to each other. Result: suicide.'†

Is that what it came down to, transcendental sex? Why else were he and Vivien such a quickly disenchanted couple? Something was lost in

* And at the New Theatre, London, from 20 January until 4 June 1949.

† Olivier's advice to a player: 'It's a wonderful part. But just remember, all you future Antonys, one little word of advice: Cleopatra's got you firmly by the balls.'

consummation; their life together was erotic only in prospect. For all Vivien's flippancy and mischievousness, there was a gravity never far off. She needed lights and people, whereas Olivier, noted Eileen Herlie, his Hamlet's Gertrude, would fall quiet at mealtimes at Notley, counteracting the quick, bold chatter about theatre and films by professing only to be interested in, as it might be, dairy farming. A harshness, a forbiddingness, started to deepen, or change, his romantic urges – to become Heathcliff, or Maxim de Winter, or Darcy, hammering out their thunderbolts. Asked, in 1982, why he didn't simply relinquish Vivien, he said, 'I can't tell you why I stayed with her so many years . . . I didn't know what else to do, but to stay along and suffer . . . You develop a very deep feeling if you have the determination to go through a terrible lot to be together in the first instance, as we did, to go through scandal, to receive awful letters from the public, to have people spitting at you in the street. It breeds in you a great determination.'

After the failure to cling on to happiness, love came to be seen as something corrupting – something which deteriorates, not grows and evolves. We must remember that they both had a religious upbringing. In what could they now have faith? Olivier concealed his aggression, and confronted his guilt and anxiety, in his acting – think of the proud, hopeless pain in his look of surprise, of enquiry, in role after role. Vivien, an odd woman, whose madness, like Marilyn Monroe's, was induced by her beauty, was searching for a fulfilment to replace the sacramental Catholic rituals and experience of her childhood. What would provide the extreme state where she could lose herself? Gardening? Canasta? Frolicking with her Siamese cats? Her obsession became Olivier – not the real Olivier, who was almost irrelevant, an impertinence; but the Olivier of her brave illusions, her tremendous illusions. She gathered framed photographs, mementoes: a shrine to a meteoric figure of genius. Paradoxically, the acting and display didn't destroy her: it tethered her to the little bit of reality she had. (Confident of being lovely, she turned exhibitionism into a kind of poster art.) To Olivier, however, she must have come to seem like an apparition, the kind that lures men to their deaths.

Chapter Seven
War Requiem

'Maybe the War will make him grow up,' Jill said to Eva, in that way she had. At a cursory glance, far from it. He behaved like an over-eager Biggles. Olivier, in Hollywood when hostilities began, took flying lessons at Clover Field in Santa Monica, clocking up two hundred hours in the air within four months; and flying would become his analogy of acting: 'I learnt a lot about a very essential factor in acting – poise, the feeling of poise – from flying an aeroplane . . . Your two enemies are tautness and ultra-relaxation . . . And [as] acting is largely a physical thing . . . it's the same equation you've got to find . . . between under-confidence or over-confidence. It's very difficult to find just the right amount. The difficulty of acting, I've always thought, is finding the right humility towards the work and the right confidence to carry it out. With flying you have to learn . . . a very exact, precise poise, between your feet being too heavy on the rudder, or your hand too heavy on the stick or too savage on the throttle. You learn a kind of very special poise. And that I've managed to bring into the acting – frightfully useful.'

By 1941, and after much lobbying, he was commissioned as an ensign in the Fleet Air Arm, and was promoted to lieutenant and put in charge of gunnery instruction. 'War or theatre, not both,' he had objected, when offered a deferment to stage a play; but his prim, schoolboyish patriotism aside, the interfusion of war and theatre, to create, literally, a theatre of war, is exactly what Olivier achieved. Ralph Richardson, who was on the Admiral's staff at Lee-on-Solent, paid a visit to him at Worthy Down and found a flawless performance in full swing. Olivier's uniform was perfect ('it looked as if it had been worn long on arduous service but had kept its cut'); his manner was 'quiet, alert, business-like'; he was fluent in people's rank and names ('They might have been his cousins and his aunts'); and he never made a mistake interpreting insignia. The tour went smoothly and, vrooming away on his motorbike, Richardson thought to himself: 'Larry did that very well indeed. I wonder if he rehearsed it?'

As with his sexuality, which didn't quite make the welkin ring to the extent implied by his stage or screen presence, so were his heroism and patriot games perfected in his art. (The actuality was crashed planes. Alec Guinness, in his address at the memorial service, drew laughter from the congregation by saying, 'He did, I believe, quite a bit of damage, but not to the enemy.') Except as an imitator, he couldn't be Nelson or Henry V, or other figures from history, like Field Marshal French, the commander-in-chief of the British Expeditionary Force, or Lord Dowding; and by the time he wrote his autobiography, he could see he'd got into uniform 'for the sake of appearances'. He could be a prince of the powers of the air – he could take flight – only through his imagination. Yet though his official war service may have been maladroit, he came to embody patrician authority and achievement – to embody Englishness and a sense of glory – that was anything but fraudulent. He had, like the admirals and generals he played, a stern sense of duty and a respect for public honours. He had an attitude of authority and he was conscious of having a position to keep up – and by making his military commanders, his organizers and patriarchs, romantic figures, I'm wondering if all this is linked to his eroticism? Olivier, with his seductiveness and scheming, appeals to men and women. He has a way of moving his neck, of tilting his head back, which is incredibly expressive of disdain – and it's less a withdrawal of affection, perhaps, than protection. Coriolanus, Crassus (in *Spartacus*), Richard III (a perversion of power): none can withstand their scorn.

Olivier the chivalric knight, the avenger, first appeared in *Q Planes*, which was made at Denham in September 1938, after the gastronomic tour and ancestral pilgrimage to France and before he departed, on 5 November, for America and *Wuthering Heights*. He plays Tony McVane, a test pilot, in a yarn Korda had concocted from a news clipping, in which he'd read about a plane which took off but never landed. It's James Bond decades before James Bond, and the plot involves cross-eyed villains on a dredger, who put on little round sunglasses and fire radar beams at passing aircraft. The beams cut the plane's engine, there's a little puff of smoke in the cockpit, and after gliding into the sea, the pilot and his machine are captured and put in the hold. Olivier's air ace, profoundly decent and good-mannered, is intensely dislikeable. He's replete with pride, contempt, a sense of superiority; he smoulders and is without softness. McVane knows that he's smarter than the other chaps on the base (he's also more good-looking than those about him: he's Sir Gawain); and Olivier is a different category of actor, too, when shoved into a ward room of gesticulating bit players. He, like his pent-up character, stands out; and it rather prophesies his own failure to mix with genuine military personnel after he'd volunteered for duty. Soldiers and airmen, who were, now I come to think about it, probably the first people he'd ever encountered who didn't wear make-up, like entertainers, or silly clothes, like the ecclesiastic fashion show at All Saints, he castigated as narrow and resentful – non-actors were the living dead: 'I found the so-called ordinary people so terribly ordinary, so lacking in imagination, I'd hate them for it. They didn't understand each other's feelings at all. I thought when I joined "How marvellous, now I shall know real people, instead of this froth that I've been living amongst all my life." My God, give me the froth every time for real people. Real people are artists. Ordinary people aren't . . . Without any pity, feeling, imagination about each other's troubles or woes or sensitivities or sensibilities. Almost inhuman, I found the real people.'

A want of magnanimity bordering on misanthropy? An honest account of the effect on his independent spirit of all life's contingencies, waiting beyond the stage door – beyond his own immediate concerns and needs? If it's that other people, ordinary or otherwise, were all externals and surface that he objected against, what did he ever see in Vivien? The fact of the matter is, other people could certainly fill him with annoyance. On Ibiza, he'd be in a relaxed holiday humour, and then suddenly formidable. For example, frustrated by illness, he started to maunder during dinner about death and oblivion. Susan Elliott, whose daughter, Jennifer, was undergoing drug rehab, and whose husband, Denholm, had been diagnosed as HIV positive, said, 'I understand, in my own way, what you are going through' – and Olivier erupted: 'What do you know? How can you possibly know about death and dying?' This is very revealing. Dominating, domineering and competitive, he had to be supreme even in suffering. His response is an accusation, hurled with a Lear-like arrogance: he knew he was not ague-proof, with his cancers and which-what; and was he also remembering the anguish he had known and fled, with his mother, and with Vivien? What emerges from this testimony is his isolation: he was a universe unto himself. Reality, others, were things to be looked at from a distance. He did try to make amends ('Are you all right, my darling?'), but he had to be ushered out of the room by Joan Plowright.

The way he could round on friends, be nasty to Susan Elliott, when previously he'd won her over by cooking – all by himself, with damaged, bandaged hands – a Thanksgiving Dinner (turkey, sweet potatoes, pumpkin pie); and not only that, he wrote to each guest afterwards, grateful that they'd been 'so sweet and brave to eat my cooking': it connects with Richardson's remarks to Peter Hall about Olivier's equivocal charm. And he repeated his assessment for Kenneth Tynan: 'I *hate* Larry. Until I see him. Then he has more magnetism than anyone I've ever met. Except Alexander Korda. I had a film contract with Korda from 1935 until he died, in 1956. I would go to see him with a furious speech about what I wanted, and what I'd do if I didn't get it. And all the time he'd be staring at my feet. When I'd finished, he'd say, "Where did you get those marvellous shoes? I'd give anything to have shoes like those." And I would be defeated.'

Richardson is not defeated in *Q Planes*. He's the secret service man, Major Hammond, who swaggers and totters through the film, jaunty and scatterbrained, and it's clear that the actor was already in a world of his own, the one cocooning him in *Greystoke* or *Time Bandits*. He conducts an invisible orchestra with his pipe, fences invisible foe with his brolly, and if Hammond was played by any other actor, I'd complain that he's overdoing the props and bits of business. With Richardson, it's as if he's not in an office get-up, but attired as a pirate, complete with parrot and eyepatch. This is the difference between him and Olivier. Richardson is quite oblivious of other people; he's happy being in that world of his own.* Olivier? His soaring consciousness, suggestive of a pastel-grey infinity of sky and sea, is aflicker with his dissatisfactions – no rest; no peace – and, like Richard III, he expects at any moment to be impinged upon. The forces of duty and responsibility (and providence)

* Olivier was to play a version of Major Hammond in *The Jigsaw Man* (1984). He's Admiral Sir Gerald Scaith, again of the secret service, who is superintending some malarky involving Michael Caine and double agents. Olivier does a great deal of looking askance. He steals scenes by swivelling his eyes in mock horror at the person or persons he's standing next to. He has gusto, there's no denying that. As a prelude to saying 'Bugger off!' he scowls, snarls and grimaces, such that, after this build-up, you expect poetry or an epigram worthy of Oscar Wilde. Sir Gerald, or Olivier, is a dissembler, a dodderer, with a thick underswell of slyness. The jigsaw of the title could refer to the way he's pieced together his performance – ordering and drinking whisky at the club, lighting a cigarette and throwing it into the Thames, flourishing his cane like it is a cutlass: it's a lively drama-school student's impersonation of old-man-with-walking-stick, and Olivier is taking the mick a bit, too. (Were his own boisterous beginnings like this?) Taking his cue from the fact he is an *admiral*, Olivier walks with a rolling gait, he has a growly voice (Robert Newton, who was screen-tested for Heathcliff, is not a million leagues off); he likes his drink, and it should be rum.

It is a Richardson role – so how does Olivier differ in it? He plays to the audience, almost to the music-hall gallery. He is conscious of his effects. Richardson's eccentricities, by contrast, are the product of that weird world perceived and created within his own mind, and to applaud him would be an interruption and an impertinence.

threaten to destroy him. But he doesn't signal his wariness by shifting his eyes about, sweating, starting at a sudden noise; he's not highstrung and paranoid, with hair standing on end like quills upon the fretful porcupine, like Irving. Olivier's unsleeping watchfulness looks almost like indifference. He surmounts difficulties with apparent ease and grace and precision – which in *Q Planes* means evading the advances of Valerie Hobson, a journalist disguised as a tea lady, who is spying on the pilots. It is her intention to seduce McVane – Olivier, as so often, in amorous matters, is not the hunter but the hunted.

The conquest of the air is ecstatic; it is a divine achievement. Korda, in 1935, conceived the idea of a documentary to celebrate and explicate the history of man-powered flight, and *Conquest of the Air* was a hotch-potch project, directed at various times and over several years by Zoltan Korda, Alexander Esway, Donald Taylor, Alexander Shaw, John Monk Saunders and William Cameron Menzies. London Film contract artistes were conscripted, as available; scenes were shot against sets left over from other movies. Eventually, five and a half hours of material was assembled, seventy-one minutes of which was cut together and released commercially in 1940.

The trouble is, it's about flying and it's earth-bound. It is also unintentionally comic: those monks with cardboard wings jumping off battlements, to the accompaniment of a plummy voice-over. Over they go, time and again, whilst the peasantry look on with incomprehension. Or the idiot boffins, scribbling calculations and making diagrams, and then strapping themselves to a kite and running and getting up speed and floating and crash-landing. Or the endless shots of biplane contraptions, piquant struts and strings and wires, which crumple to the touch . . . The film only comes alive for Olivier's brief scene, as Vincent Lunardi, a balloonist, who is all frills and foppishness – and innuendo: the ascent into the sky is an erotic experience, a thrill. Olivier, in periwig and beauty spots, is a giggling god, Mercury, say, who invites ladies into his basket as if it's a bed – the gondola is like a four-poster. His high-pitched, fast-paced enunciating toys with effeminacy, but it also contains a kind of sigh, a kind of groan, that's sexual.

Yet I never think of Olivier as a libertine, despite the fact he was a persistent adulterer: from Jill, to Vivien, to Joan, who overlapped, along with lovers like Dorothy Tutin or Sarah Miles. ('He made love, and how! Guiltily, dirtily': she's the only person to give him a gold star; but then, she's the only person outside the practitioners of tantric sex to publicize the efficacy of drinking urine.)* His transgressions, against a social and religious contract, which promulgated the guilt, are nevertheless, in terms of destruction and reconstitution, a fulfilment of natural urges. What Olivier embodies are masculine principles of domination. This is regenerative and (as such) a virtue. It's what Wyler wanted for Heathcliff, too. Rehearsals began on 28 November 1938; shooting commenced on 5 December, amongst the Hollywood heather.

Olivier has credited Wyler with teaching him how to adapt his stage technique for the camera; with getting him to simmer down: 'That was lousy over-acting. What dimension have you climbed up to now? Get off your arse and come down from that cloud. Crawl back down here to earth and join us.' But the beauty of *Wuthering Heights* is that for all Olivier has said about the lessons he learned – the humiliations he suffered at the hands of a director who was 'a marvellous sneerer, debunker' – the evidence before our eyes suggests he didn't for a single second heed the advice. Olivier, on the screen, always provides the visceral, exaggerated excitements and effects of the theatre, or opera house. My favourite example of this is the film of *Othello*, shot during a few weeks in the summer of 1965 on a set of brownish-orange cardboard. There is no attempt to be cinematic. It's as if a camera was left rolling in the Old Vic stalls. The critical wisdom is to disparage the result –

---

* In *Lady Caroline Lamb* (1972), Sarah Miles plays the name-part as a (surely satirical) impersonation of Vivien Leigh. Caroline, her face painted a greenish-white, is ill and mad. She throws shoes at her suitors; she's the hell-cat, the flirt; and she is very tiresome, as she labours to be the irrepressible, irresistible little-girl-woman. She visits an amphitheatre at night, for example, and communes with the ancient stones, responding to the savagery and colour – to the passion. Yet she's nothing but affected. Meant to be romantic and full of feeling, so intent on sensation that she holds a tryst with Richard Chamberlain's sullen, poovish Byron in a greenhouse (*what* a role for Olivier once upon a time: George Gordon, the sixth Lord Byron, of Newstead Abbey, Notts.), she is, as Margaret Leighton's Lady Melbourne perfectly observes, a 'mass of nothing – has no centre – none at all'.

There was a good story lurking in this material: a famous romantic poet, and the romance – and romantic poetry – he induces in his women. (Perhaps Olivier did play Byron, as Heathcliff?) But the problem is Sarah Miles; her Lady Caroline has the appeal of a retarded adolescent: on purpose, or because she is simply a terrible actress? When she tries to be flamboyant she is silly and embarrassing; when she's rapturous, she's stupid. She overdoes the gamine. The best scenes in the film, therefore, are with Olivier's Duke of Wellington, because this is how he treats her, not as wild and wonderful, but as the type of woman who, if she decides to stab herself during dinner, is best ignored. So he goes on drinking port. 'She tried to kill herself!' – 'Nonsense, m'boy. No difficulty in killing yourself, if you really mean to.' Olivier is magnificently, ironically indifferent. An Antony in command of Cleopatra, for once.

for you can see the joins in the wigs, the runny make-up, the crinkles in the canvas backdrops. Theatre, put on film, can look tremendously tatty and unsophisticated – coarse. But Olivier transfigures the virtual amateurishness; we attend to his physical surfaces: the skin, the eyes, the movement, the command. He doesn't underplay – and yet he's not (nor was he as Heathcliff) overacting. I don't believe it is ever possible to accuse him of that: *that's* his purpose, his style; and in *Othello*, where we see the saliva, the pores of his skin clogged with greasepaint, the perspiration, it's not that we are as close as a theatre audience, it's more like being on stage with him. We are brought into his artificial world. We look at his hands and wish to pinch him.*

Making *Wuthering Heights*, Merle Oberon complained about his saliva. 'What's spit, for Christ's sake, between actors, you bloody little idiot?' he retorted. She was dainty, like Cathy after her marriage to Edgar Linton, when she remarks about the stable-boy's grime. ('Is that all I am to you,' says Heathcliff, 'a pair of dirty hands?') Olivier might seem to have had a thing where spittle is concerned. During *Hamlet*, he noticed that Peter Cushing, as Osric, was mumbling – he'd lost three teeth owing to an abscess and his new false choppers made him self-conscious. 'You are afraid of spitting at people,' said Olivier, putting his face close to Cushing's. 'Drown me! It will be a glorious death so long as we can hear what you're saying.'

What I'm drawing attention to – what Olivier was drawing attention to – is an actor's need to be sensitive and alive. Acting is a physical discipline, dealing with hunger and thirst, with the endurance of pain, with touch and sight. Theatre has mystical dimensions, probably, but it is also of the earth world: if it is not to be filigree, an insubstantial pageant, like Prospero's trick of the light, it must connect with plants and animals, stones and flints and birds and trees and water.† This is Heathcliff, coexisting with his mastiffs, or with Pennistone Crag. This is the Olivier of *Uncle Vanya*, showing the Rosemary Harris character his maps of beautiful great green forests, with their rivers and rocks; and

* It is for these reasons I have to disagree with Michael Blakemore, the director of *Long Day's Journey into Night*, who told me that he 'didn't really approve' of the taped version because Olivier is 'over-sized for the small screen – on TV it's like seeing the back of a clock with all the works on show'.

† In his lifetime Olivier planted hundreds of trees: 'Limes, whole avenues of limes. Oaks. Willows, cricket-bat willows. Oh, divers flowering trees. I always wanted to . . . Poplars, the tall kind. An orchard of apple trees . . . "Maybe I'm just a crank but when I plant a birch tree and then watch it put forth its leaves and sway in the wind, my soul is filled with pride": Yes . . . I planted two birch trees in memory of that line' – Astrov's, in *Uncle Vanya*.

he's trying to interest her in him; and it is also his farewell. When she and the old professor have gone, he doesn't want to leave, yet there's nothing to stay for except Ilyena Andreyevna's lingering scent. Or it's the full aura of Olivier's deathbed scenes: Lord Marchmain, arranged with his muffler and rugs, or Clifford Mortimer, lying next to the bedside table, with its can of talcum powder and pasteboard boxes of little pills. Or, earlier in his career, in *The Demi-Paradise*, what I recall best is the suggestiveness of the brief scene in the café. Wilfrid Hyde-White is the waiter, and Ivan, the gauche Russian, and Ann Tisdall, his girlfriend, order sandwiches and beer. The wartime ambience is there in the starched tablecloths, the artificial flowers, and the elderly string quartet, behind the pots of ferns, playing musical comedy selections.

It is Olivier's duty to make everything appropriate to his characters look real. Not so much a matter of *being* real, as he'd be at pains to point out, so long as the acting seems real: 'Acting is illusion, as much illusion as magic is . . . I remember going to see the Actors' Studio [in New York] and . . . the Method actors are entirely preoccupied with feeling real to themselves instead of creating the illusion of reality [for the benefit of the audience]'. There's the famous story of Dustin Hoffman huffing and puffing, getting himself into a state, sleeping in his clothes, knocking himself out, appearing on the set red-eyed and in a pickle, so that his own frame of mind would coincide with Babe Levy's, his part in *Marathon Man*. Olivier glanced at his co-star, an unshaven wreck, and said benevolently, 'Why don't you try acting, dear boy, it's far easier.' Mood, for Olivier, is in the details, not the emotions. In *Rebecca*, scooping the marmalade; in *Pride and Prejudice*, the dance steps; in *Carrie*, counting the banknotes and handling the keys; in *Long Day's Journey into Night*, the way Tyrone is meanly measuring out a glass of Scotch: with Olivier, the trick of it resides in his practicality – how a cravat was tied; how the make-up was applied; how to get a revolving stage to function noiselessly; how things were done, or functioned, or were explained away.*

* 'I remember we went to Germany to see the great Berlin ensemble company. They gave a supper party . . . and Larry was asked to speak. He was taken totally by surprise. He got up and said, "I've had a marvellous experience this evening, and I was particularly amazed by" – and everybody leaned forward expecting something about the epic power of their performance . . . and he said, "how you can make your revolving stage move and make no sound. And the second thing" – and they all leaned forward again – "is that you must use some spirit gum to stick on your wigs which is better than ours because one cannot see the wig joint." That's Larry.' (Tynan to Richard Meryman, *Life* magazine, 12 August 1972.)

When I describe what Olivier has accomplished, his gesture, his posture, I find he never did anything unnecessary. He's very economical; he has an abrupt, fierce precision. Bernard Braden, rehearsing *A Street Car Named Desire,*† recalls Olivier directing Bonar Colleano and Renée Asherson in a scene that involved 'a good deal of flurried movement. Eventually he went on the stage to illustrate what he wanted them to do. It seemed incredibly simple as he did it, but somehow they couldn't reproduce it. I thought them very stupid. The same day I was rehearsing a scene with Vivien Leigh in which I was required to lift her from the floor, turn her round to a wall and lift the shade off a lamp so that Blanche could be seen in a bare light. Finally he came on stage to show me how to do it. He did it three times in quick succession, and it was like watching quicksilver. I could no more have reproduced it than fly, but I realized that to anyone sitting in the stalls it would have looked incredibly simple. I achieved a semblance of it eventually, but it was never in a class with what he did.'

Olivier was deliberate. He had a combination of stillness and alertness, common in the animal kingdom, but unique to him. (Perhaps he wasn't a realist but a sensualist.) It's to do with needs, rather than – as I said above – emotions. Indeed, 'I never trust actors who work on emotion – it's out of your control,' he stated. He is military; he is swift and decisive. Hence, Crassus, in *Spartacus*, who keeps himself apart from what Coriolanus calls the 'clutches of a mob'. Olivier spent ages telling Peter Hall that *Coriolanus* was not about pride; and in that Crassus is a version of Coriolanus, he was right. Pride is related to boastfulness, arrogance, display. Coriolanus, Crassus, Olivier: such men have no need to show off, to preen, as such. They are men who know their mind, or at least their worth. Though self-absorbed, they are not egotists; but they do suggest the autocratic nature of the artist, who can't be a democrat, who can't devolve. That's why Olivier is good at kings, princes, rulers. He's in his element enthroned and surrounded by a court, by the subservient. (There's an inadvertent joke in *Nicholas and Alexandra*: Olivier gives a speech advocating democracy, and yet as Count Witte, in a bushy beard and decorations, he is every inch an unimpeachable tsar.)

† Olivier directed Vivien's Blanche in the London production, which opened at the Aldwych on 1 October 1949. He believed himself heavily indebted to the New York production, which had starred Jessica Tandy, and so insisted on crediting Elia Kazan in the programme. The film, released in 1951, of course won Vivien her second Oscar. It is interesting to see her over-the-top gentility – which is part of Blanche's malady – and Brando is watching her; and his character is coping, and Brando is coping: it's her style of acting over against his own.

Crassus, who diverts his energy into warfare, is cruel, arrogant, indignant. Or is he? In Olivier's performance, there is a kind of longing that goes with his intensity. A weariness, a despair, a harsh tenderness; in his search for Spartacus, he wants to *be* Spartacus, in a strange way; he wants to be a man who can be loved, who inspires affection. Jean Simmons* is rescued from the battlefield and sent to his villa in Rome. Once Varinia, the slave girl, has had her hair done, once she is adorned with a tiara and necklace – she's Vivien. Olivier has a way of standing behind her, arranging her jewels, that is exactly Antony attending to Cleopatra; and to know Roger Furse designed the costumes for both the epic Kubrick film and the epical Shakespeare production helps to bolster the comparison. But there's more to it than this; more to it than togas and breastplates and Crassus and Varinia's resemblance to an Angus McBean still. You feel that Olivier is a dangerous man, especially when he is flirting. Love, death, work, recreation: these are fields of battle, and whether he is Archie in the auditorium, out-gazing the punters, Graham Weir, in the classroom, in *Term of Trial*, punishing Terence Stamp, or Crassus addressing the senate, or Henry V his troops, Olivier's men of action, no matter what different kinds of lives they may stand for, no matter what differing levels of emotion are expressed, are similar in that they are coping with turmoil and conflict.

Olivier may have mistrusted emotion, and made it his business to keep aloof and solitary (he was funny about Dustin Hoffman: 'my leading man . . . Great mobility in the lower part of his face'); he may have been pragmatic to a degree ('There is only one way to begin to do a thing, and that is to do it') – but the fact remains he filled his characters with life, his life. Heathcliff, alien and hostile, Hamlet, and his reveries, Henry V, with his spontaneous heroic deeds, all the way up to Ezra Lieberman, in *The Boys from Brazil*, or Rudolph Hess, in *Wild Geese II*,† where, past his dancing days, red-blooded passion is refined as

* Hamlet has grown up to be Claudius – or Crassus – and he has rediscovered Ophelia, who hasn't changed an iota.

† This is an example of how Olivier dominates a film even though he is not in it much. He's Rudolph Hess, and the plot is about springing him from Spandau. We see blurred photographs of him, scratchy newsreels, and we glimpse a hobbling, shuffling figure taking his exercise. He swaggers, he won't give in; it is the fast walk of an oldster who is persistent, defiant. The mysterious lone prisoner in the huge prison, refusing to die; the monster in his tower: it is a rather gothic idea. Yet Olivier wins sympathy for the caged creature. Though set free, he wants to go back – it's the only place he knows, his home. This is intensely sad. Like Clifford Mortimer with his blindness, the theme is

a lucid sensitivity, Olivier's acting is an outlet for his personal feelings and the effects upon him of relations, chance, accident; of things beyond his grasp. Principally, his mother's death ('We children never mentioned her death to each other,' said Sybille. 'It was too bad to talk about. It is really impossible to convey the chasm that there was without her'); the difficulties with his conscience over girls ('I can never rid myself,' he told Virginia Fairweather, 'of the appalling guilty conscience, not just over the split [from both Jill and Vivien] but over everything'); and, specifically, his upheavals with Vivien before the split, and the consequences of her nature, from which she could not escape, nor he be delivered.

It was the same sadness which waited to gain possession of him. Vivien reminded him of – and therefore became associated with – the earlier tragedy; and neither his mother nor the woman he'd call 'my late wife' were ever quite dead in his mind. It was Agnes who first took him to the theatre – and talk about psychic welts! As he told Dulcie Gray, 'he was very frightened . . . and they sat in the stalls. There were two sets of curtains on the stage. The blue brocade ones parted to reveal red velvet ones. As these, too, began to rise, he shivered in nervous excitement. His mother took his hand. "Don't be frightened, Larry," she said . . . Ever afterwards, in the terror of his own first nights, he remembered this, and wished his mother had been there.' Mothers, darkness, silence, vaginal flaps, noise and sudden activity: it's enough to make Dr Freud himself incoherent, had he been consulted about these exits and entrances. Olivier never discarded his mother's mementoes, testaments from the world of lost innocence she represented; and only the other day – seven years after his own death – a cache of her letters to him at boarding school was discovered in a barn at the Malthouse, Steyning.* He'd preserved the envelopes, addressed in her neat, looping copperplate, just as he'd treasured the leaves from the family album, with their hand-

isolation. It is a hide-and-seek performance: the mystery of Hess, and the special agents trying to find out about him, corresponding with the mystery of Olivier himself, the invisible object, the absent presence. Parenthetically, Olivier looks amazingly like Hess – huge eyebrows, his jaw angrily thrust forward. You might like to compare this make-up with the young Olivier at the Birmingham Rep, as Richard Coaker in *The Farmer's Wife* or Tony Lumpkin in *She Stoops to Conquer*.

* 'Olivier papers reveal a compulsive hoarder', *Times*, 4 January 1996: 'Letters to actors, playwrights, directors, family and friends run like a tireless commentary on his own existence,' the article stated. Obviously, as Olivier could only retain copies and carbons of his own outgoing correspondence, I have myself already gathered up the originals (or xeroxes thereof) from archives and individuals across the world. I have crates of the stuff.

tinted illustrations of rich-purple wild flowers and robin's-egg-blue and flamingo-pink babies in their bassinets: 'First got up from the floor & stood alone (& safe) on Aug. 29 1908. Age 15 mths.'

Vivien's letters, cut to ribbons, turned into streamers, by the wartime censor, were also hoarded. It is a single, unifying grievance circling within him. As a child, he'd seen his mother on her deathbed; in 1967, he discharged himself from hospital to see Vivien's corpse being laid out. 'I stood and prayed for forgiveness for all the evils that had sprung up between us.' His characteristics and curiosities, and romantic impulses, are trapped in his own history, which went all the way back. His history prevented him from being free, but it made him the actor he was. As he told Freya Stark, over dinner at the British Embassy in Paris, prior to Christmas 1946: 'Like all the arts . . . it is the technical part which is the hard labour, and when the instrument is ready, the inspiration comes . . . The sign of the real artist is the willingness to undergo all the pain and trouble.'

The instrument was ready for *Wuthering Heights*. It is interesting that Olivier was at his most Shakespearian* – diverse, declamatory, nuance-crammed, playing as if to impress Elsie Fogerty or Lilian Baylis – in non-Shakespearian roles. In *Marathon Man*, he's Richard III; in *Sleuth*, he's Leontes; in *Khartoum*, he's Othello; in *The Boys from Brazil*, he's Prospero; in *The Betsy*, he's Lear; in *The Entertainer*, he's Coriolanus; in *The Power and the Glory*, he's Titus Andronicus; and in *Twenty-One Days*, as I have discussed, he's Hamlet. Here, spiritually agonized, and with love being the cause of people's deaths, he is Romeo:

> When he shall die,
> Take him and cut him out in little stars,
> And he will make the face of heaven so fine
> That all the world will be in love with night,
> And pay no worship to the garish sun.

Standing guard in ballrooms, on staircases, or the other side of window panes, illuminated by candles or the moon, or a silver-grey reflected light concocted by Greg Toland, the cinematographer, Olivier is very beautiful. It is one of the great moments in movies, when Heathcliff returns, after having vanished for many years, and he confronts Isabella, Cathy and Edgar. Olivier is the natural aristocrat, and he holds the scene, the power of his reticence and the urgency of his love giving it its measure. He's poetic, and has been in mourning from the start, ever

* 'Mr Shakespeare and I are very close, you know,' he said in 1983. 'We've done a lot for each other.'

since he and Cathy frolicked on the moors and he knew then that such happiness could only be fleeting; but his performance isn't an outpouring. What it is may be deduced from his own comments on the subject: 'My emotions were in a bit of a whirl. I was most deeply in love with Vivien, and I could think of little else. Merle and I had been spitting at each other all day, in real hate, and [Wyler] suddenly made us do a love scene, which went beautifully in one take.'

Wuthering Heights contains Olivier's relationship with Vivien, who had followed him to America on 27 November aboard the storm-tossed *Majestic*. She, like Cathy with Heathcliff, was sucking the soul out of him. Vivien had wanted to play Cathy, and had been offended when Wyler offered her the smaller role of Isabella (played in the event perfectly by Geraldine Fitzgerald, one of his few leading ladies by whom Olivier was not ill-served); and yet there's enough off-putting daintiness in Merle Oberon's mishandling of the part for us to imagine how Vivien would have approached Emily Brontë's robust, ebullient heroine. Cathy belongs with Scarlett O'Hara or Lady Hamilton in the sorority of turbulent ladies who boss, flirt and manipulate; who are ultra-feminine and full of guile, who pretend to be weak, frail vessels when it suits them. No wonder Olivier, with thick curls, dark brows, and pale shimmering skin, can only take that pained, on-the-defensive look off his face when dealing with Flora Robson, who as Queen Elizabeth or Ellen Dean, the housekeeper at Wuthering Heights, has the resigned, melancholy expression of a woman who knows she's not properly or completely loved. Vain and ferocious, in *Fire Over England*, she's at least free from artificiality; she doesn't want to be something else. In *Wuthering Heights*, her scenes with Olivier have a touching domestic quality.

The skies are like an inky sea, and when Merle (or had it been Vivien) wanders the moors, you can forget all notions of the weather sympathizing with the character's seething confusion. All she's keen on is being stately. Her so-called independent spirit is compromised when she marries David Niven and becomes part of the Thrushcross Grange sodality; and doesn't she adore scampering before the painted backdrop gardens, scattering the white peacocks, and running through the empty rooms with their expanse of crystal and white paintwork? It could be Notley, especially when she exults in being an invalid, propped up before the fire, or languishing amongst feather pillows, coughing and spluttering, and getting Donald Crisp, as Dr Kenneth, to tinker with an array of medicine bottles and look concerned, as he does when nursing Lassie.

Olivier and Vivien stayed together at the Beverly Hills Hotel, until it was considered prudent for the adulterers to be more discreet, whereupon

Olivier rented a house at 520 North Crescent Drive. On 11 December came the back-lot fire for the burning of Atlanta sequence in *Gone With the Wind*. The bathos, simpering, histrionics and politicking Vivien endured to land the role of her dreams was pretty extensive*, yet the very next day Selznick was informing his wife: 'Saturday night I was greatly exhilarated by the Fire Sequence. It was one of the biggest thrills I have had out of making pictures – first, because of the scene itself, and second, because of the frightening but exciting knowledge that *Gone With the Wind* was finally in work. Myron [Selznick, Olivier's agent] rolled in just exactly too late, arriving about a minute and a half after the last building had fallen and burned and after the shots were completed. With him were Larry Olivier and Vivien Leigh. Shhhhh: she's the Scarlett dark horse, and looks damn good.' Principal photography began on 26 January 1939. Vivien was in busy correspondence with her husband, a lawyer you'll recall, to check the particulars of her contract. 'As you will realize I loathe Hollywood, & for no other part would I have dreamt of signing a contract. My agent here assures me that if the picture is a success I can make demands & get my contract altered in such a way that is impossible at this moment.' (To her mother she wrote, 'If Larry were not here I should go mad.') Leigh Holman's scrutiny of the legal paperwork couldn't have been accomplished with much thoroughness, however, because Selznick retained the right to veto Vivien's performances for years, and eventually there was a court case.

Olivier wanted to direct Vivien as Sabina, the coquette, in Thornton Wilder's *The Skin of Our Teeth*, an experimental, which is to say a tedious and chaotic, drama about the survival of mankind, as represented by the Antrobus family†, across the aeons, from the caves to modern times. As a portentous look-we-have-come-through! or message-to-the-planet epic, it connects with Olivier's final and most ingenious absent-yet-present stage appearance, when he was the hologram of Akash, the supreme being and judge, in the musical *Time*, at the Dominion Theatre in 1986. 'To know me you must truly know yourself,' he intoned, in his best Jupiter manner. 'Go forth with love.' That Olivier himself, far from going anywhere, was already snug at home, and that he'd turned up only

* The interested reader, breathless for minutiae, is directed to *Memo From David O. Selznick*, edited by Ruby Behlmer (New York, 1972) and *Showman: The Life of David O. Selznick* by David Thomson (London, 1993). There is also a TV movie, *The Scarlett O'Hara War* (1980), starring Tony Curtis and Morgan Brittany.

† In the West End, the role of Mr Antrobus was played by Cecil Parker. When the production was revived for the Australian tour, in 1948, Olivier took the part.

as a mechanical facsimile, was an irony that did not escape the contemptuous critics.

Selznick appealed not to a celestial tribunal, but to the Chancery Division of the High Court. He objected to Vivien's wanting to appear in a stage production, when in films she'd reach 'a potential audience of between fifty and one hundred million people throughout the world'. Sir Walter Monckton, for the Selznick organization, said Miss Leigh was his client's personal asset; Sir Valentine Holmes, KC, for Miss Leigh, said she was subject to national service regulations, which annulled the demands of Hollywood, and if she could not appear in *The Skin of Our Teeth*, then she'd be drafted by the Ministry of Labour and sent to work in a munitions factory – and surely Selznick would not want that to happen? One wonders why not. Vivien in her Schiaparelli chiffon manufacturing bombs would have been a sight worth seeing – preferable to her mannerisms running riot in the Wilder opus, which opened at the Phoenix Theatre on 16 May 1945.*

She's best known for *Gone With the Wind*, which must be the most cumbersome and crappy film ever made. The repetitive 'Tara theme', by Max Steiner, is enough to induce the dry heaves; and the photography, by Ernest Haller, and the design, by William Cameron Menzies, is lurid to the point of pain: the greens are greener, the reds are redder, the sunsets more preposterously orange, than any pigment outside the paint-pots of Walt Disney. (Did the technician at the Technicolor lab have one too many?) But this aside, what's very horrible is the character of Scarlett. She's the apotheosis of the self-willed, petulant, possessive wee miss, who wants the privileges normally accorded men – she wants to dominate – but, then again, she's seeking that strong, devil-may-care fellow who'll slap her around – who'll dominate *her*. I can't do better than quote Noël Coward on the subject: 'Ah me! The ladies. God bless them. What silly cunts they make of themselves.'

Scarlett oscillates between two men, as Vivien did between Holman and Olivier. Ashley Wilkes (Leslie Howard), who has sandy hair and a sad countenance, who chops wood, who is useful and good; and his opposite number, Rhett Butler, dressed in black, with a polka-dot tie, a quizzical smile, and who is piratical and heroic – 'with enough courage you can do without a reputation,' he says. It is a grinning, cavalier performance. Scarlett says she loves Ashley, yet she is aroused only by

* Tynan – presumably with Olivier's blessing – corresponded with Wilder about revising, and reviving, the play as a vehicle for Maggie Smith at the National. Nothing came of this.

Rhett. The more he spurns her, the more she dotes on him, coming on strong with her eyelid-fluttering little-girl act. Eventually she wins him and she's thrilled by his continuing off-handedness and the way he calls her 'my child'. (When he kisses her, in order to gaze up at him, Vivien's head is inclined so far back it's at ninety degrees to her spine – she's virtually decapitated.) He carries her up the vast red staircase as if to a human sacrifice, or a ceremonial rape. 'I want you to faint,' he says, the Deep South suddenly Transylvania. 'That's what you were meant for.' We cut to next morning, and Vivien is smiling and waking up, full of joy. Has she had her first orgasm? Does marital rape agree with her? Or is it that Mammy's breakfast eggs were perfectly boiled?* Rhett likes to treat his wife as a whore, and she relishes his misbehaviour; and when he calls her 'my dear' it is a put-down, an insult. (He's only really at home away from her, playing cards in the local cat house.)

Scarlett is meant, of course, to be his kindred spirit – a woman who is told, 'You'll never mean anything but misery to any man', i.e. because she is tempestuous and has high spirits to burn. But where Scarlett is forward and lively, Vivien is jerky and artificial. (She pokes her tongue out and pouts when upbraided by Mammy – what a long way she's come from *Look Up and Laugh* with our Gracie.) We hear her being told, 'You have so much life', yet what is intended as passion registers as caprice, wilfulness. Her vivacity is put on; she never naturally comes alive. Rhett has confidence; she has self-consciousness. When she is tearful, the glycerine droplets glide perfectly down her cheeks. (Ovate, please, for the make-up supervisor, Monty Westmore, whose father, George, did Valentino's hair.)

The Civil War rages; Atlanta is a cliff of flame; Tara is despoiled; and Scarlett weeps in the vegetable plot: 'As God is my witness, I'll never be hungry again!' The cyclorama goes yellow, apricot and crimson; the screen is filled with spectacular dawns and conflagrations, and all the while, Scarlett and Rhett are meant to be cut out for each other, making love amongst the ruins. With Vivien flaring her nostrils like a filly, however, we can have no interest or sympathy in their plight; and Clark Gable, clicking his dentures, grinning and grimacing and proud of his gums, is simply brutish. So it is facile to say Rhett = Olivier, Ashley = Leigh Holman. A more accurate analogy would be to suggest

* At Notley, Vivien liked to be in charge of the guests' breakfast trays herself: poached eggs, toast, honey, orange juice, a folded newspaper, fresh rosebuds in a slim vase, all set out upon an immaculate lace cloth embroidered by nuns, which later you could no doubt use to hide your knickers under. Would she have been happier, do you suppose, running a Cotswold country-house hotel?

that Olivier was an amalgam of Gable's ability to charm and disarm and Leslie Howard's tenderness and restraint; of Rhett's individuality and Ashley's patriotism; of the one man's liveliness and confidence and the other's philosophic gloom. As luck would have it, Olivier did get to play Rhett Butler to Vivien's Scarlett, during their Australian tour. In October 1948, and for £5,000, they spent two days recording an adaptation of *Gone With the Wind* for Harry Alan Towers. The result was broadcast on Australian radio.*

Scarlett: Rhett! Rhett! Where are you going?
Rhett: I'm going to Charleston, back where I belong.
Scarlett: Please – please – take me with you!
Rhett: No. I'm through with everything here. I want peace. I want to see if somewhere there isn't something left in life of charm and grace. Do you know what I'm talking about?
Scarlett: No. I only know that I love you.
Rhett: That's your misfortune.
Scarlett: Oh, Rhett! Rhett! Rhett! Rhett! Rhett! But Rhett, if you go what shall I do? Where shall I go?
Rhett: Frankly, my dear, I don't give a damn!

We are on Gable's side when he walks out on his Scarlett; and we commiserate with Olivier, also. Gable delivers this dialogue in throw-away fashion; he's interested only in leading up to the inevitable, notorious last line: 'Frankly, my dear, I don't *give* a damn!' Nor does he. He's supremely indifferent. Mentally, as it were, he has already departed – he's going through the motions of a farewell. (No guilt or uneasy conscience for him!) Olivier, by contrast, can't be rugged and inconsiderate. He's equally as thrilling – but there's also the appeal to his loneliness, to his vulnerability. As you can guess, his version of Rhett is conveyed not by the pejorative exit (so abrupt that it gives Scarlett hope, tomorrow being

* I have disinterred several forgotten Olivier/Vivien tussles – where their real-life relationship is questioned and allayed. At the Recorded Sound Reference Centre (a division of the Library of Congress, Washington, DC) there may be found, in the NBC archives, a fragment from the stage production of *Romeo and Juliet*, recorded for *Women's Salute* and aired on 26 May 1940. On 30 September 1951, Olivier and Vivien performed scenes from Shaw's *Caesar and Cleopatra* for *The Big Show* – again as part of the local publicity for their theatre production.

Two complete dramas exist, adapted for radio. First, Shaw's *Pygmalion*, for the Campbell Playhouse series; broadcast on WABC on 27 December 1940. Secondly, Coward's *Private Lives*, a Screen Guild Show in aid of the Motion Picture Relief Fund, and with music supplied by the Oscar Bradley Orchestra. An excerpt from this Gulf Radio Theater production was released on the disc *Hollywood on the Air: The Feminine Touch* (Star-Tone Records ST205); though I can't ascertain a precise date, this again is *c.* 1940.

'another day'), but by the longing, the hunger, carried in his desire for peace – 'I want to see if somewhere there isn't something left in life of charm and grace', words which Clark Gable gallops past in embarrassment. Olivier is a seeker after that which is always on the edge of disappearing and cannot be quite met with in this world; and in his voice, which they all think they can imitate – O'Toole, Finney, Hopkins – but which they've not listened to properly, because it was never a weapon, a missile hurled at the audience, but a withdrawing roar, Olivier signifies a hero's aloneness amongst the wind and sun, rock and water.

Olivier's voice, one of the century's great noises, and more to my taste than Gielgud's pleasant flowers, was not a headlong shriek; neither was it a retreat or a death howl. Rather, it's expressive of Ibsen's trees, fires, mines, high places (in addition to Halvard Solness, Olivier, wearing Irving's tie-pin, played the eponymous John Gabriel Borkman in a production broadcast live on television in 1958); of Chekhov's romantic dreams; of Shakespeare's Merry England – and what Hazlitt called the materiality of English sports and recreations, cutting a stick, mending a cabbage net, digging a hole in the ground, hitting a mark, turning a lathe. Olivier liked to vanish to his garden, being busy, always pottering, cleaning out the goldfish pond, pruning the lime trees. He had a special simplicity at times. Yet the way he receded into himself, outwardly cordial and inwardly hard-headed and subtle, is not unconnected with his being one of those people incapable of love and friendship. His conception of Astrov, 'a very favourite part of mine', is instructive. He can't love Sonya, even though he sees her goodness; she has a yearning, which he can't respond to. Astrov is a chuckling, ironic man, with lots of layers and perspicacity. He has outgrown his ideals, and he won't replace them with sentimentality or nostalgia. (He is elegiac – but that is a different quality.) He has seductive powers, and he could be callous, or cynical; and there is a pitilessness. He can see how Ilyena will turn heads; she is pretty and flirtatious, but perhaps in the end not worth much. His kisses and lovemaking are only really half sincere. Ultimately, he has to be practical, as Richard III is, needing a horse.

There's one magical scene: the two women stand at the window; and the bleached black and white photography of a pioneering television recording imparts a paleness, an opaqueness, that's like the frost and cold of Russia: a permanent twilight, with no sunsets or dawns, with no altering weather. The characters seem to float – are translucent – like lost souls. They are people left out, or left behind, whose lives are suspended, who are indeterminate. Sonya, as played by Joan Plowright in a Yorkshire-ish accent, rather overdoes her plainness; and Ilyena,

Rosemary Harris, with her white lace parasol, is almost a parody of the self-centred beauty. The sun is white. The screen is ash and white and grey, suggestive of death and the blurring of distinctions, of identities. But if, in *Gone With the Wind*, Scarlett was not just poised between two men, but two sorts of men; so too are the two girls in Astrov's life more or less like the ones in Olivier's: Joan is, well, Joan. Ilyena is Vivien, a fantasy figure, distant and not quite real; and Astrov knows this, and is wryly aware of his foolishness in falling for her. It is as if, in the Chichester production of 1962, which built upon the Old Vic's attempt of 1945 (when Joyce Redman and Margaret Leighton played the women), Olivier was bringing to the doctor – and he's good at doctors: Chebutikin,* in *Three Sisters*, Dr Spaander, in *A Bridge Too Far*† – his own private knowledge of entanglements with an erotic nemesis. (Ilyena is rather empty; she lacks personality. Is this what Olivier was less deceived by, after the drama of Vivien?) Taking one insight and experience,

* When he was at RADA, Kenneth Branagh, who was to play this role, wrote to Olivier – creep, creep – asking for advice. The Great Man replied by return, explaining that characterization 'is entirely at the disposal of your own thoughts and workings out . . . If I were you, I should have a bash at it and hope for the best' (10 February 1981).

† On 15 May 1931, Olivier alarmed Eva, his first mother-in-law, by intermixing an account of Jill's appendectomy and bulletins about her ovarian cyst with the news that he enjoyed watching operations. '[Jill] was operated on at 12.30 p.m. and Bertie Eskell said the last thing she said was: "Promise the incision won't show" . . . Next day . . . I watched Bertie perform an operation – and I was so interested that I stayed for a second one. It was awfully funny, Mum, I'm not really a bit squeamish and I stood for two hours, watching Bertie sawing people's insides about, without turning a hair.' In the next paragraph, reverting to Jill, he tells Eva that 'she's got more guts than anybody I've ever met' – which under the circumstances wasn't the most propitious choice of words. He's so intent and gleeful about what he's deriving from the experience, his insensitivity to what Eva must think, or what Jill's enduring, is nearly winning.

In *On Acting*, the theme is taken up again: 'I have always been fascinated by surgeons . . . The theatricality of the surgeon in the heat of the operating theatre fighting for the life of a patient under the winged shadow of death is drama at its height . . . I had a friend who was a fine surgeon and I begged him for some time to let me attend one of his operations . . . I feel actors should know more about their bodies than perhaps they do. Maybe they should have a copy of Gray's *Anatomy* on their bookshelves along with Shakespeare . . . It wouldn't be a bad idea . . . to see and be aware of the way the motor works, the blood and the pound of flesh . . . You might think this morbid or macabre, but not at all. I simply wanted to know more about myself. I wanted to get under the make-up, really beneath the skin. I wanted to know every part of me. Every inch, duct and vessel.'

Dr Frankenstein? Dr Faustus? Olivier is in this brotherhood of exuberant scholars. It is something of a surprise that in 1977 he turned down half a million dollars to play Sir William Gull, the sinister surgeon of Queen Victoria, in a film about Jack the Ripper.

adding it to another; accumulating, gathering, discriminating amongst circumstances, Olivier's way of responding to what was happening around him was to perfect it – and distance it – by his so-potent art.

Vivien had signed her contract with Selznick on 30 January 1939. In the absence of succinct counsel's opinion from Holman, Olivier himself attempted to intervene, complaining that the suggested fee of twenty thousand dollars was too low; and there were also complications involving Korda's participation, agents' deductions and Christ knows what. Selznick, mindful of the way Olivier's demurrals had queered Jill's pitch over *Bill of Divorcement*, said, 'Larry, don't be a shit twice.' *Wuthering Heights* wrapped as *Gone With the Wind* lensed (to adopt the parlance of *Variety*), and Olivier had to leave Hollywood altogether, to appear in S. N. Behrman's *No Time For Comedy*, with Katharine Cornell, at the Ethel Barrymore Theater, New York. What can I discover about this drama? Only that, as Gaylord Easterbrook, Olivier was a world-famous playwright torn between his aptitude for revues and lightweight farces and his ambition – during these dark days of the thirties with wars looming ('The action of the play takes place in 1938') – to write sombre, tragic epics, in keeping with the spirit of the age. Put bluntly, the play was about Noël Coward wondering if he should be Franz Kafka; and a verbose, specious turkey it was, too. Olivier transformed his character, and riveted the audience's attention, by introducing a repertoire of odd little stunts: he balanced a glass of water on his head, jerked it into the air and caught it with his teeth; he then balanced the by now empty glass on his chin. He also made much of perching on the sofa and leaning forward to fiddle with his socks, pulling them up, and adjusting his laces – this to register the character's profound indecisiveness, apparently. ('This homely touch is so convincing to audiences that from time to time kindly ladies send him garters.') He'd then collapse backwards, comically exhausted by this strenuous activity.

It was during the pre-Broadway try-out, in Indianapolis, on 30 March, that Olivier heard of his father's death. (After a lifetime of scrimping and saving, Gerard left an estate valued at precisely £286 2*s.* 11*d.*) One of their last conversations had had to do with sex. Ibo had gone off the boil: 'after ten years of marriage, she at fifty-five "didn't want it any more", but he at sixty-five was full of beans and this withdrawal of tender intimacies was distressingly saddening to him . . . One felt piteously sorry for the old boy, but one does know how it is with girls between fifty and sixty.' (That worldly final clause is rich: *how* did he possess such knowledge?) Olivier was at last an orphan; he was severed from any family disapproval of his actions. But he was also severed from Vivien, who was working all hours in California, *Gone With the Wind* proceeding 'at snail's pace, and now they've taken to dawn shots – which is *v.* exhausting and miserable,' as she informed Holman. She and Olivier communicated by long-distance telephone and, resourcefully, by trans-continental radio: Olivier would attend Sunday-night concerts in New York which were broadcast live and Vivien, tuning in, would listen for his pre-arranged coughs and claps.

Gone With the Wind finished shooting on 27 June, and that same month Olivier signed the contract for *Rebecca.* At her own insistence Vivien screen-tested twice for the Joan Fontaine role, but she could never be demure enough. (As I have already argued, in *Rebecca* she's Rebecca.) Though, on the whole, we share the Joan Fontaine character's embarrass-ments, and sympathize with her – she is appealing – we do get a bit much of her stumbling lost about the house, fainting or bursting into tears. She's diffident, compliant, taken over – Rebecca is insistently everywhere: her address book, engagement diary, clothes, choices of menu; Manderley is still full of her routines. The second Mrs de Winter, by contrast, has no character of her own; and Max loves her for this. Olivier manages to make his sullenness and bossy lines ironic, so that he is not bullying; and there are elements in his performance of his springy, watchful light-comedy manner, from *No Funny Business.* He's a man so self-enclosed, he didn't see Rebecca for what she was until too late – just as he fails to see what it is doing to Joan Fontaine to abandon her in Manderley and expect her to duplicate Rebecca's mistressy duties. And why, now we are on the subject, does he keep Mrs Danvers on – she creeps about like a ghoul? Joan Fontaine is the coy, awkward girl – very much a child, to be ordered about, to be formed. This is Rhett's view of Scarlett; Othello's of Desdemona; Caesar's of Cleopatra; Higgins' of Eliza. Is it what Olivier wanted of Vivien? An unquestioning and inexcitable loyalty and devotion? But it didn't work out like that. The second Mrs de Winter is passive, retiring – she's Virgilia* to Coriolanus: 'my gracious silence' – whereas the second Mrs Olivier was deliberately provocative, a showgirl to his prince.

Wuthering Heights had opened at the Rivoli Theater, New York, on 13 April, and its success confirmed Olivier as a matinée idol; he was mobbed by fans as he made his way to the stage door for *No Time For Comedy.* Once, declining to give an autograph, a girl gave chase. 'I think she would have scratched my eyes out. Those people hover on a thin dividing line between love and utter loathing.' Vivien's stardom was assured by

* Vivienne Bennett in 1938; Mary Ure understudied by Vanessa Redgrave in 1959.

the gala première for *Gone With the Wind* in Atlanta: motorcades, costume balls, civic receptions. The ballyhoo was repeated in New York (where it opened at the Capitol and the Astor on 19 December) and Los Angeles (at the Cathay Circle on 28 December). As Vivien's secretary told Vivien's mother: 'If you can just imagine the greatest thing that has ever happened in all the world – that's "your little Vivien" . . . She is all over every newspaper everywhere . . . She is so unspoiled by it all and is still, and will always be I know, the same sweet girl. Larry is so proud of her . . . Believe me they are both "tops" right now and all of Hollywood envies them.' Thus began the remorseless mythology of The Oliviers. Gone were the days when reporters felt it necessary to inform readers 'the name is pronounced Oh-live-ee-ay in the French fashion'; now publicity acquired a degree of mawkishness and high-temperature schmaltz not seen since Ezra Pound's* translation of Remy de Gourmont's *The Natural Philosophy of Love*.

A sample:†

> . . . it is in America that Olivier and Mrs Holman, now known to all and sundry as the Vivien Leigh who is playing Scarlett O'Hara, apparently have worked out their personal problems. The columnists say Olivier and Vivien are going to get married, that Olivier and Jill Esmond either are or soon will be divorced.
>
> In Hollywood the publicity departments believe the public does not want its screen favourites to marry. Whether or not the publicity departments are right, Olivier will do as he likes. He doesn't give a damn.
>
> Speaking frankly, he doesn't give a damn for anything much except being a really great actor, living the abundant life, and Vivien Leigh.
>
> *August 1939*

> Olivier says: 'I don't suppose there ever was a couple so much in love.' Vivien Leigh says: 'Our love affair has been simply the most divine fairy tale, hasn't it?'
>
> Some moralists may object that the fairy tale of Laurence Olivier and Vivien Leigh leaves something to be desired since they are not married to each other. This is obviously true. On the other hand, they intend to get married as soon as their divorce decrees become final . . .
>
> They will soon join the select company of great American lovers – the

---

* '. . . the brain itself is, in origin and development, only a sort of great clot of genital fluid held in suspense or reserve,' claimed the translator in his postscript to the limited edition deckle-edged laid paper watermarked 'Antique de Luxe' copy in my possession.

† Quotations taken from the likes of *Life*, *Movie Mirror*, *John Bull*, *Cavalcade* and *Harper's Bazaar*.

Duke and Duchess of Windsor, John Barrymore and Elaine Barrie, and John Smith and Pocahontas, who lived before their time.

May 1940

This is love such as our grandparents knew, the love that shares alike and gives alike and cleaves unto no other person or thing . . . They were thinking, not that their love story had come to a happy ending, but that it was beginning its dearest chapter, the chapter of Mr and Mrs Laurence Olivier going on forever and ever, till death should them part.

November 1940

Not with Vivien and Larry do career, success, the spotlight of solitary fame come ahead of everything else. Here, for once, are two people who love each other so completely that it is the success of the other that is put first . . .

January 1941

[Alan Dent] would go to the piano and strum, whereupon Olivier would come and sing Handel with tremendous mock-seriousness . . . finishing up with: 'I say, that was jolly good!' It was then Mrs O's turn to sing – Handel again – in a sweet little high voice as incredibly pure as a choirboy's alto. That done, the two together would sing sweet old English ballads in unison, an especial favourite being 'The Lass that Loves a Sailor' . . .

c. *October 1945*

Six years ago the Oliviers found that they could not live without each other. They are still content.

'We find it very easy, this living together,' says Olivier, lounging comfortably in a chair in his wife's dressing-room at the Piccadilly Theatre. A Siamese cat called New is asleep in his arms.

'Yes,' says Vivien, resting on a couch, assessing him with her grey-green cat's eyes . . . Can she find fault with him, even some minor flaw, like pressing the toothpaste at the wrong end? No. She won't admit any. 'I think he is the perfect husband,' she says.

Olivier does not refute it. He smiles. The Siamese cat changes over and goes to sleep again at Vivien's feet. Vivien's legs are trim in black stockings.

November 1946

. . . if ever a couple were in love it was these two. It might have been a long scene from a romantic play, except that the emotions were real. Nor did it ever sink into bathos, for when the mood took them they could be as gay and amusing as Molière.

May 1947

It is characteristic that he keeps a beautiful miniature of his wife on his dressing-room table, telephones her every lunchtime from the studio, and looks forward to making films and producing plays in which she will star – perhaps as Desdemona in *Othello*?

When one reviews the unique position they hold in the world of the theatre and of cinema, it isn't surprising that they should frequently be referred to in the American Press as 'Britain's Royal Family of Stage and Screen'.

January 1948

They're a perfect match – like tea and crumpets.

c. *June 1948*

His marriages can best be explained in theatrical terms . . . Jill Esmond made an exit as Vivien Leigh made an entrance. It was as if Larry's career was a play. Charming and talented as Jill was, the piece wasn't at its best with her as leading woman. The moment Vivien took over the part, we all knew it was as right and inevitable as it has proved to be.

c. *April 1950*

Marriages among the high-strung people of the stage are ordinarily about as stable as gelatin dessert. The Oliviers are astonishingly exceptional. After 17 years of knowing each other and 12 of marriage, they are still deeply in love. Their conformity to familiar matrimonial customs is borne out in every facet of their lives, even in pet names. To him, she is 'Puss' or 'Pussy'; she calls him 'Ba' or 'Baba'.

Some time ago a confirmed bachelor friend of the couple stopped visiting them for no apparent reason. 'Why don't we see you around the Oliviers' any more?' another friend asked.

'To tell you the truth, they make me nervous,' the bachelor said. 'They act so blasted loving, you'd think there was something to this marriage nonsense after all!'

January 1953

That such a happy and serene façade was maintained for so long is a credit to Olivier and Vivien's joint theatrical genius; also to the collusion of the press, who were as keen on fostering the image of perfection – the Oliviers as darlings of the gods – as their modern equivalents would be on exposing the sleaze, the madness, the diabolic realities.* The

* The actuality of Olivier's life with Vivien is chronicled succinctly in Noël Coward's diary: 'Larry is worried about Vivien, who is having a sort of suppressed nervous breakdown. Had a long talk with her and tried to convince her that nervous exhaustion is the result of physical exhaustion, and that she needs a long rest' (20 April 1952); 'We are all dreadfully sad about poor Vivien. She is in a mental home and has been asleep for a week. She had apparently really gone over the edge, poor darling. Larry, wisely, has gone away to Italy' (28 March 1953); 'I had a mysterious telephone message from a Miss Hartley. I called back and it was poor, darling Vivien . . . It was a heart-breaking conversation. She started in floods of tears and then made a gallant effort to

problem, in essence, was that the Oliviers were not only a fiction for the public; they were fantasy figures to each other. Olivier, especially, disappeared into his performances – one after the other, Heathcliff, Maxim de Winter ('His face was arresting, sensitive, medieval in some strange inexplicable way, and I was reminded of a portrait seen in a gallery I had forgotten where, of a certain Gentleman Unknown,' wrote Daphne du Maurier); and now Darcy. *Rebecca* had begun production on 8 September; Olivier signed for *Pride and Prejudice* in November, and Aldous Huxley's adaptation of Jane Austen's novel was before the cameras in the New Year, 1940. Vivien had tried to coax Louis B. Mayer to cast her as Elizabeth Bennet, but Selznick insisted that she play Myra, a fallen woman, opposite Robert Taylor's dopey aristocrat, Roy Cronin, in *Waterloo Bridge*.

Pride and Prejudice, being about Darcy and Elizabeth's troubled courtship, their raillery and skirmishes of wit, is a war film, in its way. (The story also involves the local garrison, troop manoeuvres, the glamour of the military life and, distantly, the Napoleonic Wars.) Lady Catherine de Bourgh, kitted out as if in black sails and billowing topmasts, is like a battleship in pursuit across the oceans – she is belligerent – and Mrs Bennet and her rival, Lady Lucas, pillaging the draper's shop and racing home to set up appointments for their daughters with any eligible bachelor, would surely slit throats to achieve husbands and dowries.

---

be gay and ordinary, but the strain showed through . . .' (12 April 1953); 'It is really discouraging to reflect how needlessly unhappy people make themselves and each other. They are now going to start afresh down at Notley, which may work or may not. I shall be surprised if it does. Attractive and enchanting women can certainly wreak havoc when they put their silly minds to it. I am sorry for him and for her. They both have so much and are so lacking in common sense' (22 April 1953); 'I went back to the house with them and observed, to my true horror, that Vivien is on the verge of another breakdown. She talked at supper wildly . . . Her voice became high and shrill and her eyes strange . . . Larry came and talked to me . . . She has begun to lose sleep again and make scenes and invite more and more people to Notley until there is no longer any possibility of peace. Their life together is really hideous and here they are trapped by public acclaim, scrabbling about in the cold ashes of a physical passion that burnt itself out years ago' (7 April 1955).

There are dozens of such entries, culminating in the note for Sunday 8 February 1959, written on board SS *Queen Elizabeth*: 'Vivien is in despair about Larry leaving her. I had a long quiet session with her. She was very pathetic and perfectly sane and sweet, and I feel that the shock of Larry packing up and going may have done her a power of good. [It did not.] It is difficult to resist her charm and pathos when she turns them on. I cannot understand why she should be surprised at Larry popping off after all the ghastly scenes . . . It is depressing to reflect that two such talented and enchanting people should torture each other so.'

(The galloping of the horses, the pursuit by open-topped carriage, is a Charge of the Light Brigade.) Olivier plays his character as angry, irritated. He's like a general forced into civilian attire, who attends formal functions, whose movements are stiff and commanding; who has no small talk and is thus ruled out as taciturn and insolent. Once he meets Greer Garson, however, we view Darcy as she does – as a man with considerable diffidence, who enjoys her poise and wit, her liveliness and spark. When the soldiers from the regiment in the region pursue her sisters, and Wickham elopes with Lydia, Darcy is the fellow who steps in and preserves the family honour.

Thus did Olivier imagine himself stepping in to help England in her hour of need. Drake's drum had been banged, and here he was. When war had been declared in Europe, Olivier, Cary Grant and Herbert Wilcox, on behalf of the British artistes in Hollywood, flew to Washington to see the ambassador at the British Embassy and ask for instructions. Lord Lothian told them to 'Go back [to California] and get on with your job. It's important to keep the English idiom and way of life before American audiences. Don't violate the Neutrality Act, but do everything you can to help. And tell those of military age to get back to England and take their part.' Olivier, as a thirty-something, was beyond the call-up limit; but according to Wilcox he telephoned Vivien in some indignation and said, 'We've been advised to stay in Hollywood and get on with the job. Get packed, darling, we're going back to England.' This is apocryphal – unless it did take fifteen months for Vivien to parcel up her gowns, hats, gloves, frocks, shoes, slacks, kimonos, boleros, cardigans, petticoats and bloomers. They didn't leave for London until 28 December 1940, when they boarded the American Export Liner *Excambion*, east-bound out of Jersey City for Lisbon, Portugal. The *New York Times* sent a reporter to see them off: 'I know London is not the safest place in the world right now, but it is still my home and that's where I want to be,' said Vivien. Olivier patiently explained that he had indeed volunteered for service with the British Government shortly after war began, but he'd been advised by the War Office and the military attaché at the embassy in Washington to remain 'in this country for the present . . . England's need was for machines and food rather than man power. [Now however] Mr Olivier said he would offer his services to British officials "for whatever they think I can do"' – and, as we know, he'd been taking all those flying lessons; and if the Ministry of Information hadn't released him from the Fleet Air Arm to make *The Demi-Paradise* and *Henry V*, there'd have been several years more added to the war and tuppence on the rates.

They remained in America for the acclaim (Vivien was presented with her Oscar by Spencer Tracy on 29 February 1940 at the Coconut Grove in the Ambassador Hotel); and in order to be out of the way of Jill and Holman, who might have tried, if not to win them back, then to maximize their guilt and sense of shame. Vivien kept up her stream of chummy letters, of course, writing to her husband in the style of a little old lady sending succour to our brave boys at the Front: 'I am knitting Balaclava helmets . . . Would one be of any use to you and would you like it?' (17 January 1940); and I can only wonder at what she thought she was up to. Trying to make Holman think semi-well of her, to ease her guilt over the desertion of him and Suzanne? In the over-zealousness of her knitting, crocheting, sewing and shopping if not for herself then for friends, Vivien confided her malady. Rather like her rigid domestic rules, over the 'placement', or the cutlery, or her party games and manic hospitality, Vivien's anxiety to be seen doing good, her refinement, actually adds up to a refusal to reflect. Seeking for certainties (she enjoyed crossword puzzles, Chinese chess, problems that can definitively be solved) and seemingly looking strong, she was really rather a mess.

Olivier, too, had had the shine taken off perfect happiness. When I've speculated about sources for his great guilt and of his understandings of pain, I've assumed that this goes back to the death of his mother; or to what he did to Jill; or to the horror of Vivien's crack-up ('it has always been impossible for me not to believe that I was somehow the cause of Vivien's disturbances, that they were due to some fault in me'); or to the fact that he was away in America when war was declared on 9 September 1939; or perhaps it was simply a metaphysical crisis, like Orson Welles': 'You know that you're absolutely great . . . but have you chosen the right road? . . . It is not self-doubt; it is *cosmic* doubt! What am I going to do – I am the best, I know that, now what do I do with it?'

Olivier doesn't mention it in any of his memoirs, perhaps because the things that really count go too deep. There must be a superstitious hush. That he could jabber about Vivien, and dramatize her tragedy, suggests it didn't reach him, in quite the same sense. But I think it was the impending death of his three-year-old son, in the winter of 1939, that undermined his sense of himself and embroiled him in nightmare. Tarquin went down with meningitis, and Jill's long letters on the subject – 'From your cables I gather you are interested so I will tell you the whole story' – make terrifying reading. The cold, damp cottage in Sussex where she and the child were living, away from the Blitz; the pains in his neck and spine; the screams; the high temperatures; the coma; the impossibility of finding a doctor ('Of course all the doctors are in the army'); the snowdrifts; the dropping of the precious medicine bottle; the panic-stricken consultations with specialists across faulty telephone connections; the chances of blindness or deafness as after-effects; the car which won't start; the trying to cope . . . Little wonder that this profound sock put any extra-marital shenanigans into perspective. On 29 January 1940 Jill filed her petition in the Probate, Divorce and Admiralty Division of the High Court of Justice, requesting a dissolution of her marriage on the grounds that 'Mr Olivier and Mrs Holman had committed adultery at Christchurch Street, Chelsea'. That she attempted to make light of it to Olivier only underscores Jill's sense of defeat. 'The whole proceeding took place in a very poor set. Perfect but dull casting, for Judge and Counsel.' Jill was handed a photograph of Olivier for her to identify. 'The Judge had a look at the picture, looked at me with surprise, and then gave me a Decree Nisi straightaway.'

Jill was granted full custody of Tarquin (as Holman was of Suzanne); and we mustn't underestimate the sheer danger of those times for the two of them, ill and cold in Britain, and there's Larry and Viv, safe and mollycoddled in America, planning their Irving/Terry *Romeo and Juliet*, which opened in New York in the May. It was decided that Tarquin should be evacuated to California; and he and his mother, braving German submarines, sailed across the Atlantic at the end of June. By one of those quirks of fate which, had it befallen in a novel, would make the reader burst with impatience, also aboard the Cunarder, *Scythia*, were Suzanne and her granny, Gertrude. They didn't speak. The ship docked at Halifax, Nova Scotia, and Olivier met up with Jill and Tarquin in Toronto. 'He got on well with T. but didn't seem really interested and never asked about his illness,' Jill was to say, chagrined. But this wasn't indifference, in my opinion, but an affective, reticent silence; seeing Tarquin, and confronted, as it were, by an innocent he'd abandoned, was too disconcerting for comment. Also, he wouldn't want to seem obligated or connected to Jill, over what she'd endured; he didn't want to be seen to share in the emotion, or the responsibility. What with Vivien there too, polluting the air with Joy de Patou, bestowing cold kisses and, for all her sumptuousness and lavishness, being in reality narrow and shrill, it is no surprise that Olivier appeared cool or incurious. This is how men are when they've done wrong; it is how they behave when they are ashamed.

Sub-Lieutenant Holman of the RNVR, on receipt of his balaclava, had also filed for divorce, naming Olivier as the co-respondent. He could see that fame, though it hadn't changed Vivien as such, had had the effect of confirming to her that the admiration of the world was her birthright. There was now no need for him still to be there in her life, as a refuge, had all this acting nonsense failed – though that is what he continued to be in a sense, her emotional safety net. To be able to write coyly, breathlessly, like this – 'I do so hope you will not have a very unpleasant time at the divorce thing Leigh darling. I understand it's tomorrow' – suggests that under the bright, trivial tone there is considerable feeling for him, as to a father. And one of the manifestations of her barking madness, Olivier has said, were the times she treated him, too, as a father-figure. Of the period when they were performing the Shaw and Shakespeare double bill, he recalled, 'She started to be like a slightly frightened daughter . . . it seemed a funny little child-like, clinging need for protection.' He'd married Jill and she turned into a superior mother surrogate; a virago. He married Vivien and she reverted to the nursery; she became one of those ghastly manipulative child-woman invalids from a Victorian ghost story. The effect on Olivier was to bring out in him the competitive, spoilt youngest child, which he might otherwise assume he'd expiated when he'd played Katharina at Stratford-upon-Avon in 1922. Even on their way to the wedding ceremony, held in secret at midnight on 31 August 1940,* at a hotel in Santa Barbara, called Ranch San Ysidro, they squabbled like kindergarteners. 'It was absolutely hilarious,' Garson Kanin told Hugo Vickers. (Kanin, his chickabiddy, Katharine Hepburn, the county clerk, Jack Lewis, and the municipal judge who performed the ceremony, a drunken Fred T. Harsh, who exclaimed 'Bingo!' as the groom kissed the bride, were the only people present.) 'They started quarrelling rather bitterly. She was sharp-tongued. Larry was tough as hell. They were scrapping all the way to the banns.'

And this is how they were when not acting, which is to say when not working; and they were always working. The post-war Old Vic tour of Australia and New Zealand was one long playground dispute. In the Birmingham Repertory Theatre Archives, I found the following letter to Sir Barry Jackson from Eileen Beldon, who in the long ago had been Helena when Olivier was Parolles, and who was now Mrs Candour in *The School for Scandal*, Margaret of Anjou, widow of King Henry VI, in *Richard III*, and Mrs Antrobus in *The Skin of Our Teeth:*

* Jill's decree had become absolute on 5 August, Vivien's on 26 August: 'We were married as quietly as possible, and I wired you as soon as it was done and would have written beforehand if I had known myself it was going to take place as soon as that' – Vivien disingenuously to Holman, 4 September 1940.

At Present Brisbane
Midnight August 26th 1948

Dearest BJ

. . . I wish I could send you a luscious juicy steak that I have never been able to eat since I got here, I am so revolted by the amplitude! But best of all I wish I could send you the flowers – besides their own rare and peculiar blossoms of sub-tropical growth there are roses, sweet-peas, stocks and freesias and daffodils and violets and all our spring flowers blossoming, at the same time. My room is like a flower show and so it has been all the while – this I shall remember – this and the cleanness of the atmosphere so that in the country it is possible to see for eighty miles and think you could walk it in a few hours; the very sunlight is reflected from the glossy leaves of the gum trees and the red baked hills [. . .]

The tour has been a tremendous success. In Melbourne the theatre held sixteen hundred and four thousand people were turned away for every performance. In Sydney it cost them £2,000 [in postage and extra secretarial assistance] to return £118,000 – that is the financial side alone.

I believe Larry has been disappointed by the reception especially of *Richard III*. I gather the enthusiasm has not reached the peaks of London, New York and Paris. But we have been handicapped by the barns of theatres we have had to play in, and an audience completely unused to live theatre. Personally, I don't understand what he complains about. I think Australians are wonderful [. . .] Apart from Larry there is no one as good as [a list of Birmingham Rep players] and I think we shall all get our ears slapped down when we come to London. Personally it has been a curious unforgettable experience which I wouldn't have missed for anything.

Have you read Henry James' *The Turn of the Screw*? Well, Larry and Vivien remind me of the two children in that – charming, talented, exquisitely mannered, diabolical and bewitched, and completely immature. I can neither believe in nor trust them to behave like adults. The slightest criticism throws them into sulks and despair which is really comical.

In spite of his undoubted ability I can only think of Larry as a little boy playing with the theatre like a toy and ready to break it any minute. But one gets terribly tired of even the most charming children and I shall be glad now to get home.

[. . .]

All blessings,

Ever,

*Eileen**

* This edited transcript of one of Eileen Beldon's letters to Sir Barry Jackson is reproduced by kind permission of the Sir Barry Jackson Trust.

Between the divorce, in the New Year, and marriage, in the summer, came the Victoriana *Romeo and Juliet*. It was previewed on the West Coast, the *San Francisco Call Bulletin*, aware that here we had Scarlett and Heathcliff in the flesh, making the observation: 'An audience with expectations of real-life fervor in the play's romantic passages was not disappointed. No pre-nuptial embrace, for instance, has been more torridly prolonged in the Bard's most famous love-story . . . The current presentation gains interest because Miss Leigh and Mr Olivier are very much in love and are to be married when divorce decrees become final.' When they reached Chicago, the company travelling in reserved Pullman cars, crowds mobbed the couple at the Union Station, where banners and streamers proclaimed, 'SEE THE GREAT LOVERS IN PERSON'; and in New York, at the Fifty-First Street Theater, the posters exclaimed, 'See Real Lovers Make Love in Public'.

That Olivier (who was presenting, producing, designing and directing: he lost his shirt)* and Vivien intended to identify with the star-crossed teenage lovers is rather curious. Romeo and Juliet meet, fall in love, separate and commit suicide, all in the space of four days. There is no happy-ever-after:

> For never was a story of more woe
> Than this of Juliet and her Romeo.

It was as if, already, they were trying to relive the early days of their romance and convince themselves that they were still smitten. Olivier decided that Romeo was a boy who matured into a man as he coped with the tumultuous emotions; and Juliet, he decreed, was 'little more than a child'. Vivien was to stand on tiptoe, indulge in girlish games – she still has a wet-nurse after all – and in the Capulets' garden, whilst delivering the Act II, Scene v soliloquy, she was to bounce a ball, beating time, killing time:

> Now is the sun upon the highmost hill
> Of this day's journey; and from nine till twelve
> Is three long hours . . .

Olivier informed his sister Sybille, 'I shall never love a part as much as Romeo again!'; yet if he was in love with love, real life was about to smash its fist through the gossamer of his reveries. The reviews, especially the judgement of Vivien's contribution, were catastrophic. Her character-

* Despite what has always been assumed about the loss of their joint savings, it was only Olivier who had invested his accumulated film earnings in the production. 'Vivien did *not* put one penny of *her* money into it. She has more sense,' said Jill waspishly.

ization was deemed 'immature and shallow'; 'Miss Leigh . . . dashes through the [lines of] poetry . . . with little indication that she has ever bothered to understand them'; 'she is not yet accomplished enough as an actress to go deep into the heart of an imaginative character wrought out of sensuous poetry'; most of all, she was inaudible – though those that did hear her mouse-squeaks complained of 'the thin, shop-girl quality of Miss Leigh's voice'.

Such criticisms – variously skirted and seasoned or more diplomatically put – would surprise Vivien always. The man she exasperated most was Tynan, who couldn't abide the blind belief that just because she was pretty therefore she could act. 'Coldly kittenish', he dubbed her; 'this silly woman', 'a pale featherweight beauty', 'a small personality', 'an attractive child endlessly indulged at its first party', were some of the other things he called her. 'Niminy-piminy' summed her up. 'Miss Leigh is sweet; but when you have said that half a dozen times, you have said everything.' But his contempt had serious implications – these were that Vivien was bad for Olivier, that he reined in his genius to accommodate her talent. 'Blunting his iron precision, levelling away his towering authority, he meets her halfway,' was how Tynan put it; and of *Antony and Cleopatra* he said, 'Antony climbs down; and Cleopatra pats him on the head. A cat, in fact, can do more than look at a King: she can hypnotise him.'

Which all could have been ignored or shaken off, except I think that Olivier concurred with the assessment. Tynan saw through Vivien; and one of the reasons for the love–hate relationship Olivier had with the critic has to do with their seeing eye to eye as regards her charms. (Vivien had kidnapped him with her glamorous life; her life of surfaces.) Olivier confronted Tynan personally: 'I told him that he had been directly responsible for at least one of Vivien's nervous breakdowns' – which rather implies that he himself gave occasion for the others? Olivier was wholly self-absorbed, such that he could never give himself to another person – except, almost, to Vivien; she was his sole, and fateful, surrender. I don't think she impaired his acting, however, which was Tynan's fear; what happened is that the values were changed. Now that he was famous, and had lost his privacy, not only his successes, but his weaknesses, were to be on show – so he was strangely (and attractively) vulnerable, and able to show the frailty and fragility of great authority, in his kings and conquistadores. I don't mean by this that, as an actor, shifting, slanting, dispersing, Olivier was suddenly beset by insecurity. I mean that the nature of his vulnerability was his awareness of not being invincible; and that's a quite different thing.

What is it that connects one human being with another? Olivier was always detached and proud, and with Vivien sin and grief became their sacred bond, and he'd deluded himself into thinking it was love. He'd adored her flattery and beauty; he'd been transfixed by the boisterousness of her sex drive (though that would pall: 'all *that* had gone into my acting, and you can't be more than one kind of athlete at a time'); and when Jill had become pregnant, he'd scarpered, preferring the dream show life with Vivien. But where was the transformation scene? Olivier was waiting for it to become real, and it never did. He expected a reality of tenderness and trust between them, but she went insane and he felt himself to be guilty of her trespasses against him – her nymphomania and damage and darkness. Her brittleness wasn't Juliet's innocence; she was already Blanche, the tormented angel. As the public queued up for their money back on *Romeo and Juliet* ('Much scenery; no play' – 'tepid and tedious' – 'heavy and tangled'), they fled to Katharine Cornell's house ('that terrible house', as he described it to Anthony Quayle when they drove past it years later) in Sneden's Landing. With them went Olivier's understudy, Jack Merivale, with whom Vivien would set up home after the end, though nobody would have guessed this from what happened next. Olivier was busy with his flying manuals,* so Vivien, bored and scratchy, decided to challenge Merivale to Chinese chess. When he looked like winning she accused him of cheating. 'You invite yourself here and then you cheat!' she screamed. Merivale, trying to calm the atmosphere, appealed to Olivier – semi-jokingly. 'Larry, stop her! She doesn't mean that!' Vivien then let rip: 'Don't you come between us! Nobody's coming between us. Don't you try.' Olivier, sitting a few yards away, never once stirred from his book. Vivien turned Merivale out the next morning.

The play closed on 8 June. Olivier, from the telephone at the stage door, tried to reach Duff Cooper at the Ministry of Information, again begging them to accept his services.† He was told, in effect, don't hurry home. You may be more useful where you are. A few days later this message was reiterated in a cable: 'THINK BETTER WHERE YOU ARE STOP KORDA GOING THERE.' Korda! He had wanted to exploit Vivien and Olivier's relationship in *Twenty-One Days;* he was about to propose a repeat performance in a film provisionally entitled *The Enchantress,* about Emma Hamilton's affair with Admiral Lord Horatio

* 'I've still got my log book, registering about 250 hours of circles and bumps on the Hudson, while the sands of our *Romeo and Juliet* were running out,' he said in 1982.

† In Olivier-speak, to make this telephone call was 'This deed I'll do before this purpose cool': why did he quote Macbeth, for heaven's sake?

Nelson; though, in fact, what became *That Hamilton Woman* is not really about eighteenth-century maritime adventures and the order of battle at Trafalgar at all; it's about the spirit of Englishness in the anticipation of a German invasion. It is blatant propaganda: 'Look out Bonaparte! By Gad we shall lick you now!'

Korda had been recruited to the British secret service. Claude Dansey, deputy head of MI6, and later on the board of London Films, had encouraged the Prudential Insurance Company to put up money for the Denham Studios; and MI6 officers went there to acquire film-making skills as cover for their official activities. In 1940, Churchill created British Security Co-ordination, to gauge American intentions concerning Europe, and to see what the Germans themselves were doing as regards the United States. Korda, travelling on military aircraft, gathered the intelligence in New York and returned to brief Churchill in person. On his missions to America he worked with the Office of Strategic Services, a forerunner of the CIA, and this had been set up by William Donovan, who just happened to be Korda's lawyer. If Churchill wanted to incite America into the war – on our side, I should add – and to stir up support for Britain and to attack appeasement, what better than to enlist the skills of a couple of petulant mummers in their wrinkled tights?

Work began in Hollywood on 18 September;* and the magic of *That Hamilton Woman* is that it *remains* in Hollywood. Sir William Hamilton's villa and the Neapolitan royal apartments are a studio palace (designed by Vincent Korda), with vast black shining floors, garden terraces and a starlit cyclorama; and there, in the distance, beyond the toy boats bobbing on a silver sea in the miniature bay, is Vesuvius puffing away. Vivien reclines in a huge boudoir, with curtains and draperies ruched and scalloped like the satin tabs of a thirties Odeon. It's tarty, that ornate bed, big enough for six ('Why, I've never tried,' was Vivien's saucy response). These are theatrical movie star sets, twinkling and shimmering in unison with Vivien's costume jewellery and the gold

* During the previous twelve months, in addition to the hotels and trains of the *Romeo and Juliet* tour, and the weekends at Sneden's Landing, or the trip to Toronto to see Tarquin, the Oliviers had moved thrice: 606 North Camden Drive, Beverly Hills; 1107 San Ysidro Drive; and now 9560 Cedarbrook Road, Goldwater Canyon. This would be hectic by anybody's standards, yet it replicates the pattern of Vivien's childhood. Like an heiress in Henry James, she was always travelling from one luxe hotel to another – always a guest (and later she'd be the perfect hostess); and with no roots, no real room of her own. Hence the propagation of emotional insecurities?

braid on Olivier's uniforms; and the story is constructed as a series of theatrical, movie star set-pieces, with Miklos Rozsa's mournful, woozy violins heightening the romantic, moonlit mood. (Were Korda and his English cast parodying the atmospherics of an MGM musical?) Nothing, from the King and Queen of Naples living in a bedlam of children and dogs to Nelson's death on the *Victory* is ever less than a *performance*.

Vivien is at her least awful in the prologue – as an aged woman of the streets, stealing a gin bottle in Calais. Made up to be old and ugly, she stops forcing her prettiness upon us; and her deep, growly voice, as she sadly recounts her past (from a prison cell), is more natural than that elocution-lesson tinkle o'bells, that bell clinking from the chapel top, which she normally treats us to. (She's at her best as an adulteress or a prostitute – perhaps because then she saw the links between harlotry and acting: putting out, giving it all up.) It takes no more than a flashback, however, for us to be back in an abyss of artificiality, as the youthful Emma capers around the sets, showing off her wardrobe. She leans against pillars, sobs, squeezes out tears, and skips with an affected refinement. She has a painstaking beauty; she has masks of virtue – but these are exactly the qualities that appeal to Sir William Hamilton, the aesthete, who is apparently warm and charming, but who actually possesses Emma. She's merely another exhibit in his collection, 'another ornament for your home – like that vase'.* Later, he loses his treasures (and thence his wits) in a storm. 'Where's the good of trying to fight the elements,' he says philosophically, referring to the rough crossing – but not only to that. Like St Joseph, he accepts being a cuckold because Emma and Nelson's amorous tag is almost virtuous; it embraces nature. (Emma eulogizes Nelson as 'a force of nature'.)

Sir William has a limp and a walking stick to symbolize his impotence. Olivier, who like Vivien shows off his wardrobe – his cloaks, plumed hats, dress uniforms, gaudier than the Lord Mayor's coach; and with all those medals and orders, which are the death of him, because he's easy for the French snipers to pick out – is also progressively disabled. In each scene there's less of Nelson (an eye, an arm); but the heavy make-up paradoxically releases something in Olivier, as the Richard III get-up does. He is progressively disfigured (and progressively decorated: baron, viscount and Duke of Bronte) and increasingly authoritative. His voice is richer – darker-tinted –

* Are you paying attention, Larkin scholars?

and gone are those high-pitched yelps, the staccato, of his younger roles. Indeed, it is only through Olivier's voice that we appreciate Nelson's heroism or feel that he is on an epic scale. We never see any action – his right eye injured during the storming of Calvi, in Corsica; the loss of his right arm at Santa Cruz; his bravery in expeditions under Lord Hood (whom Olivier was to play in *The Bounty**.) As with Dowding, in *Battle of Britain*, Nelson's great chivalrous quality is his forbearance.

Olivier's voice carries his sexual attraction, too. Whatever the extent or demerits of the historical verisimilitude, *That Hamilton Woman* is an accurate depiction of its stars' romance. 'I know I must not come back,' says Nelson to Emma, 'and I know that nothing in this world can keep me away.' Here we have the distinguished (and married) public man, led into sexual temptation and making goo-goo eyes at a trim, coiffed Circe who is out to get him: 'That Hamilton woman,' it is observed, 'never leaves him alone for a moment' – exactly Vivien's tactic with Olivier. Not that Nelson's scruples melt like hot marzipan. Though he's warned off Emma because she's the sort of siren that's only interested in men for what she can get out of them, Nelson doesn't perceive her that way; and he is intrigued by a creature who is aroused by volcanoes and battleships. He feels freshened by her – less taciturn. His patriotic fervour seems to intensify as the love affair deepens; and as Vivien prattles about dancing in Capri in the moonlight, Olivier turns Nappy into Hitler: 'You will never make peace with Napoleon,' he tells Sir William and the assembled courtiers. 'Napoleon can never be master of the world until he has smashed us up, and he means to be master of the world.'

Bonaparte and Hitler combined cannot have been more indomitable than Gladys Cooper's Lady Nelson, the erstwhile Mrs Nesbit, who is as root-faced as a Pilgrim Father. (It's no surprise Nelson doesn't mind not seeing her for seven years.) Officially married to him, and ruling out divorce, she tries to possess her husband as Sir William does his wife. This is not love – though it alters not when it alteration finds – but a contractual, binding agreement. And adultery, the seeking of a life without constraints, is of course a moral crime, and as Nelson rises and

* Samuel Hood (1724–1816) was a Lord of the Admiralty and commander of the Mediterranean fleet during the revolutionary wars. In *The Bounty*, Olivier reprises his Nelson costume, and looks as stern as hell as Anthony Hopkins surrenders his sword before the bigwigs at Captain Bligh's court martial.

rises, and is ennobled, Emma gets to be progressively penniless. (It's the woman who pays.) The majesty of Olivier's conception of the role, however, is that even when delivering those Churchillian, impassioned, patriotic speeches to the Lords of the Admiralty ('You cannot make peace with dictators! You have to wipe them out!'), Nelson's rhetoric has an undercurrent of pleading and elegy. Vivien might be doing her butterfly act in her corner of the film – 'Lady Hamilton is using you for her own ambition and conceit,' says Gladys Cooper. 'Everything is calculated and cold-blooded' (did Jill have a hand in the script?); but Olivier has the poetry and solemnity of a doomed lover. Who can forget the scene where they are on the terrace in full fig, overlooking the toy ships and the smoking mountain. It is midnight on New Year's Eve 1799. 'Now I have kissed you through two centuries,' says Nelson. It is not – it couldn't be – true to life; and other actors could make the clinch ridiculous. But Olivier makes the moment magnificent and sensual.

They live alone in the country with their idealized love until Napoleon's proposed invasion of England means that Nelson is obliged to return to duty – indeed, no sooner is he pacing the poop than he puts out the flags: 'England expects that every man will do his duty.' It has been idyllic; and idylls have to end. Emma knows he'll not return. 'He'll never come back,' she informs her mother. Nelson's last moments below decks on the *Victory* are staged as the tableau in A. W. Davis' famous genre painting (it's a *pietà*) which hangs in the National Maritime Museum – the Admiral in his billowing white shirt, pale and decorous, reclining dramatically amidst his kneeling officers. (In one take, Olivier's wig was ignited by an able seaman coming too near with the hurricane lamp.) We even hear history's most famous misquotation, 'Kiss me, Hardy', for 'Kismet, Hardy.' Hardy goes to tell Emma the news, which gives Vivien her big chance to pantomime her grief. Her eyes glare into the middle distance, her mouth goes tight, she stops doing her needlepoint. As if in a dance – or trance – she pulls the curtains closed and drops to the ground, sinking down like a wounded swan. 'His last thoughts were of you, milady,' says Hardy. 'That you should be cared for.'

In his dotage, when it slipped his mind that he was married to Joan and had started to call her Vivien, or to refer to Vivien as 'my late wife', Olivier was found weeping before the television set – 'This, this was love. This was the real thing.' He'd been watching *That Hamilton Woman*. So did he cry for Nelson and Emma, or for himself and

Vivien? Or had the distinction become blurred? Whatever the answer, this film was to be the last time they ever appeared together on the screen.*

---

* Though this was not intentional. Olivier only gradually gave up hope of their playing the Macbeths together – a film to have been based on the successful stage production at Stratford. A screenplay had been prepared, locations scouted for in Scotland, and Olivier grew a beard which emerged, claimed Vivien, in weird gingery strands. The project collapsed for want of cash. However, an indication of what might have been can be deduced from Glen Byam Shaw's 1955 prompt book for the theatre version; and it is interesting to notice how his descriptions of Shakespeare's character can be taken as straightforward observations of Olivier himself – indeed, what was Byam Shaw's mind actually on? The play or the actor?

> Macbeth – 42 years old [Olivier was 48]. A superb leader & soldier with the courage of a lion and the imagination of a poet. A man of iron discipline and will-power & an almost hypnotic personality. There is something marvellously mysterious about him. The sort of man who can make one nervous by just looking at one. No one would ever dare to slap Macbeth on the back or be jolly with him. Even his friends find him a bit over-powering & his soldiers & servants are terrified of his anger. He is tremendously proud and confident, but never shows off or blusters. When he speaks other people remain silent.

Lady Macbeth, according to the director, was to suggest a suppressed sexual excitement about the idea of the murder; the blood and the violence arouse her – and it is this ecstasy which becomes the agony of her breakdown:

> His wife takes the daggers back herself, but it seems to me that the supreme effort needed to do so undermines her mental and physical strength for ever . . .

Later, Byam Shaw remarks, of the somnambulism scene:

> Lady M. is fast asleep, & unconsciously says things that no torture in the world would drag from her if she was conscious.
>
> Her mind is diseased, but she is not mad.

The anarchy of love and sex? Vivien, anyone? Byam Shaw was to exculpate Macbeth with a similar discrimination – illness being a mitigating circumstance: 'He is like a man who is mentally diseased, but the magnificence and courage of his nature remain till the end.' As if to counterpoint the idea of derangement, the set was a lath-and-plaster edifice of dark tunnels, ravines, battlements and caves – askew arches, wonky vistas, everything sloping, listing, toppling, to indicate twisted vision, and hence twisted reason, I expect.

Chapter Eight
The National Theatre as Metaphor

On 20 July 1971, draped in chains and robes, Olivier delivered his maiden speech in the House of Lords. He referred to his Uncle Sydney, the Baron of Ramsden, as 'incomparably much more deserving, virtuous, illustrious, and in service to his country richer than I can ever hope to be'; and he seems to have had a Goonish idea of how blue-bloods are meant to speak. India, for example, he decides to gloss as 'one of the richest jewels in the Imperial Crown and which now sounds perhaps almost quaint to the retrenched ears whose lobes can only boast the holes to show where once such lush gems hung.' This is like a bad literal translation from a manuscript that unfortunately survived the great fire at the library of Alexandria in the time of Caesar and Theodosius. Yet Olivier was proud enough of his effort to reproduce it as Appendix B in his memoirs. It is so apparently amazingly badly written – the mock courtesy; the excessive fawning and genuflections; the flat jokes; the Blimpish (or Bloodnok-ish) patriotism and platitudes – it has to have an inner purpose; and so it proves. We are seeing Olivier at his own valuation.

Pretending to throw himself on their mercy – 'I must beg to suggest to your Lordships that it would be most contrary to the chivalry for which your Lordships' House is so famous to withhold your gallantry and refuse a maiden of sixty-four' – what the speech reveals is that Olivier regards himself as even above this. Seemingly fantastically modest – 'it does not take all that multi-repeated persuasion, that seethingly passionate ardour [from Harold Wilson, who'd nominated him for a peerage] to make even the [here comes that rib-tickling epithet again] coyest maiden of sixty-four to wonder what on earth she thinks it is she has got to lose' – the tone of the diatribe is actually contemptuous. This is Richard III apeing spinsterishness and delivering a sly oration to the citizens and court.*

* Another example of Olivier saying one thing whilst implying another: his delivery of the opening announcement on Ulster TV: 'It is my privilege – my rare privilege – in

Olivier is never more imposing than when appearing plaintive and out-at-the-elbows. In *Three Sisters*, for example, everybody else is faded, stylized, reciting and almost chanting their lines; the atmosphere is drooping, dead, overwrought. The teachers, post office workers and soldiers complain about boredom, headaches and neuralgia, justifying their unadventurousness and watching their lives run out. They are lazy and talkative and full of themselves – and where Chebutikin could be the cynic, the drunk, Olivier twinkles and chuckles. Chekhov's lassitude is so alien to him – to his fire – and he's the only one with sap, the only one in those pale-pink rooms, with the bowl of pale-yellow roses on the piano, to be in colour, despite the grey tunic he wears. He has panache. Similarly, in *The Entertainer*, the muttered comments of the scornful audience and the reluctant applause; the information we are fed about Archie by his family – that he is an undischarged bankrupt, a flop, a disaster: this doesn't quite fit with what we see, starting with those cut-outs, photos and posters by the theatre, which are of Olivier's Kabuki face – with its black-magic powers. His music hall, likewise, is not a run-down shack but a grand red plush and gilt fun palace. Archie is expert with his make-up; his clothes are spotless; and he is a seducer. Shirley Ann Field's Tina Lapford falls to him as Claire Bloom's Lady Anne does to Richard.

Olivier seems to be there, vehement and distinctive, in all he undertakes. Amongst his last things was Harry Burrard, the defiantly awful stand-up comedian in *Lost Empires*, broadcast in 1986. 'His day is done,' we are told in Colin Firth's voice-over, as Harry, garishly accoutred in a ginger Hitler wig and an out-size baby romper suit, follows the acrobats and jugglers with his terrible jokes – which he inflicts on the audience, like Lear inflicting his love games on his daughters, or the artist in *The Ebony Tower* singing rude songs to Roger Rees. 'Poor Harry Burrard – you could see the despair in his eyes.' Not in Olivier's eyes – there you'll find only rage. 'I'm not lying down – I'm not giving in, not Harry Burrard,' he tells the boy on the train; and instead of being pathetic, which is what J. B. Priestley's novel intended, Olivier is entirely credible – and limitlessly ferocious. Such sentiments are his hymn to life, like that speech in *A Voyage Round My Father* about the 'sheer persistence of nature' – the earwigs, mayfly and beetles in the garden; and also of course Clifford Mortimer himself, keeping going, against adversities;

---

fact it is my unique privilege to be the first person to appear before you on Ulster Television and it makes me extremely happy to share in your pleasure in the fact that Northern Ireland is now a member of the Independent Television Network.' He licks his lips and wriggles; it's all very saturnine.

and, too, Olivier's own persistence which, with its propulsiveness, is heroic.

In *Lost Empires*, nobody talks to him or greets him backstage – because his failure and boredom are contagious? Or because, as when Olivier was Richard, there was a supernatural aura? He is meant to be going mad and thinks he is being followed by mysterious, menacing figures; he gets aggressive and has to be escorted off the stage. The audience cat-call him and throw vegetables – it is a blood sport. But Olivier rises above the humiliation, with his skipping and bowing. There is a fleeting cut-away to his laughter with a dwarf in a Pullman carriage, as the company tours from one town to the next. I think we are meant to register: poor outcasts, hiding unhappiness and pain with the tat of theatre. But with Olivier (like his Van Helsing) appearing in clouds of steam at the station, attired in a flapping coat, a check suit and grey gloves – i.e. as a dandy – what we feel is not pity; it's more like awe. If Olivier had a fondness for playing fops and flops, it's not because these people were unlike himself, and they were a diversion. There's no spirit of condescension. Nor is it that, were it not for his brawn and determination, he'd actually have ended up as Archie or Harry – or, for that matter, as the beggar in *Carrie* or the schoolmaster squirming on an assault charge in *Term of Trial* whom, in his big scene in the dock, he turns into Wilde responding to Carson: 'I'm not damn well guilty and the girl knows it. You've condemned me . . . because I tried to be gentle; you've condemned me because I tried to protect her vulnerability and her youthful pride . . . Sex was never on my mind . . . but a pure love – purity.' What connects all these characters together, from the sad majesty of the music-hall artiste, to Hurstwood creeping backstage to see Carrie Madena, star of *Ladies in Waiting*, to Graham Weir, addressing the court, is Olivier's instinctive sense of his public. The spring of their nature, their vivacity, which was his, is the certain knowledge that they are being observed – if only, as is the case with the priest in *The Power and the Glory*, by God.

Olivier's immediate theatricality, the pleasure he gets us to share in what without his frankness, or slight apprehensiveness, might seem a very artificial or insincere kind of world, allowed him not only to transform characters whom Priestley ('His life was burned into every line of his tortured face') or John Osborne ('He trails off, looking very tired and old') had meant to represent failure; he could also, at the other end of the social scale, be more regal than royalty. When he and Vivien toured Australia and New Zealand, women would drop a curtsey to them and chaps lift their hats. Olivier delivered patriotic speeches ('When a man is British, he is constantly finding himself proud of being so') and was convincingly Henry V in a suit. In the newsreel *British News: No. 336*, the first item is entitled 'Their Majesties Visit Leicester'. King George VI inspects the municipal mace and stutters so much when making his address, I thought the celluloid had jumped off the sprocket. Queen Elizabeth, in her clompy shoes, wanders around a factory and fingers its output – garden gnomes. Next on the Court Circular agenda: the gala première of Powell and Pressburger's *A Matter of Life and Death*. Celebrities in the audience line up for the monarchical handshake, and there, next to Bud Flanagan and Will Hay, are Olivier and Vivien, who look more – literally – glorious than the dumpy Queen and the shuffling King. It reminds me of Henry James' *The Real Thing* – a genuine pair of aristocrats, posing for their portrait, seem fake; much more impressive, in bearing and mood, are some rounded-up servants. By the same token, 'Their Majesties Visit Leicester' is an Ealing comedy starring Margaret Rutherford and Naunton Wayne, whilst at the gala première it ought to be Olivier and Vivien, 'God and the Angel', as they were dubbed in Australia, receiving the homage.

Hence, at his induction into the House of Lords, Olivier acts the part to perfection whilst his sponsor, Lord Goodman, looks like a ropey extra or a drunken Donald Wolfit dragged in out of the rain; and if we can scrape the barnacles off his speech, what he was trying to say, in a succinct nutshell, was that he remained proud of Britain; to his mind, despite the depredations of the socialists, the country would always be *Great* Britain: 'I believe in Great Britain and in keeping her great under the Sovereign.' (There's much more in this vein.) By Britain he means, of course, England. (When Christopher Fry contemplated moving to Wales, Olivier went into a flap: 'You are not to go and live in Wales, you are *not* to go and live in Wales, you are absolutely not to go and live in Wales . . .')* His vision of Englishness is related to Betjeman's, whom he met in Ireland when making *Henry V*. There is a reverence for railway stations, town halls, the Brighton Belle, breakfast kippers, the details of gothic church architecture, chancel screens and the liturgy, gaslit streets, seaside boarding houses (with 'bottles of sauce and Kia-Ora and squash/Awaiting their owners who'd gone up to wash'); or the cultural properties belonging to events like Derby Day, the Henley Regatta, Cowes, dog races, darts, Wensleydale cheese (which Andrew

---

* When Tarquin was first shown around Notley, he said it reminded him of Cors-y-Gedel. 'To hell with Wales. This is England,' snapped his father.

Wyke picks at in *Sleuth*), beetroot in vinegar (a staple of the Rice family), and the music of Elgar and Handel.*

Olivier and Betjeman have similar sensibilities.† Olivier would have been Actor Laureate, had such a post existed; he was created a member of the Order of Merit instead. 'It wouldn't be difficult for him to accept – and play – the role of the rather grand Establishment actor,' commented John Osborne in 1973. Yet though he was elevated to the peerage and given the OM, though he was, at thirty-nine, the youngest actor ever to be knighted, there is more to Olivier's superior sense of Englishness than his pride in being recognized with strings of honours (Hon. D.Litt., Oxon, Manchester, Sussex, Edinburgh and London). As with Betjeman, things mattered to him: 'I believe that in a great city, or even . . . a village, a great theatre is the outward and visible sign of . . . culture . . . I believe in anything that will keep our domains, not wider still and wider, but higher still and higher in the . . . hope of quality and probity.' Yet where Betjeman was nostalgic, hankering for a life which may have disappeared, Olivier of course, or shall we say his spirit, *survived* from such an era – Camelot or Merry England – and therefore we cannot quite declare it lost. I know this example is Scandinavian, but it helps to prove my point: in *The Dance of Death*, Olivier becomes young and dapper, as Captain Edgar jigs to 'The Entry of the Boyars' – we see right before us the gleaming Sir Gawain he once was. As Laughton told him, 'You *are* England'; and England, as embodied in Olivier, was no fantasy island, no reverie. As with Churchill, or Margaret Thatcher, those other bequests to the nation, there's an onward thrust to his activities. Urgent, keen, assertive, if there is one thread which runs through Olivier's career – from his impassioned early days in the West End and on Broadway to the high spirits and miraculous foolishness of his final cameos in those blockbusters – it is the strength of his ambition. He was consumed with ambition, like a Shakespearian king. (He had the concomitant guilt and doubt, too: can you be a good man and a strong king?)

He was superabundant, his acting full of turbulence and striking effects. 'His attitude is that he is making history, particularly English

---

* That other self-consciously English Englishman, T. S. Eliot (b. St Louis, Missouri), discusses or at least catalogues such occasions in, I think, *Notes Towards a Definition of Culture*.

† Similar, too, were their recollections of a reputedly loveless, lonely childhood: 'Deep, dark and pitiful I saw myself,' wrote Betjeman in his verse autobiography, *Summoned by Bells*. Olivier's theatricalities and Betjeman's eccentricities (he was quite a performer) seem devised to keep back the distress of private feeling.

history,' said Osborne. How paradoxical, therefore, that the most English of Englishmen should be in America at crucial moments – the declaration of war, the death of George VI, his weddings to both Vivien and Joan, the latter being held at Wilton, Connecticut, on 17 March 1961. The propagandistic *That Hamilton Woman* came into being at the General Services Studios, Los Angeles; Daphne du Maurier's spooky Cornwall in *Rebecca* was reconstructed in Hollywood, with the assistance of the head of the Hollywood Raj, C. Aubrey Smith, as the quintessentially English magistrate, Colonel Julyan; and Jane Austen, as English as beef, is fundamentally Americanized in *Pride and Prejudice*: that haberdashery, where we first meet the Bennet girls, aswirl with ribbons, muslin, damask and bows, is in a Wild West town; the ladies who gossip are from the Old West; and in the carriage chase and other exteriors, the terrain is Californian scrub. Luckily, the MGM set-decorators uprooted the cacti, as they are seldom found in Winchester or Bath. As with *Wuthering Heights*, which should unfold in damp Yorkshire, nothing could be done to regulate the sunshine.

Olivier told Eileen Herlie, during the filming of *Hamlet*, that 'there are some subjects which should only be filmed in Britain [because] they are either British by authorship or historically associated with Britain'. Which would rather tend to rule out his own career and the adaptations of literary classics and pageants he'd personally been associated with, from Heathcliff to Nelson; and when he was asked, as he boarded the *Excambion*, 'Why do you [propose to] stay in England when Hollywood is ready to give you the world?', he answered simply, 'It's my home.' It is ironic therefore that when, in January 1943, the Air Ministry, as surely they must have done, pleaded with the Ministry of Information to prevent Sub-Lieutenant Olivier of 757 Squadron from crashing any more planes (he bumped into aircraft parked on the ground whilst taxiing), and to take him away, it was to play – a Russian. Ivan Kouznetsoff is a Soviet marine engineer who comes to England, where a propeller he has invented will be manufactured at Felix Aylmer's foundry. 'Quite simply it was a propaganda film,' Olivier told Puffin Asquith's biographer. 'The purpose of the propaganda was to make the English love the Russians who had just come into the war.'

I don't think the Russians had much to do with anything* – *The*

* Though being Russian had a lot to do with Olivier's work for Asquith. Puffin directed him in *Moscow Nights* (1935). Olivier was Captain Ignatoff, recuperating in a military hospital and charming the nurses. He's bright and snappy, with a high, explosive laugh. Though Russian, he's like an English officer; and he's very seductive, getting a kiss from a nurse when she's helping him to walk. He fixes his gaze on her – and it was *Moscow*

Demi-Paradise extols the English to the English. Young Kouznetsoff is the pretext; an excuse to see ourselves, as it were, with a fresh pair of eyes. For what Olivier's character takes in is what the English were fighting the war to preserve; the film is an anthology of national foibles: rain, cramped railway compartments, snobbery, bad cooking, tyrannical landladies, trolley buses, a glass of sherry before dinner, cricket scores, advertisements for Sandeman's Port, Guinness is Good For You, Black & White Scotch Whisky, and the Women's Institute. But this is not a documentary; it is an hallucination. The office boy with the pencil behind his ear is George Cole; the lady selling charity flags is Margaret Rutherford; the housewife in a headscarf on a pushbike is Joyce Grenfell; the man in the box office is Miles Malleson. When Kouznetsoff walks along the high street, it is a scene to make Pevsner weep for joy – the master butcher, the guildhall, the tea rooms; and all of this cavalcade was constructed in the studio.

Olivier's character is like the straight man or stooge; England, where Felix Aylmer recites Bradshaw and take snuff ('Care for a pinch?') is his comic feed. Not only does he have a thick Russian accent, to distance him, he's also a man who has to think each word before he says it – he's not at ease with the language, nor with the people who speak it, i.e. with the grammar of their ways. But he's not befuddled – he's no slow-witted dope. Indeed, he has the intense concentration, the anxiety to learn and progress through trial and error, of a child – and when he's the boffin, puffing on a pipe and designing his prototype propellers, the incongruity of a grown-up's pipe in that fresh, open face is what's most striking. It is a bashful performance. When he helps Penelope Dudley Ward off with her coat, and does so with a flourish, and she smiles at the funny foreignness of him, Olivier half colludes with her

---

Nights that first caused me to notice how Olivier can move his eyeballs and eyelids independently, so that he looks at you twice, and he's looking at you deeper.

In 1967, Puffin Asquith was to have directed Olivier in *The Shoes of the Fisherman*, in which this time he plays a Russian politician, Piotr Ilyich Kamenev, who does the world a service by banging up Anthony Quinn for twenty years and delaying his becoming Pope. Owing to illness, however, the production was taken over by Michael Anderson; and Olivier was left to read the lesson at Asquith's memorial service at St Margaret's, Westminster, in the spring of 1968: I Corinthians, Chapter XIII, which apparently he delivered very slowly and deliberately, with huge pauses. Was he resisting the temptation to be Russian? ('Charity envieth not; charity vaunteth not itself, is not puffed up, doth not behave itself unseemly, seeketh not her own, is not easily provoked, thinketh no evil; rejoiceth not in iniquity, but rejoiceth in truth; beareth all things, believeth all things, hopeth all things, endureth all things.')

(yes, that was rather a cossacky gesture, wasn't it?), but he also perceives that her response to his gallantry is a bit patronizing. Alert to every nuance, as he apprehends this new country and its means, Kouznetsoff finds that just when he thinks he has their measure, the English have a tendency to vanish, or slip away and gabble about irrelevancies. At dinner, he wants to discuss his propeller; Felix Aylmer and his dotty cronies divert discussion to gardening, or the sea, or golf. The Russian is bewildered by the ironies, the lack of directness, the twinkling sideways-on courtesies. 'I don't understand the English!' he explodes eventually, his attempts at talking business – or shop (bad form) – rebuffed. 'You are living in the past – because that's more easy for you, more comfortable; but you are losing the present.'

On that outburst, a fast-fade – and a flash-forward. It is now a few years later and war has been declared. Felix Aylmer is still in his frock coat, polishing his pince-nez, except what had seemed fuddy-duddy Victorian sentimentality (his engineering firm's motto is 'Duty and Service') now represents the deeper English virtues. 'Tradition,' he says, 'it's a living thing'; and as if to prove his point, Margaret Rutherford, who though she's still Madame Arcarti and Miss Marple is actually called Rowena Ventnor, organizes a historical pageant, to raise funds for Kouznetsoff's beleaguered home village. In her tweed cloaks, a helmet, carrying a spear, and with her jaw thrust out and chins wobbling magnificently, she's a reincarnation of Britannia. Other characters portray Roman soldiers; Queen Elizabeth I glides into view on a barge. Then, in a moment of blissful surrealism, a hush falls across the lawns and terrace, the characters fall back, and a lone cellist starts to accompany a pair of nightingales. Microphones secreted in the boskage relay the birdsong to Broadcasting House. Searchlights rake the sky, bombs are soon going to fall; but before the chaos, this weird peacefulness. When he'd first arrived, Olivier's character would have been flummoxed. This time around he is absorbed into the magic. The English *like* being alone, against the Germans; they relish being a tight little island. (If this wasn't a real Russian visitor's view, it's certainly Olivier's.)

His propeller is a success – the factory works non-stop to cast and fit it ('We said we'd get the job done – it's only another proof of this country's determination to do everything possible to help our friends and allies, the brave Russian people' – over in Hollywood, a brought-up-to-date Holmes and Watson, having routed German agents, were being similarly stirring;* and everybody sings 'For He's a Jolly Good Fellow'. Kouznetsoff becomes an honorary Englishman. Before he departs, he tells the assembled throng: 'Much of the world thinks you are perfidious and hypocritical – and you are warm and kindly. It amuses you – your sense of humour – for people to think otherwise. If you can laugh at life and yourselves, you can be tolerant. You love freedom – for there is no laughter where there is no freedom . . .' In that Englishness is about humour and understatement, this would be the mood of, for example, *A Voyage Round My Father*, where the daughter-in-law, played by Jane Asher, is the outsider newly arrived in the Chilterns demi-paradise; and she will never belong, and nor does she want to. She is exasperated by the blind tyrant; the others are enchanted, or are willing to pretend to be. The nature and purpose of English feigning is explored here; our apparent indifference – and all the time, the tenderness and intimacy is going on beneath the apparent indifference. Jane Asher's Elizabeth has no irony, no lightness, and can't see this – she's the one that's blind. (Is she an American?)

Olivier has one long scene which is wonderful.† He's taking tea outside, and he's telling jokes, and trying to provoke debate, decrying foreign travel, saying how overrated sex is, etc., barking out answers to the crossword in asides, fending off a wasp (with real panic); he's vulnerable, crotchety, impossible, the undisputed centre of attention. Like Lear, he's entertaining and wanting to be entertained, and a bit bored – and Elizabeth, who refuses to be impressed by the recitative, cuts across him. Why do they all bother, she wants to know? Why talk

* In February 1921, Olivier went on a choir school outing to see *Henry IV Part Two* at the Royal Court: 'Prince Hal. Oh, that magical Prince Hal, the most beautiful male I have ever laid eyes upon. His profile was that of a god, his figure pure Olympiad, his voice the most beautiful instrument I had yet heard, and even his name suggested the utmost in glamorous masculinity – Basil Rathbone. To me he had it all, and more, and represented a collation of theatrical virtues that I could never hope to attain.' Hyperbole? It is the case that Olivier never played Holmes, but was a spiderish Moriarty, in *The Seven Per Cent Solution*.

† A clue to how he accomplishes it, controlling and varying the tempo and ensuring he fixes our attention (and that of the other characters), may be found in his description of his method in *Uncle Vanya*: 'I have a horror of a performance becoming mechanical, automatic, and I watch like a hawk for signs of it . . . When you play your role just a little differently, it surprises your fellow actors and keeps them alive. There is a time in *Uncle Vanya* when Sonya is distraught that I am drinking vodka all through this scene. She watches me pouring it down and at a certain time I pick my glass up and go to the cupboard to get more. At that moment she offers me some cheese to try and stop me drinking. Now I vary the timing of my move so that she has to watch me very carefully. It keeps her in the reality of the situation.'

about the garden and the colours when he's blind, for heaven's sake? She accuses the family of being trivial, and Olivier says, 'What?' – and there's a flash of Richard III in his chill inflection, a glimpse of incredible power. It lasts no time at all, but the fire is there. We might compare it with Clifford in court, with his theatrical rage and his love of conflict and argument. But those are staged battles. With Jane Asher's Elizabeth, real anger is provoked, and he's thrown. Clouds gather in those blind dark eyes; in those blind phantasmagoric eyes, which constantly change colour: hazel brown, with pale-grey rims, like planets, edged with mists, or deep black, coal black, surrounded by red.

Clifford Mortimer is a compendium of Olivier's Englishness: he never allows himself to be abandoned; he's not a person you'd want to contradict – or, in connection with Olivier's harsh judgements on his younger self, you'd best not really agree with him. This elaborate game of self-mockery and underplaying – the sum of all the parts adding up to self-assurance or, if it goes wrong, to self-satisfaction: this is what the tigressy, impersonal, sceptical Elizabeth can't enter into; she can't understand the nature of the relationship between Alan Bates and his pa. She thinks they tell jokes, evade issues, refuse to be serious or direct – yet the truth and feeling of the father–son bond is in the silences, or in the grain of Olivier's voice when he lists in a letter what's been going on in the garden. As with Astrov – another Russian whom Olivier converts into an English gentleman – Olivier can talk about one thing whilst ostensibly talking about another.

Kouznetsoff not only travels physically from Russia; he goes on a mental journey from exclusion to acceptance. He stops being foreign. By the end, he's virtually a son to Felix Aylmer: it's the bond of *A Voyage Round My Father*, and Olivier's open face, black hair, and combination of clumsiness and canniness pre-incarnates Alan Bates. Eradicate the Danny Kaye-calibre Russian dialect, give him a tonsure, put him in tights and on horseback – and with those happy-breed, band-of-brothers speeches, he is Henry V. Which is not surprising, as during the making of *The Demi-Paradise*, preparations were underway for *Henry V*; and perhaps Olivier had always been preparing for *Henry V*, which makes me wonder. (The Dauphin calls Henry 'a vain, giddy, shallow, humorous youth', which could be a description of any of Olivier's earliest roles.) Captain Ignatoff, in Puffin Asquith's earlier Olivier effort, *Moscow Nights*, has a petulant streak. 'I'm damned if I'll take anything from a filthy profiteer!' he says to the nurse, hitting the milk jug over. He's angry because she is engaged to a chap he loathes. How quickly his charm can fade, and he becomes bumptious; Ignatoff expects to get his way. (When he sees the nurse and her fiancé together, the whole breakfast tray goes on the floor.) He is described as 'an almost perfect young man': the officer and a gentleman who, when he gambles at the casino or plays heads-and-tails against himself, believes he should be lucky. (He has considerable conceit.) Olivier speaks his words with an almost bitter clarity of enunciation and in moments of rage his voice acquires the high-pitched rat-a-tat of Richard III. Alternatively, the soft way he can say 'I see' freezes the air, like Clifford Mortimer's 'What?' Either way, shouting or whispering, Olivier is derisive, cutting, and one day this will culminate as the suave and unnerving Andrew Wyke, in *Sleuth*, with his mock-military swagger and his hectoring, contemptuous snarls and snorts.

The jaunty quick-step walk (and the way he bounds up a staircase), the bark in his voice, the command; and then the exaggerations, such as the cravat, the fastidiousness, the genteelisms, make Wyke queerish, absurd, camp. (Olivier gives off a glee.) *Sleuth* is of course about confidence tricksters (fake burglaries, an insurance scam, attempted murder), and so after a fashion was Shakespeare's *Henry V*. 'The mirror of all Christian Kings' is, in the original play, a war-mongering bully whose army consists of rapists and cut-throats who go forth to France because 'profits will accrue'. The bishops urge war because of the benefits to church revenues; war with France will divert attention from local difficulties (Henry intends to 'busy giddy minds with foreign quarrels'); and the expounding of the Salic Law, Henry's legal claim to the French throne and dukedoms, is so specious and pettifogging, Olivier has to play the scene for comedy, with Felix Aylmer, as the Archbishop of Canterbury, and Robert Helpmann, as the Bishop of Ely, filling the stage with quires of foolscap, dusty folios and sheaves of documentation. Shakespeare's point, of course, is that the King has already made up his mind to invade the continent; and when he gets there, look what he does: threatens to pillage Harfleur, executes an old friend ('We would have all such offenders so cut off'), and after Agincourt 'the King most worthily hath caused every soldier to cut his prisoner's throat. O 'tis a gallant King!' And Brutus is an honourable man.

Olivier removed all the nasty and bloodthirsty references, especially those to genocide, or ethnic cleansing as it is now called. His Henry is not a despot or a spoiled brat ('France being ours, we'll bend it to our awe/Or break it all to pieces'); and when he's called 'a royal captain' leading 'choice-drawn cavaliers', the 'Star of England' who speaks in 'sweet and honey'd sentences', all irony is quite obliterated. We could ascribe this to adroit editing. The government was sponsoring the film of *Henry V** and, wishing to ennoble the forties, and give England its moral triumph, violence and disaster – what Shakespeare calls 'the dogs of war', 'famine, sword, and fire' – are suppressed. 'The pull of this play as popular propaganda, I could see, might be potent,' said Olivier. But there's more to it than this; it isn't textual tinkerings or slants which manage to show Henry in a good light. Olivier wasn't an apologist for Henry V; rather, *Henry V* adapts itself to Olivier's clarion style. When Henry says he'll be the sun-king who, after voyaging across to Normandy, 'will rise there with so full a glory/That I will dazzle all the eyes of France', *dazzle* is what Olivier does. He is not vainglorious; he is, as we know, Jupiter – 'in fierce tempest is he coming,/In thunder and in earthquake, like a Jove.' I doubt whether the oratory of these big speeches has taken flight like this ever before (it certainly hasn't since) – 'Once more unto the breach, dear friends, once more' or 'We few, we happy few, we band of brothers' or 'God for Harry! England and Saint George!': Walter Pater said that all art constantly aspires towards the condition of music, and in Olivier's performance acting achieves that ideal. (It's as if he's lustily singing hymns.)

It is his most poised characterization (to recall his aeronautical analogy). Too much one way, and Henry would be priggish, and thus his heroism debunked; too much the other, and we'd be in the land of parody. Urgent and keen, and with a cherishing voice, in the court scenes, and a voice like the noise of battle rolling among the mountains, when he is out of doors, Olivier presides over a public celebration. The fight scenes, with the cart-horses in fancy dress, denote vigour and valour, not brutality. *Henry V*, i.e. the film produced by Olivier, directed by Olivier and starring Olivier, as opposed to Shakespeare's more ambiguous drama, sees war as an adventure, a jape. During this 'scrambling and unquiet time', England will be left with the Home Guard – Dad's Army: 'grandsires, babies, and old women'; and by an amazing sleight of hand, which has to do with what was on people's minds during the Second World War, when Exeter says to the King of France that he must 'divest yourself and lay apart/The borrowed glories that 'longs/To him and to his heirs, namely the crown', you think that he is rebuking the Nazis, who had been laying claim to peaceable countries and neighbours. It is

* As Walton's fanfares get underway, and after having been informed that here is 'A Laurence Olivier Production', this pops on to the screen: 'To the Commandos and Airborne Troops of Great Britain this film is dedicated, the spirit of whose ancestors it has been humbly attempted to recapture in some ensuing scenes.'

indeed a contemporary war film,* and Henry's belligerence is transferred to Hitler – for when 'he bids you then resign/Your crown and kingdom', that's what the Germans would do, not the British; and the British have as much right to be in France as the Germans during the Occupation. That the film was released on 12 July 1944, soon after the D-Day

---

* The screenplay is included in *Masterworks of the British Cinema* (London, 1990), along with Hitchcock's *The Lady Vanishes* (1938) and Coward and David Lean's *Brief Encounter* (1945). Though, as I have been arguing throughout this book, Olivier had an isolating personality, and was unique and apart, his work belongs with the spirit of the age in which it was produced; his achievements are contextual, environed, and explore a race of people who are shy and difficult, like the themes of the other English directors. Hitchcock's film, like *Henry V*, is a war film: trains, spies, Balkan intrigue, and Czechoslovakia and Poland are threatened by Germany. Though it is terrific comedy, the idea of vanishings, the question of identity and non-existence, is menacing and strange – and is related to the nightmare of secret police making dawn raids and arrests. Michael Redgrave, who has a nervousness and eagerness that is almost embarrassing – he's always helpless, out-pointed, ineffectual – here gives an early version of his Vanya.

Brief Encounter is the serious partner to *Private Lives*: two people who ought to be together, but aren't; or maybe here we have Victor Prynne and Sibyl? The film is about goodness, and a desire to do good, starring Tristan and Isolde in the refreshment room at Milford Junction. Romantic passion, and feeling released, and then having to part: here are the wartime themes of sacrifice, duty and relinquishings. Laura and Alec may be quintessentially English and middle class, but here they are, feeling intense emotions: joy, ruefulness, shame, deception, love and pain. 'Nothing lasts really – neither happiness nor despair – not even life lasts very long,' says Celia Johnson's Laura, in her anguished voice-over, with its slight note of panic – of incipient hysteria. Celia Johnson has a sympathy, a sweetness, which Vivien, with her over-strong sense of refinement – her being delicate and her social smiles – could only contrive.

Trevor Howard's Alec is quite unlike the roaring brute he became later – Henry Rawlinson, or Lord Cardigan, or Captain Bligh. He has a delicacy – not dissimilar to Olivier's; though he is kinder, gentler than Olivier. He has ease and power and assurance – and a sort of shyness, which is quite different to Olivier's scowling reserve. (Howard was second in line for Archie Rice had Olivier for some reason not been able to make the film version of *The Entertainer*.) *Brief Encounter* is about what it means to be a happy twosome, and Vivien and Olivier *did* fulfil Laura's daydream – waltzing, or being in a theatre box peering through opera glasses, or reclining in a gondola, or driving through beautiful countryside, the wind blowing her hair, or leaning on a ship's rail, looking at a tropical beach in the moonlight. But the daydream is a nonsense; it is a cruelty to prolong it. Reality is hurtling express trains, the screams of train whistles, billows of sulphurous steam – which is the mood of an extract from Olivier's private wartime diary: 'I think the thing that hits one so when hearing of a war is not the thought so much of the horrors of it, but the terrible irremediable mess that everyone's lives are to be turned into until the thing is over . . . It means the whole earth is under a sort of pall of sickness, distress, and anxiety and self-disgust in some way or other . . .'

Landings, added to this confusion. Harry's band of brothers became the Allied invaders – except Harry doesn't intend to liberate France; quite the reverse. All credit to Olivier, in his silver armour, that this is got away with – everybody was taken in, because Henry V was actually a version of Richard III; and if he wasn't exactly clothing his naked villainy with odd old ends stolen forth of holy writ ('And seem a saint when most I play the devil'), though there's a bit of that, Olivier's Henry, dealing with actualities and practicalities on the one hand, and myth-making and rhetoric on the other, floats free of history, and the original dramatist, to become a portrait of the actor himself as a young man. Henry's watchfulness is Olivier's; likewise, his reticence and his hints of concealment.

Making the movie was a military campaign. In February 1942, Olivier had silenced an unruly mob of Fleet Air Arm service personnel by falling to his knees in the canteen and saying, hands clasped in prayer: 'O God of battles! steel my soldiers' hearts/Possess them not with fear', and the following May he recited the 'Crispin' and 'Harfleur' speeches on a radio broadcast called *Into Battle*; and Dallas Bower, the producer, followed this with a full wireless adaptation of *Henry V*, which Olivier recorded in Manchester. His voice was heard by the inaugurator of Two Cities Films, Filippo Del Giudice, who proposed a version for the cinema. Bower, who had wondered about a television play, had the beginnings of a script to hand, and he joined the project (at Olivier's insistence) as the associate producer. J. Arthur Rank put up the finance. William Wyler was to have been the director – would he have made Henry, like Heathcliff, emerge from a forest in a fairy tale? – but on 1 March 1943, after he had completed the fourteen-week shoot on *The Demi-Paradise*, Olivier was announced as being the one who'd handle the megaphone. He promptly hired the technicians he'd got to know on the Asquith film – principally, Reginald Beck, the editor, and Paul Sheriff and Carmen Dillon, the art directors – and Roger Furse, currently on the staff of the naval officers' training station at Lancing, was released from service to design the costumes.

To Furse fell the task of researching medieval illuminated manuscripts, which gave the film its Bayeux tapestry appearance – the rather flat, sideways-on stylization. He also superintended the construction of the miniature London, with the Thames and toy theatres. This artificiality I enjoy; the early sequences in the Globe, with the actors acting, are inspired. (Can you spot Shakespeare himself backstage, lending a hand as a dresser?) Leslie Banks comes on as the Chorus, and there's a sense of occasion.* Olivier, however, had this Victorian passion for veracity – an almost childlike belief in making things real, when of course theatre and film are make-believe – and you can bet that the coats of arms for the knights are authentic, the fifteenth-century wooden saddles would fool a fifteenth-century wooden saddle maker, and the colours for the costumes have been brewed from vegetable dyes dating from the Middle Ages. This literal-mindedness gets in the way of the imaginative faculties; but it did allow Olivier to pretend that film-making was on a par with Operation Overlord.†

He left for Ireland to shoot the Agincourt sequences on 28 May. At Enniskerry, Lord Powerscourt, the Irish Commissioner of the Boy Scouts, had facilities for campers and outward-bound enthusiasts in his park. Olivier was now in command of hundreds of people, hundreds of horses, the cookhouse, latrines, wardrobe and props. Not Harry, but Larry had his army; and as the extras and riders were drafted from the Irish Local Defence Force, it was in fact the Irish Dad's Army.‡ Like the King in his tent, Olivier wrote to Vivien by candlelight from his caravan, praying for victory. 'I am on top of a little hill – very solitary – where I can see the whole layout of the camp and the location.'

Cameras rolled on 9 June, and Olivier, riding his horse Blaunche Kyng, which he later took home and put out to grass at Notley, cantered around the set, lining up his shots. He worked long hours and resented those who couldn't match his stamina – 'I shall get rid of him, or anybody who doesn't pull his weight,' he'd snap. He complained about how long it took the men to get into their armour; he complained about the drowsiness of the animals; and – the one element beyond his control – he complained about shifting cloud formations, which ruined continuity. Two weeks were completely wasted by rain and fitful sunshine.

But then it came together; the weather improved, and a procession scene 'was really lovely and gave me a great lump in my throat at each of the two takes we made'. The horses swished their tails; they galloped and retreated. Reinforcements surged into view for dramatic clashes, and the horses lying down in the water, pretending to be dead, didn't flinch. The unit returned to Denham on 24 July, with fifteen minutes of film,

* I've heard it said that Puffin Asquith suggested these scenes – if so, and Olivier was never again so inventive as a director, then they are equal to the nightingale sequence in *The Demi-Paradise* for whimsy and exuberance.

† Leslie Banks said: 'Larry ended up fighting his war with the making of *Henry V*, and he won a more glorious victory than most of the Field Marshals of the British Army.'

‡ One member of which named his donkey 'Vivien Leigh', and you can't ask for greater glory than that.

and the studio slog began on 9 August – finishing, or wrapping, on . January 1944. Editing, scoring and which-what took until the summe When released, the film ran for eleven unbroken months; it was similarl successful in America where it opened in April 1946 and the followin year Olivier received an Oscar for 'his outstanding achievement as acto producer and director in bringing *Henry V* to the screen'.

Olivier didn't so much play a king as embody in himself those qualitie of imperiousness and dissociation which had inspired Shakespeare t create such a character in the first place; and a king has to have hi castle. Notley, a picturesque ruin when he first saw it, was purchased i late 1944, with monies advanced by Del Giudice.* He and Vivien neede somewhere to settle, as Durham Cottage had sustained bomb damage - what Ralph's rockets and Catherine wheels began, the Luftwaffe com pleted – but a sixteen-room grey stone pile surrounded by brambles? I looked like Manderley after Mrs Danvers has torched it. However, a Olivier himself said in 1986:

> Notley Abbey was near Thame, halfway between Stratford and London, and was very, very beautiful. Of all the houses I've lived in over the years, Notley is my favourite. It was absolutely enchanting, and enchanted me. At Notley I had an affair with the past. For me it had mesmeric power; I could easily drown in its atmosphere. I could not leave it alone, I was a child lost in its history. Perhaps I loved it too much if that is possible.
>
> It had been built by Walter Giffard, Earl of Buckingham, during the reign of Henry II, 'in order that the souls of the King, his Queen Eleanor of Aquitaine, his own soul and those of all his family, might be prayed for in perpetuity.' Whenever I returned to Notley after a period away, I felt safe and secure . . .

The Abbey was further endowed by Henry V, a fact which thrille Olivier;† and instead of Augustinian monks (whose skeletons were unear thed during the restoration work), Olivier and Vivien – especially he – filled the place with theatre friends. Once, she invited the entire cas of *Oklahoma*, the showgirls and Howard Keel. Katharine Hepburn an

---

* He paid Olivier £15,000 not to appear in any other film for eighteen months, s that his publicity value and exclusivity for *Henry V* could be maximized, and so that, i effect, Olivier would not be competing against himself. Plans for *Cyrano de Bergerac* havin come to nothing, Olivier didn't work in the cinema again until *Hamlet*, in 1948; an then only the cameo in *The Magic Box*, *Carrie* and *The Beggar's Opera* until *Richard III* i 1955.

† Henry remained his hero. On 21 October 1971, the anniversary of Agincourt, h attended Evensong at Westminster Abbey and declaimed the 'St Crispin' speech at th tomb of the warrior king.

Marlene Dietrich would be found weeding the roses; Orson Welles would be typing *Mr Arkadin*; Rex Harrison would be discussing the role of the Duke of Altair, in *Venus Observed*, which Olivier was to direct in New York. William Walton composed *Troilus and Cressida* in the guest cottage. The hall, study, three cavernous reception rooms and five principal bedroom suites were soon crammed with cut flowers and bibelots. Especially cut flowers. The country-house life was well observed by Susana Walton:

> We would arrive with other guests on Saturdays, after their matinée and evening performances, for a seated, sumptuous meal. The table would be decorated with bowls of floating passion-flowers, and we would be served exquisite food and wine. Larry used to droop by three in the morning, but Vivien never tired. The house was always full of flowers from the conservatory. I vividly remember our room, with curtains chosen to match the sheets, as well as the breakfast set, and the colour scheme continued down to the loo paper. It was sybaritic.
>
> Despite parts of the house being very old, Vivien did not think twice about tearing out an ancient staircase and replacing it with a handsome one, bought at a house sale, that she liked better. She also loved the garden, and I enjoyed gardening with her when I was there.

Evening dress was expected; there were drinks in the library before dinner, which was announced by a butler. Cream and butter were supplied by the Notley herd, which also supplied the White Tower restaurant in Percy Street. (The seventy acres of grounds were managed by Olivier's brother Dickie, whom he had generously put through agricultural college after the rubber planting in India proved a fiasco.) There was the lime walk, which Olivier planted and pruned; a fast-flowing brook. It was a pop-up-book idyll of England.

So why do I find it creepy? Since returning from America, the Oliviers had lived in a succession of rented places, at first to be near the airbases and later to be near the film studios. Hawksgrove, at Fulmer, near Denham, was one such address; Old Prestwick, Gerrards Cross, Bucks., was another. They were anxious to put down roots – and at Notley, which started to become habitable in February 1945, Olivier could imagine his roots reaching down to entwine with those of huge personalities and eventful history. However, it's not the corpses laid out under what was once the high altar which worry me – indeed, it's when Notley Abbey sounds like Northanger Abbey that I'm ready to put in a bid. Nor am I put off at the idea of Robert Helpmann parading in a leopard-skin jockstrap. A clue to my concern is to be found in that image of the guests assembling for cocktails in the library. It's as if the curtain is about to go up, and they are all suddenly in a play. And the Henry V associations – it is as if life here is an extension of a performance. There's no reality. Tarquin was to the point when he wrote, 'there was an exhausted sexuality about the place': exactly. It was a shrine to a lost love.

Whilst Olivier was knocking the wings off planes, making *The Demi-Paradise* and, without a pause, launching into the logistics of *Henry V* ('he's overworking and like to have a nervous breakdown', claimed Oswald Frewen), Vivien had endured a long provincial tour in Shaw's *The Doctor's Dilemma*, which began in August 1941 and arrived in London on 4 March 1942, where it ran for over a year. She toured North Africa for three months in 1943, entertaining the troops in Gibraltar, Algiers, Tunis, Tripoli, Cairo and Alexandria with a Binkie Beaumont revue called *Spring Party*. Despite the insects and heat, her round-the-clock volubility never abated. She started making *Caesar and Cleopatra* in June 1944, with Claude Rains, but the production, for which she'd been preparing since the previous November, was delayed when she suffered a miscarriage – that a woman in her condition was to be found beating the slave and chasing him around the Memphis Palace, running around the throne room and leaping on to the dais to proclaim, 'I am a Queen at last – a real, real Queen! Cleopatra the Queen!' could not have helped matters; and indeed it was two days after slipping and falling during a take that she lost the baby. Olivier, with his unnerving detachment, examined the foetus, marvelling at how beautiful and perfectly formed it was. 'It had a penis, and would have been a little boy,' he told Tarquin, who'd have been its half-brother. Vivien recuperated in the London Clinic, but was never completely well ever again.* Like a

---

* In the book of the film, *Meeting at the Sphinx: Gabriel Pascal's Production of Bernard Shaw's Caesar and Cleopatra* by Marjorie Deans (London, 1945), we are led to believe that Vivien was perfection in the part, mainly because she herself had 'a personality which is notably clear and unshadowed, giving a brilliant, princesslike quality of assurance and poise which, for the part of Cleopatra, has an obvious value . . . The exciting thing about Shaw's Cleopatra is that you watch the process by which a child turns into a woman, and a foolish nursery-kitten into a highly controlled and dominating queen. Could Vivien Leigh interpret that transforming experience? Could she show us the struggle and emotional strife through which alone it could take place? I think she has done so triumphantly.'

I couldn't say. In a shameful dereliction of critical duty, I could stand only five minutes of her titting about between the paws of the plaster-of-Paris sphinx before switching off the video and finding something better to do. I didn't know it at the time, but I was virtually following Shaw's precedent. At a private screening of the film he did nothing but mutter, 'Oh, she's ruining it . . . That was a delightful piece of comedy. It goes for nothing now.'

worm in the bud, her illness fed on her damask cheek; she pined in thought and succumbed to a green and yellow melancholy, as Viola says to Orsino. She lost weight alarmingly, especially during the run of *The Skin of Our Teeth*, which opened at the Phoenix Theatre on 15 May 1945 (and was revived in the September of the following year). A tubercular patch on her lung was diagnosed. She spent six weeks at University College Hospital – and thence to Notley, where she was cloistered for nine months.

Notley, therefore, was not so much a home as a sanatorium; later, it was to be an asylum, with Vivien hurling abuse or crumpling into a heap, sobbing inconsolably, and Olivier there, looking on helplessly. What her activities since the return from America also reveal, in addition to her fading health, is how much her work, and Olivier's, kept them apart. He in Ireland; she in Manchester, Liverpool (where she met and dined with Leigh Holman), Leeds, Blackpool, Leicester, Glasgow or Edinburgh; he at Denham whilst she trekked the desert; he in Germany with an Old Vic tour when she had her spontaneous abortion. They did their utmost to meet at weekends and she read her way through the novels of Dickens, traipsing by train to their rendezvous. But the non-proximity is only a symptom, not the cause, of what went wrong. What went wrong was what was going right with Olivier's career. On 1 November 1945, James Agate* sent her one of his appalling *Ego* volumes with a covering letter saying 'Hurry up and get well or people will think Larry thrives in your absence. *He is becoming a great actor.*'

She hardly needed this to be rubbed in. Call it consumption, an infection of her lymphatic system, an immunodeficiency disorder, a combination of genetic, hormonal or uterine abnormalities; label her a manic-depressive psychotic and squirt her full of anti-depressant drugs; give her two or three blasts of electro-convulsive therapy per week to induce such brain seizures she's sexually excited by a pop-up toaster; tot up her fevers and chills and monitor her intake of gin and tobacco: what she was dying slowly from was a broken heart, and nobody can convince me otherwise. She became vituperative and unmanageable because she wanted to claim Olivier's love exclusively, and as Peter Glenville, who directed him in *Becket*, and *Term of Trial*, and who had appeared with Vivien in *The Doctor's Dilemma*, said: 'his love [for Vivien] was second – a close second, but still second to his obsession with

* Agate, the *Sunday Times* drama critic, required his catamites to urinate into a whisky glass, which he'd then savour and knock back. Overdue at his seat after the interval on the first night of *The Skin of Our Teeth*, he was thumped by Olivier: 'You're late, damn you!'

acting the great parts'. And as somebody once said in another context, second is nowhere. When Marcel first meets Albertine he realizes, 'I knew that I would not possess this young cyclist if I did not possess what was in her eyes.' Vivien never possessed what was in Olivier's eyes. Her outbursts were aroused by her love; the madness and mess of her was the fault of her love – and Olivier's anger and passion and indignation was the result of his not being able to reciprocate to a like degree. If, at one time, they were mutually in love, like Romeo and Juliet, their sensations and ideals had been dealt a blow by the contingencies of real life: the war; their careers; being back in Britain. Vivien couldn't cope with the end of the perfection, and threw herself into napkin folding, flower arranging, or preparing those breakfast trays. (She'd be the perfect hostess.) For her, the ideal of love remained; and Olivier, not wishing to be devoured, grew to be afraid of her love for him.

Yet it is the violence and darkness, provoked by her serious disabilities, which pursued him at Notley, at parties, backstage with people watching, all over Australia, in New York hotel rooms, and at the stage door of the Royal Court Theatre, where one particular tirade ended with her rounding on George Devine* ('I was always very fond of you, George. But I could never stand that fucking awful pipe. If you'd been married to me, you would have had to smoke it outside in the garden'), which was what now began to flood his acting, and he gave performances which appeared fierce and careless, full of pain, suffering, dying, agony, sound and colour: the Button Moulder, Richard III, Astrov, Hotspur, Oedipus, Lear, Hamlet, Caesar, Antony, Malvolio, Macbeth, Titus Andronicus, and Archie Rice. Vivien had offered herself to him – like a standing sacrifice – and in real life he'd become imposing and dignified and withdrawn. How else could he have coped with her cycles of euphoria and despair, her off-putting mix of domination and submission? Her intensity and attentions had impressed Olivier early on, when she first saw him, but now she was discolouring his world. The simplicity and innocence he appeared to have created at Notley was filled with dread and fear, yet it is exactly the swinging back and forth between rapture and agony, privation and enormous bliss, which forms the truth and purity of his performances.†

---

* Devine was Mr Antrobus in the September 1946 revival of *The Skin of Our Teeth*. He's Peachum in *The Beggar's Opera*, and as the artistic director of the English Stage Company, at the Royal Court, he produced *The Entertainer*.

† I've often wondered what it must have been like for him, in *A Long Day's Journey into Night*, with all those scenes where Tyrone confronts his frail and coughing tubercular son, Edmund, on the one hand, and his hyperactive wife, who is burning herself up, on

He had anticipated, after the completion of *Henry V*, to return to the Navy. In March 1944, however, John Burrell and Ralph Richardson turned up at the film studios and asked him to join them in reviving the Old Vic Company, which had become depleted during the war. Indeed, the actual theatre, in Waterloo, had been bombed, and so plays were to be performed at the New Theatre, St Martin's Lane. Money was provided by the Council for the Encouragement of Music and the Arts, and the First Lord of the Admiralty ('with alacrity') granted Olivier's permanent release from the armed forces. Tyrone Guthrie helped to choose the repertoire and directed *Peer Gynt*; Burrell directed *Arms and the Man*, *Richard III* and *Uncle Vanya*. In the second season, *Henry IV Parts One and Two* and the *Oedipus/The Critic* double-bill were added to the stock of pieces. (Burrell directed the Shakespeare, Michel St Denis the Sophocles, and Miles Malleson the Sheridan.) In the third season, which opened on 24 September 1946, Olivier added his own production of *King Lear*. The year 1947 was taken up with the film of *Hamlet*, and Eileen Herlie commented: 'When it's time for him to jump into the scene, he's *in* it! "Just give me a minute", he'll say. But he needs only a few *seconds* to get into the mood, have his lines ready and come forth in full emotion.' He reported at the studio at seven; broke for lunch at one, when he telephoned Vivien at Notley. He'd shoot until seven fifteen, and then settle to watch the rushes. Vivien got it into her head that he was having an affair with Jean Simmons, and this was why she hadn't been cast in the part: 'Larry is fucking his Ophelia . . . I'm sure of it, I'm losing him to a bloody child. Well, I shouldn't be surprised. I was barely out of my teens when Larry started fucking me.'

Olivier missed the Royal Première at the Odeon, Leicester Square, attended by the King and Queen, the princesses and the Duke of Edinburgh, who sat in a garlanded Royal Box,* because he was out being

---

the other. The members of the family try to be good-natured, but there are resentments and dissatisfactions not far under the surface. The light, jokey atmosphere only increases the tension; and in a flash they are insulting and scolding each other, intermingling banter and complaints. Then they pause before the next round – 'Who started us on this . . . ?' They are people who find it impossible to be kind to each other, making up only to squabble again. In the Tyrone household, illness is the product of restlessness and despair. ('Your mind is poisoned by your own failure,' growls Tyrone to Jamie, the elder son.) There is an atmosphere of suspicion and gloom and sulks and insinuations that's worse than the pestilence in Oedipus' Thebes.

* I don't know about their majesties, but I personally can't work up much enthusiasm for the *Hamlet* film, which like *Henry V* won so many accolades, including, in 1948, Oscars for Best Picture and Best Actor. Roger Furse (production designer) and Carmen Dillon (the art director) also won Academy Awards. My first objection is that the long scenes

monarchical in Australia on the Old Vic Tour, which lasted for ten months. And there'd been no need to cast Vivien as Ophelia because she *was* Ophelia, pitifully bawdy, pent-up, crammed with panic and fear. On the antipodean tour she handed out wild looks, was found to be coughing a lot, drank champagne and Guinness, wrote letters to her cat, New, refused to sleep, or to allow the others rest, and flirted with Dan Cunningham, who was playing Richard's avenging angel, the Earl of Richmond. In Sydney, the Oliviers met Peter Finch, to whom they offered the chance of work, should he ever be in London; and Vivien began an affair with him. His appeal? He was like an Olivier with a weaker will – an Olivier she could command. He enjoyed late nights and drinks and had a loucheness which complemented Vivien's moods when she was demanding to be amused.

The thing about Finch is that in essential ways he was *unlike* Olivier.

---

with the camera snaking around corridors, through windows, along ramparts and platforms and up stairways suggest an imitation of an Orson Welles film – without the power and suggestiveness with which only Welles can imbue light and shade. Looking at the fogs and smoke and emptiness, I just thought: Elsinore must be a draughty place. It always looks like a set, or a model of a set. Then there's the pounding heartbeats and wobbly focus for the Ghost, who generates no blood or soaring excitement. Of the non-spectral cast, Basil Sydney, as Claudius, is a fairy-tale king who keeps his crown on at all times and looks terrible in those rumpled tights; Felix Aylmer does his ponderous and twinkling old shag act as Polonius, hopping and skipping in his robes, and with a Father Christmas beard: we get no sense that he is paternal, that he cares about Ophelia, who is indeed played by Jean Simmons as if she's Vivien. With her blonde tresses, she's Hamlet's twin – and I wonder if Shakespearian scholars have considered the ramifications of *that*? The Players aren't so very different from the court who are already in fancy dress; and apart from Stanley Holloway, who is superb as the beaming grave-digger, there are only two moments, in 155 mins., that I like: Hamlet patting the dog ('O, my old friend!') and the boy actor putting on the blond wig, and it's Ophelia.

The main problem, however, is the Principal Boy, whose presence in the film is an embarrassment – because 'the story of a man who cannot make up his mind' (i.e. the tale of a flusterer) is absolutely alien to Olivier, who was decisive, non-vacillating, active, insistent. The softish focus he uses for the close-ups of his luminous face makes him look vacant and vague. We can't believe he has intense feelings; he's pale and helpless, slack and with no tension. In those moments when he can blaze, he's a different fellow: gone is the abstractedness – e.g. when getting his friends to swear they'll not divulge news of the Ghost; or in the duels, when he is allowed to be furious, and it seems he'll win. When he's sonorous, he's Fortinbras, Laertes, even Claudius. But as Hamlet he is monumentally miscast, because Hamlet is not heroic. When this Hamlet's eyes dart in anger, I ask myself: why is this character so stricken? Hamlet's eyes should be full of fear, because of life's void, but it is against Olivier's nature to succumb to metaphysical desolation.

Finally, am I alone in thinking the curtains of Gertrude's bed are spread like the lips of a giant vagina?

His performances (as Boldwood, in *Far From the Madding Crowd*, Dr Hirsch, in *Sunday, Bloody Sunday*, or Howard Beale, in *Network*) droop. He is languid, gaunt and good at grief. My personal favourite is the hero of *The Trials of Oscar Wilde*: Olivier could never have sustained that note of crumpled dignity – Olivier would have to catch fire and be Carson or Queensberry. Finch was a bruised, sombre personality; and Maxine Audley was in the right of it when she said he had 'no evil in him'. This is why, despite the fornicating that went on, Olivier knew he was no threat. Indeed, he was almost useful, keeping Vivien entertained and comforted whilst Olivier got on with his career. As he told Kenneth Clark, 'I just want to act well. Nothing else.' Then again, it was humiliating to be a cuckold; and though he could reason that Finch was 'doing what I had done to her first husband seventeen years ago', that he was to be bracketed with the prosaic Holman, and that history in a sense was repeating itself, was no consolation. The mixed feelings of relief and humiliation are conveyed in *Sleuth*. Wyke hates his wife but can't really allow anybody else to possess her. Raging around the house like Ford in his Master Brook disguise at the Garter Inn, taunting Michael Caine's young whippersnapper, and pretending to be genial, Olivier's performance is a whirlwind of self-parody. Even the mock-Tudor fun palace is like Notley, with the costume hampers for treasure hunts and fancy-dress games ('There is virtually no end to the concealment of identity'), the automata, chess, puzzles and clutter. In a basement den are model theatres, complete with Roger Furse's stage designs and models. When Caine's Milo says Marguerite never mentioned any of the parties, Wyke is fleetingly, openly Olivier when he says, 'it was all some time ago', with a note of regret.

Wyke may wince at the thought of the adultery; what reaches him most, as with Olivier, is the thought of cuckoldry ('the devil himself hath not such a name,' says Ford in *The Merry Wives of Windsor*). It is belittling. It means you can't satisfy your wife. It implies impotence or infertility. Olivier's motivation, for the character of Wyke, is to remind his rival that he's superior. He confronts his wife's lover, and what I remember from the movie is Olivier's contempt and incredulity. This happened in reality. Finch duly came to London and was put under contract by LOP in March 1949 (he played Iago, naturally, in Olivier's presentation of Welles' *Othello*). He had sherry and biscuits at Durham Cottage and was invited to Notley, where he became a permanent fixture. He tried to elope with Vivien a few times – Olivier on one occasion discovering them hiding at Ginette Spanier's apartment in Paris. He took off his tie and, advancing menacingly, handed it to Finch: 'Dear boy, I forgot to get you a Christmas present.'

Finch and Vivien held hands at Stratford and at parties – to make Olivier the public cuckold – and one night at Notley, Vivien left the men in the library. 'This is between you two. You must decide who is to have me.' Olivier, as he did when dangerous, went all servile and fawning, bewildering Finch with a full-dress performance of a doddering butler, from whom he'd not derive any sense, or expect any quarter. Finch attempted to become a haughty duke, in his turn, fiddling with a cigarette case. It must have been excruciating. Vivien was soon back, choking for a shag. 'Which one of you is coming to bed with me?' I don't know the outcome; but you don't have to be Anaäs Nin or Henry Miller to imagine a few permutations or cross-fertilizations, so to speak. Perhaps they sat down and watched television.

In 1953, Olivier and Vivien were to appear together in *Elephant Walk*; Olivier, however, withdrew, as he continued to be busy on *The Beggar's Opera*.* Vivien ran around to Finch's flat in the middle of the night, starkers under her mink, begging Finch to accept the role, of a tea planter, in Olivier's stead, and to come out to Ceylon within the week for the location shoot. Once in the tropics, she cracked up. Olivier had to fly across the world to rescue her. They moved to Hollywood for the interiors. Vivien stripped naked and swam around George Cukor's swimming pool chasing John Buckmaster, Jack Merivale's stepbrother. Again, Olivier flew across the world to rescue her – and this time the studio doctors were threatening to have her incarcerated. Back in Britain, she was put into a mental hospital in Surrey. The first item she requested when she emerged from her daze was a leg-depilator. 'She was now more of a stranger to me than I could ever have imagined possible,' said Olivier, from the safe distance of the Waltons' villa in Ischia.

Vivien dropped Finch once she and Olivier finally divorced, which suggests that one of his unwitting principal functions was to taunt, to degrade, to outrage; he was one of her stratagems to win her husband back (by making Olivier jealous) whilst, at the same time, his presence was allowing her to relive, after a fashion, the feelings of an exciting new romance. He was a reminder of happiness. She used him, when all is said and done, and yet, typically wan and patient, he bore no ill will. Finch's tribute when she died was beautiful: 'I remember her most now

* He wrote to Christopher Fry, who had adapted John Gay's operetta, to say that 'the film progresses as most films do, disseminating frustration and flouting cohesion but Peter [Brook] is bearing up very well under the strain' (6 October 1952). In another letter he complains that the role of Macheath 'just isn't *digestible*'.

walking like an eager boy through temples in Ceylon; walking in the wind near Notley. I always see her hurrying through life.' Hamlet might have spoken such words at Ophelia's memorial service. Olivier's only comment on the Finch episode was to write: 'Somehow, somewhere on this [Old Vic Australian] tour I knew that Vivien was lost to me.' By which he means he'd become conscious of having given her up.

The practicalities of leaving somebody involve a right tangle of emotions. Not the least of it is the burden of guilt, and a deep resentment at feeling guilty, because you know you'll never be able to shake off the past and live completely carefree. Your purchase on joy and felicity is going to be tenuous. Olivier's plan of action, his way of coping with what was cooped up within him, made him look both calculating and helpless. Along came these women – what else could he have done? Yet there is an inevitability about the fate of his relationships that is almost devious. He left Vivien for Joan in exactly the way he'd left Jill for Vivien. The public scandal; his connections to a wife and her belief in him; the hide-and-seek with the press. Olivier reconsidered the past by reliving it. This double nature, the past echoing the future, occurs in his work, too.* Hamlet's swallow-dive off the battlements on to Claudius' head may be seen in those home movies from the thirties, where Olivier leaps off the prow of a yacht; Mr Halpern, when he attends his wife's funeral, in *Mr Halpern and Mr Johnson*, is carrying a single pink carnation, like Othello, who comes from his wedding to Desdemona toying with a long-stemmed rose. Olivier felt he'd been neglected by his own father – so he neglected Tarquin. He even came out with Farve's lines. 'Come here, Tarkey,' he said at Notley. 'Get outside that and you won't be doing badly,' and he offered the boy the top off his breakfast egg. Gerard had been preoccupied preaching; Olivier had his own cathedral – the National Theatre. 'Even when at home Larry was unavailable,' said his second son, Richard. 'It was like the theatre was his eldest child and we were all somehow second best.'

Olivier dealt with private pain in public ritual; and Vivien's personal tragedies intermingled with his high achievement. If he, as he would say

* Olivier implicitly made the connection when he explained to Tynan how he could be Hotspur *and* Shallow, Oedipus *and* Mr Puff: 'it was at first difficult to be in love with two characters at the same time. Just as it's difficult to be in love with two women at the same time. But then I discovered the trick of it. I realized that the reason you fall in love with one woman is because you are no longer able to love the woman who came before and yet you still have all this love in you. And that's what I did with Hotspur and Shallow. Once finished with a performance of Shallow, I would put him out of mind. I forced myself not to love him [and] I turned all my love to Hotspur . . .'

to her 'at odd moments after we had got back home " . . . *lorst* you in Australia"', and if he didn't actually get around to separating from her until the summer of 1959,* when had it all really started to be over? All the way back in 1944, when Tyrone Guthrie wouldn't allow her to join the Old Vic Company. 'She is not a good enough actress,' he said succinctly. So instead, along with Olivier and Richardson, it was Sybil Thorndike, Harcourt Williams, Nicholas Hannen, George Relph, Joyce Redman and Margaret Leighton whose names were printed on the mustard-yellow posters.† They opened on 7 August with *Arms and the Man* at the Opera House, Manchester. This was the occasion of the Guthrie 'if you can't love Sergius, you'll never be any good as him' story; the full implications of which now become clear. If Vivien, shipping water fast, was expelled from his affections, then he could justify to himself his absorption in his characters – he'd fall in love with them instead. As Cecil Beaton observed, 'when Larry started the business of falling in love with his characters, he began to fall out of love with Viv. We often heard him talk about it, and it always struck me . . . that he used [acting] as a substitute for his flagging love for her.'

His fabled artistic integrity and confidence were the product of personal callousness and cunning, it could be argued. He was wedded to his craft, to his vocation, like the celibate priest, who needs no family distractions, is another way of putting it. The way you weave yourself into the lives of other people, and the two extremes of work and home, ambition and domesticity, selflessness and selfishness, contentment and

---

* On 23 May 1960, Vivien issued a press release: 'Lady Olivier wishes to say that Sir Laurence has asked for a divorce in order to marry Miss Joan Plowright. She [who?] will naturally do whatever he wishes.' Decrees for Vivien and Joan's husband, Roger Gage, were granted on 2 December and became absolute the following March.

† Dame Sybil we have met before; Williams was King Charles VI in the film of *Henry V* and First Player in *Hamlet*; Hannen was the Duke of Exeter in *Henry V* and the Archbishop in *Richard III*; Relph, who was to go on the Australian tour, was a frequent partner on stage, e.g. Herbert Reedbeck in *Venus Observed* and Billy Rice in *The Entertainer* (Olivier left his widow, Mercia, £1,000 in his will); Joyce Redman was to be Emilia in the National Theatre's *Othello*; and Margaret Leighton, who was to be Lady Melbourne in *Lady Caroline Lamb*, was Lady Percy in the stage production of *Henry IV Part One*, and she recalled how Olivier would be altering and perfecting details up to the last minute, telling her on what line to take a breath, so that he could carry her more easily – the audience would see Hotspur literally sweep her off her feet. Leighton in real life was married to the briefly famous Laurence Harvey. Olivier came to supper one evening and Harvey started to bad-mouth a number of famous actors. Olivier would have none of this and let go a torrent of magnificent Derek and Clive invective: 'Call yourself an actor? You're not even a bad actor. You can't act at all, you fucking stupid hopeless snivelling little cunt-faced cunty fucking shit-faced arse-hole.'

agitation, quite quickly become moral issues, and out of the turmoil of these times came Richard III, first displayed before the public on 13 September 1944. What comes over in that characterization, and in *Marathon Man*, is the sheer happiness of being evil; its seethings; its lightness, which it took Olivier to find in the darkness. It's as if, as Richard, he is no longer having to hold down his violence. Olivier is in his element. But what is that? A secret admiration for blood-lettings and the irrational? Partially. What's more interesting are the ways Richard is defying limits, creating and destroying, overcoming limitations, and what it adds up to is an intensity. And what is chilling about Richard, Macbeth, or the demon dentist, is that, with Olivier thinking and suffering and feeling, living through each moment, and drawing us in, they can *still* commit their deeds. 'I just simply went through it,' he explained.*

Olivier played Richard off and on for over ten years, concluding with the film in 1955; except it's not a film, it is a pantomime. The slapstick starts with Walton's score. Given his official compositions for the coronation of George V, etc., the music for the crowning of Cedric Hardwicke is like a parody of regal pomp, especially when the climax of the ceremony – it's almost endearing – is Sir Cedric uncertainly trotting off on a cart-horse that is probably two men inside a suit. The titles unfurl on parchment scrolls, and there is an attempt to put us in the picture – yet it is always a bugger's muddle, the Shakespearian network of cousins, uncles, factions, associates, Lancastrians and Yorkists. This is followed by an attempt to be pictorial: the banners and flags and the women of the court floating by with their wimples. But the effect is tatty. The costumes look like they were found mouldering in Henry Irving's carriage loft – wrinkled tights, dim cloaks, mildewy velvets, Chico Marx hats – and the sets seem unpainted: pale blue or green tints or a grey wash. With the large empty spaces (throne rooms, chapels) and the empty sky, it is as if the camera was left running on an empty back-lot. The film has a pallor, the palest pinks or brown; and the

* People were perhaps ready to respond to Richard, for as Olivier said, 'I had got a lot of things on my side, now I come to think of it, from the point of view of timeliness. One had Hitler over the way.' But what is particularly interesting is the element of self-portraiture, as suggested by these words from his interview on *The Dick Cavett Show* in 1980: 'From all this [accumulation of mannerisms and detail] you begin to sort out those things that seem to be true to the character you've been forming . . . And since it is really you, you begin to love this new side of your own character as you have loved the old side. Possibly you love it more, since it is all so new and different . . . [and] you let the character eventually impose himself on your being.'

lighting is bleached or overexposed. Where is the cold and dank medieval world? Why, within Richard. It is all muted, underdone, blurred and far-off, the better to exaggerate Olivier, who talks to us, like Archie Rice, in a direct address. He comes and goes from the thrones and seats – though he never sits down – and he throws open the shutters to show silent movie extracts: Cedric Hardwicke's Edward IV, sagging backwards, clutching at his heart; or, another interpolation, the monks inscribing Clarence's death warrant and sprinkling the wet ink with sand. (Another silent movie aspect: Pamela Brown – in real life Michael Powell's mistress – flitting about as Mistress Shore, the strumpet shared by Hastings and Edward IV.)

As the story concerns removing people, wiping them out, here's another justification for the visual austerity. (The screen is often etched with little except Richard's shadow, cast on doorways, corridors, the bars of Clarence's cell, or following Lady Anne into her room.) One of the delights of the film is the way Olivier himself seems to be decimating the opposition, getting rid of rival actors. Robert Stephens has argued that 'Olivier's one great fault was a paranoid jealousy of anyone whom he thought was a rival – he couldn't bear not to be the one on top and so he clung to power.' There is plenty of evidence for this. Who can forget Olivier's psychopathic expression on the newsreel footage when the crowds go wild for Vivien at the Atlanta première of *Gone With the Wind*? There is something, too, of the tenacity and lunacy of the self-made man in Olivier's Malvolio and James Tyrone. And, not wanting his Othello to be outmanoeuvred by a charming, conniving Iago, he cast Frank Finlay as his nemesis, instructing him to be drab, monotonous and colourless. (When he'd played Iago to Ralph Richardson's Moor in 1938, Olivier naturally stole the show.) He didn't want anybody but himself winning over an audience. (Alec Guinness said that as the Fool to his Lear he benefited from the lighting 'that always surrounded him as he kept the Fool close to his side'. Hence, Archie Rice, the failed music-hall comic, is a nightmare version of Olivier: what he feared he'd be reduced to. He hated Maggie Smith for knocking him off balance in *The Master Builder* – and, it's true, her flirtatiousness and briskness matched his own in assurance. As Stephens, her former husband, says, 'not many people ever did that to Larry and lived to tell the tale'. Even ostensibly mild roles, such as the doddery old Jews he went in for in his last pictures, *The Boys from Brazil* or *The Jazz Singer*, are quite capable of rage. Olivier was never placable. Macbeth, Antony, Titus Andronicus, other classical kings and generals, he considered to be *his* roles, aspects of his astonishingly varied majesty; so when Stephens, and his compeers, were ripe for such plays, Olivier denied them their chances. He'd sack people, tell them they were too big for their boots. 'I'm afraid, my darling, as I can't persuade you to change your mind, that's about it.'* Others simply fled the country – Maggie Smith went to play Shakespeare in Canada; Anthony Hopkins went to Hollywood, to drown his sorrows in a few mini-series.

Olivier collected young actors and, in RADA alumnus Joe Orton's words, 'he doesn't give them parts, he has them playing the set'. He preferred to promote mediocrities, who presented no challenge; and despite the promptings of Kenneth Tynan, who drew up many a plan, he refused to act alongside Gielgud, Richardson or Scofield and indulge in any clash of the titans. How like his own Richard III he seems, made strong by resistance, seldom disposed to be 'in the giving vein'. Your error, with both Olivier and the villains he played, was to think him a friend, to drop your guard. Stephens and Hopkins made this miscalculation. (Is that why they got in the grip of the grog throughout the seventies? Creative frustration?) So, inexorably, did Tynan, who received his comeuppance when he prepared a *New Yorker* profile which he presumed to expand into Olivier's biography: 'The book I have in mind will be a belated act of thanksgiving,' he gushed from California, where he was dying of emphysema and poverty ('Forgive handwriting – shaky due to illness'). Olivier was quite deaf to entreaty. He said he'd collaborate with the project, only to withdraw his consent, and Tynan was forced to return the advance to Simon and Schuster. 'He called me about an hour ago with the rather shattering news that he didn't intend to cooperate with me in any way,' Tynan told Joan Plowright, his bowels turned to water.

This 'sudden and chilling change of heart' destroyed the critic – as Hal's rejection of Falstaff destroyed a well-intentioned companion. Tynan was Iago to Olivier's – Iago. It was a marriage. From 21 May 1963, when the critic sent the artist ideas for a 'possible repertoire' (*Hay Fever*, directed by Olivier, *The Crucible*, with Scofield, or *Sergeant Musgrave's Dance*, with Olivier), up to and including Olivier's letters in November 1973

* The repercussions of his rewards and/or non-favours continue to this day. Julie-Kate Olivier, interviewed in the *Mail on Sunday*, 31 March 1996, said: 'It can be a great disadvantage being an Olivier. My sister Tamsin once auditioned for a director who didn't give her the role. He told her later: "I auditioned for your father once and he didn't give me the part. Now you know how it feels." It's frightening. When I go for an audition I wonder: "Did my father sack you?" Even now his myth is still with me.'

to Max Rayne, over the issue of Tynan's severance pay,* they wrote to each other every day. Tynan, it goes without saying, was the first person for Hall to exterminate when he came near the National. In 1972, he'd asked it to be minuted at a board meeting that a condition of his accepting the helm was that 'Tynan should go'. As he tells himself in his diary three years later, 'Tynan was a truly passionate devotee at the Court of Larry'; he then muses: 'I wonder what happened to that love affair, for love affair there was in the artistic sense.'

Tynan, in miniature, suffered the same rule of fate as Jill or Vivien. He challenged aspects of Olivier's power; and in coping with the realities of that power he was diminished. What does the farce over Hochhuth's *The Soldiers* seem, in retrospect? Tynan called the play 'one of the most extraordinary things that has happened to the British theatre in my lifetime', which on its own is embarrassingly hyperbolic enough. Was it a noble battle to challenge the Lord Chamberlain and end censorship? Or Tynan showing off? (There was charlatanry in the air: Hochhuth didn't speak English; Tynan didn't know German – which makes me sceptical about his enthusiasm for Brecht.) And from what mixture of motives did Tynan insist on embroiling the patriotic Olivier in the staging (or non-staging) of this anti-Churchill farrago? (*The Soldiers* accuses Churchill of war crimes and the sending of the Polish leader, Sikorski, to his death.) I think we should remember Tynan's enthusiasm for bull-fighting – and he must have thought of Olivier as the magnificent gleaming black bull, hurtling into the ring, stuck with spears and streamers, dying beautifully and symbolically. This may indeed be the Olivier of the Old Vic – it's Othello – and the Olivier of Tynan's dreams and reviews; but it is curious to say the least to goad and humiliate Olivier in reality – for that was the effect of what Olivier called 'L'Histoire de Hochhuth' (to bring in another tongue none of them could speak). As head of the National he had to defend his deputies, their decisions and convictions. It seems the most dreadful set-up.

Olivier credited Tynan with making him tackle Othello; that he credited the critic with also causing one of Vivien's breakdowns is of course connected. Tynan once knocked on her dressing room door at Stratford after *Macbeth*, glared at her, strode past not saying a word, and greeted Olivier effusively. Vivien (reports Dulcie Gray) crumpled into 'frightened tears'. The way he showered Olivier with praise and denied

* 'Quite honestly this severance arrangement is entirely new to me,' Olivier said to Tynan. 'I have never had any such in my life and I don't look for one now . . . But as you ask it of me I will as ever do all I possibly can to help.'

Vivien one particle was a cartoonish summary of the gulf that separated husband and wife in any event; and Tynan boasted to Victor Stiebel that he'd 'split the Oliviers'. Did he fear that, otherwise, Olivier would become Alfred Lunt to Vivien's Lynn Fontanne? Terry to her June? Or is it that he was personally jealous of her association with Olivier; jealous of the woman, like Iago having to destroy Desdemona? It is all of these things, plus the love–hate bond that unites the critic and the artist. Ideally, the former explains and, in his writings, perpetuates (or derides) the activities of the latter. The critic completes the circuit – and, if it is Hazlitt or Coleridge on Kean, Kemble, or Macready, artistry is interpreted in works of art; the critic overtakes the artist, as Norman Mailer does in his biography of Marilyn Monroe. More usually, however, it is a tempestuous partnership, like this exchange between Irving and Shaw:

> I have read lots of your droll, amusing, irrelevant [irreverent, surely?] and sometimes impertinent pages [wrote Irving], but criticism containing judgement and sympathy I have never seen by your pen.
>
> If you knew the trouble your performances give me [replied GBS] – you are in some ways the most difficult subject a critic can tackle, and quite the most exasperating for an author-critic – you would be astonished at my patience and amiability.

Without question, Olivier and Tynan respected – *loved* – each other's talent (and let's face it, Olivier couldn't write and Tynan couldn't act), despite the personal antipathy and wariness; but they were alike, here, too, in not wanting a personal closeness from people. They preferred a distance. Tynan, as Literary Manager at the National, gave Olivier his words to speak; and Olivier, on the stage, could act out Tynan's desires. (Is that what a star does? Gives us a vicarious existence in fantasy?)*

---

* Olivier and Tynan were linked well enough in the public mind (like Holmes and Watson, Laurel and Hardy) for hate mail to be addressed to the pair of them. Here, misspellings and all, is an extraordinary outburst, preserved amongst Tynan's papers, and it refers to the production of *The Merchant of Venice* – and particularly to Olivier's Shylock:

> Olivier,
> So you enter the lists as a typical jewish puppet responding to the strings of the ever increasingly powerful international jewish mob, but it does not surprise me as, if there was ever an overrated person it is you with your pompous and arrogant demenour [*sic*].
>
> The encredible [*sic*] impudence of your statement that 'I am sure that I may be allowed to speak on behalf of our profession in England . . .' is indicative of your character.

What brought them together, and what finally drove them asunder, may be exemplified by that production of *Othello* which Tynan had suggested. Watching a run-through at the Haymarket, in April 1964, he scribbled reams of notes, which he had typed up and distributed to the cast. His suggestions were pertinent: 'Keith Marsh has a very unmistakable face and voice – is there a risk of a laugh when, having just been seen as a senator, he reappears as a Cypriot?'; . . . 'Will people notice that Iago simply hasn't had time to get the three gallants "flustered with flowing cups"?'; . . . 'L.O. must make it clear earlier on that this is a new interpretation. That is, make Othello obviously egocentric. Otherwise audiences will think not that this is an egocentric OTHELLO but that this is an egocentric PERFORMANCE'; . . . 'Othello must be still for "Farewell the tranquil mind" – it's a considered declaration, he shouldn't roam about.' There is a great deal more, including a few pages of detailed cuts (he must have known the text by heart). Tynan was painstaking – but you can see the flash-points. He'd virtually usurped the role of director; he was telling Olivier what to do. The critic was trying to become an artist.

Tynan had got above his station, as he did over the Hochhuth nonsense; and it was his cocksure attitude which made folks simmer with impatience. Olivier, who seemed to believe that the Literary Manager's job had vaguely to do with the press department or editing the souvenir programmes,* replied to the circulated notes on 12 April. His tone is that of a firm-but-fair headmaster, stuffing his briar with shag, and caught between admiration for a bright sixth-former and a need to control the wildness. He is also exasperated. 'My dear Ken,' he begins, thanking him fulsomely for 'your helpful suggestions'; he compliments Tynan for drafting the National's press releases; for being on board ship, and so on. Then he does his best to explain to him, as to a child, 'the livid state of inflammation that the nerve ends have arrived at' in the run-up to opening night, and that actors could really rather do without this

---

> Your friendship and association with that character Tiernan [*sic*] is another indication of what you are, and it will be a relief when you no longer occupy a position which you sully with such an article supporting that thrice accuresed [*sic*] race. Do you ever consider the suffering of thousands of Palestinian refugees and the countless millions all over the world who suffer by exploitation of the jews. Names such as hyams, maxwell, bloom, berstein etc mean nothing to you but they are typical of the tyrannical parasites which constitute the jewish race.

* Dear Larry: About your memo on leaflets and bills: I long ago surrendered any control of or interest in these subjects . . .

(15 October 1965)

judgematic intervention of his. It had plainly never occurred to Tynan that people would take his report amiss; focused on the play as a whole, he'd forgotten, if he ever knew, that actors had personal feelings which could be hurt; or even that they had personal feelings at all. (Hence, the unrelenting disapproval of the Dresden-dainty Vivien.) 'One has just got to know when to apply the throttle and when the brakes; in other words, one has got to drive with more care than you did,' Olivier tells Tynan,* whom he finds precipitate, insensitive, lacking in common decency and common sense. In today's jargon, Tynan was clueless about man-management. It is worth allowing Olivier to speak for himself – he delivers the chastisement rather well; in fact this is unanswerable:

> Let me put it this way. I do not think that you would now say that it was not on the cards or in the nature of things that Colin Blakely could now be a leading actor. A hasty approach to this problem, or anything other than the most cunning pressures put on at the right times, would have fucked this probability up for keeps.
>
> I have got a feeling that you may think I am a bit soft with people, or even weak. If this suspicion of mine is correct, then I must ask you now to have faith in me and to believe that I know pretty shrewdly what I am about. I am not an amateur in the business.
>
> Nobody could or should attempt such a job as mine, alone. Well, I suppose I could if I never acted at all, but apart from any other considerations, as you know, I believe that a leader of a troupe should be one of them. It is therefore absolutely essential that I know the natures of those with whom I am dealing; it is, in fact, essential that we all do.
>
> You will know, for instance, by now that Johnnie D's† immediate reaction to the smallest difference of opinion was to regard it as a personal attack and lose his temper. W. G.‡ has a far wiser sort of nature, more equable, but could very possibly be lastingly hurt though much better gifted to defend himself and more capable of beating you in an argument.
>
> I have known Georgie D.§ all my life and very intimately. He is almost over-weeningly proud, but wonderfully valuable.

---

* One of Tynan's oft-quoted aphorisms is that a critic is a man who knows the way but can't drive the car.

† John Dexter, the director of *Othello*, and an associate director of the National Theatre. He died in 1990. His posthumously published autobiography, *An Honourable Beast* (1993) contains much material on working with Olivier.

‡ William Gaskill: like Dexter, an alumnus of the Royal Court. An associate director of the National, 1963–5, he worked with Olivier on *The Recruiting Officer*. He recalled that, at George Devine's funeral, 'the door opened and a formally dressed figure beckoned us. It was Olivier, looking like an undertaker; he always knew how to transform himself.'

§ George Devine, he of the pipe that so offended Vivien, came to the NT to direct Beckett's *Play* – and Tynan had voiced his reservations about the production.

> I like you, I like having you with me, apart from it rather tickling me to have you with me, but you can be too fucking tactless for words. It may be that such criticism as you received when you were young did not hurt you much, or it may be that you've had so much of your own back since, that it has all got obliterated, but you should realise your gifts for what they are and your position for what it is and like a wise jockey not always let these things have their head.
>
> As a writer, your job is to make your readers' blood tingle, and you do, no matter how you may make the arses tingle of those you may be writing about.
>
> George is, in fact, quite right and reasonable when he says 'If you had talked to me'.
>
> As to your position, neither of us has been able to define this very clearly as yet. This is mostly my fault, I am sure, but like so much more to do with such an enterprise, it has to find definition as it goes along. I hope more than I can say, that you will have the patience to let this happen. *Certainly it was a basic understanding between us that you were to be responsible to me for the face and image of the theatre.* [Italics added.] Perhaps it is taking rather a high-handed view of this to say 'on behalf of the National Theatre' to one of the directors. What emerges clearly enough to me and I hope to you too, is that you ought to keep a bit closer to me, to send your memos to me, to be a little quicker in letting me have your thoughts and a little slower in imparting them to the others. If I don't answer, or don't react at once, it does not mean I am not thinking about whatever it is, or discarding it. The political what and when is, after all, my pigeon.

Olivier had made it plain who was boss; and in *Richard III*, amusingly, Gielgud and Richardson are the ones cast as underlings who are killed off. Gielgud is especially simpering. He is bedecked with rings and jewels and dangling pearls. In his big scene in the Tower, when he confides his nightmare to Brackenbury, the dream-of-drowning speech is too much of a set piece. It is like Gielgud is auditioning. Clarence's hallucinations, moreover, are not connected with the visual and emotional style of the rest of the film – nor with Shakespeare's play, come to that, which involves omens, guilt, ghosts, portents, surreal animal imagery; the boar, tigers, dragons. (And there's lots of bird-flight imagery, too, in the text: wrens, eagles, hawks.) Anyway, we are glad to see the murderers, Michael Gough, as a cheerful Shakespearian clown, and Michael Ripper, the Hammer stalwart, pop-eyed and taciturn, who come and pinion Gielgud to the bed and give him a brutal clubbing. His body is up-ended into a barrel of wine, which splashes everywhere and slops down some steps and runs into the Thames.

Olivier then sets about Lady Anne, the role Vivien had played on the

Australian tour. When she spits at him – twice – it's the only act of direct defiance against Richard in the film: he's impressed; and now she's worth destroying. 'Why dost thou spit at me?' he asks, only after the second time. She sees the danger in him – and he sees the spirit in her. He slowly, seductively, bats his eyelids for emphasis. Olivier holds and prolongs the moment, like a dancer. The scene unfolds choreographically, erotically: 'It was thy heavenly face that set me on,' he says. Richard maintains that he killed to win her. Love and death, and sex and violence, are the same thing to him. Claire Bloom is querulous – we can imagine that she's meant to be aroused and fearful – as she watches his sword play. It's like Leda and the swan, as he twines about her – slow ballet movements, culminating in his slipping a ring on her finger. (After this conquest, Richard appears in finer clothes, trimmed with ermine, and Claire Bloom, with pale brows, practises her nobly suffering face in readiness for *Brideshead Revisited*.)

Even when not literally or figuratively tormenting the cast, Olivier ensures that Clive Morton (Rivers), Douglas Wilmer (Dorset), Laurence Naismith (Stanley) and Stanley Baker (Henry Tudor), look like clowns. In the court sequences, or in Edward IV's deathbed scene, when Cedric Hardwicke is seen off through sheer old age and a surfeit of Hollywood epics, the characters are eyeing each other up nervously; there are lots of handshakes and apparent reconciliations and 'deeds of charity' – but Richard knows it will be child's play to set the families and factions off against each other again, to inculcate betrayals, treacheries, and to inflame self-interest. Yet as the cousins and uncles crowd into the room (it's like the cabin scene in *A Night at the Opera*), I don't think it is the ending of their feuds that they are worried about. It is who is the most absurdly dressed – and the winner of the coconut is: Ralph Richardson's Buckingham. With his blue velvet derby at a jaunty angle, and those cocked, quizzical eyes of his, he's Mr Micawber.

Richardson's staring, unblinking eyes can be sinister, knowing, surprised; he fractionally absorbs shocks, and gives nothing away to the other characters – but, paradoxically, he gives everything away to us, the audience. The King is the more frightening because not even 'deep revolving, witty Buckingham' can cope with his misbehaviour any longer. (He decides to make his escape to Brecknock,* his family seat in Wales, 'whilst my fearful head be on'.) It is one of cinema's blood-freezing moments – like Karloff's turning round to face the skylight and giving us our first glimpse of the monster, or Hannibal Lecter sitting bolt

* Brecon, where this book is being written, incidentally.

upright in the ambulance – when Richard accepts the crown and swings down the bellrope and thrusts out his black-gloved hand, enforcing homage. It is like a graphic mime of subjection and power, and the rays emitted by Olivier's eyes can expunge you quicker than a shove on the beezer. Richardson can do nothing but glance away fearfully. His humiliation is completed when Richard is not in his giving vein and Olivier comes out with one of his shrieks – which works *because* of Richardson's embarrassment and best attempts at a dignified exit. It has fast dawned on him what a lunatic tyrant he has aided and abetted.

The King is increasingly isolating, and isolated. Like Macbeth, he has many enemies, and success is uncertain, and sleep is fitful. He acts upon his dreams – the 'mockery of unquiet slumbers' – and Hastings is accused of witchcraft, and the bastardy of the little princes in the Tower is inferred. The fetching of the boys from Ludlow is a strange episode – the snow, the horses, London in the distance – for there is no cold, no atmosphere. It is neither natural, real, nor artificial. Similarly, fires in rooms give no heat; wine jugs seem empty. In London, there aren't any people filling the cardboard streetscapes, nor is there any litter, nor any signs of life. Buildings are flimsy doll's houses. We are told that the Queen has sought sanctuary, but the entire film is sealed off, in quarantine. When George Woodbridge, as the Lord Mayor of London, refers to 'troops of citizens', we wonder if he is having us on. But the effect of this drabness is to make us depend all the more on Olivier to give us his gusto. When he returns with the princes, he leaps from his horse with agility – we marvel at the physical side of this actor. Dressed nattily in crimson and black, he is every child's favourite uncle, not a pipe-puffing old bore, but an adult who is daring and dangerous. Notice how Olivier does not laugh, when he is conveying geniality, but simply opens his mouth wide, like a mask. His jollity, like the protestations of love to Lady Anne, woos people into a false sense of security; he affects intimacy, people think he's understood by them, but he has no intimates, no family life in the usual and natural sense. Relatives are there to be killed off. One of the princes goes too far, making a joke about Richard's misshapen shoulder. Walton's soundtrack produces a dissonant shriek (it's Walton-as-Stravinsky); and yet, though it is *intended* as a flash of genuine anger – Richard for an instant not playing games – and despite the make-up, the build-up, with Richard's melodramatic recoil and the child's backing away – what we get, for a split second, is a glimpse of Olivier's primitive power, a glimpse at the abyss inside him.

At last – for him; for us – Richard is crowned. During the coronation, he keeps his back to the camera. He is a golden cloak, which swishes past and snatches at Claire Bloom like she's a rag doll. Later, he looks troubled (he's Macbeth) and he doesn't seem to see Lady Anne, who keels over, poisoned. (It is a mime of the rejected and neglected wife.) The mood isn't of celebration – of success – but of rage. As in those *looks* (at Buckingham or the little prince), when Olivier doesn't have any actual lines to say, he'll express the bits between the lines, he conveys the inner life of the lines; and when this connects with Olivier's own nature, when it is his imagination responding to the meaning, then he is at his most perturbing. John Mortimer has spoken of 'the danger, the genuine fear' which his presence could impart at National Theatre board meetings, when though besuited and bespectacled he was like Othello waving a scimitar at the Venetian senate. Here, in *Richard III*, he sits in state, working things over, and he is a picture of mastery and concentration. The murder of the princes is arranged (he demonstrates the smothering by holding a cushion against Patrick Troughton's face); he talks to us in whispered confidences; he sends soldiers after the 'circumspect' Buckingham; and at the moment of assuming maximum power, power is ebbing. 'What's the news?' he demands. The nobles are starting to revolt. Men run in and out with torches . . . Suddenly, we are on the plain in Spain, for the Battle of Bosworth. (There is a mention of the weather being bad, but it is bright and the grass is scorched; it's like Olivier's Hamlet going on about the speech he wants inserted by the First Player, who then proceeds to give us 'The Murder of Gonzago' in dumb-show.)

If Richard and Richmond are emblematic of good and evil, the problem is that the latter, Stanley Baker with a terrible haircut and a Welsh accent, has no charisma. (He needs to be Olivier's Henry V.) Their prayers for victory, with trumpets and fanfares calling across the field during the night, go for little, because Olivier's script excised Richard's moments of doubt and soul-searching. When the chalky ghosts of Gielgud, the princes, Claire Bloom and Hastings float across the coppery and cobalt cyclorama, that is like a Dali painting, and tell him to 'despair and die', his bad dreams are no more than indigestion. His rallying cry to the troops is comparable with 'Once more unto the breach', and it's hard to remember that this is meant to be the losing side:

> Fight, gentlemen of England! Fight, bold yeomen!
> Draw, archers, draw your arrows to the head!
> Spur your proud horses hard, and ride in blood!
> Advance, our standards! Set upon our foes!
> Our ancient word of courage, fair Saint George,

> Inspire us with the spleen of fiery dragons!
> Upon them! Victory sits on our helms.

The battle is a foxhunt. Richard is cornered in a sandy hollow edged by willows and there he is struck by wave upon wave of soldiers. As shot from above, when they come at him and tear him apart they are like hounds.

Had he survived Bosworth, however, and been spirited away to Uruguay, the usual form with dictators, he'd have become Dr Christian Szell, who in his immaculate white suit is a prosperous dentist – a prosperous *Nazi* dentist, with cabinets in his lair that contain sinister skulls and fangs. What concerns him are the boxes and drawers in the New York bank vault that contain the diamonds he stole from the Jews; so he disguises himself as the washerwoman (like Toad) to escape the jungle and take Manhattan. The pleasure of *Marathon Man* is Olivier's purring courtesy – and arrogance – and his professional *calm*. Dustin Hoffman is tethered to a chair in the middle of the room, and look how neat and fastidious Olivier is, hanging his jacket behind the door, going to work. He unfurls his set of gleaming prongs, needles and drills, and with his eyes enlarged behind the silver spectacles, he brings an infinitude of inflexion to the query 'Is it safe?' Presumably he means the diamond hoard, though who knows for sure? *Marathon Man* is aswim with unanswered questions, loose ends, implausibilities galore. (What is Dustin's brother's relationship with the Nazis? With the CIA? What is the mystery of Dustin's dad's suicide? Why do bombs go off in Paris? Who is after whom? Who is double-crossing whom? We never know. It's a film you shouldn't think about too hard.) The sole joy is Olivier being open and suspicious and malignant; and after hours of shoot-outs and torture sequences we arrive at the reason why I'm discussing the film at all. It is an astounding scene. Szell is in and out of jewellery stores, trying to determine the value of his sparklers. He walks down the street, and old Jews start to recognize him from the concentration camps. He's the nightmare creature they've all been expecting to reinvade their lives. One old lady, who has a pouchy, tormented face, a suffering face – it's a great piece of casting: she's identified as Lotta Andor-Palfi in the credits – starts ranting in German and points him out as the 'white angel' from Auschwitz. Olivier's fear and fury, as he picks up speed, hobbling and unable to believe that this is being allowed to happen to him, the indignation, are related to Richard, and to Archie Rice, and to Coriolanus – or to any of Olivier's characters who have their superiority questioned: 'You common cry of curs! Whose breath I hate/As reek o' th' rotten fens . . . *I banish you!*'

A diamond merchant comes after him out of his shop – 'I know who you are, you murderer!' – and Szell releases the blade he keeps up his sleeve and slices his pursuer across the throat. (Attached to his wrist, the retractable bayonet is like a claw, or Richard III's nose: an aggressive limb.) He flees in a cab to his bank, to be met outside by Dustin Hoffman, and he's forced to walk up through Central Park, past the zoo, for a show-down in the waterworks. (That long walk is the scene which Hoffman made Olivier pointlessly improvise in rehearsal. The runtish star* needed 'to put himself on at least an equal footing with this sick old man,' claimed William Goldman, the screenwriter.) The diamonds tinkle down the grating – money thrown away – and Szell has to swallow those that remain, and Olivier goes from compliance to contempt. The film finishes when he falls down a spiral staircase, and he impales himself on his own dagger. He's soon back, however, as Moriarty, Ezra Lieberman (good to Szell's evil), Loren Hardeman Sr, etc. As Coriolanus' line continues: 'I banish you [i.e. as it were the likes of Hoffman]; thus I turn my back/There is a world elsewhere.'

Olivier's characters may have unruly desires, but they always keep a hold on their identity. There's no things falling apart, centres not holding; Olivier is the headland against which the waves break and break. His majesty is that of the osprey to the fish, who takes it by sovereignty of nature; and it was in the forties, and with the Old Vic, and the war, and Vivien, that he became aware of this. After the Manchester previews, in the late summer of 1944, the company played in London until 12

* It was a tremendous shock to Gregor Samsa, in *Metamorphosis*, waking up to find he'd become a cockroach; but Hoffman has been insectile from the word go. The moment he pops on the screen I want to grind him underfoot – I can already hear the juicy, cracking, squishy sound; I can see the black essence. A heavy boot had evidently knocked the life out of him *before* this film gets underway, for he totters around Central Park with a throbbing throat, looking like Piglet from *Winnie the Pooh*. (It's his panic and snuffles and Olivier's shaven head and German accent that the movie comes down to being about.) What he's trying to impart, no doubt, is the sweat, anxiety and despair of Babe Levy as he runs for his life; except that Hoffman is breathing heavily and looking tortured from the beginning – when Olivier is still in Uruguay.

Olivier and Hoffman working together is reminiscent of the encounter between Olivier and Monroe, in *The Prince and the Showgirl*. It is a confrontation – a mismatch – of acting styles, of different kinds of fame, of attitude. As the Regent of Carpathia, Olivier (a parody of Englishness) was super-efficient, immaculate, confident, unfeeling. Monroe had her blend of dizzy chaos and directness; she's waddling, pouting, parading, wiggling and giggling. Monroe wouldn't submit to Olivier – and neither would the showgirl to the prince. At the end, nothing has altered. Nobody has yielded. You know they'll not meet again.

April 1945, when they took their productions to Europe and performed under the ENSA banner at Antwerp, Ghent, Hamburg and Belsen. The Shakespeare histories, *Oedipus* and *The Critic* then opened in London between September and October, and in the summer of 1946 the productions travelled to New York* aboard the *Queen Mary*, with a thousand war brides destined for Nova Scotia, and with Vivien, who was coming along as a camp follower. ('I'm just going to enjoy myself,' she told reporters.) Was she the one, I wonder, leading the chants of the two and a half thousand fans who'd scream, 'We want Larry! We want Larry!' at the stage door? He'd regularly have the buttons torn from his coat. Ingrid Bergman, Paulette Goddard, Olivia de Havilland, Mary Martin and Ronald Colman attended his performances. One night there were ten curtain calls; another night, merely nine. 'Most of the acclaim was for Laurence Olivier, but there was enthusiastic approval too of the playing of Ralph Richardson,' said a paper – no wonder Richardson harboured murderous thoughts.

Henry V was running on Broadway concurrently. Olivier, whose day wear comprised a double-breasted suit of grey flannel, a hand-made shirt, an Indian print tie and a soft green pocket handkerchief, had a suite at the St Regis piled with crates of grapefruit, bottles of vintage cognac, and fifteen vases of flowers, all gifts from admirers. The company were allowed five dollars a day each for food and lodging; Olivier and Richardson were permitted an additional twenty-five dollars a week for shad roe, lobster and strawberry ice cream. He was conscious about having the luck of the devil. 'I wanted to make something of a name as an actor. I suppose I can say I have,' he said in September 1946. 'I wanted to have a house in the country . . . Now . . . I think I can honestly say that I would like to "give" something to the theatre instead of taking something out of it . . . I would like to help found . . . a steady and strong Old Vic Company – so steady and strong that it doesn't matter a bit if either I or Ralph Richardson or anyone else retires from it. Something that stands on its own feet and can tell us both to go to hell.'

Here we have the germ of an idea for a National Theatre; and the irony of the above proclamation is that Olivier and Richardson were indeed dismissed by the governors of the Old Vic in late 1948, when Olivier was in Australia. 'The governors felt that the administrator

---

* Olivier made two radio adaptations in America: *The Tragedy of King Richard III* was broadcast by CBS on 2 June 1946; *Peer Gynt* on 9 June – both plays being presented under the *Columbia Workshop* banner.

should not be an artist,' the press were informed in January 1949. Llewellyn Rees, director of the Arts Council, was made the new administrator. Hugh Hunt, of the Bristol Old Vic, became the director. Olivier made a huge song and dance about this; his belief that it was a personal betrayal – like a king being usurped – lies behind his attitude to Peter Hall and the succession at the National decades later. Olivier was more than an actor-manager, or an artist who wanted to keep his eye on the profits and loss; a theatre was his city state, his domain. Indeed, the appeal of management, and why it was satisfying to him,* is related to his kings and generals, whom he played on stage and for the cinema; there is an intimate connection between the sorcerers and men who master the world, whom he embodied, and the proud and confident way he ran his companies. What was once acted (or enacted) now had to be known. This was no longer a representation of power, but a putting into practice of government. The politics in the plays might seem to be about the dark stratagems of politics in reality.

You can see it coming, can't you, the way to interpret Olivier and the creation of a National Theatre? ('If he weren't a great actor,' somebody said, 'what a dictator he would have made!') The king and his courtiers; Olivier wanting to soar and show off, hogging the limelight like Irving; the plots and counter-plots. This is the atmosphere of Peter Hall's *Diaries* ('The Story of a Dramatic Battle'), where it's the Wars of the Roses still, and people behave like rival barons. 'Tomorrow, legally, I ascend the throne,' he says, as he takes over from Olivier on 1 November 1973. 'The war clouds are already gathering,' he trembles, as feuds break out amongst the trade unions. ('Fascism is theatre,' wrote Genet,† mean-

* Many of his colleagues, with some justification, felt that Olivier was wasting his gifts attending committee meetings and attending to his administrative duties – which he did diligently because (a) the chores were something of a self-imposed penance and (b) he wanted to be in complete control of each and every detail, right down to the design of the posters and leaflets. Michael Hallifax, the executive company manager of the National (1966–74), has revealed that, regarding programmes, publicity materials and performance schedules, Olivier insisted on their being printed in 'red and green for the Christmas season, lighter hues for summer, and it always had to be purple during Lent'. This conscientiousness is fully commendable, but it is hard to deny Tony Richardson's complaint that 'no one should allow Larry to do anything except act', and that by diverting his energies into management problems, financial worries, the press and quarrels with the board he denied us the opportunity to see, and himself the time to play, further great roles. But just how much can you expect of a person?

† A full-dress exegesis of *Spartacus* could be made here: the battle formations and Roman uniforms – white and red leather straps and gold buckles; the wrestling and physical combat. Olivier manages not to be brutal; we sense his courage and authority. When he becomes the dictator, and talks of restoring order to Rome and its territories, he is

ing the control of the players, the surrender of the audience, leaders and followers, the costumes, uniforms, drill.) But there are other ways of interpreting events. Olivier, I think, thought of himself as the resourceful Henry V or Hotspur, his actors being a band of merry men – a happy few. This had been the composition of Laurence Olivier Productions Limited (telephone, Whitehall 0239; telegrams, Vivier, Piccy, London; registered office, Byron House, 7–9 St James St., SW1), when in the fifties Lovat Fraser could send off polite letters like this example, to a golden codger (b.1879) who'd once toured with Ellen Terry and Forbes Robertson:

> To:
> A. Hylton Allen
> Manor Cottage
> Brighton Road
> Horley
> Surrey
> 30/i/51
>
> Dear Mr Allen,
>
> Sir Laurence has asked me to thank you for your letter of January 25th. He has asked me to tell you that he will certainly not forget you when he is casting for the Festival [of Britain] productions, and in particular for 'Caesar and Cleopatra' . . .*

(Allen had played Apollodorus in *Caesar and Cleopatra* in the first production of 1906.)

Chichester, where he'd once gone to film the cathedral bells for *Richard III*, was Olivier's dress rehearsal for the National. 'My plan is to demonstrate the versatility of the stage through a range of styles, conventions and periods,' he'd declared. He assumed responsibility for the technical aspects of the new theatre, which opened on 5 July 1962. He enjoyed discussing the plans and blueprints with carpenters and bricklayers. Problems with fire regulations, inadequate funds, a sceptical board; the multiple responsibilities of directing, acting and choosing a com-

more impressive than Kirk Douglas's pro-democracy nonsense: 'We're *free!*' Kirk leers, and in spirit only, he must mean, because Crassus' army is coming at them from three directions and the slaves face certain death. (Henry V, Nelson, etc., Olivier's pro-freedom protagonists, have, as their distinguishing quality, patriotism; which is Crassus' concern, also. Spartacus, by contrast, is very *American*; he's at one with Forrest Gump, or Chance the gardener – the slaves and fools attaining power without effort.)

* And was Mr Allen remembered? Alas, he was not. Olivier's cast for *Caesar and Cleopatra* (and *Antony and Cleopatra*) included instead Robert Helpmann, Harry Andrews, Wilfrid Hyde White and Niall MacGinnis.

pany; the long-term planning and artistic policy: all this would be his life at the National. *Uncle Vanya* began at Chichester; *Othello* transferred from the National to Chichester. Until John Clements took over in 1966, Olivier used the Sussex festival as his personal outpost – like Sir Barry Jackson, who'd had productions travelling hither and yon from the Birmingham base. In London the ramshackle Aquinas Street hutments, with rain pouring through the roof into buckets, appealed to him; the disasters of the first production, O'Toole's *Hamlet*, brought out the Dunkirk spirit. Sometimes, Olivier had to go before the tabs and apologize to the audience, or he had to ascend to the fly-tower and hoist the curtain by himself. He relished overcoming these problems – and there is an element of comedy in many of the disputes. There was a furious quarrel in Gielgud's dressing room with Peter Brook about the gold phallus which was unveiled at the end of Seneca's *Oedipus*. 'Larry was hysterical about the phallus.' He thought it 'childishly insolent', 'an incomprehensively infantile lark'. And he was right. *Oedipus* isn't about sex, lawful or otherwise, it's about destiny. Having played the part, he knew this. His schoolmasterly affront is funny, though, as is his grief over the abandonment of the National Anthem before curtain up, as is what has been labelled the 'saga of succession'.* Olivier knew the job was too much for him, but he was not willing to yield his power – that much we know. But he took it into his head to give Joan his crown. 'I told him he really mustn't be so silly,' she said. 'I wasn't Helene Weigel [Brecht's widow] and it wasn't the Berliner Ensemble.' He then came up with a scheme to form a regency council – Joan, Tynan and the associate directors, with himself at one remove in an honorary capacity. 'That was unacceptable to everybody,' said Max Rayne.

Olivier tried to stay at the National like an oldster being ingenious and mischievous to avoid being put in a home. You can understand why the board did not take him into their confidence over appointing Hall and negotiated behind his back; you can appreciate, too, that he felt, as Joan stated, 'wounded, humiliated and furious at having been kept in the dark'. It was as if he'd been told to accept his decline and fall,† and he played up to this – giving people the performance they expected?

* Or in Hall's phrase, 'Larry's obsessional anxiety – the succession.'

† Proving that the day wasn't over, that night was not drawing nigh, Olivier betook himself to television, where between 1976 and 1978, David Plowright, his brother-in-law, the managing director of Granada, enabled him to produce and star in Pinter's *The Collection*, Williams' *Cat on a Hot Tin Roof*, *Hindle Wakes* (directed only), Inge's *Come Back, Little Sheba*, Bridie's *Daphne Laureola*, and de Filippo's *Saturday, Sunday, Monday*. (Note the reduplication of a LOP repertoire.)

When Hall was living in a penthouse at the Barbican and Olivier inhabited a tower in Victoria, it tickled him to telephone Hall and ask if they could see each other flash their lights on and off. On another occasion, Hall goes to stay at Brighton, and Olivier and Joan have forgotten about the appointment; then, in the middle of the night, Olivier clatters into the guest bedroom with a wake-up call and a breakfast tray, having quite mistaken the time. At board meetings, Olivier ('He looked awful – tired and worried') veers off into irrelevant diatribes, as it might be denouncing microphones in theatres, for then 'all the gallantry was gone'.

Had not the heat-seeking rocket killed Nicholas Tomalin on the Golan Heights in October 1973, he'd have written a brilliant book about the history of the National. It was his belief that the creation of such a theatre 'provided, in miniature, a portrait of our times'. Quite so. The story would no doubt have begun with Victorian grandees and their architectural palaces, designed by Lutyens; and look what we got in the end: Lasdun's concrete turd overseen by representatives of the government. Instead of imperial splendour, a post-war drabness. Peter Hall, on his *Aquarius* television show, said: 'During [1976], a major public building will begin its life – a building by which the seventies will certainly be judged in the future.' Well, how were they to know then that the terraces and walkways linking the place to Waterloo Bridge would become piss-stained rat-runs full of beggars and AIDS victims?

Though, in fact, what we now think of as the National was not formally incorporated under the Companies Act until 8 February 1963, Henry Irving's Lyceum had in effect been the National; as had Lilian Baylis' Old Vic; as had the spirit and achievements of Sir Barry Jackson, Tyrone Guthrie, and Sir Fordham Flower, the chairman of the Shakespeare Memorial Theatre, at Stratford. Hall, the artistic director at Stratford, which in 1961 had received its charter to become the *Royal* Shakespeare Company, is the man we must credit with the sense and skill to pull the disparate elements together – 'the vast company, the immense repertoire, the constant output, the excitement, the disasters' – and formulate a grand plan. As Peter Brook described it in the RSC Annual Report for 1968, Hall 'was trying to create a living organism, where flexible imaginative conditions were related to flexible imaginative individuals in key positions'. What this all meant in practice was a huge bureaucratic machine; and Hall's *Diaries* are a record of the elation and depression (mostly that), being its ringmaster involved. But we can see at once why Hall and Olivier could never be compatible. It is rivalry all the way. Stratford vs. London; Hall the Cambridge-educated director and policy-maker vs. Olivier the actor and law-giver operating by instinct ('I am one of the least educated men you ever met,' he said in 1969); it is almost a dispute between prose and poetry, sense and sensibility, and what connects the two men is that main element which drove them apart: the scale of their ambition.

Youth and age also divided them. The *Diaries* note Olivier's every cough and splutter. 'He sounded vague and another person' (18 February 1975); 'a virus has attacked the muscles of his throat' (25 February 1975). Hall sees him in the audience at *Heartbreak House* and thinks, 'he will clearly never play a major role on the stage again' (29 July 1975). A few days later, Olivier has rallied: 'Larry . . . alert, humorous, with a mind dancing from subject to subject much as in the old days.' But luckily – 'the scale of him seems to have been pressed, reduced . . .' (1 August 1975). Olivier comes to *No Man's Land* and complains that he can't hear a word . . . He dithers about speaking the prologue to *Tamburlaine* . . . He decides the National should be opened with a grand ball, like something out of *The Prince and the Showgirl* . . . He fails to congratulate Hall on his knighthood . . . And so on endlessly.

Hall himself, as if developing Tomalin's thesis, suggests that a theatre company 'is subject to all the pressures and all the illnesses of society at large'. Thus, the embattled National is shaped and formed by trade union disputes, inefficiency, inadequate funding, broken machinery, defunct computer systems, litigation, stupidity and boredom. As Hall says, the 'country is running down. The trains are late. Petrol is short. Electricity cuts are imminent. The stock market is jittery.' The miners are on strike; there are frequent bomb scares. Hall certainly reflects this mood of breakdown and lassitude, his doctor finding him 'over-tired, over-stressed, and not in good shape'. The health of the National depended on Olivier's fitness, too. Peter Lewis, in *The National: A Dream Made Concrete,* examines revenues, the tone of reviews, the general public expectations for the place, and claims, 'the dips in the company's standards all coincided with Olivier's serious illnesses and incapacity'. I wish to extend or alter this idea – that the National was symbolical – allegorical? – of the nation's health, and that it was also determined by Olivier's health; by his dreams and desires; by his impress.

He began to suffer from stage fright during *The Master Builder*; he was convinced he'd forget his lines. (It must be a bit like sex: if you fear you'll not be able to do it, you'll not be able to do it, the erection goes.) During *Othello* he instructed the other actors not to look him in the eye, in case he'd be thrown; and when Othello was on stage alone, he wanted Frank Finlay in the wings as a reassurance. Before the opening night of

The Merchant of Venice, he told Joan, 'I'm going to walk out [of] that stage door and get on the first bus that comes'; and as she explained: 'His reputation is so big and vast now that to have to live up to that . . . and when you're head of the National Theatre and you've got all those young actors looking up to you saying, show us the way . . . and then his roles always seem to have special moments that everybody's read about, and he fears terribly that he will dry up . . . or [he] won't be what people expected. With *Long Day's Journey into Night* – that was the first big . . . part since his cancer and his thrombosis – he was very worried that he might not have the power in the voice any more. A year after his cancer treatment, Larry had his appendix out, and during the operation the cancer team was there and, as they told me afterwards, "We took the liberty of having a look around." The cancer had completely disappeared. I remember his reaction when he first learned of the cancer. It wasn't shock. He felt something like it was his due – it was something that had been meted out to him. It just came a bit before he expected it.'

So, along with all those leaps, romps, sportive tricks and pledges of virility, a corresponding quantity of maladies, infirmities, grievances and diseases? ('Olivier Suffering From Cancer. Wife Sees Good Chance of Cure' ran the headlines around the world.) But perhaps stars should suffer more – for the point of them is that they are larger than lifesize? Acting is about athleticism and stamina; and Olivier was in addition a libidinal actor: his sensuality and lingerings; his rush and vitality. It isn't that he simply wore himself out, however, that is at issue. It wasn't the normal processes of time and age that brought along disability and disaster. A clue may be found in the television production of *The Moon and Sixpence,* made by NBC in 1959. Olivier plays Charles Strickland, a painter based on Gauguin; and the drama concerns the sacrifices he makes, in human terms, to succeed as an artist – the poverty and illness he endures; finally, the disfigurements of leprosy. The idea is that genius comes at a price; you have to pay. And pay Olivier did, the last twenty-five years of his life being the encroachment by death; an unbroken (even overlapping) sequence of complaints: prostate cancer, involving an obstructed uretha and retrograde ejaculation (think it over), cured by radiotherapy; appendicitis; pneumonia; gout; piles ('too charming'); a thrombosis in his right leg; a tangle in the tubes connected to his left kidney; and – the killer – dermatomyositis, an inflammatory disorder of the skin and underlying tissues, including the muscles, where the fibres frayed and broke down. This condition had been preceded by fevers, malaise, and difficulties in rising and walking; and the appearance on his face, eyelids and knuckles of a fine, scaly rash, which was later accompanied by severe swelling. The problem lay in his collagen – the protein that is the principal constituent of white fibrous connective tissue. The condition is also often associated with internal cancer.

With Olivier, though, it is a more complex issue than balancing the profit (his career) against the loss (being an invalid); and he overcame his indispositions time and again, incorporating his pinched features and high-pitched voice in his film parts: Lear's waning; Ezra Lieberman's one last chuck of the dice against the forces of darkness; Clifford Mortimer, forlorn and very empty, gazing at blooms and butterflies he never saw. (You almost have to admire the *energy* of Olivier's illnesses.) Olivier outraced death. Acting was where the resurrections took place; and you don't have to be too ingenious* to see how illness and theatre are metaphors of each other, Olivier mutating, evolving, transforming, like a virus; and the way he approached new characters was as if he's capturing an organism's genetic code and altering it. However, what happens with Olivier is that his interest in the mystery of the body, its strengths and weaknesses, his devotion to acting as a physical discipline, is bound up with his awareness of the spirit. The battle between good and evil, order and catastrophe, is continued in the fight between sickness and health.

Illness, he felt, was a moral contamination, a pollution – and if we want an example of how Olivier represented his era, and changed with his era, first there's his Old Vic Oedipus, in the forties, when Thebes' pestilence suggested totalitarianism and barbarism in Europe. Fascism was the disease of the hour and the plague was a punishment for wickedness. Then, in the post-war era, came *Titus Andronicus*, which Jan Kott, seeing the production in Warsaw in 1957, could recognize as strangely being about recent disturbances and wars. *The Entertainer*, also, is about post-war exhaustion and decay. The realness and importance has gone out of Archie's life and art; through this Osborne tries to represent the decline of the empire and the ending of England and Englishness. It's all an inversion of Olivier's lordliness, kingship, greatness; Archie is a hopeless businessman; he can't hold an audience, run a theatre, or earn respect and love. Olivier gives him a lot of vigour that's used to no purpose. Archie is always shrugging, smiling, grimacing, working his eyebrows, his mouth, his elbows, or flourishing his stick or waggling the microphone stand. He's a parodic anthology of Olivier's performances, those to come as well as in the past. The off-putting

* Though that is exactly the word to describe Susan Sontag, in her book *Illness as Metaphor* (Harmondsworth 1978), Jonathan Miller, in his study, *The Body in Question* (London, 1978), and anything by Oliver Sachs.

dapperness and mirthless grins and smirks (*Sleuth*); the rage and the over-enunciation (*Richard III*); the lisp which creeps in occasionally owing to the false teeth (*The Merchant of Venice*); the humiliations (*Term of Trial*); the sorrow (*Hamlet*); the song-and-dance act, when he swivels from the hips and gyrates in a blue suit (*Othello*); the painted lips (Nelson, in *That Hamilton Woman*); Archie and Phoebe's mutual hatred, and yet you can't imagine they'd live apart (*The Dance of Death*;* *Long Day's Journey into Night*).

Archie's tragedy is his self-awareness. He knows how lacking in humour he is. Unlike Billy, the role Olivier originally wanted to play, he doesn't belong to the Edwardian world. (Billy is impersonated by Roger Livesey: Colonel Blimp himself, with that groaning, wheezing, low, hooting voice.) Billy has a faded grandeur (he cherishes his Agate clipping) and in the pub he can deliver his Kipling-era ditties with conviction; whereas Archie's routines are flat, because he is self-conscious. His Britannia tableau and patriotic jokes don't work. He's the comedian who hates himself, his audience, and his material; his skits and routines are slick and professional, but nobody responds. His ballad to the hostile house, 'Why should I care, why should I let it touch me?', is heartbreaking, for the trouble with Archie is that he does care – about the death of his son, for one thing, when his sob of grief modulates into a rendition of the Negress' song, dredged from memory. Tony Richardson keeps this scene in long shot – because Olivier, through his simply being Olivier, was too good? A 'pure and natural noise', Archie calls it; and if only he could do one thing as authentic as that – and Olivier, playing

---

* 'Hatred and love!' wrote Strindberg. 'All is one. The same source of energy. Sometimes positive, sometimes negative electricity. But one and the same.' This is the direction in which Olivier and Vivien were headed towards the end of their marriage – a sort of emotional melt-down witnessed (exacerbated?) by Tynan, who remarked of *The Dance of Death*, 'there are whole passages that take me back to dear old Notley'.

In the play, Edgar and Alice drain each other of self-respect; their life together is a routine of monotonous card games interspersed with acts of violence: the husband shoots six bullets through a portrait of his wife, throws bottles at a closed window, sobs, snickers, and at the close, wrenches himself out of his wheelchair to spit at Alice full in the face.

Illness and suffering, the seizures and convulsions, are all too neatly symbolic of moral collapse. It took Olivier to invest this Nordic melodrama with greatness – in his performance loathing and misery became an expression of intense love. The production was directed by Glen Byam Shaw, who'd piloted Olivier through the Stratford *Macbeth*.

It was filmed in 1969, but never released. Gary Meyer, manager of the University of California Theater in Berkeley, found the print in the Paramount vault, and it was screened at an Olivier Festival in 1979. 'Laurence Olivier for marquee, but theme makes outlook tough. Okay for card-carrying intellectuals,' said *Variety*, bestowing the kiss of death on *The Dance of Death*.

this scene, is as authentic as that. Vivien watching him first realize the scene in rehearsal couldn't stop weeping. 'The production had . . . become a vehicle containing all her sense of loss to come or already endured,' wrote Osborne. We can't have Archie being transcendent. Archie cares, and is touched by the plights of others, but he has to cover up. He's always seeming to be in a rush. All the fecklessness, the jabber, is to conceal his feelings. He's fast and light, giving the illusion of being busy; he's the same back at the digs, pouring drinks, flirting, teasing, telling stale gags and, to intensify the neurosis, there's Phoebe weeping and creating. 'He's funny,' she says sarcastically. 'You're so rich. You're such a big success.' Archie responds to this with silent laughter and chortles, an open-mouthed hiss. (His glances conceal his anger.) We *can* see it, though it is black and white, the red mouth, the blue suit, and the slightly greenish skin, translucent like a fly's wing.

The atmosphere of *The Entertainer* is like a psychological sickness; the soundtrack jangles with pit bands or bursts of echoey pianola music. There is a sense of guilt, laxity, contamination. Vivien was desperate to play Phoebe in the original production at the Royal Court and, to everybody's consternation, attended rehearsals, arriving at Sloane Square in her chauffeur-driven Rolls. She thought a rubber mask could be made, to make her look blowsy and common. 'What about that!' laughed Tony Richardson as soon as he dared. 'Rubber masks! Oh, my dear God. Rubber masks!' Phoebe! A monotonous and complaining drudge, wheedling and apologizing, who lives on tea, cigarettes and gin (she's well gone in drink); of whom Archie says, 'She's tired – and she's tired of me'; and who says of herself, when asked of her proudest achievement: 'I made him want me'. (The autobiographical parallels proceed apace. Archie asks Jean, played by Joan Plowright, 'What would you say to a man my age marrying a girl your age?' His daughter answers: 'You can't do a thing like that to Phoebe.'*) Richard Olivier has suggested

---

* Notley was advertised for sale in *Country Life* (13 August 1959), when Olivier was commuting between Stratford, where he was appearing as Coriolanus, and Morecambe, where he was making *The Entertainer*. The property was purchased by a Mr Arnold Swanson: 'All for £30,000! You know what? We stole it from them. It's worth £75,000 – and I'd have paid it. I'd have paid anything for this house. It's got charm. And peace. I like that. It was sort of invested in the building by the monks.'

All the furniture was thrown in with the purchase price, including a huge gilt mirror flanked by Nubian slaves and a marble garden table, which itself had cost £1,800. Mr Swanson cheerfully scrapped the Oliviers' theatrical touches: 'Right now we're cleaning the place up. We haven't decided on our staff yet, but the Olivers had a Portuguese couple. The man was marvellous at flower arrangements. He seemed to do it all the

that his father's mysterious viruses, attacks of gout and one ailment after another, began in earnest when, in 1949, Vivien made the announcement, casually over lunch, that she didn't love him any more. 'I felt as if I had been . . . condemned to death,' he'd stated. 'It was as if I had been rendered forever still inside . . .'

When Vivien, the name of the enchantress who bewitches Merlin, incidentally, said she didn't love him she meant the impersonal man he had become, who only ever pretended to drop his command. She loved his talent; she loved the person he once was – the person he was again being with Joan. But what was there to love in the newly knighted Sir Laurence, who was out of reach; who in his art attained a heaven that was shut to her? He saw his illnesses as divine wrath for his emotional faults and transgressions; for leaving his wives and abandoning his children.* He'd have cancer; Vivien had her consumption. Thomas Mann said that TB is 'a disguised manifestation of the power of love; and all disease is only love transformed'. W. H. Auden, in 'Miss Gee', says that cancer is 'like a hidden assassin, waiting to strike at you . . . as if there had to be some outlet for foiled creative fire'. Olivier's creativity was not thwarted. Far from it. Real life is what he renounced; fragility, mortality and the contingent are what he fought against. Constructing his compan-

---

time . . . We'll have a ballroom, more land, get a herd of beef. We'll join the local hunt, settle down here permanently. We'll join in the local life okay. We live simply, you know' [Mr Swanson was a Canadian].

Olivier told his sister-in-law, Hester, who lived at Notley Mead, the guest cottage, 'I'll miss Vivien every day of my life.'

* Olivier had separated from Joan, too, towards the end, and had begun flinging woo at Marcella Markham, his dialect coach. He gave her jewels and a gardenia. (As a septuagenarian slippered pantaloon, he got nowhere. Ms Markham politely repelled his advances.) On 6 March 1980, Joan asked Richard Olivier to announce, through the family lawyers, that she would 'neither attend award functions for her husband nor accompany him on trips'.

Richard Olivier only saw his father when he was ill, and therefore off work and forcibly recuperating. His first memory is of Olivier blacked up for Othello; all that courage and endurance – which contrasted with the 'real' man, languishing in hospital rooms later on. Not that he was a tractable patient. Maddened by his medicines, there was 'the devil in those eyes' – which we can well believe.

Julie-Kate's recollections are similar. 'I think I missed out a lot because he was rather old when I was growing up . . . He'd been ill for so long and it was so hard watching him fade away. So it was a release when he actually died because I loved him. But it also made me feel glad that people weren't pursuing me because they wanted to meet my father.'

Owing to his complex cocktail of pills and opiates, Olivier was meant to reduce his consumption of whisky. When his daughter refused him a refill he said loudly: 'I can't believe a sperm from my testicle ever created such a cunt.'

ies, mounting his plays, the disbanding, the regrouping, the separations: this was analogous to family life, and it did duty for family life.

He was born on 22 May 1907. (Dorking is no more than twenty miles away from Ashurst, where he was to die, eighty-two years later.) I haven't researched the meteorological detail, because I want to continue believing that it was a close day, and that there was a nervous hush before the storm. His last words were, 'I don't want this'; his first articulate utterance was '*Damn!*'

Appendix A
A Battle Plan

Throughout this book, I have made large claims for Olivier's athleticism, particularly on stage. Here's a precise example, courtesy of The Shakespeare Birthplace Trust. Olivier was forty-eight when he did this eight times a week. The Macduff was Keith Michell; he had to remind Olivier that Macbeth was not meant to win.

Macbeth: Stratford-upon-Avon, 1955
Fight between Macbeth and Macduff

TEXT: Macduff: '. . . Than terms can give thee out!'
Macduff cuts to L flank.
Macbeth parries and flicks over to disarm. (L to R)
Macbeth cuts to R flank. Macduff parries.
Macbeth grabs Macduff's sword wrist, places his sword-arm elbow under Macduff's sword arm, swings him round (R to L) to reverse positions.
Macbeth cuts to R cheek. Macduff parries.
Macbeth cuts to head, direct. Macduff parries 6th.
Macbeth cuts to R flank. Macduff parries.
Macbeth moves in to a lock.
TEXT: Macbeth: 'Thou losest labour . . .'
TEXT: Macbeth: '. . . mayest thou the entrenchant air . . .'
Macbeth cuts L to R. Slices to Macduff's head. Macduff ducks.
Macduff cuts to R flank. Macbeth parries.
Macduff cuts direct to head. Macbeth parries 6th.
Macbeth envelops to low line (R to L) on:
TEXT: Macbeth: '. . . Let fall thy blade . . .'
BREAK. Macduff retreats up-stage.
Macduff cuts to L cheek. Macbeth parries.
Macduff cuts to R flank. Macbeth parries.
Macduff cuts to R cheek. Macbeth parries.
Macbeth moves in to lock and pushes Macduff up against rostrum on:

TEXT: Macbeth: ' . . . To one of woman born.'
Macbeth moves in to lock and Macduff pushes him away on:
TEXT: Macduff: 'Despair thy charm . . .'
TEXT: Macduff: ' . . . Untimely ripp'd.'
CRISIS. From here on, Macbeth fights desperately. Macduff coldly.
Dialogue down to TEXT: Macbeth: ' . . . HOLD ENOUGH!'
Positioning: Macbeth C up-stage. Macduff R slightly down stage.
Macbeth cuts direct to head. Macduff stands ground and Macbeth is forced into a lock.
They struggle and turn round.
Macbeth knees Macduff to stomach which breaks lock.
Macbeth slices upwards. Macduff avoids cut.
Macduff cuts to L flank. Macbeth parries.
Macbeth cuts direct to head. Macduff parries.
Macbeth cuts to L flank. Macduff parries.
They hold each other's blades on the turn. MACDUFF TO FOOT OF STAIRS.
Macbeth cuts to R flank. Macduff parries.
Macbeth cuts to R cheek. Macduff parries.
Macbeth cuts to R flank. Macduff parries.
Macbeth cuts to L flank. Macduff parries.
MACDUFF ON ROSTRUM LEVEL.
Macbeth springs on to rostrum.
Macduff lunges as Macbeth does so. Macbeth parries.
Macduff grabs Macbeth's sword wrist and brings his own hilt into Macbeth's shoulder.
Macbeth pushes Macduff back. Macduff up one step.
Macbeth cuts to L flank. Macduff parries. Macbeth follows with L hand to throat. Push up steps. Macduff pushes off with R foot.
Macbeth slices up, L to R. Macduff avoids cut and cuts direct to head.
Macbeth parries, envelops L to R and slices up, R to L.
Macduff retreats up steps and Macbeth lunges.
Macduff disarms, and draws dagger (R hand), stabbing down.
Macbeth draws dagger with L hand, transfers to R hand, catching Macduff's stab with L hand.
Macduff grabs Macbeth's dagger wrist, LOCK. They struggle up to level.
ON LEVEL. They struggle and Macduff gives way, going down on R knee.
Macbeth falls over him on to steps. Positions reversed.

Macduff pushes Macbeth's dagger with his own, grabs his wrist with L hand and pushes his R forearm under Macbeth's throat.
Macduff pushes Macbeth off.

Appendix B
The Olivier Theatre

Life magazine called him 'one of the stately homes of England'; I don't think he was quite that – the Olivier Theme Park, complete with slumbrous lions and a designated picnic area – though he did become a train: British Rail named a locomotive after him in May 1980; and he did become a theatre. Throughout the sixties, a Building Committee would meet to discuss and plan what the National should eventually look like; and on the subject of auditoria, Tynan (in a letter to Olivier dated 4 May 1966) suggested a fan shape, 'with a quarter-circle stage', seating approximately one thousand punters. He had in mind the amphitheatres of the Greeks. Amongst his papers I found this transcription of an interview between Peter Hall and Denys Lasdun, transmitted on ITV on 29 February 1976; but more interestingly, I also found the drawings Lasdun mentions, which I append herewith.

LASDUN: After listening to everybody for . . . two years, I suddenly did a drawing, I remember vividly doing it – I got a piece of paper out and I said 'really what you're all asking for is a room' – and I drew a square – and a stage in the corner – and there was a sort of silence . . . because it was very basic and I said – of course you'd put seats around it like that – and that is really what you're talking about – and somebody tried to take the drawing away from me but I grabbed it back because I knew that we were onto something but I knew it was simplistic and we had a long, long journey ahead of us before we found out what it was. So then everybody was very excited and we began to develop it and we began to try and find out where . . . on that stage would every pair of eyes of that audience pass through a single point of command, as it were of the actor – and conversely where would that actor stand, so that without moving his head he felt he was addressing and signalling to everybody without moving towards the back [of the stage]. And we argued and argued and discussed and discussed and discussed and in the end we arrived at a position, it's not of course an exact position—

HALL: It's an area—

LASDUN: It is a zone – now it's a very interesting zone because when you come to look at the Olivier Theatre [as] we have built [it], and if you look at that black line [on Fig. ii] and go on with it, as it were, extend it – you have made the right angle of the room – [and] that is what is left of that doodle . . . years later. We [have a] position where . . . an actor . . . forward on the stage is within an angle of about 120 degrees – which is within the span of his eyes – and he can see everybody, and furthermore, nobody, no member of the audience, is looking across the stage at *other* members of the audience. Now, there's a lot more to this room than that, but to come back to your initial question, how did we start – this is where we started; we then developed the Olivier room, until . . . we arrived at [its present] form and that form generated the whole building.

Figure (i)

	The Rt Hon	Address	The Archway
	Viscount Chandos PC DSO MC		10a Aquinas Street
	Sir Laurence Olivier		London SE1
Manager	George Rowbottom	Telephone	Waterloo 2033
	Kenneth Rae	Cables Telegrams	Thenat London SE1

The National Theatre

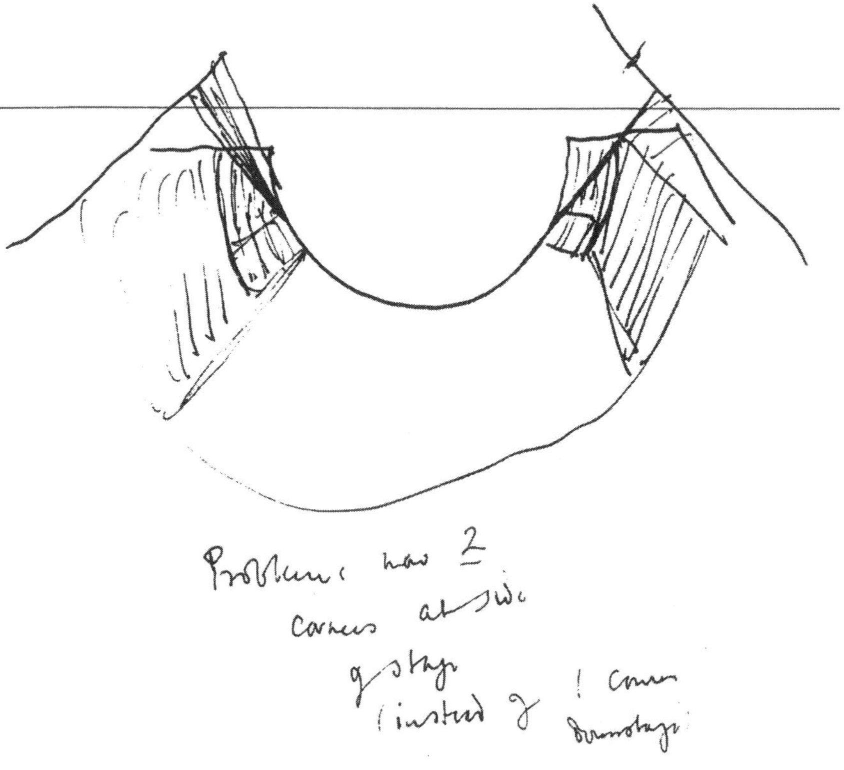

Figure (ii)

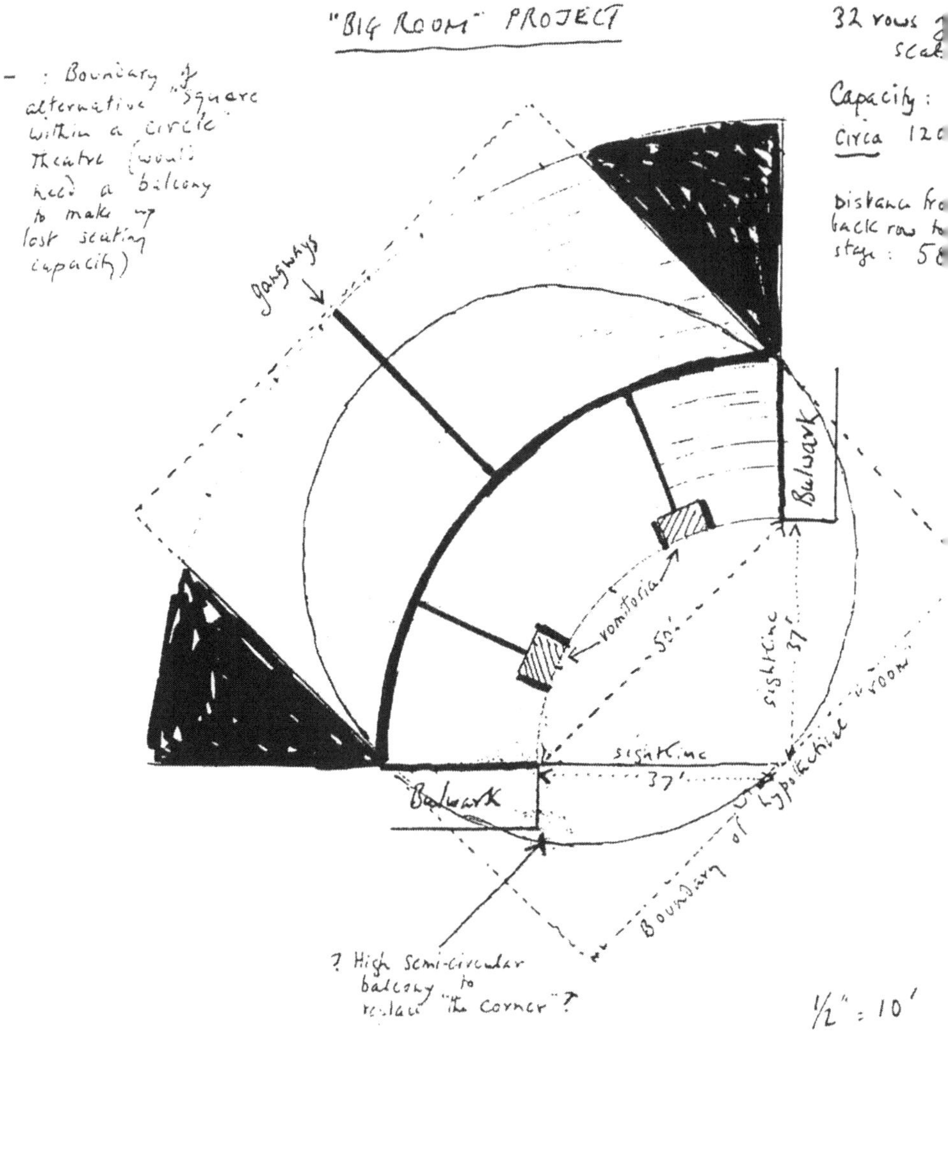
"BIG ROOM" PROJECT
32 rows
Capacity :
Circa 12
Distance fro back row to stage : 5
– : Boundary of alternative "Square within a circle" theatre (would need a balcony to make up lost seating capacity)
gangways
vomitoria
50'
sightline 37'
sightline
37'
Bulwark
Bulwark
Boundary of hypothetical "room"
? High semi-circular balcony to replace "the corner" ?
1/2" : 10'

Sources and Acknowledgements

Had I been *extremely* precocious, I may well have met Olivier. In April 1964, he came to Cardiff's New Theatre with his National Theatre Company productions of *Othello* and *Uncle Vanya*. People who had failed to obtain tickets at the Old Vic travelled down to Wales – one man coming from Finland and another from Paris ('he arrived just as the audience were settling in their seats after the national anthem', wrote the *Western Mail*).

The shows proved a mixed blessing, as Roy Todds, the booking manager, explained: 'No one was really keen to follow Sir Laurence' – so, in subsequent weeks, patrons at the New Theatre had to endure Norman Vaughan, the Beverley Sisters, Ivor Emmanuel and Ted Rogers. Full-blooded Shakespeare and crepuscular Chekhov were superseded as it were by rivals of Archie Rice.

I never saw him – so at least I was set free to imagine him, which I started doing as a child, when shabby-genteel uncles (the kind that dished out dud premium bonds for birthday presents) would inform me that the bogeyman was going to get me. The bogeyman? A floating chartreuse bedsheet with big hollow eye-sockets? No – I found the bogeyman waiting for me in a book about Tudor history, published by another uncle who ran the Wayland Press. What elicited from me the primal scream was a plate of Olivier's Richard III.

Normally, when frightened (by Karloff's sagging jaw, Christopher Lee's fangs, or Kevin Bacon's nose), I fall back on remembering that this is *acting*, with a film crew standing by, etc.; yet for all the deliberate artifice, with Olivier there was something beyond acting: something real, and in his heart. He knew this, too. When he assured John Mills that Richard was certain to be a disaster ('It'll be terrible, terrible. I want you to know as one of my old friends'), what he meant was that his performance was going to be experimental; he'd not be bad, but different – hazardous, in his pace and pitch.

This book, my response to Olivier's vehemence and great interestingness, is indebted to the following catalogue of books, articles, archives and individuals. Olivier has long been a heavy industry for critics and biographers, but the first effort (Barker's) is unsurpassed for information and intelligence. Vermilye's conspectus of the screen career is similarly superb. Vivien, also, is well-trodden ground. Hugo Vickers' study glistens as a lone scarab in the sand. As regards newspaper and magazine pieces, there are of course millions of reviews, interviews and features. I have listed only those that actually proved useful. May I direct the reader to the 'Bibliography of Laurence Olivier's Life and Stage Career' by Frank E. Mello, which is published in *Theatre Notebook* from time to time, for a more complete picture. The 'selective list of books and articles' appended to Holden's dull tome, prepared for that author by the Society for Theatre Research, is likewise comprehensive. My final section is a gathering of those persons with whom I personally discussed Olivier, or who helped with this opus in other vital ways – the Islington flat of one of them, situated in the former fly-tower of the Collins Music Hall, was my research headquarters during the summer of 1994. And it was to the Collins that Olivier himself had come, hunting for a real-life Archie Rice; and where Vivien, resplendent in the stalls, had caught a semen-filled hankerchief plumb in her lap, hurled from somewhere in the auditorium.

1. Printed Books on Olivier

BARKER, Felix *The Oliviers* (London, 1953).
Laurence Olivier (Kent, 1984).
BRAGG, Melvyn *Laurence Olivier* (London, 1984).
COTTRELL, John *Laurence Olivier* (London, 1975).
DANIELS, Robert L. *Laurence Olivier: Theater and Cinema* (San Diego, 1980).
DARLINGTON, W. A. *Laurence Olivier* (London, 1968).
FAIRWEATHER, Virginia *Cry God for Larry* (London, 1969).
GOURLAY, Logan (ed.) *Olivier* (London, 1973).
HAILL, Lyn (ed.) *Olivier at Work: The National Years* (London, 1989).
HIRSCH, Foster *Laurence Olivier on Screen* (Boston 1979; 1984).
HOLDEN, Anthony *Laurence Olivier: A Biography* (London, 1988).
KIERNAN, Thomas *Sir Larry* (London, 1981).
KORDA, Michael *Curtain* (London, 1991) [a fictionalization of Olivier's life: he is Robert Vane, Vivien is Felicia Lisle, Danny Kaye is Randy Brooks].
MORLEY, Margaret *The Films of Laurence Olivier* (New Jersey, 1977).

O'CONNOR, Garry *Darlings of the Gods* (London, 1984).
Olivier: In Celebration (London, 1987).
OLIVIER, Laurence *Confessions of an Actor* (London, 1982).
On Acting (London, 1986).
OLIVIER, Richard *Shadow of the Stone Heart* (London, 1995).
OLIVIER, Tarquin *My Father Laurence Olivier* (London 1993).
SILVIRIA, Dale *Laurence Olivier and the Art of Film Making* (Ontario, 1985) [dedicated 'For Lord Oliver'].
TANITCH, Robert *Olivier: The Complete Career* (London, 1985).
VERMILYE, Jerry *The Complete Films of Laurence Olivier* (New York, 1992).
WHITEHEAD, Peter, and BEAN, Robin *Olivier: Shakespeare* (London, 1966).

2. *Printed Books on Vivien Leigh*

DENT, Alan *Vivien Leigh: A Bouquet* (London, 1969).
EDWARDS, Anne *Vivien Leigh* (London, 1977).
McBEAN, Angus *Vivien: A Love Affair in Camera* (Oxford, 1989).
ROBYNS, Gwen *Light of a Star* (London, 1968).
TAYLOR, John Russell *Vivien Leigh* (London, 1984).
VICKERS, Hugo *Vivien Leigh* (London, 1988).
WALKER, Alexander *Vivien* (London, 1987).

3. *General Bibliography*

— *Masterworks of the British Cinema* (London, 1990).
— *Five Seasons of The Old Vic Company: A Scrap-book record of production for 1944–1949* (London, n.d.) [includes the chapter 'From Gin Palace to National Theatre' by Olivier].
AGATE, James *The Contemporary Theatre 1944–1945* (London, 1946).
AUERBACH, Nina *Ellen Terry: Player in her Prime* (New York, 1987).
BACALL, Lauren *By Myself* (London, 1978).
Now (London, 1994).
BEHLMER, Rudy (ed.) *Memo from David O. Selznick* (New York, 1972).
Inside Warner Bros (1935–1951) (London, 1985).
BERGMAN, Ingmar *The Magic Lantern* (London, 1988).
BILLINGTON, Michael *Peggy Ashcroft* (London, 1988).
BRANAGH, Kenneth *Beginning* (London, 1989).
BROOK, Peter *The Empty Space* (London, 1968).
The Shifting Point (London, 1987).

BROWN, Ivor (ed.) *Shakespeare Memorial Theatre 1954–1956: A Photographic Record* (London, 1956).
BURTON, Hal *Great Acting* (London, 1967).
CALLOW, Simon *Being an Actor* (London, 1984).
Charles Laughton (London, 1987).
Orson Welles: The Road to Xanadu (London, 1995).
CASSON, John *Lewis and Sybil: A Memoir* (London, 1972).
CASTLE, Charles *Noël* (London, 1973).
CHRISTIE, Ian *Arrows of Desire: The Films of Michael Powell and Emeric Pressburger* (London, 1994).
(ed.) *The Life and Death of Colonel Blimp* (London, 1994).
CLARK, Colin *The Prince, the Showgirl and Me* (London, 1995).
COOK, Judith *The National Theatre* (London, 1976).
COVENEY, Michael *Maggie Smith: A Bright Particular Star* (London, 1992).
COWARD, Noël *Autobiography* (London, 1986).
CROSS, Brenda *The Film Hamlet: A Record of its Production* (London, 1948).
DAVIES, Anthony *Filming Shakespeare's Plays* (Cambridge, 1988).
DEANS, Marjorie *Meeting at the Sphinx* (London, 1945).
DEXTER, John *The Honourable Beast: A Posthumous Autobiography* (London, 1993).
DRAKE, Fabia *Blind Fortune* (London, 1978) [Foreword by Olivier].
DUNCAN, Barry *The St James's Theatre: Its Strange and Complete History 1835–1957* (London, 1964).
DUNDY, Elaine *Finch Bloody Finch* (London, 1980).
ECKERT, Charles W. *Focus On Shakespearean Films* (New Jersey, 1972).
ELSOM, John, and TOMALIN, Nicholas *The History of the National Theatre* (London, 1978).
EVERSHED-MARTIN, Leslie *The Impossible Theatre* (Chichester, 1971) ['Prologue' by Olivier].
The Miracle Theatre (London, 1987) [Foreword by Olivier].
FERRIS, Paul *Richard Burton* (London, 1981).
FINDLATER, Richard *The Player Kings* (London, 1971).
(ed.) *At The Royal Court* (London, 1981) [includes the chapter 'The Court and I' by Olivier].
FORBES, Brian *Ned's Girl: A Biography of Dame Edith Evans* (London, 1977).
FOWLER, Gene *Good Night, Sweet Prince: The Life and Times of John Barrymore* (New York, 1962).
GASKILL, William *A Sense of Direction: Life at The Royal Court* (London, 1988).
GIELGUD, John *Early Stages* (London, 1939).

Backward Glances (London, 1989).
GOLDMAN, William *Adventures in the Screen Trade* (London, 1983).
GOODWIN, Tim *Britain's Royal National Theatre* (London, 1988).
GOTTFRIED, Martin *Nobody's Fool: The Lives of Danny Kaye* (London, 1994).
GUINNESS, Alec *Blessings in Disguise* (London, 1985).
GUTHRIE, Tyrone *A Life in the Theatre* (London, 1960).
In Various Directions (London, 1965).
HALL, Peter *Peter Hall's Diaries* (London, 1983).
Making an Exhibition of Myself (London, 1993).
HARWOOD, Ronald (ed.) *The Faber Book of Theatre* (London, 1993).
HAWKINS, Jack *Anything for a Quiet Life* (London, 1973).
HAY, Peter (ed.) *Theatrical Anecdotes* (Oxford, 1987).
HAYMAN, Ronald *John Gielgud* (London, 1971).
Playback (London, 1973).
The First Thrust: Chichester Festival Theatre (London, 1975).
HESTON, Charlton *The Actor's Life: Diaries* (London, 1978).
HOBBS, William *Techniques of the Stage Fight* (London, 1967).
Stage Combat (London, 1980) [Foreword by Olivier].
IRVING, Laurence *Henry Irving: The Actor and his World* (London 1951; 1989).
KEMP, T. C. *The Birmingham Repertory Theatre* (Birmingham, 1943).
KITCHIN, Laurence *Mid-Century Drama* (London, 1960).
KORDA, Michael *Charmed Lives* (London, 1979).
KOTT, Jan *Shakespeare Our Contemporary* (London, 1965).
KULIK, Karol *Alexander Korda* (London, 1975).
LEAMING, Barbara *Orson Welles* (London, 1985).
LEFF, Leonard, J. *Hitchcock and Selznick* (London, 1988).
LESLEY, Cole *The Life of Noël Coward* (London, 1976).
LEWENSTEIN, Oscar *Kicking Against the Pricks: A Theatre Producer Looks Back* (London, 1994).
LEWIS, Peter *The National: A Dream Made Concrete* (London, 1990) [dedicated to 'the Memory of Laurence Olivier'].
LEWIS, Roger *Stage People* (London, 1989).
MADSEN, Axel *William Wyler* (London, 1974).
MANVELL, Roger *Shakespeare and the Film* (London, 1971).
MEYER, Michael *Not Prince Hamlet: Literary and Theatrical Memoirs* (London, 1989).
MILES, Sarah *A Right Royal Bastard* (London, 1993).
Serves Me Right (London, 1994) [dedication 'For Lionel Kerr', i.e. Olivier].

MINNEY, R. J. *Puffin Asquith* (London, 1973).
MORLEY, Sheridan *Tales from the Hollywood Raj* (London, 1983).
The Other Side of the Moon: The Life of David Niven (London, 1985).
Our Theatre in the Eighties (London, 1990).
MORTIMER, John *In Character* (London, 1983).
Murderers and Other Friends (London, 1994).
MOSELEY, Roy *A Life with the Stars* (London, 1982).
MOSLEY, Leonard *Battle of Britain: the making of a film* (London, 1969).
NIVEN, David *The Moon's a Balloon* (London, 1972).
NOBLE, Peter *Profiles and Personalities* (London, 1946).
O'CONNOR, Garry *Ralph Richardson: An Actor's Life* (London, 1982).
ORTON, Joe *The Orton Diaries* (London, 1986).
OSBORNE, John *A Better Class of Person* (London, 1981).
Almost a Gentleman (London, 1991).
PAYNE, Graham, and MORLEY, Sheridan *The Noël Coward Diaries* (London, 1982).
PAYNE, Graham, *My Life with Noël Coward* (New York, 1994).
POWELL, Michael *A Life in Movies* (London, 1986).
Million-Dollar Movie (London, 1993).
QUAYLE, Anthony *A Time to Speak* (London, 1990).
QUEENAN, Joe *If You're Talking To Me Your Career Must Be In Trouble* (London, 1994).
REDFIELD, William *Letters from an Actor* (London, 1966).
REDGRAVE, Michael *In My Mind's Eye* (London, 1983).
RICHARDSON, Tony *Long Distance Runner: A Memoir* (London, 1993).
ROBERTS, Peter *The Old Vic Story* (London, 1976).
ROBOZ, Zsuzsi, and GEBLER-DAVIES, Stan *Chichester 10: Portraits of a Decade* (London, 1975).
ROSS, Lillian and Helen *The Player: Profile of an Art* (New York, 1962).
ROSSI, Alfred (ed.) *Astonish Us in the Morning: Tyrone Guthrie Remembered* (London, 1977) [includes a long interview chapter with Olivier].
SANDERSON, Michael *From Irving to Olivier: A Social History of the Acting Profession in England 1890–1980* (London, 1984).
SINCLAIR, Andrew *Spiegel: The Man Behind the Pictures* (London, 1987).
SINDEN, Donald (ed.) *The Everyman Book of Theatrical Anecdotes* (London, 1987).
SPOTO, Donald *The Life of Alfred Hitchcock* (London, 1983).
SPRIGGE, Elizabeth *Sybil Thorndike Casson* (London, 1971).
STEPHENS, Robert *Knight Errant: Memoirs of a Vagabond Actor* (London, 1995).
STOCKHAM, Martin *The Korda Collection* (London, 1992).

TABORI, Paul *Alexander Korda* (London, 1959).
TANITCH, Robert (ed.) *Ralph Richardson: A Tribute* (London, 1982).
Gielgud (London, 1988).
THOMSON, David *The Showman: The Life of David O. Selznick* (London, 1993).
TREWIN, J. C. *Peter Brook: A Biography* (London, 1971).
TYNAN, Kathleen *The Life of Kenneth Tynan* (London, 1987).
TYNAN, Kenneth *He That Plays the King* (London, 1950).
Alec Guinness (London, 1953).
Curtains (London, 1961).
Tynan Left and Right (London, 1967).
The Sound of Two Hands Clapping (New York, 1975).
A View of the English Stage (London, 1975).
Show People (London, 1980).
Letters (London, 1994).
USTINOV, Peter *Dear Me* (London, 1977).
VICKERS, Hugo *Cecil Beaton* (London, 1985).
WALTON, Susana *William Walton: Behind the Façade* (Oxford, 1988).
WILCOX, Herbert *Twenty-Five Thousand Sunsets* (London, 1967).
WILLIAMS, Harcourt (ed.) *Vic-Wells: The Work of Lilian Baylis* (London, 1938) [includes the chapter 'Over the Water' by Olivier].
The Old Vic Saga (London, 1949).
WILLIAMS, Kenneth *The Kenneth Williams Diaries* (London, 1993).
The Kenneth Williams Letters (London, 1994).
WORSLEY, T. C. *The Fugitive Art: Dramatic Commentaries 1947–1951* (London, 1952).
ZEFFIRELLI, Franco *Jesus: A Spiritual Diary* (New York, 1984).
Zeffirelli: The Autobiography (London, 1986).

4. Periodicals

'Titus With A Grain Of Salt' by Evelyn Waugh, *Spectator*, 2 September 1955.*
'The Big Step I'm Taking' by David Lewin, *Daily Express*, 18 November 1958.
'The *Observer* Profile: Laurence Olivier' [unsigned], *The Observer*, 8 May 1960.

* Waugh knew the Oliviers socially – he liked it when Vivien boomed into the bell of his ear-trumpet – and he went backstage after *Titus Andronicus* to pay his respects. In his diary he noted how Vivien caressed members of the cast 'provocatively'.

'Larry and Me – by the first Mrs Olivier' by Herbert Kretzmer, *Sunday Dispatch*, 30 April 1961.
'Olivier, My Life, My Work, My Future' by Harold Hobson, *Sunday Times* [*c.* October 1963].
'The Great Sir Laurence' by Richard Meryman, *Life*, 1 May 1964.
'Knights in the Theatre – Sir Laurence Olivier: The master builder' by Peter Roberts, *The Times*, 5 December 1967.
'Olivier' by Terry Coleman, *The Guardian*, 1 June 1970.
'First Lord of the Stage' by Richard Meryman, *Life*, 8 December 1972.
'Henry Irving and Laurence Olivier as Shylock' by Richard Foulkes, *Theatre Notebook*, xxvii, 1973.
'Lion in the Realm, A Pussycat at Home' by Richard Meryman, *Detroit Free Press*, 8 April 1973.
'A Man Who Won't Stop Acting' [transcription of Olivier and Joan Plowright's interview with Barbara Walters on NBC TV's *Today Show*], *The Sunday Times*, 15 July 1973.
'Olivier: the unsatisfied man' by Irving Wardle, *The Times*, 27 October 1973.
'How I Escaped from Genteel Poverty' by Ian Cotton, [n.p., *c.* 1973].
'What Makes Larry Run?' by Margaret Laing, *The Sunday Times* magazine, 28 November 1976.
'Oliviers: Distinct, Separate, Yet One' by Michiko Kakutani, *The New York Times*, 27 February 1980.
'The Times Profile: Laurence Olivier at seventy-five' by Alan Hamilton, *The Times*, 17 May 1982.
'Lord Rayne replies to Lord Olivier', *The Sunday Telegraph*, 3 October 1982.
'Confessions of a Real Actor' by Gerald Clarke, *Time*, 15 November 1982.
'Actor for the Ages' by Richard Meryman, *Life* [*c.* 1983].
'Obituary: Lord Olivier' by Mark Amory, *The Independent*, 12 July 1989.
'The Acting Monarch' with contributions from Michael Blakemore, Melvyn Bragg, Simon Callow, Trevor Griffiths, Derek Jarman and Ronald Pickup, *The Independent*, 13 July 1989.
'Olivier's Heights' by Scott Berg and Harold Hobson, *The Sunday Times*, 16 July 1989.

5. Institutions

(a) United Kingdom

All Saints, Margaret Street, London, W1N 8JQ (Dr C. C. G. Rawll, archivist).

Ashmolean Museum, Oxford (Katharine Eustace, Assistant Curator, Department of Western Art).

Birmingham City Council (Department of Leisure and Community Services) – The Central Library (Philippa Bassett, Senior Archivist, and Paul A. Woodward, Assistant Librarian, Arts, Languages & Literature Department – for The Sir Barry Jackson & Birmingham Repertory Theatre Collection).

British Film Institute (Ros Cranston and James Griffith, Cataloguers); National Film and Television Archive (Alison Strauss, Administrative Assistant).

The British Library, Department of Manuscripts (Sally Brown, director – for the Olivier/Tynan papers).

Chandos Records Ltd. (Paul Wescott, Press Officer – for material on William Walton).

Chichester Festival Theatre (Lucy Brett, Publicity Department).

Christie, Manson & Woods Ltd. (Philip Harley, Department of Modern British Pictures).

CTE (Carlton) Ltd. (Mick Lachman, Publicity Department, and Karen Henson and Coral Nicholas, Business and Licence Managers – for the films of Alexander Korda).

Granada Television (Adrian Figgess, Traffic and Library Manager – for the archive of correspondence, casting notes, contracts, production files, cuttings and budget details pertaining to Olivier's television work).

Hatfield College, University of Durham (W. A. Moyes, Director, Hatfield Trust).

Imperial War Museum (Michael D. Moody, Department of Art – for information about Herbert Arnould Olivier).

Lambeth Palace Library (R. J. Palmer, Librarian).

Merton College, Oxford (S. J. Gunn, Fellow and Tutor in Modern History and College Archivist – for information about Gerard Kerr Olivier).

The National Portrait Gallery (Judith Flanders, Publishing Manager).

The National Sound Archive (Lee Taylor, Information Service Assistant).

The New Theatre, Cardiff (for cuttings relating to the visit made by the National Theatre Company in 1964).

The Raymond Mander & Joe Mitchenson Theatre Collection (Richard Mangan, Administrator – for an extensive gathering of reviews, programmes, feature articles, correspondence and theatrical history).

The Shakespeare Birthplace Trust, Stratford-upon-Avon (Marian J. Pringle, Senior Librarian – for prompt books, news cuttings, photographs, programmes, set designs, music and associated production materials to do with all Olivier's appearances at the Shakespeare Memorial Theatre).

Sotheby's (Susan Kent, Department of Modern British and Irish Pictures).

The South Bank Show (Melvyn Bragg, Editor, and Bob Bee, Producer).

St Edward's School, Oxford (Helene Van Rossum, Archivist – for information about Olivier's school plays, including programmes for *A Midsummer Night's Dream*, signed by the cast, and *The Merchant of Venice*, 1921, when Olivier sang 'A Hymn to Cynthia' in Act V).

The Theatre Museum, Tavistock Street, London (Janet Birkett, Librarian – for reviews of Olivier's London performances; photographs amassed by *The South Bank Show*; an album of snapshots of Olivier at Elsinore in 1937, given by Phyllis Hartnoll; photographs of the National Theatre and Chichester actors and productions, and of the National Theatre Company in Moscow, given by Richard Lyndhurst; boxes of general cuttings and articles; the Olivier/Christopher Fry correspondence; and scrapbooks on Olivier's career 1944–9).

University of Bristol Theatre Collection (Christopher Robinson, Keeper).

(b) United States of America

Academy of Motion Picture Arts and Sciences, Margaret Herrick Library (Kristine Krueger, Information Service – for Samuel Goldwyn Collection, Hedda Hopper Collection, press materials, scrapbooks, and correspondence).

The Billy Rose Theater Collection, the New York Public Library for the Performing Arts.

Boston University Special Collections, Mugar Memorial Library (M. Goostray and Howard B. Gotlieb, Curators – for Olivier's correspondence with Eric Ambler, G. B. Stern, Bette Davis, Julian Blaustein, Mildred Buchanan Flagg, Franc Marcus, Irene Selznick and Robert Speight).

The Carpenter Center for the Visual Arts, Harvard University (Chris Killips, Director).

The Celeste Bartos International Film Study Center, Department of Film, The Museum of Modern Art, New York.

George Eastman House, International Museum of Photography and Film, Rochester, New York (Kathleen MacRae, Administrative Assistant, Film Collections).

The Library of Congress, Washington, [i] Motion Picture, Broadcasting and Recorded Sound Division (Edwin M. Matthias and Madeline F. Matz, Reference Librarians); [ii] Manuscript Division (James H. Hutson, Librarian – for correspondence typescript carbons of five letters from Joshua Logan to Olivier; three typewritten letters from Olivier to Logan; and one long handwritten epistle; also, three typewritten letters from Olivier to George Middleton).

The Museum of Television and Radio, New York (Jonathan Rosenthal, Researcher).

National Center for Film and Video Preservation, at the American Film Institute, John F. Kennedy Center for the Performing Arts, Washington (Zoran Sinobad, Archives Assistant).

National Film Archives at College Park, Maryland (Shirley Williams, Archives Specialist, Motion Picture, Sound, and Video Branch).

UCLA Film and Television Archive (Lou Ellen Kramer, Reference and Outreach Co-ordinator).

University of California, Berkeley, University Art Museum & Pacific Film Archive (Nancy Goldman, Head of PFA Library).

Wisconsin Center for Film and Theater Research (Crystal Hyde, Jen Venzke and Anne Wilkins, Archivists).

6. *Plates*

The plates in this book emanate from the following sources, to whom the publishers gratefully offer acknowledgement:

BFI Stills, Posters & Designs: 11, 14, 20, 24, 26; Zoë Dominic: 29; Ronald Grant Archive: 5, 15, 27, 28; Angus McBean Photograph, Harvard Collection: 1 (photo. courtesy NPG, London), 19 (photo. courtesy Shakespeare Centre Library, Stratford-upon-Avon); Hulton Getty: 8, 9, 10, 18, 31; Kobal Collection: 3, 6, 7, 16, 22, 25; National Portrait Gallery, London: 21 (photograph by Howard Coster); Billy Rose Theatre Collection, New York Public Library at Lincoln Center: Astor, Lenox and Tilden Foundations: 17 (photograph by Van Damm

Studio); Bob Penn: 4; Popperfoto: 23; Thames Television: 30; John Vickers Archives: 2

The author and publishers have made all reasonable efforts to contact copyright holders for permission, and any omissions or errors in the form of credit given will be corrected in future printings.

7. *Individuals*

In Oxford I am beholden to Suzanne Anderson, John Bayley, Roy Boulting, Constance Cummings, Iris Murdoch and Jon Stallworthy; in London to Chris Beetles, Michael Blakemore, Simon Callow, Peter Evans, Leslie Gardner, Michael Gough, Kenneth Griffith, Ronald Hayman, Barry Humphries, Philip Kemp, Herbert Kretzmer, Wolf Mankowitz, Steve Masty, Alec McCowen, the late Sir Robert Stephens, and Francis Wheen; and elsewhere in Britain to A. E. Cox, Christopher Fry, Michael Herbert, and John Walter Skinner, of the Celebrity Information Bureau. Lady Susana Walton invited me to Ischia, to see out-takes of Olivier talking about Walton for the Tony Palmer documentary *At the Haunted End of the Day*. The book took shape inside my head when I was in Manitoba watching and discussing *Hamlet* with Lewis Baumander, Blair Cosgrove, Keanu Reeves and Joan Stephens – my thanks to Alison Macdonald and Jeremy Langmead, of the *Sunday Times* 'Style' section, for sending me on that assignment. I have also benefited from discussing Olivier with Bruce Bradley in New York. My London editors, Mark Booth, Simon King and Kate Parkin, consider my work God's greatest gift to the gaiety of Random House since the advent of Joan Collins, the gothic novelist. Anna, Tristan, Oscar, and Sébastien Lewis looked after me in France; Heather and Milo Boorman pampered me in Powys.

R. L., Easter Monday, 1996

Index